American

Pentimento

PUBLIC WORLDS

Dilip Gaonkar and Benjamin Lee, Series Editors

PATRICIA SEED

American

Pentimento

The Invention of Indians

and the Pursuit of Riches

PUBLIC WORLDS, VOLUME 7

UNIVERSITY OF MINNESOTA PRESS

MINNEAPOLIS LONDON

Additional maps and Internet links related to this book may be viewed at
http://www.upress.umn.edu/americanpentimento.html

Copyright 2001 by the Regents of the University of Minnesota

Maps copyright Patricia Seed.

Published by the University of Minnesota Press
111 Third Avenue South, Suite 290
Minneapolis, MN 55401-2520
http://www.upress.umn.edu

Library of Congress Cataloging-in-Publication Data

Seed, Patricia, 1949–
   American pentimento : the invention of Indians and the pursuit of
riches / Patricia Seed.
      p. cm. — (Public worlds ; v. 7)
Includes index.
   ISBN 0-8166-3766-0 (HC : alk. paper)
   1. Indians of North America—Land tenure. 2. Indians—Colonization. 3. Indians—
Civil rights. 4. Land tenure—Government policy—America—History. 5. Right of
property—America—History. 6. Europe—Colonies—America—Administration.
7. America—Colonization. I. Title. II. Series.
   E59.L3 S44 2001
   970'.00497—dc21
                                                                    2001001828

Printed in the United States of America on acid-free paper

The University of Minnesota is an equal-opportunity educator and employer.

12 11 10 09 08 07 06 05 04 03 02 01   10 9 8 7 6 5 4 3 2 1

Contents

Maps

All maps of the Americas are Lambert Azimuthal Equal Area projections, centered midway between the two continents (at roughly San José, Costa Rica). The world map is a Robertson projection centered on the original prime meridian, located in the Madeira Islands.

Preface

> But why should I mourn at the untimely fate of my people? Tribe follows tribe, and nation follows nation, like the waves of the sea. It is the order of nature, and regret is useless. Your time of decay may be distant, but it will surely come.
>
> Chief Seattle, 1887[1]

> Men make their own history, but they do not make it just as they please; they do not make it under circumstances chosen by themselves, but under circumstances directly found, given, and transmitted from the past.
>
> Karl Marx, *The Eighteenth Brumaire of Louis Napoleon*, 1852

One need only cross any international border to see that history, unlike fiction, rarely transcends international boundaries. Having spent summers over the past ten years haunting bookstores in Europe, South America, Africa, Australia, and New Zealand, I am no longer surprised to find popular American fiction in translation or bound in different covers for foreign editions. Nor am I surprised to find Portuguese or Dutch versions of familiar books on computer programming languages, Web design, and Internet marketing. But in the sections labeled "history," the majority of authors and subjects differ profoundly from those in comparable U.S. stores. Fiction travels well, as do the ubiquitous books on programming, but history rarely does.

For years I have written successfully for scholarly and popular Spanish-speaking and Portuguese-speaking Latin American audiences on a variety of historical and cultural issues. And I was especially familiar with what Spanish-American readers in particular would require of a book dealing with the early history of relationships between natives and colonizers in the New World. I knew that they would demand, as they have in the past, that my story tell of powerful natives standing defiantly together in the face of overwhelming odds. Any narrative of mutual learning would need to be definitively subordinated to the dominant story of colonial exploitation and native resistance. In both popular and scholarly writing in contemporary Mexico, for example, the well-known figure of La Malinche, Cortés's mistress and translator who mediated between Spaniards and Aztecs, is rarely portrayed in a positive manner. Indeed, in everyday popular speech her name is synonymous with the most vulgar slang expression for being done in, the very graphic exposition of what happens to someone who tries to cross boundaries or help the colonizers.

To tell the story of the Mayflower Pilgrims in the way contemporary Mexican readers would expect, one would need to convey how the heroic Wampanoags resisted the devastating English invasion; how Squanto betrayed his people by saving the beleaguered Pilgrims rather than letting them die, as they deserved; and how he had finally let his own people down by translating for Winthrop rather than using his knowledge and experience to help them understand how they could better resist the invaders.[2]

Yet this is not how the story is told in the English-speaking United States. Squanto is a hero for having helped save the struggling Pilgrims, rather than a traitor who saved the invaders. Furthermore, there is an immensely popular national celebration (Thanksgiving), formally created by Abraham Lincoln, that today celebrates an entirely different tale—of mutual interaction and learning between colonizers and Indians.[3]

If you look at the facts, there is no reason to prefer one story over another. William Bradford first landed soldiers in Massachusetts, so the history of his arrival could as equally well be told of the English invasion of North America as of a peaceful encounter between the two. Both accounts are equally probable and improbable. But hearing Squanto's story told as betrayal of his people is as unlikely an experience for American audiences as the story of a heroic Malinche is for Mexican readers. What national readers will and will not find plausible in the histories they choose depends largely upon how they perceive themselves and how they wish to see their past—and, in the case of this book, how they prefer to view their relationship to aboriginal peoples.

Such differing national expectations of historical narratives are frequently incompatible, so writing history for multinational audiences requires a new set of approaches. In this book, therefore, I will not retell either popular tale about the encounter between American natives and Europeans. I will not recount how natives heroically resisted European incursions any more than I will retell how the parties interacted peacefully and learned from each other. Nor will I conclude with any of the competing patronizing fantasies about how English, Spanish, or Portuguese colonists treated "their" Indians better. Rather, I will trace the history of cultural assumptions behind contemporary unself-conscious declarations about the rights of Europeans (and later Americans) to certain native resources.

Historians are not yet trained to examine critically differing national or regional expectations of narratives, themes, and subjects in the writing of comparative history. Yet such a step is necessary for history to transcend national boundaries. Therefore in this book I employ an anthropological lens in order to compare historical processes and perspectives. Such critical awareness is particularly imperative for the subject of this book, the aboriginal peoples of the Americas, who have been invariably depicted through the prisms of national languages and national cultures.

My thanks go first of all to Peter Hulme, who invited me to the "Fourth World" conference at the University of Essex in 1992. Participating in those weeklong conversations was an unforgettable experience. Second, I would like to thank a smaller group of people who attended a miniconference I organized at Rice University on indigenous peoples—Margaret Dunaway, Claudia Briones, Kathryn Milun, and Russel Barsh. Several visitors to the Rice Anthropology Department have been extremely valuable interlocutors, notably Brazil's Alcida Ramos and Australia's Jeremy Beckett. Another memorable opportunity was an invitation to Stockholm to meet Maria Estela Lobo and Rio-based physicians who have struggled to provide the Yanomami with health care in the devastating first years after contact. Additional thanks to Dominique Buichellet, Jean Jackson, Elizabeth Leeds, Patrick Harries, Marysa Navarro, Pam Smart, and George Marsical. Parts of this manuscript have been presented orally to the Anthropology Department at MIT, the Harvard-MIT Seminar on International Development, the History Department at the University of Cape Town (South Africa), the International Congress of Historical Sciences in Montreal, the American Historical Association, the American Studies Program at the University of Houston, the Sawyer Mellon Seminar at Johns Hopkins University, the Medieval and Renaissance Studies Conference at the State University of New York–Binghamton, the Literature Department at the

University of California, San Diego, the History Department at Dartmouth College, the John H. Parry Lecture at Harvard University, and the New Zealand Anthropological Association meeting in Dunedin. Thanks to those who have read the manuscript: Silvana de Paula, Jennifer Hamilton, Susan Kellogg, Linda Lewin, Lauren Lisabeth Marshall, Stuart Douglas, Mikkel Venborg Pedersen, Harold Hyman, Wendy Pond, and Jean Williams Brusher, who wonderfully restructured its awkward moments. And above all, thanks to my husband, George Marcus, whose work is a continuing source of inspiration and who has usually patiently endured rereading parts of this manuscript.

American Pentimento: An Introduction

pentimento. In painting, a trace of an earlier composition or of alterations that has become visible with the passage of time.

Oxford English Dictionary, second edition

On a wintry afternoon in November 1992, I was sitting in a conference room at the University of Essex listening to a group of activists on behalf of indigenous people. Many were themselves natives, others their allies from the United States, Europe, and the United Nations. Together they were trying to forge a common ground for international action on behalf of native peoples.

Yet despite the tremendous desire for shared ground, I kept hearing and observing people talking past each other and missing significant cues in others' speeches. When a representative of one of Guatemala's Maya communities began to speak about "human dignity" as the foundation of contemporary native struggles, I observed some participants rolling their eyes in irritation, dropping their eyelids to half-mast, or rummaging discreetly in knapsacks and briefcases for other things to do. Yet these same bored or even exasperated people snapped to attention when the next speaker shifted the topic to land rights. They dropped their unfinished work into briefcases and knapsacks and popped their eyes open.

But another group, those who had been listening eagerly to the Guatemalan speaker, seemed taken aback by the sudden switch in topics. And as the next speaker continued in the same vein, their expressions slowly dimmed from enthusiasm to patient endurance as he continued to dwell on the subject of land rights.

As speaker followed speaker down the long row of chairs, a pattern began to emerge in the faces of those in the room. Those springing alert during lengthy discussions of land ownership all came from English-speaking nations, whereas those stoically enduring those same speeches resided in Spanish-speaking nations.[1] Despite the considerable differences that separated the Maya from the Argentine Mapuche speakers, they responded with the same enthusiasm for discussions of human dignity while merely tolerating their counterparts' discussions of the principal place of land rights. On that cold, rainy November day, members of contemporary aboriginal communities and their political allies were expressing modern agendas dictated in places and even in times far distant from the present.

The separate aims expressed in that Essex room—human dignity and land rights—indicted radically different colonial systems. The English had conquered property, categorically denying the natives' true ownership of their land. Spaniards, on the other hand, had conquered people, allowing sedentary natives to retain their terrain in exchange for social humiliation. Thus regaining soil comes first on the agenda in aboriginal communities once dominated by England, whereas seeking human respect is central to contemporary aboriginal struggles in regions once controlled by Spain.

Thus the past exists in the present. It is reproduced without great care or even particular knowledge. Different histories made themselves known in that Essex commons by the way people sat or fidgeted restlessly in response to the discussion of certain issues, the way they embraced certain questions enthusiastically and dismissed others as merely tedious. History appears at its most seductive (and most coercive) when it reproduces the past without words, in the daily expectations and unself-conscious behavior of members of a society.

Arriving from increasingly overlogged forests, Europeans saw seemingly endless woodlands promising unending supplies of timbers for ships, charcoal for heat, and logs for construction.[2] Accustomed to endemic shortages of coins, the Europeans found that the New World contained quantities of silver and gold not simply for money but for decorative objects and even buildings—a scale no European had ever previously imagined. Far from desiring either neutral or scientific information about the New World, Europeans intensely coveted ownership of the natives, their land, and/or their possessions.[3]

All Europeans, however, did not covet the same things in the same ways. Coming from a region in which land was a central concern, English colonists assumed that the objective of colonization could only be to own the natives' land. In contrast, Spanish and Portuguese settlers equally took it for granted that control of people (and their labor) was the only goal that mattered. Although the differences between the Spanish and English colonizations of the Americas have long been recognized, these differences in economic ambitions are rarely acknowledged.

Regarding the distinctive English preference for land in the New World, people educated in the United States are usually taught, for example, that the differences between English and Spanish colonies were rooted simply in the demographic and ecological accidents of historic encounters. The argument, roughly stated, is that English colonists found hunter-gatherers in North America, whereas the Spaniards encountered large civilizations, such as those of the Aztecs and Incas. But this safely satisfying rationale simply cannot account for the facts. The Portuguese, for example, never found any indigenous societies other than the same types of mobile farmers and hunter-gatherers the English did. Yet whereas English colonists firmly believed that the hunting and farming practices of the natives entitled the English to take over native lands, Portuguese colonists neither made such arguments nor drew the same conclusions from identical native practices.[4]

Another story familiar to those educated in the United States varies the same theme, also arguing that Europeans' takeover of natural resources was dictated fundamentally by the natives themselves. This thesis suggests that the groups Europeans first encountered determined what the Europeans' practices would be toward all natives.[5] But this version of the "accident of encounter" explanation is simply not true, for all Europeans initially encountered the same kinds of people as did the British in North America.

Spaniards, Portuguese, Englishmen, and Frenchmen, for example, all first happened upon small-scale agricultural and hunter-gatherer societies in the New World: the Spaniards encountered Lucayos or Tainos in the Caribbean; Englishmen and Frenchmen confronted Algonquian-speaking tribes in eastern North America; and Portuguese and Frenchmen located Tupis on the eastern rim of South America. Neither the characteristics of native peoples nor first contact can explain the dissimilar ways Europeans pursued wealth in the Americas. Rather, cultural traditions about valuing, transferring, and allocating riches emerged in Europe long before the colonists' quest for riches in the Americas.

Beyond frowning upon greed and prohibiting usury, the Roman

Catholic Church had little interest in fixing moral standards for regulating financial or commercial transactions. And Roman traditions regarding exchange, transmission, and seizure had long since been profoundly modified by Scandinavian and Germanic incursions in the north of Europe and Arabic and Berber invasions in the south.[6] Thus traditions regarding commercial exchanges differed sharply between northern Europe, where Scandinavian and German conquests had influenced local customs, and southern Europe, where Arabic and Berber conquests had similar effects.

Rules regarding owning, buying, and selling goods therefore did not originate in a shared European tradition but rather grew out of a hodge-podge of regional customs and practices, often shaped by interactions with the conquering powers of the Middle Ages. These largely local or regional rules for conducting exchanges, both formal and informal, often were further shaped by people's experiences in trading with neighboring villages and towns, and occasionally by the experiences of individuals who ventured to faraway lands.[7]

In the later Middle Ages, European cities, towns, and states began to gather rules and regulations together, to iron out differences in existing practices and customs, and to create more uniform guidelines for the exchange and acquisition of goods.[8] And although concepts from long-forgotten Roman legal traditions were sometimes reintroduced, traditional customs remained the core of these regulations, expressed in the usual languages of the people.[9] By the sixteenth century, culturally distinct guidelines governed the means of exchanging, transmitting, and acquiring wealth in timber, gold, silver, tin, furs, and agricultural land in separate parts of Europe.[10]

All Europeans' ideas about the lawful pursuit of riches overseas in the sixteenth and seventeenth centuries originated in this quotidian conflation of the everyday, the obvious, and the proper.[11] In seizing resources from peoples they had not known of before 1492, colonists and their supporters extended this amalgamation by describing their reasons for seizing economic assets as fundamental *international* maxims.[12] But what they characterized as "international" or "universal" were simply their own distinct European cultural traditions applied overseas.

Sustaining the belief that their own cultural premises regarding wealth were "universal" allowed Europeans to justify seizing the assets of peoples in distant lands—peoples whose resources they had never dreamed existed prior to 1492. Equally important, calling such ambitions "universal" reinforced the unstated internal agreement among colonizers about what they would seize, how, and why. Such a consensus permitted members of

Anglo-Saxon culture, for example, to pursue a common goal of owning native land without destroying themselves with internal divisions over the legitimate ends of colonization in a hostile overseas environment.

But indications that their own economic ends and methods were not universal already appeared in New World conflicts over economic objectives among colonists from different European economic cultures. Colonists from each separate culture vociferously and angrily denied that other Europeans had legitimate rules for gain. They customarily attacked other European cultures' approaches and rationales for obtaining wealth as mere fakery, vivid confirmation that their competitors were looking for any excuse to justify patently unacceptable conduct. Such unambiguous hostility to dissimilar European methods of acquisition surfaced repeatedly. Tolerant acceptance of other points of view emerges only when no major benefits are at stake, and in the New World significant European political and monetary interests were at risk.

Given the extent of mutual misunderstanding and hostility occurring even among Europeans, it is not surprising that an equally oblivious misapprehension of culturally distinct economic principles applied to European judgments about aboriginal peoples. In confiscating natives' goods and using their land or their labor, all Europeans severely judged Native Americans' failure to observe the familiar guidelines of the Europeans' own particular cultures concerning what resources could be owned, by whom, and how. Europeans uniformly explained that they were displacing Native Americans and seizing their labor, land, and other valuable commodities because the conduct of the indigenous peoples failed to conform to the Europeans' expectations of society. Finding that the natives failed to value or to exploit the resources the Europeans believed to be profitable, the Europeans declared the natives to be ineffectual or unworthy users of their riches.

But in thus rationalizing their seizing and retaining the New World's resources, Europeans did not automatically invoke the practical reasons they were able to achieve their aims of wealth. The deadly European combination of microbes and militaries in fact wiped out many of the indigenous peoples, who initially lacked defenses against both types of invaders. But Europeans found neither military victories nor the biological near extinction of native peoples sufficiently gratifying explanations for their continued ownership of the New World's riches.

Like most successful colonizers, Europeans wanted to create a morality tale from the facts of success. Conquerors feel more comfortable believing they are entitled to the benefits, the acquisitions—territorial or economic—

that have come their way. Rather than seeking to justify their gains as resulting from their own distinction, however, Europeans in the New World reversed the process, claiming that their qualifications stemmed from the inferiority of the "Indians."

To assume, however, as do many critics of colonialism, that these harsh judgments of aboriginal peoples were always either spitefully or arbitrarily created is to misrepresent their more complex historical and cultural roots. Although part of Europeans' desire to understand their ambitions as universal was motivated by greed, another part stemmed from traits that we might today call classically narcissistic.

Self-centeredness was and is not necessarily intentionally malicious. Many and perhaps even most Europeans saw themselves as holding their own ends above those of others, justifying their aims on their own terms without regard for the interests of others. Selfishness—disregarding or remaining oblivious to the interests of others—is not the same as planned and premeditated malevolence. True evil, intentional and calculated, is thankfully rare, even though colonialism seems to have generated more than its share. But intense self-absorption is not intrinsically the same as great evil. Therefore ordinary Europeans did not seize other peoples' assets simply because of a stark will to power or a desire to oppress, as critics of colonialism often declare;[13] more often they did so because they were fundamentally and self-interestedly following familiar rules for appropriating assets.

But this approach has far more troubling implications than the attribution of such motives to obscene desires for power and riches. By ascribing the expropriation of natives' resources to colonists' coarse lusts or to other Europeans' crude desire for gold, we safely distance our own present-day and presumably more modest and benevolent goals from those more malicious ones that we impute to earlier generations. Therefore to consider that expropriation of natives' possessions stemmed simply from familiar modes of thinking about acquiring resources is vastly more unsettling than to attribute it to suitably distant and avaricious European colonists. It is infinitely more comforting to accept that past conduct and motives differ from present ones than it is to consider the potentially disturbing continuity in economic motives and methods between our colonial past and our national present.[14]

However, for two different reasons, it is imperative that we undertake the process of rendering self-conscious cultural differences in economic methods and objectives, despite an instinctive discomfort with such proceedings. First, in a world that is increasingly linked together economically, confronting distinct cultural assumptions in economic activities is profoundly important. Dispassionate understanding of the historical divergences in cultural economic traditions is necessary for successful economic negotiation across boundaries.

The second reason is more directly related to the aboriginal peoples of the contemporary Americas and is the focus of this book. Because the dominant languages and legal cultures throughout the Americas are European, citizens of the modern Americas today often instinctively share many of the historical and cultural attitudes the colonizers brought with them. Such unself-consciously shared convictions remain embedded not simply in language but in popular cultures as well as in legal systems. And these usually mechanically repeated expressions in law and popular culture today provide continuing stumbling blocks to natives' ownership and management of the same natural resources that the original colonists targeted throughout the Americas. Today land is as difficult for the Shoshones to retain in the contemporary United States as gold is for the Yanomani of Brazil. The economic object may be different, but in both cases members of modern nations share an absolutely unshakable conviction that Indians do not have a right to land (the United States) or gold or oil (Brazil) if the nation or its citizens want it. Although many or perhaps most inhabitants of the contemporary Americas have no idea where these assumptions that the nation owns the land or the gold originated, they still retain the unwavering belief that if settlers or their nation wanted either the land or the gold it was, and still is, rightfully theirs. The basic seductive power of history resides in the denial of its existence—the unreflective assumption that it is simply what is "right," "obvious," or "reasonable." But definitions of the right to own certain resources stem not from the transparent domain of the everyday but from the past, and from an amalgamation of cultural choices made long ago, but that continue their effects in the present.

This book's focus on colonialism's continuing impact in the Americas raises yet another set of distinctions. Studies of such long-term influence on the postcolonial world have tended to focus upon the more recently decolonized (and often more narrowly upon the Anglo-Indian) world.[15] But rapidly growing middle classes in India currently seem to be altering that nation's central political directions in ways that cannot be understood from the vantage point of its postcolonial past. The English impact upon national systems of governance thus appears to be fading in regions where colonial rule began only in the past century. But the impact of nineteenth- and twentieth-century European colonialism on the Americas seems to be more vigorous. The fundamental reasons for this greater vigor, however, are both medical and economic.

Although Europeans took over Africa and Asia in the nineteenth and early twentieth centuries by force of arms, they did not also exterminate the inhabitants of those continents with microbes.[16] In the Americas, Australia, and New Zealand, native populations were decimated (reduced by 90 percent) during the first hundred years.[17] A few native communities, such as those led by the sixteenth-century Tupac Amaru, were able to conceal themselves in remote mountain hideaways, but no large group could keep out of sight effectively for long. And those who reemerged, along with the 10 percent who had survived the ravages of disease, were not always those most familiar with their groups' cultural traditions or most able to reconstitute their networks. The decimated remnants of once-thriving native communities had to reinvent themselves and their societies within sight and sound of numerous armed and healthy invaders, their weapons, and their demands for wealth. Overwhelming military force combined with the loss of 90 percent of the entire native population to ensure that European economic demands played a fundamental role in restructuring native communities to serve European dreams of gain.

The long-term dominance of a single colonial tradition has further preserved distinct European economic objectives in the Americas. Unlike both Africa and Asia, where first Dutch, then French, and then English replaced Portuguese colonizers in the same regions during the seventeenth and eighteenth centuries, English, Spanish, and Portuguese legal and economic systems have uninterruptedly and uncontestedly dominated separate major areas of the Americas for hundreds of years. And in the contested regions—only in three territorially small sections of Canada, the southwestern United States, and the Caribbean—multiple layers of European economic rules have imposed themselves on top of each other and the same native peoples. Yet, rather than superimposing their requirements upon earlier ones, as in Africa and Asia, Europeans in the Americas nearly eradicated the economic basis and organizational forms of earlier colonial systems. English colonists ignored earlier Dutch colonists' insistence upon formal contracts for land with native peoples after defeating Peter Stuyvesant in 1666; the British destroyed the French trade-only system after 1763, replacing it with their own distinctive land-occupying policy, even in trading territories in the Ohio Valley. And when the United States conquered a third of Mexico in 1848, officials and U.S. settlers were profoundly unhappy with the Iberian/Mexican approach to both mining claims and landownership, and rapidly replaced both approaches with those derived from Anglo-Saxon traditions.[18] Finally, in the Caribbean, English colonists pursuing their lands summarily exiled the aboriginal peoples once kept near Spanish settlements for their labor. The result has been an especially powerful colonial legacy of the distinctive forms of European rule not in a safely distant subcontinent, but within the boundaries of modern American nations, and in the relations of such nations to the natives of our Americas.

Therefore, in order to explore the contemporary predicaments of the aboriginal peoples of the Americas with respect to natural resources, I will concentrate in this book on the European colonies whose rules for acquiring riches have most profoundly influenced the present-day options of most natives of the Americas: England, Spain, and Portugal.

The first three chapters cover English colonization. Chapter 1 describes how English colonists came to desire land and later rationalized their owning and profiting from this, their most desired asset. Chapter 2 explains how the term *wasteland* came into the English language, and its connection to the popular fable of vanishing Native Americans. Chapter 3 follows the history of the social distinctions between hunters and farmers that led to the English-language partial political fiction that natives were "hunter-gatherers." But the chapter also shows how Anglo-Saxon ambivalence about hunting—dating from the Norman Conquest—also continued in the New World, generating vicious and occasionally violent hostility toward Native Americans, despite hunting's function as their assigned (fictively universal) economic role.

Chapters 4 through 6 address Spanish colonization. Chapter 4 discusses the distinctive Iberian rules governing ownership of valuable subterranean resources and the resultant demand for native labor to mine the earth. Chapter 5 examines the costs (in terms of human dignity) of official Hispanic protection of native lands from seizure by colonists. Chapter 6 explains how and why Spaniards justified their culturally legitimate objective (use of native labor) in terms of a different political fiction.

From specific detailed comparisons, chapter 7 moves to establish the common cultural logics that sustained both English and Spanish settlers' perceptions of an impassable boundary between themselves and natives and contributed to the belief in enduring entitlements to specific New World resources. Chapter 8 moves back to the specific cultural history of economic objectives in the Portuguese colonial world, a domain close to, but often wrongly characterized as identical with, the Spanish colonial empire. Chapter 9 briefly examines the differences in the ways both former Ibero- and Anglo-American colonies structured their postindependence relationships with the natives. Chapter 10 highlights the continuities between colonial and national relations to Native Americans. Finally, in my

Map 1. European origin of contemporary American legal systems. The pattern of horizontal lines represents areas whose legal systems were based on that of England; the pattern of white diamonds, in Central America and western South America, shows areas based on the Spanish legal system; and the area of South America covered by the pattern of dense black dots based its legal systems on that of Portugal.

conclusion I look at the different approaches to human rights and resource rights for native peoples today.

Throughout the Americas, Australia, and New Zealand today, native communities' rights to wealth are governed by a host of modern regulations that seem to have deleted traces of the earlier colonial rules. But underneath more recently imposed standards, traces of earlier ones can

often be seen. The result is a history that more closely resembles the slow- |
ly changing surface of a sixteenth-century painting than the usually script-
ed historical theater of actors on a stage.

Over time, the covering pigment on a canvas sometimes becomes
transparent, allowing glimpses of an earlier drawing or painting to show
through. The artist's original lines or paintings are called *pentimenti*; sometimes, but not always, they signal an artist's changed intentions.[19] Throughout the twentieth century, traces of earlier compositions began to appear in
many paintings created during the sixteenth and seventeenth centuries—
the floor in Pieter de Hooch's *Interior*, the hat brim of Rembrandt's *Flora*.[20]
And this phenomenon, which we have observed in art in our own times,
we can also see in our societies. Over the centuries, and particularly in the
aftermath of independence, national law codes and administrative and
judicial decisions have attempted to obliterate traces of the original
sixteenth- and seventeenth-century approaches to native peoples by over-
writing them. Yet as the twentieth century progressed, the outlines of
these original colonial intentions reappeared, becoming visible through
contemporary codes.

Each colonial power invariably deprived American natives of one or
another of their riches because they had the misfortune to inhabit a terrain
rich in gold, silver, precious stones, fertile agricultural land, abundant
forests, plentiful fish, and people.[21] European yearnings for riches—
unleashed in the Americas—traced the outline of native peoples as some-
how not entitled to own the riches they possessed. Therefore, underneath
the subsequently layered-on regulations governing natives' access to natural resources can often be seen vestiges of the original colonizer's economic
aims—a colonial pentimento.

1

U.S. MORTAGE CULTURE!

Owning Land by Labor, Money, and Treaty

When a representative from one of the many native communities at the 1992 Essex conference introduced the subject of land rights for indigenous peoples, individuals in the audience from English-speaking regions of the Americas responded enthusiastically. Securing land rights, they agreed, should be the first priority for Native Americans. In the years since, however, I have heard identical sentiments uttered in Hindi- and Urdu-inflected English, with rounded Kikuyu and Swahili vowels, in Australian drawls, and in rhythmic Polynesian cadences. Regardless of continent or accent, English speakers from far-flung corners of the earth are talking about obtaining land to right the wrongs of colonization. This unanimity among citizens from East Africa and Polynesia, South Asia, and Australia is less astonishing than it first appears. All these people have been colonized by an English legal system, and in an English legal system landownership is, and has been since the sixteenth century, the principal objective of colonization.

The underlying reasons for the preoccupation with possessing land lie deep in England's past. "In the Middle Ages," writes William Holdsworth, "the land law was the most important and the most highly developed branch of the common law."[1] The eminent English legal historian S. F. C. Milsom observes that the first legal textbook in England (1496) dealt with land law and that it took "nearly four centuries before text-books were written on other branches of law."[2] The foundation of the English legal system resided in the ownership of soil.[3]

In English law of the sixteenth century, only the monarch enjoyed full dominion over land and hence the ultimate authority for control over land.[4] Queen Elizabeth's letters patent—the first official legal act of English sovereignty for the New World—established this pattern. Sir Humphrey Gilbert and Walter Ralegh were entitled to "have, hold, and occupy and enjoy . . . all the *soyle* of all such lands, countries, and territories . . . and of all Cities, Castles, Towns and Villages, and *places* in the same."[5] It was soil and places that Gilbert and Ralegh first received the right to hold and enjoy. Furthermore, as these first English patents for the New World both state, these lands were granted "with full power to dispose thereof, and of every part in fee simple or otherwise, according to the order of the lawes of England."[6] In other words, the land of the New World was given to select men to use and to distribute "according to . . . the lawes of England."

Landownership constituted not merely the official but also the cultural heart of Englishmen's invention of America as theirs. Owning the New World's land crosscut social classes and established a socially desirable practice for individuals as well as a worthy public goal. Upper classes as well as landless farmers could legitimately aspire to own the soil of the New World.

Even when English-speaking critics attacked England's policy in the New World, they limited themselves to criticizing the means, not the ends, of land acquisition. Roger Williams criticized the royal letters patent as well as the popular Puritan belief in the eminent domain of English agriculture, arguing only for a different process of acquiring native lands. William Penn in the seventeenth century likewise altered only the means, not the ends, of English colonization of the Americas. And while the objective of landownership was unique, so too were the means that Englishmen used to acquire it.

The Means to Landownership

Alone among Western European traditions, English law did not require a written procedure for claiming ownership of land until late in the seventeenth century.[7] Until then, Englishmen could claim that they had acquired ownership of land simply by exchanging other commodities and by doing physical labor on the land. Therefore English colonists overseas (in contrast with other Europeans) understood actions such as handing over money, building a house, putting up fences, and planting crops (which they customarily called "labor") as establishing legal ownership of a terrain, just as they had in England. Such belief in the transparent meaning of particular actions (without benefit of either a speech, such as in the Spanish Requirement, or written document) made it possible for hundreds of illiterate or barely literate people to acquire title to plots of ground at the start of English colonization.

Furthermore, authorities in England did not require that settlers seek their permission to obtain land during the first century of English colonization. Although a few local communities insisted upon strictly controlling the assignment of land, settlers soon left the restrictive districts in search of more lenient ones that allowed actions to indicate ownership.[8] English speakers often used specific words to convey their confidence in the capacity of physical actions alone to create ownership of land. Many echoed John Winthrop, who declared, "Land was free to any who would possess it."[9]

Owning through Actions (Labor)

The popular English-language proverb "Actions speak louder than words" first appeared in the middle of the nineteenth century, but its sentiments were widely established earlier.[10] "Your Actions . . . make you a lyar," Lord Herbert wrote in 1648, thus conveying the widely held idea that an action is more telling than spoken or written words.[11]

More important, however, English law also established this principle. Usually communicated by the legal phrase "The thing speaks for itself," this doctrine allowed ordinary Englishmen sitting on a jury to render judgment based upon neither written documents nor verbal assertions, but simply upon their construal of the meanings of actions. "It is apparent," wrote Sir George Croke (1560–1642), "that the money was lent for Interest, and is more than the Statute permits; Wherefore . . . if . . . the matter is apparent to the Court to be usury, there the Jury needs not to shew that it was corruptly, for res ipsa loquitur [the behavior speaks for itself]."[12]

Yet another uniquely English concept prevailed in understandings of property rights. Roman law, the foundation of many European laws on possession, separated physical control and intention to possess (conveyed in spoken or written words). But in English law, and English law alone, physical detention usually implied legal possession and ownership as well.[13] This thought was and still is often expressed in the peculiarly

English saying "Possession is nine-tenths of the law." That adage originated in a slightly different form in the middle of the seventeenth century, when Englishmen first began to seize land overseas. Initially the phrase was "Possession is eleven points of the law," when "the law" contained twelve points. The timing of this saying's origin raises suspicions that perhaps it originated to rationalize a colonial practice.[14] Regardless of how the expression began, it shows that the mere physical detention of land was sufficient among Englishmen to establish a claim to formal ownership.

English colonists believed that planting was the action that best established ownership. To farm, one expended strenuous and often painstaking effort.[15] Tilling the soil, or "laboring," meant striving against an obstacle, especially when the effort was painful or compulsory; farming was a struggle rather than an effortless success.[16] Embedded in this understanding of cultivating the New World was a sense of striving that the English believed entitled them to own the land upon which they toiled.

Fifty years later, John Locke made an even more straightforward statement of this position. "As much Land as a Man Tills, Plants, Improves, Cultivates, and can use the Product of, so much is his Property." More famous still is his general statement, "Whatsoever then he removes out of the State that Nature hath provided . . . [and] hath mixed his Labour with . . . makes it his Property."[17] This has become known as the labor theory of property, a thesis that became even more widespread in the English-speaking world in the eighteenth and nineteenth centuries. Yet such theories were not popular outside of England.

Scholars such as Samuel von Pufendorf, Locke's contemporary, rejected the idea that labor itself could create ownership. For Pufendorf, as for other continental Europeans, state permission was necessary. In the Netherlands, for example, even a farmer's permanent improvements did not entitle him to own the improvements, let alone the land upon which they were placed.[18] Englishmen, however, believed that state validation was unnecessary.

Capital That Labors

One of the most perplexing cultural concepts for those not raised speaking English is the difference between *labor* and *capital*. Native speakers often use the words as if they are synonymous, speaking or writing of capital "working." Modern advertisements convey the belief that "you can put money to work for you." But the idea that capital (an abstract form of money) can actually "work" as if it were a person is unique to English. In all the languages spoken by the other European colonizers—Spanish, French, Dutch, and Portuguese—capital produces only "returns to capital," profits, and gains. In all of these languages it makes no sense to speak of capital "working" because capital cannot be personified.[19]

The characterization of capital as a person, however, allows English speakers to conceive of money as "laboring" just as humans do. As early as the seventeenth century, Englishmen expressed beliefs that their capital, just like their labor, toiled, and therefore merited the rewards customarily given to those who struggled. An example appears in John Locke's elaboration of the merits of the labor theory of property. "The measure of Property," Locke wrote, "Nature has well set, by the Extent of Mens Labour. No Man's Labour could subdue, or appropriate all . . . so that it was impossible for any Man, in this way to intrench upon the right of another."[20] Thus landownership seemed to be constrained by the physical capacity of a single man.

But the owners of very large properties in England did no actual physical work. Rather, they paid others to weed, clear the fields, plant, harvest, and glean. But because money was thought to "work," the landowner could be considered as "working" because his money was laboring for him. Therefore, Locke added, "the Grass my Horse has bit; the Turfs my Servant has cut . . . become *my* Property."[21] "Labor" thus meant the money paid the employee ("servant" in seventeenth-century English) or slave who actually labored. Hence, strictly speaking, the true limits of a man's terrain were defined not by his labor but by the extent of his capital.[22] Literary critic Ambrose Bierce satirized this idea at midcentury. *Labor*, he said, is a noun: "One of the processes by which A acquires property for B."[23]

The monetary form of labor enjoyed a superior status to actual physical effort in claiming land. In sixteenth-century England, for example, cooperatively organized farm laborers were unable to claim that they worked and therefore owned the land by virtue of their toil. However, the enclosing landowners, who hired others to work for them, claimed that they "worked" vicariously through their money. And their "labor" created preferential rights to ownership over those working with noncompensated labor.

Juxtapositions: An English Right

While claiming that their seizure of New World lands was meritorious because they had exerted effort for it, English colonists did not recognize anyone else's labor as creating ownership rights. Neither Dutch farmers nor Native Americans who farmed (and adopted European methods) had ownership rights based upon work.

In June 1639, the commander of the Dutch fort at Hartford asked a prominent Dutch colonist, David de Vries, "to make a protest against them [the English], as they were using our own land. . . . I told him [the Puritan Governor] that it was wrong to take by force the Company's land, which it had bought and paid for. He answered that the lands were lying idle."[24] But even that was untrue. For the next year, as another well-placed Dutchman, Adriaen Van Der Donck, observed, the English settlers "forcibly [threw] into the river [Dutch] ploughs and instruments, while [Dutch settlers] were on the land for the purpose of farming, and have put [Dutch] horses in the pound. . . . The [English] also seized hogs and cows."[25] If the land was "idle," why were the English throwing Dutch ploughs into the river and impounding the Dutch settlers' horses, hogs, and cows? The land was clearly already being cultivated.

When Dutch settlers built breweries, or planted, or even when they performed those actions that created property rights, English colonists and their leaders refused to recognize those rights. The right to take over land by farming was an English right that did not extend to other Europeans.

Englishmen believed that paying the wages of or the transportation for indentured laborers or slaves created ownership of New World lands for the men who paid the wages or transport.[26] Wealthy capitalists could and indeed did bring thousands of indentured servants and slaves to the New World, largely in the southern colonies.[27] But these ownership beliefs did not prevail among the indigenous peoples of the Americas.

In the Americas, natives of different groups frequently labored for one another without any payment. Even in the most sophisticated New World empires, tribes and communities often toiled on each other's terrain in exchange for assistance in time of war or famine.[28] Because the natives lacked a cash nexus for services rendered, Englishmen categorized the natives' actions as forms of labor inferior to those that were compensated. Like the cooperative forms of farming that English landlords had displaced at home, reciprocal work obligations lacked any role for cash and therefore failed to enjoy the highest status of "labor," which entitled the "laborer" to own the land.

In much of the southern United States, Englishmen evicted Indian farmers in order to use their own slaves for farming, thus enabling the English to own Native American lands. After defeating one of the largest groups of sedentary natives in the southeastern United States, the peach-tree growing Apalachees, English plantation owners used the Apalachees as slaves, because by owning them as labor the English could claim their land.[29] This convoluted belief that capital was a higher form of labor was also tied to a broader perception of the cultural superiority of money.

Using Money

A definition of money is hard to pin down. Glyn Davies describes the difficulties in the recent book *A History of Money.* Money is a medium of exchange, a measure of value, a means of payment, and an abstract unit of account.[30] It can be property or possessions of any kind viewed as convertible into money or having value expressible in terms of money. According to the *Oxford English Dictionary* (second edition), money is "a commodity accepted by general consent as a medium of economic exchange. It is the medium in which prices and values are expressed, it circulates from person to person and country to country, thus facilitating trade, and it is the principal measure of wealth."

The Englishmen in the New World seemed to think that money was a source of their superiority over Native Americans. As John Locke memorably remarked, the day laborer in England was better off than the Native American "king of a large and fruitful Territory in America" because the day laborer had money.[31] Locke thus explicitly characterized the mere possession of (as opposed to the use of) money as a fundamental source of English supremacy over Indians.

Locke's allegation that the natives lacked money, in the sense of a generally accepted medium of exchange, was mistaken. Regional currency systems abounded in the New World. In the northeastern woodlands, small clamshells called *wampum* passed as a local form of currency. The value of goods could be expressed in terms of wampum. A beaver skin or a canoe could be traded for wampum. Wampum could be drilled through the center and threaded on string. In Central America, the Mayas used cacao beans, as a form of money. Maya traders throughout the entire Central American region used these small tough seeds as currency.

Furthermore, the colonists themselves often adopted these Native American media of exchange. In 1637, Massachusetts declared white wampum legal tender for sums up to one shilling, a limit raised in 1643. The terms *country pay* and *country money* referred to crops such as tobacco, rice, indigo, wheat, and maize. Tobacco was used as money in and around Virginia for nearly two hundred years, lasting about twice as long as the U.S. gold standard. But these regional forms of money were not universal, or what Marx called the "general equivalent."

Purchase

Inhabitants of the Americas, however, did not value all goods through a system of local currency. In particular, Native Americans did not appraise land by such means prior to the arrival of Europeans. Among peoples of the eastern woodlands of both North and South America, land was usually a symbolic manifestation of kinship. It was often temporarily exchanged for access to different resources—a hunting ground traded for one with different animals, or a place exchanged for one where different crops would grow. Permanent alienation (abandonment) occurred only in extreme circumstances: in times of war, famine, or population growth beyond the carrying capacity of the land.[32] Such permanent departures resulted from obvious factors, such as military occupation or the inability of the soil to yield enough to feed the population.

English colonists interpreted their giving of money to natives as meaning that the natives permanently lost their terrain. Yet this interpretation of the exchange ritual was initially alien to Native Americans. Writes George Snyderman: "The first grants of lands [by natives] were merely grants to the use of land during good behavior."[33] As a result, Indians sometimes "sold" the same tracts to different "purchasers," most likely in anticipation of a temporary alliance or temporary conveyance, whereas the English invariably regarded such exchanges as the permanent renunciation of all rights to land.

But what was and still is called a purchase belongs to a broader category of exchange.[34] In most systems of exchange, presents are part of efforts to establish continuing relationships with other persons. Giving generates an obligation to reciprocate, thus creating a continuing cycle of exchanges.[35] But the object of "purchasing" is not to return the item to the person who had given it, but to permanently remove the item from further exchanges.[36]

The second distinctive characteristic of purchase as a form of exchange was the presence of a valuable commodity such as money.[37] English settlers often interpreted giving any form of recompense as a permanent and binding sale, despite evidence to the contrary. John Smith declared, "If this [improvement] be not a reason sufficient to such tender consciences; for a copper kettle and a few toyes, as beads and hatchets, they will sell you a whole Countrey; and for a small matter, their houses and the ground they dwell upon."[38] The idea that a copper kettle and a few toys were sufficient to purchase an entire country suggests a profound misunderstanding of the nature of the Native Americans' patterns of transfer. Smith's arrogant "soothe tender consciences" suggests that he understood payment as an unnecessary step, one that might be used in extenuating circumstances to avoid possible difficulties or, as Smith more sarcastically considered, to placate those endowed with an excess of scruples.[39]

Purchase was rarely contemplated in projects for colonial settlement.[40] Funds for the acquisition of land from native inhabitants were rarely part of the expenditures allocated for the New World—and such portions were usually referred to as "trifles." Roger Williams and William Penn, legendary figures who now represent beneficent English colonialism, supported payment as the ideal means of dispossessing the Indians.[41] Although exchanging cash for land can indeed be understood sympathetically, given that there was no formal requirement for them to do so, their supporters have characteristically managed to fail to consider that their "charity" was a means of achieving their own primary economic ambition.

Furthermore, the considerations of purchase that we now understand to be associated with that concept—the rights to refuse to sell, to seek the most favorable terms, and to obtain restitution (through force if necessary) in the case of failure of the other party to adhere to the contract—did not apply to the "purchases" of native land. Puritan John Cotton in 1647 declared, "If they [the Puritans] sit downe [settle] upon the Possession of the Natives, [the Puritans have *a right*] *to receive the same* [*the land*] from them by a reasonable Purchase or free Assignment."[42] The key part of Cotton's phrase is his understanding of Englishmen's rights. Once the Puritans arrived, by virtue of their mere presence they had a right to receive the land from the Indians.

As a result, the options Englishmen envisioned for the original inhabitants were few. Cotton *permitted* natives to give the land to the Puritans for free ("free assignment") or for payment ("reasonable Purchase"). Given only these two options, it is easy to see how English settlers were able to cast their payment as a form of benevolence. Any sum they provided was a clear example of their "generosity." But the invention of payment as munificence concealed an absolute sense of entitlement. Once the Puritans arrived, Native Americans lost the right of refusal. In Cotton's formulation, natives did not have a right to insist upon holding on to their land or to reject Puritan attempts to settle.

The standards of sales (including the requirements of consent, right of refusal, good faith, and fair dealing) that existed among Englishmen and that the Dutch required of contracts with Native Americans did not apply.[43] Undue influence and unconscionable conduct were the rule rather than the exception. One common technique of inducing sales was to summon the Indians to a council whose sole purpose was to induce land cessions. Veiled and open threats often accompanied these negotiations, verbal misrepresentations were frequent, and the right of refusal was denied.[44] At one session, Legro, a Miami chief also representing the Potawatomie, the Wea, and the Ottawa, replied:

> You have made a request of us for our lands which we have already refused. . . . I told you our situation. . . . We have a right to trade or exchange our property, if we can agree, and if we cannot agree to trade, we can separate in peace. But it is not so here, for you ask us after we have refused. . . . We can never sell it. . . . Therefore that we wish you to understand for all. That is all we have to say."[45]

The Native Americans were never free to contract in this respect. Under most international conventions, the absence of a right to refuse is called forcible expropriation, not purchase, but the English colonists showed no concern for indigenous consent. Natives had a right to receive money, but not a right to refuse consent. The English nonetheless persisted in endeavoring to label the exchanges they made with natives "sales," because buying was a legitimate means of gaining ownership according to *their particular code.*

English leaders did not insist upon introducing cash into the native economy or encourage colonists to strive to put all their economic dealings with Native Americans on a monetary basis. Rather, Spanish-American colonies developed programs to institute monetary economies among natives.[46] Because possession of "money" guaranteed a form of superiority, Englishmen would severely restrict Native Americans' access to money. Only when indebtedness could be used to force natives to sell their land did English colonists include them in the realms of cash, but more often natives were caught in the treacherous webs of credit.[47]

Juxtapositions

Land purchases as politically self-congratulatory practice were uniquely English, for English conceptions of "purchase" were as alien to the French, the Dutch, and other Europeans in the same area of the New World as they were to the natives. Noticeably absent from the French picture of relations with the Indians is consideration of purchase of land.[48] French colonists in what is now the United States did not usually buy land from the natives; rather, as the natives repeatedly told English colonists, the French simply asked for permission to reside with them.[49] Native leaders understood that the French colonists had not paid a price for the lands and considered that the French had understood this as well. French-Native American relations centered on the politics of the gift—a politics of exchange, not a politics of purchase.[50]

Nor did Netherlanders endow money with the same cultural significance. A Dutch preacher in New York State in 1644 remarked how several northeastern Indian communities remained indifferent to European money despite several decades of contact. Johannes Megapolensis described how "I once showed one of them a rix-dollar; he asked me how much it was worth among the Dutch; and when I told him, he laughed exceedingly at us. We were fools to value a piece of iron so highly; and if he had such money he would throw it in the river."[51] Accordingly, when trading, the Dutch tried to offer goods that the natives desired.

The story of the Dutch acquisition of territory has been rewritten as the story of purchases in order to suit the cultural imperatives of an English narrative history. The tale of Peter Minuit's purchase of Manhattan Island for twenty-four dollars has grown from a minor side note (part of a sentence) in the Dutch versions of the acquisition of Manhattan to the central element of the story.[52] It has been retold in countless elementary classrooms in the United States and has become solidly entrenched as part of U.S. folkloric history. The English-language version focuses on the presentation of money—and a pitifully small amount of money at that—as the central reason the Dutch owned New York (and the English by right of conquest from the Dutch).

In the Dutch version of the event, several matters are particularly stressed (these matters are omitted in the popular English-language versions of this tale). First, the presentation of money was accompanied by a written document, a prerequisite of a sale in every European nation except England. Second, proper authorization was required for the contract to be valid. Appropriate Dutch authorities had to approve any such acquisition before an exchange could take place, and such formally sanctioned exchanges were the only legitimate means of acquisition.[53]

In contrast, no English authority ever required settlers to pay for land that they acquired. Dutch colonists were often highly critical of English practices of "purchase" because they lacked formalities and written records. Furthermore, neither farming nor "treaty" was a legitimate method of acquiring land in the New World regions controlled by Spain, France, the Netherlands, and Portugal. And requirements for purchase were far more stringent in Dutch, Portuguese, and Spanish colonies than in English ones. Dutch irritation at Englishmen's acceptance of lax and nonbureaucratic procedures expressed itself in a complaint that talking to the English about the legality of their land acquisitions was, as the Dutch proverb goes, "knocking at a deaf man's door."[54]

When confronted with the Dutch contention that they had a prior, properly concluded purchase for lands around Hartford, the English leader claimed that in his own opinion the lands were "uncultivated" and that was a superior claim to Dutch contracts.[55] English colonists lacked any profound respect for other colonists' purchases from natives (reserving "purchases" as a means of settling disputes among themselves over claims to land).[56]

Finally, contracts, which require consent and a lack of coercion, dominated Dutch ideas of payment. Instructions to Dutch colonists from the leaders of the quasi-governmental West India Company demanded that natives freely agree to contractual sale of land. Other oft-repeated instructions declared that fraud, trickery, and other deceptive means were not to be used, because such methods would backfire into subsequent antagonism.[57] Such attitudes were notably missing in English purchases.

But the decentralized process of acquiring Native American lands through individual actions—labor and purchase—produced endless conflicts among settlers claiming to have "labored" on or "purchased" land from Native Americans. For nearly two centuries, Englishmen sued each other in a never-ending battle over the legitimacy of their "acquisitions" from Indians.[58] Such widespread internal dissension eventually led authorities to insist upon consolidating control over the acquisition of land from Native Americans. First colonial and then national officials at the end of the eighteenth century insisted upon the transfer of land through centrally written and authorized agreements, which they called *treaties*.

Treaties: English New World Purchases

The word *treaty* has a distinctive origin and unusual history in English, one that gives it a uniquely different meaning. Whereas in other European languages *treaty* came from the word meaning "to deal with in person and face to face," in English the word originally meant "writing"—as opposed to speaking, or gesturing, or participating in a ritual.[59] From the fourteenth century, when the word first appeared in the language, until the middle of the seventeenth century, the word *treaty* primarily meant a form of inscription: a story, narrative, or written account, treating a subject in writing; a (literary) treatment; a discussion.[60]

Any written agreement between two English subjects could be and indeed was called a treaty. Not until the mid-seventeenth century (roughly around the time of the Peace of Westphalia) did the word *treaty* in English become commonly used to refer to an agreement between states.[61] Hence the earliest "treaties" between English colonists and Native Americans were simply written agreements. The 1621 "treaty" between Massasoit, leader of the Pokanoket, and the Plymouth colony was not necessarily an accord between nations; rather, it was an agreement that was recorded on paper.[62]

In the other European languages, the word *treaty* usually referred to personal contacts or dealings with a person. In Spanish, Portuguese, Dutch, and French, the word came from the verb *to treat*, meaning "to relate to or deal with someone personally." A treaty was thus something arranged in person, as opposed to communicated anonymously or over great distances. Treaties therefore could result only from direct personal contact between one group and another.[63]

A second unique dimension to the English use of the word *treaty* in the Americas concerns its objective. Overseas Portuguese—and then later French and Dutch—traders started to use treaties in the sixteenth century to acquire from the natives everything from sugar to shellac.[64] These formally negotiated agreements served primarily to regulate the flow of trade goods.[65] The Dutch adopted these Portuguese practices as they displaced the Portuguese in the African and Asian trade in the seventeenth century. And as Dutch influence itself waned in Africa and Asia, both British and French trading companies subsequently imitated their predecessors' practice of acquiring trade goods through treaties.[66]

The Spanish empire also used treaties in a slightly different context. Accustomed to signing truce agreements when they could not win wars against Muslims in Iberia, Spanish officials began to use written agreements in the Americas under similar circumstances. After the major conquests had ended, Spaniards increasingly encountered large Native American groups who practiced what Diego de Almagro christened "guerrilla" strategies, raiding Spanish supply and communications routes. Realizing that full-scale continued war was a fruitless effort, Spanish officials signed agreements not to launch hostilities in order to ensure the continued flow of goods and services through regions dominated by hostile tribes. They commonly termed these truces *pacts* and later sometimes *treaties*.

But in the New World, English officials did not customarily use treaties principally to acquire beaver skins, canoes, or other trade goods, as had the Dutch and Portuguese. During the second half of the seventeenth century, English officials occasionally signed agreements to end hostilities, as did the Spanish. After the early eighteenth century, English officials most often used treaties to acquire or fix the boundaries of land.[67] On the face of it, there was little in these English-language treaties to distinguish them from purchases. English "treaties" frequently involved the exchange of money for land and resulted in the permanent loss of ownership by natives.[68] Coercion and threats frequently occurred in the course of treaty negotiations when natives refused to release their land.[69]

But two significant factors did separate treaty purchases from simple purchases. First was the political standing of the signatories: purchasers were private individuals, whereas treaty signers were government representatives. Under a treaty purchase, the crown (and later the national government) formally authorized the acquisition of land. After the Norman Conquest, all title to land was held from the sovereign. When English sovereigns or their representatives signed written agreements with the natives, such accords constituted the most secure legal title to native lands under English law.[70] Furthermore, the treaty purchases had the added benefit of creating state control over the distribution of an economic asset widely desired by the state's subjects and later citizens, thus enabling public officials to dispense new land grants and put an end to ceaseless squabbles among colonists.

Second, the practices surrounding the signing of written documents (treaty purchases) differed notably from the previously popular strategies of labor and purchase, both of which lacked ritual content.[71] Negotiations and signings of land treaty purchases often included elements of indigenous ceremonies: a circulating peace pipe, lengthy speeches, even the proper decorum during speeches (silence).[72] During these formalized treaty purchase negotiations, Englishmen participated in Native American rituals to guarantee their power to bind the natives to the surrender of land, despite the native peoples' own understandings of the agreements they had concluded.[73] The incorporation of native ceremonial devices did not create bilaterally binding agreements.[74]

The incorporation of native rituals into the discussions did not mean that natives had any greater control over the terms. Governor Clinton of New York reminded the natives of "smoking our Pipes together" when telling them that the deed they signed had no resemblance to what they had been told they were signing.[75] In 1790, three Oneida leaders wrote:

> We returned home [after treaty negotiations] possessed with an Idea that we had leased our Country to the People of the State, reserving a Rent which was to increase with the increase of the Settlements on our Lands

until the whole Country was settled, and then to remain a standing Rent forever. This Brother was our Idea of the Matter. We supposed that we had at the same time reserved a sufficient Tract of Country for our own Cultivation; but since we had time to consult the Writings and have them property explained, and have seen the Proceedings of your Surveryors, we find our Hopes and Expectations blasted and disappointed in every particular. Instead of leasing our Country to you for a respectable Rent, we find that we have ceded and granted it forever for the Consideration of the inconsiderable Sum of Six hundred dollars per Year."[76]

In particular, English colonists disregarded the reverence that Native Americans had for the spoken word. Instead, Englishmen relied upon their own new eighteenth-century rules, which largely rendered the once valued oral agreements worthless in comparison to the written text.[77]

Juxtapositions: The Labor (and Capital) Theory in Comparative Perspective

Two of the other European nations colonizing the New World also accepted a role for labor and capital (accompanied by a written statement) in claiming overseas possessions. Both Portugal and the Netherlands recognized forms of labor and capital as creating valid rights to monetary rewards. But leaders of both powers asserted that such efforts could apply only to sea-lanes and commerce, not land.

Whereas English colonists remained convinced that labor meant farming, and that farming (and planting plus capital) entitled them to appropriate *land*, Portuguese and Dutch colonists believed that labor only really meant taking risks at sea. High-seas navigation was the most hazardous peacetime work of the fifteenth century. Even in the early twenty-first century, going to sea is the riskiest occupation around. According to the U.S. government, even commercial fishermen face a risk of death on the job that is up to thirty times greater than that for any other occupation.[78] For these two major seagoing powers, ownership-making labor and capital were expended only at sea. Therefore labor and capital could create rights only over new ocean routes—never over land.

In slightly different and competing ways, both the Portuguese and the Dutch asserted that labor performed at sea created the right to control the new maritime approaches they had discovered.[79] Both further concurred that the labor and capital expended on finding new ocean routes at sea could legitimately create exclusive sailing and trading rights in distant parts of the world.

The Netherlands States General in 1614 described the "diligence, *labor,* danger, and *expense*" of oceangoing discovery, as well as the "outlays, trouble, and risk" involved as a legitimate justification for exclusive commercial privileges. The States General often referred to "great expenses and damages by loss of ships and other dangers" as exclusively entitling Dutch citizens to gain.[80] Both the labor and the expense of oceangoing voyages of exploration were often described as "due to our own efforts" and "at the cost of our own Netherlanders."[81] And in all cases, the States General assured Dutch citizens that they were entitled to financial rewards (in the form of exclusive rights to trade) for their expenditure of labor and funds on the high seas.

Portuguese kings also spent significant amounts of their treasury on voyages of discovery, and they also insisted that such capital outlays created ownership of those discoveries. Portuguese legal scholar Seraphim de Freitas declared, "He who makes the preparations or publicly known expenditures . . . is held as the owner" of newly accessible resources.[82]

Portuguese monarchs and subjects also argued for economic rewards because they had taken considerable risks. Sailors and pilots were risking their worldly goods, as well as their lives, and hence believed themselves entitled to significant compensation. Navigator Duarte Pacheco Pereira declared that Portugal was entitled to exclusive use of maritime routes because "the discovery [by sea] of these lands . . . cost . . . the deaths of many men."[83] Once ensconced overseas, Portuguese colonizers never considered farming to be as risky as sailing, hence it remained undeserving of the economic rewards that seaborne navigation merited. In fact, Portuguese colonists shared a history of derision for farming. Portuguese colonists saw themselves as forward-looking investors employing capital to improve agricultural production and to market exportable commodities overseas. They understood themselves as commodity brokers and marketers, not as farmers.

Wrote a leading Portuguese humanist, Clenardo, in 1535, "If agriculture was held in contempt anywhere, it was incontestably in Portugal."[84] Portuguese colonists derided farming as stupid and backward-looking—it was an occupation for losers. "Only with some reservations can the term 'agriculture' be applied to the processes of exploitation of the earth widely established in the country with sugar mills," observed one of Brazil's leading historians, and the use of iron plows in Brazil produced drastic agricultural failures.[85] Even when agricultural goods have been a major source of international revenue for Brazil (sugar in the seventeenth and eighteenth centuries, coffee in the nineteenth and twentieth), the nation has never identified itself with agricultural production.[86]

Such scornful attitudes contrasted acutely with deeply engrained Anglo-Saxon prejudices. Cotton Mather, for example, referred to the semidivine nature of labor with plows ("It seems to be at the Plow, is to be where the Influences of Heaven may find us").[87] But such divine inspiration failed to descend on planters elsewhere in the Americas.

Other Europeans mocked English claims that they had a right to the New World because they "farmed" it. Dutch colonists characteristically scoffed at this English rationale, and conservative Spanish critics found such efforts equally unbelievable. "Mere theft," declared Juan Ginés Sepúlveda, the most conservative advocate of Spanish colonialism in the sixteenth century.[88] Yet whereas other Europeans found implausible the explanation that one could own the land by merely farming it, giving money (with or without native consent),[89] or signing a private agreement, Englishmen did not. And whereas other European colonists considered such explanations to be deliberate efforts to deceive others, in fact, English colonists needed only to convince themselves.

2

Imagining a Waste Land; or, Why Indians Vanish

When Queen Elizabeth first formally authorized New World colonization, she alluded only to spaces, not to people. Declaring that Englishmen were entitled to take over "Cities, Castles, Towns and Villages," she said nothing about the people who already lived there.[1] Cities, towns, and villages were implicitly inhabited, but Elizabeth did not acknowledge their residents. Thus Indians first vanish in the formal history of English colonization. Their presence on the land is omitted in the initial and all subsequent official authorizations for settlement.

Two powerful associations with the word *land* led English colonists to assert that the New World land was uninhabited. The first such usage is well-known. For much of the twentieth century, literary and social critics repeatedly noted the ways colonists gendered the land as female. Walter Ralegh and Richard Hakluyt frequently labeled the land "virgin," linking uncultivated terrain to a lack of sexual experience.[2]

Calling uncultivated land "virgin" land frequently encouraged a masculine fantasy of the initial plowing as a carnal act. Descriptions of tilling the ground regularly appeared as a male erotic role—plowing the field or furrowing. And imagining sexual intimacy between male colonists and the land effectively excluded others from the relationship, including the natives.

Englishwomen also employed metaphorically erotic images of the landscape. Images of hilly terrain were described as "nature's bosom." Slightly different metaphors of intimacy appeared among women colonizers, including the intimate entwining of cultivated vines and houses.[3] The intimacy of garden and house also expressed an exclusive emotional bonding with the landscape that rendered natives equally invisible.

A second powerful association of the word *land* with even more significant consequences for the natives was that of "waste land." Long before a single Englishman ever set foot on American soil or even claimed a square inch of New World territory, Sir Thomas More invoked this expression as justification for Englishmen's seizing of others' lands. More, inspired by Amerigo Vespucci's partially fictional best-seller about his voyages to Brazil, described an imaginary new world he named Utopia. Using as a speaker a make-believe member (Raphael Hythloday) of Vespucci's voyages, More included in his story a description of an island off Brazil's coast inhabited by *"a people which does not use its soil but keeps it idle and waste* [and] nevertheless forbids the use and possession of it to others."[4] Upon finding such lands, More's Utopians were entitled "by rule of nature" to take over and farm so "that the ground which before was neither good nor profitable . . . is now sufficient and fruitful." Should the existing residents object, the Utopians "[may] drive them [the natives] out. . . . For they count this the most just cause of war."[5]

Modern analysts rarely see More as laying the groundwork for overseas takeovers. Rather, they customarily class him as a humanist—someone attaching primary importance to human beings and their values. The name of his fictional world, *Utopia*, has become synonymous with an ideal society. But despite his lack of intentional malice, More unself-consciously justified a right to colonize that wholly disregarded the rights of the original inhabitants of a land.

More's ideas were distinctive in another way that is rarely noted: his statements were based on information from the New World. Despite relying upon Vespucci's accounts of what were, in fact, Portuguese voyages to Brazil, More's approach had nothing in common with that of his Portuguese contemporaries. His fellow humanist João de Barros wrote scathingly of *Utopia*. It was, Barros declared, not for all people, but "a modern fable . . . to teach the English how to rule."[6]

Utopians' desire to settle and farm relatively unused terrain would be echoed by generations of subsequent English colonists. And yet when More formulated these ideas he lacked any direct, firsthand knowledge of the New World. He called it "waste" because in English history, and in the

English language of the sixteenth century, it was customary to describe underutilized terrain as waste land.[7]

Waste

Although More described the original inhabitants of Utopia as keeping their land "idle and waste," the word *waste* did not acquire its usual modern meaning of "trash" or "refuse" until the eighteenth century. Rather, the words *waste* and *land* originally came into English from two different languages. *Land* is shared with Norwegian, Dutch, Swedish, Danish, Frisian, and German. *Waste*, on the other hand, is common in the Romance languages, and came into English from French. Thus the combination of *waste* and *land* was a hybrid concept produced in the wake of the Norman Conquest. Forty years after the Norman victory, the term *waste land* was first used in English.[8]

In its initial deployment, *waste* referred to the density of settlement, signifying uninhabited or relatively underinhabited ground. Despite subsequently acquiring other meanings, the word has retained this original sense.[9] Its other early meanings included "wilderness" and "an uncultivated terrain." Thus from its earliest use in twelfth-century English, *waste land* did not simply mean unused ground. Rather, it signified specifically terrain that was not being farmed, and with few or no people.

During the fourteenth century, the negative connotations of *waste* grew, but not so far as to mean "refuse."[10] In addition to signifying uncultivated land, it meant ground yielding little by way of either woods or forage.[11] But *waste* (sometimes rendered in Latin as *vacuum*) soon became entangled with yet another and different set of ideas, those relating to ownership.[12]

Although it may at first seem odd that use and ownership customs might be attached to the meaning of waste, the logic is not hard to follow. Beginning in the ninth or tenth (but not later than the eleventh) century, Englishmen began to use animal power to help plow fields.[13] Horse-drawn plows worked well in light soils, but mules and oxen were required as draft animals in order to break up heavy clay soil so that seeds and tiny plants would have room to send out roots.[14] The move to animal power was aided in large part by the widespread availability of mules, oxen, and horses.[15]

Employing such large farm animals required feeding them. Nearby unplowed ground was often covered with tasty grasses that animals could devour at no additional cost to the farmer. And because many farmers needed to feed their draft animals, uncultivated land close at hand began to be shared. Although someone might own such land, a local lord perhaps, it was his "waste"—that is, his uncultivated land—that was being used.[16] Hence by the start of the fifteenth century, the common feeding of animals often took place on "waste"—unfarmed land that was shared ("in common").

The idea of common land added two new dimensions to earlier understandings of "waste." First, *common* meant something belonging to or shared by the community, something to be used by all. *Common* defined not just what the land was being used for, but who was using it. According to the *Oxford English Dictionary, common* signifies "belonging equally to more than one; possessed or shared alike by both or all (the persons or things in question)" and "a common land or estate; the undivided land belonging to the members of a local community as a whole."[17] Thus *common* added the concept of shared use or shared ownership to the idea of waste.

In the Middle Ages, English farmland—as opposed to waste land—was usually designated by a variety of physical indicators. First, boundary markers often noted its contours and were one of the principal visible signs by which people could recognize privately held farmland or pasture-land. Second, cultivated ground was usually turned under, either to aerate the soil or to prevent weeds from acquiring deep roots. Since Anglo-Saxon times, Englishmen had plowed by hand (and later using animals) even land that they were not going to plant. If a plot of land was to lie fallow for a year or more it was plowed, "broken up and cleared as firmly as any arable."[18] Sometimes even pasture was tilled.[19] Thus another unique feature of English fallow land was that it retained the marks of plowing in between bouts of use.

In England, allowing plowed land to return to its natural wooded or meadowed state (even when lying fallow) was considered worse than simply failing to use the land; it was an act of destruction subject to legal action. Land lying fallow without the markings of plows had clearly been abandoned. If a tenant let the land grow weeds, the landlord was entitled to compensation for an economic loss. "If a tenant converts arable land into wood or meadow, it is waste," wrote Sir Edward Coke.[20]

Improvement

More endorsed Utopians' taking over land that was "idle and waste." He rationalized their actions of making such terrain "sufficient and fruitful" by using labor on it (farming). Englishmen understood their farming as creating a betterment, or, as they called it, an improvement. However, when sixteenth-century Englishmen used the word *improvement,* they often meant something far more concrete.

Initially, *improvement* meant only financial gain, investing or using money to make a profit.[21] Like *waste*, which retained one of its original meanings while acquiring other divergent meanings, the word *improvement* also maintained the principal meaning of profitability while adding several other seemingly unrelated connotations over the years.

During the 1300s, the word *improvement* came to signify making profits in agriculture. Specifically, it denoted the landowner's profitable cultivation of his terrain, resulting in revenues for the king.[22] Over the next hundred years, this sense—generating profits from farming—overwhelmed the word's more general connotations. By the mid-fourteenth century, English landowners had begun finding another way of increasing their farms' profits: reclaiming "waste" or unoccupied land.[23] And the coincidental timing of this historical event led to the creation of yet another, linguistically unique meaning for *improvement*. For the first time, the word began to be associated with fencing.

Farmers in England had always taken great pains to define the edges of their properties with fences, stones, or hedges of thorns or other impassable materials.[24] Thirteenth-century Anglo-Saxon elites started erecting fences to contain semiwild animals so that they could be more readily hunted, a practice that imitated a method used by their Norman rulers.[25] Thus the verb *to enclose* first meant "to seclude" or "to imprison," because the action trapped semiwild animals.[26] By the fifteenth century, however, the word became broadened, signifying generally "to surround with walls, fences, or other barriers so as to prevent [both] free ingress or egress."[27] The word that once meant hemming animals in came to mean keeping people and animals in as well as keeping them out. Thus the fence, symbolically delimiting boundaries of property (culturally of great weight in English society), during the fourteenth century also became a means of denying communal farmers access to terrain they had once used.

By the first decade of the sixteenth century, *to enclose* most usually meant to erect a fence that would prevent farmers and herders from entering formerly cooperatively or communally held ground.[28] Fenced "common" or "waste" land was now used for private farming or herding, and for profit.[29] Hence the word *improvement* had become identified with fencing, excluding traditional users from "waste" or common lands.

Erecting fences also rationalized a particular cultural allocation of profits: only the person who did the fencing had a right to the profits. English enclosures did not want communal and cooperative tillers of the soil in England to become more efficient and profitable producers. Rather, they were enriching themselves alone—as the values of their culture suggested they had a right to do—by evicting the previous legal users of the terrain. Even Thomas More wrote that those Utopians who transformed "ground which before was neither good nor profitable" into terrain that was "sufficient [and] fruitful" were not obligated to share the profits with those people whose land the Utopians took in order to become wealthy. This implied understanding of the right to profit from seizing others' "waste" lands was unique to English language and culture.

In the languages of other European colonizing nations, the term *waste land* was unappealing. French and Dutch—the languages of the two other nations colonizing the same region of North America as the English—did not link *waste* with simple underutilization. *Braakland* is simply lying fallow; *onvruchtbaar, infertile,* and *onbehouwd,* uncultivated; and *woest*—the closest in sound to the English *waste*—has connotations of savagery and fierceness. These were not exactly appealing associations for potential colonists. Although French comes closer to English in implying a relatively uninhabited land, the terms *terre désolée* and *désert* also connote desolate, devastated, and desert—all of which suggest an unattractive land, unfit for human habitation.[30]

The New World as Waste

Englishmen frequently repeated More's characterization of the New World as a "waste land." William Strachey characterized the terrain as "the waste and vast, uninhabited growndes." So too did Robert Gray: "so great a Circuit [lies] vayne and idle."[31] Yet English colonists and advocates like More who had never even seen the New World claimed that America was a "waste" or "idle" land because it matched their cultural images of waste land. Englishmen reading about or laying eyes on the New World discovered a terrain without plow marks made by draft animals, without boundary monuments, and without significant numbers of people.

Englishmen thus noted the absence of plow marks they expected to see in a productive landscape, whether actively cultivated or temporarily unused. Native Americans, however, did not leave such traces upon the landscape. In the New World, natives customarily allowed temporarily inactive ground to return to its natural state of meadowlands or woodlands, making it appear unused to Englishmen. Also in no part of the Americas did there exist any indigenous animals capable of pulling plows. The closest were the pack-bearing alpaca and vicuña, neither of which was suitable for use in farming.[32]

Natives tilled the soil by hand. Samuel de Champlain noted that the Massachusetts Indians "cultivate and till the ground . . . [with] an instrument of wood, very strong, made like a spade . . . planting three or four grains in a place . . . then planting again as much as three feet off and so on."[33] Another writer observed a slightly different process of planting: natives made "heaps like molehills" that "they sow or plant in April with maize."[34] Hence New World lands, even when planted, were not plowed by animals and therefore did not appear to have been farmed "properly."

Englishmen's next visual clue that the New World was an uncultivated or waste land was the absence of boundary markers. Physical objects, animate or inanimate, rarely defined the limits of terrain used for hunting or farming in any area of the New World. English colonists consequently concluded that the natives either were occupying limitless terrain or, more likely, were treating it as a commons.[35] In 1690, John Locke explicitly characterized the New World native as "the wild Indian who knows no enclosure and is still a tenant in common"—that is, someone "still," in spite of everything, owning land communally.[36]

Native land in the New World was in fact a complex mixture of individual private property and communally held land. It was subject to communal use rights and individual usufruct, depending upon the region, the tribe, and the community.[37] The Hurons, for example, considered forests, plains, and uncleared land as common areas, but they regarded cleared land as family property as long as those who cleared it used it.[38]

The final visual clue signaling the New World's status as waste land was its relative underpopulation. Colonial advocates endlessly mentioned disparities in population between England and the New World in order to establish the legitimacy of English settlement. Wrote Walter Ralegh, "If the title of occupiers be good in land unpeopled, why should it be bad accounted in a country peopled over thinly?"[39] Anglican preachers William Symonds and Patrick Copeland argued for the settlement of Virginia because "Our Countrey aboundeth with people: your Colony wanteth them."[40] Another prominent colonial advocate, Samuel Purchas, wrote in 1624, "His Majestie hath . . . disposed the overflowing numbers of his Subjects . . . in the spacious American regions (some thinly, others not all inhabited)."[41] The rationale for seizing New World lands because they were relatively unpopulated was often stated forthrightly. Richard Eburne wrote in 1624, "When finding a Country quite void of people . . . we seize upon it, take it, possesse it, as by the Lawes of God and Nations, lawfully we may hold it as our owne, and so fill and replenish it with our people."[42]

Stressing population disparities reinforced Englishmen's perception of their legitimate actions in occupying a "waste" land. If the land was considered settled, then their title to the New World was, in Englishmen's eyes, somewhat less legitimate. "I like a plantation in a pure soil; that is where people are not displanted, to the end to plant in others; for else it is rather an extirpation than a plantation," wrote Francis Bacon in 1625.[43] Therefore English colonists had powerful reasons for minimizing the extent of native settlements.

Labeling this (actually unique) desire to settle relatively uninhabited land as a "Law of God and Nations" was one strategy for claiming universality for an English cultural phenomenon. Another approach was to assert that such a principle could be found even in nature.[44] And one of Englishmen's favorite nature metaphors involved bees. Eburne wrote, "It is time, and even high time, that [Englishmen] like stalls that are overfull of bees or orchards overgrown with young sets, no small number of them should be transplanted into some other soil and removed hence into new lives and homes."[45] Walter Ralegh observed, "When any country is overlaid by the multitude which lie upon it, there is *a natural necessity* compelling it to disburden itself and lay the load upon others by right or wrong."[46] But as a claim to a principle of nature, let alone a universal axiom, such a statement did not hold up to scrutiny. Only Englishmen believed that a large population size justified their "disburdening" of some of that population onto the lands of others.

Modern observers are often surprised to learn that when the English occupied the New World, both the Netherlands and France were far more densely populated than England.[47] Yet neither French nor Dutch colonists justified their overseas settlement by citing either "overpopulation" at home or population disparities overseas. On the contrary, French political leaders believed that keeping people at home preserved the wealth of the country, and they feared that emigration might lead to depopulation.[48] Nor was empty land as appealing to the French as it was to their English counterparts. Frenchmen principally migrated to a few small Caribbean islands rather than to vastly less populated reaches of what is now Canada.[49]

The single most densely settled European country of the seventeenth century, the Netherlands, sent the smallest total number of colonists abroad.[50] But the economic and political climate of the Netherlands was vastly different from that of England. Perhaps the most tolerant region in Christian Europe, the Netherlands continually welcomed religious dissenters from other nations (including the Puritans, who lived in Leiden for many years). They also welcomed forcibly converted Portuguese Jews and Spaniards fleeing the Inquisition. Nor had the Netherlands undergone the kind of massive social disruption and concentration of wealth in the hands of increasingly fewer landowners that reduced or eliminated economic opportunities in sixteenth-century England. The Netherlands economy was booming; citizens could be persuaded only with difficulty to leave domestic comfort for insecurity overseas. The States General noted in 1633 that "those who will labor in any way here [in the Netherlands] can easily obtain support, and, therefore [they] are disinclined to go from home on an uncertainty."[51]

England had not excess population but surplus labor, relative to the employment opportunities at hand. England alone of the European powers was shunting long-term farmers off the land, leaving them and their skills redundant. The sudden increase in unemployed and homeless people in England resulted predominantly from the enclosure movement that had abruptly severed thousands of people from the only way of earning an income that they and their forefathers had ever known.

Rather than attributing the sudden rise in the unemployed to the recently created enclosures, English elites blamed the victims, holding the displaced rather than the enclosures culpable for "diverse kindes of wrongs." These people were portrayed as "a contynual cause of dearth and famine, and the very originall cause of all the Plagues that happen in this Kingdome."[52] Robert Gray in 1609 warned even more ominously of "mutinies, sedition, commotion and rebellion, scarcitie, dearth, povertie, and sundrie sorts of calamities" that such individuals might create.[53] The solution that Englishmen conceived for this excess not of population but of labor was to send the unemployed abroad to find work.

Richard Hakluyt recommended sending "our superfluous people [i.e., labor] into those temperate and fertile parts of America."[54] For English elites, the New World would provide a convenient dumping ground.[55] Englishmen characteristically understood the injunction to colonize as, in Shakespeare's words, "having the world for your labour."[56] The thought would have been more explicit had he written, "having the world for your labor surplus." By using the word *waste* for New World lands, English elites could provide this "surplus" labor with an objective they considered desirable—farming the land of the New World.

Improving the New World

Englishmen believed that their actions would have a positive effect on the New World "waste" lands. Like More's Utopians, they were to take ground that "before was neither good nor profitable" and make it "sufficient and fruitful." Anglican clergymen Richard Hakluyt and William Strachey would express similar sentiments, as would Puritan leader John Cotton and famous Elizabethan men of action including John Smith and Walter Ralegh. Smith declared in 1631 that the New World had "more land than all the people in Christendome can manure [farm], and yet more . . . than all the natives of those Countries can use and cultivate. . . . Where . . . so much of the world [is] uninhabited . . . [it is] a good . . . were it manuered and used accordingly."[57] "If a people does not use its land, but leaves it infertile," wrote William Strachey, "possession [should be held] by those who would make use of it."[58] Puritan John Cotton in 1647 declared that the king had a right "to take possession of the voyd places of the Countrey by the Law of Nature, (for Vacuum Domicilium cedi occupanti)."[59] Walter Ralegh claimed, as did More, that occupying underutilized land was "the most just cause of war."[60]

Countless English colonists thus understood themselves (and their fellow countrymen) as people "who would make use of" the New World land, or, as they often said, as people who "will possesse and improve it."[61] Both sets of expressions identified Englishmen as effectively using the terrain, laboring on it, tilling the soil, planting crops, and raising domesticated animals, concretely making the ground "fruitful." "Indians," Puritan Robert Cushman alleged in 1621, "are not industrious, neither have art, science, skill or faculty to use either the land or the commodities of it, but all spoils, rots and is marred for want of manuring, gathering, ordering, etcs. As the ancient patriarchs therefore moved from stranger places into more room, where the land lay idle and vast, and none used it . . . so it is lawful to take a land which none useth and make use of it."[62]

By the end of the seventeenth century, such sentiments about Englishmen's right to expropriate "waste" had become English political orthodoxy. In the second of his *Two Treatises of Government*, John Locke stated, "In distinct Parts and parcels of the Earth: yet there are still great Tracts of Ground to be found, which . . . *lie waste*, and are more than the People, who dwell on it, do, or can make use of," adding that such land "is *free to any that will possesse and improve it*."[63] Locke, rather than advocating warfare as did More and Ralegh, asserted that unused excess capacity could be expropriated (implicitly without payment) to anyone who would make productive use of it. The means that English colonists used to improve such land were those they had learned in England.

Farming, cultivating the soil with plows, and raising large animals for food and transportation all constituted the labor of improving the New World. Colonists were quick to use fences to enclose and thereby claim their cultivated ground, pointing to the physical object as concretizing their labor.[64] As historian William Cronon notes, the fence "to colonists represented perhaps the most visible symbol of an improved landscape."[65]

That belief was not shared by all European colonists. Dutchmen customarily used polder or dikes to separate land in the Netherlands, but in the New World they often used fences—in part because timber was more readily available than in the Netherlands. But fences were not part of the ethos of claiming new terrain in Dutch settlements, nor were they seen as visibly demonstrating labor or "improvement." Rather, fences had to be placed in accordance with surveys of the land, materializing the formal boundaries fixed by writing.[66]

To Englishmen, however, fences terminated the rights of communal landholders. Thus laying out boundaries, building stone walls, and putting up hedges created the reliable sensation of familiarity and rightness among English colonists dispossessing "communal" Indian landowners in the New World. These actions led some historians to describe "colonization . . . [as] a struggle to define boundaries on the landscape."[67] But defining boundaries meant excluding Native Americans.

The oldest and most traditional meaning of the word *improvement* was, in the words of Walter Blith, to "convert the land to the best profit."[68] The *Oxford English Dictionary* (second edition) defines the verb *to improve* in terms virtually identical to Blith's: "to turn land to profit, to enclose and cultivate (waste land); hence to make land more valuable or better by such means." But the word carried a distinctive cultural understanding of the social allocation of profits—an expectation of who had a right to profit from an enclosure.

According to English culture, only the person who did the fencing had a right to the profits. The English carried this belief to most of their successful overseas colonies and never considered options that became common elsewhere in the Americas.[69] The English could just as easily have taught the natives how to make profitable uses of the land, or they might have introduced the natives to more profitable products and allowed them to cultivate such crops, as did Iberian colonists throughout the Americas[70]— but the English did not.

English settlers in Maryland and Virginia took away natives' lands in order to produce themselves—at a handsome profit for nearly two centuries—a Native American crop, tobacco.[71] English colonists assumed that they alone held the right to receive the profits from land, and they felt neither a moral nor a social responsibility to share those earnings with the aboriginal peoples whose land they had taken. English colonists in the

Americas were thus reproducing the social allocation of wealth that had been legitimate in their home society, where enclosers had neither economic nor social responsibility for those they displaced.

Inventing themselves in the familiar and emotionally powerful role of "improvers" had a final significance for English colonists. In thus identifying themselves, English-speaking settlers rationalized their enduring economic success as the result of their own efforts rather than the dispossession of others. Thus they could vicariously partake in the sense of supremacy shared by enclosers in England. In the New World, all colonists were evicting landlords and all aboriginal peoples were the expelled. Ordinary Englishmen, sometimes even the formerly evicted, could replicate overseas their dispossessing landlords' powerful emotional conviction of superiority. Thus English colonists and their leaders likewise lacked any interest in helping natives in the New World achieve profitability.

There was an additional motive for the lack of interest in promoting native agricultural development. English elites were inspired to support overseas colonization partly by the goal of ridding the country of a potentially politically troublesome excess of labor. Training aboriginal inhabitants to develop their own agriculture would have reduced the number of superfluous English workers and dissidents that could be shipped overseas. Indigenous labor was not the English elites' concern; English labor was. Therefore the English colonists' primary interests lay in displacing native peoples' labor, not in helping it to become profitable or in joining it with that of English producers.

Like many colonizers, Englishmen were ambivalent about their efforts overseas and the consequences of those efforts. But they only regretted the loss of open space, the disappearance of the waste land they were occupying.

History and the Loss of the Commons

As enclosures slowly reduced the amount of communally held waste land in England, many on Albion's soil lamented the loss of common land. Among those mourning this disappearance was Thomas More, whose Utopians owned land in common—even though they first had to eject the original inhabitants ruthlessly in order to do so. More's attitudes reflected nostalgia for a fast-disappearing moment of communal landownership, which was linked to a desire to re-create this communal ownership overseas.

Even more famously than Thomas More, John Locke linked America to England's vanishing past, noting with yearning that "in the beginning, all the world was America." By "all the world was America," Locke referred to the Native American system of communal landownership. Thus "in the beginning," Locke claimed, all people held land in common. But this characterization misrepresented indigenous communities.[72]

Both the natives' "communal" landownership and the enclosing English landlords operated at the same historical moment, the sixteenth and seventeenth centuries. But referring to the natives' actual practices as "all the world's" in the beginning meant characterizing the natives' existing customs as more than backward, as belonging to the past. But like so many colonial assertions, this invention of communal landownership as a historical anachronism was uniquely English. Only in seventeenth-century England was communal "waste" land being transformed into privately owned terrain. Locke was inserting the natives' actuality not just into history, but specifically into English history.

In misrecognizing the natives' present as England's past, Locke was also mislabeling English colonists' individual ownership as belonging to the future. If Native Americans represented the past, then English colonists represented the world to come. What Locke characterized as the future, however, was in fact merely a continuation of the English present—the ongoing (sixteenth- and seventeenth-century) transformation of "idle" land into "profitable" ground through fencing and other acts of "improving" landlords. Just as such misrepresentations allowed landlords in England to understand their own ends as forward-looking, overseas Englishmen could rationalize seizing land from Native Americans with the same logic. If in America the past of England's communal landownership still existed, settlers could envision themselves as bringing inescapable historical progress to "communal" landholders. In Locke's formulation, colonists did not need to believe they were the wicked dispossessors of Native American farmers; rather, they were the slightly apologetic bearers of unavoidable historical and economic progress.[73]

But regret alters only sentiments, not necessarily practices. The vision of themselves as reluctant bearers of progress allowed colonists to express feelings of loss while continuing to dispossess the natives of their terrain. This sentimental nostalgia that depicted the American present as England's own past ("in the beginning") provided Englishmen with a powerfully persuasive way of sidestepping any sense of responsibility for expropriating "communal" native landowners. And there were good reasons for so doing.

From the time that More penned *Utopia* until the first sustained English settlement in the New World, numerous critics vocally expressed reservations about the considerable social consequences of enclosure-induced evictions in England. Whereas an "improvement" signified increased profitability for the fortunate few who owned land, "improvements" removed thousands of less fortunate individuals from their lands and their livelihoods, leaving them unemployed and homeless. And although some publicly questioned the social worthiness of a system that drove thousands of formerly hardworking people into unemployment, many more, including government leaders, responded vindictively, even passing measures demanding the enslavement of the dispossessed.[74] By late Elizabethan times, such vengefulness had diminished, resulting in the adoption of a series of measures—the "poor laws"—aimed at providing a minimum level of social assistance for those expelled from the land by the enclosure juggernaut.

However, neither the hostile public criticism of enclosures' inevitable disruptions nor the concern for the dispossessed transferred overseas. Rather, the colonists identified themselves with the enclosing landowners and continued to utilize the term *improvement* to justify their New World activities, long after such a rationale had outlived its usefulness in Britain.[75]

Not surprisingly, the *Oxford English Dictionary* notes that this fencing and enclosure-based meaning of *improvement* continued to be used in America long after it ceased being popular in England. This meaning, "*especially* used of the lord's inclosing and bringing into cultivation of waste land," enjoyed greater longevity in America than in England. It was "retained in the 17th–18th centuries in the American colonies," thus revealing the enduring attractiveness of enclosing landlords' rationales in the English-speaking New World.[76]

This lack of concern for the fate of the dispossessed overseas became one of the hallmarks of English colonial thinking, separating colonial attitudes from those at home. In England, public approval of the landowner's superiority and sole right to profit had been widespread but not universal. The enclosures provoked a small but thoughtful strain of criticism from some of England's elites, but this capacity for empathy with the dispossessed stopped at England's shores. Englishmen were either unable or unwilling to acknowledge identical consequences or to empathize with people overseas who neither looked nor sounded like them.

Furthermore, English colonists settling in the Americas viewed themselves as displaced by pressures for religious conformity and lack of economic opportunities; thus they often identified *themselves* as victims in the New World. And, as frequently happens with those portraying themselves as victims, they felt entitled to minimize, if not forget, any social responsibility for people they in turn were victimizing. Portraying themselves as sufferers contributed to their lack of empathy for the natives. Therefore, the English colonists were able to ignore the fact that they themselves were inducing poverty and homelessness among people whose lives and livelihoods had once stood secure.[77]

In rationalizing their entitlement to the New World, the English were doing, in a fundamental way, no more and no less than other Europeans who understood their victories overseas as fundamentally deserved and merited. But the English were unique in understanding their seizure of relatively uninhabited terrain to be justifiable, and they were alone in viewing their superiority over natives as residing in farming and making profits.

The least savory consequence of Englishmen's desire to find relatively vacant land was their lack of concern for, and even the occasional celebration of, Indian deaths from disease. On the American frontier, biological warfare was an ideal strategy.[78] It killed people but did nothing to harm the productive capacity (and potential profitability) of the land. One English inhabitant of Long Island in 1670 wrote, "It hath generally been observed, that where the English come to settle, a Divine Hand makes way for them, by removing or cutting off the Indians, either by Wars one with the other, or by some raging Mortal Disease."[79]

James I of England, in his letter patent for the Plymouth colony dated November 3, 1620 (old style), wrote:

> Within this late yeares there hath by God's Visitation raigned a Wonderfull Plague . . . to the utter Destruction, Devastacion and Depopulation of the whole Territorye, so that there is not left for many Leagues together in a Manner any [person] that doe claim or challenge. . . . Whereby We in our Judgment are persuaded and satisfied that the appointed Time is come in which the Almighty God in his great Goodness and Bountie towards Us and our People hath thought fitt and determined that those large and goodly Territoryes, deserted as it were by their naturall inhabitants should be possesed and enjoyed.[80]

Not only did the English king not mourn the native deaths or take them (as had Charles V) as evidence of unjust and tyrannical conduct by colonists, he actually embraced them. To James I they were proof positive of divine intervention on behalf of the English.

Settlers as well as monarchs echoed similar sentiments embracing native deaths as a clear demonstration of divine intervention in their favor. John Winthrop suggested that the infection that hit the natives just before the Puritans arrived was evidence of God's hand in creating a vacant land:

"God hath consume the Natives with a great plage in those parts so there be few inhabitants left."[81]

Not all Europeans welcomed the disappearance of Native Americans from the landscape, however. Many Spaniards, including the monarch himself, viewed disease and other causes of native deaths as evidence of God's disfavor toward the colonists. Charles V in 1523 ordered Hernán Cortés to take into consideration "the monumental harm and losses received by the said Indians through their deaths and dwindling numbers and the great disservice that Our Lord has received because of it."[82] In a similar royal order to Ponce de León two years later, he added, "Not only has our duty to God Our Lord not been performed because such a multitude of souls have perished . . . but we ourselves [the crown] have been ill served by it as well."[83] The devastating loss of people threatened the basis of the Spanish monarch's collection of a per capita tax on Native Americans, but the English understood those same deaths as evidence of divine favor toward an empire that sought its overseas wealth in owning land.

3

Gendering Native Americans:

Hunters as Anglo-America's Partial Fiction

A unique characteristic of early English-language writings on the native peoples of the Americas is their fixation on the gendered division of labor. In North and South America there were many societies in which women were the farmers, planting and harvesting crops close to home, while men trekked further afield in pursuit of fish, game, fowl, or exotic plants that could be traded. All the societies encountered by the Portuguese in three hundred years of settlement shared this characteristic, as did many of the communities encountered by French, Dutch, and Spanish colonists. Yet this gendered division of labor is rarely mentioned outside of the English-language tracts.

During their first twenty-five years in the New World, Spaniards encountered only peoples with agricultural technology similar to that of the inhabitants of the northeastern United States.[1] Upon entering what is now the southwestern United States, Spaniards also found similarly equipped and organized societies. Yet Spanish tracts on the peoples of the Caribbean and the Southwest make only glancing reference to the division of labor, if they mention it at all. The early writings of the Portuguese Jesuits on the

Tupi-speaking peoples, which today occupy more than a thousand tightly printed pages, contain only three very brief mentions of the gendered division of labor.[2]

Yet derogatory comments on the identical division of labor—Native American women's farming and men's hunting—fairly leap off the pages of English-language writings and are hard to avoid.[3] To understand why gender should assume such a large position in English colonial writings, we need to examine what was at stake in the division of tasks between men and women.

The central reason Englishmen identified Indians as hunters lies in the nonverbal English theory of landownership: whoever farmed the land owned it. If men farmed the land, they owned it. Whereas in the Old World this individualism favored men, in the New World it potentially favored women, given that farming was predominantly a female occupation in the woodlands of eastern North America.[4] In the absence of the "deep-cutting plow pulled by large draft animals," historian James Axtell neutrally notes, native "women could easily hand-plant, hoe-weed, and harvest (with male help) the vegetable crops for the village."[5] Thus, according to the English theory of property, Native American women might be entitled, individually and personally, to own North American land because they cultivated it and labored on it.

Native women cultivators were performing the tasks that Englishmen needed to perform in order to rationalize their rightful ownership of the New World land. English male colonists did not wish to characterize their imperial ventures as a struggle against women overseas. Therefore for the English the dominant image of Native Americans would have to be identifiably male.

English male colonists were also afraid that Englishwomen would be inspired by Native American women to farm the New World lands themselves. Of course, if they farmed it, they would own it. Therefore English propagandists set out to make the life of the Indian woman seem so horrifyingly difficult that English female colonists would abhor the prospect of adopting native women's roles. Englishmen created the highly effective political myth of the "squaw drudge."[6] William Wood declared, "Their employments be many: first their building of houses . . . troubled like snails to carry their houses on their backs . . . planting of corn, [weeding] gather[ing] . . . covering it." His list goes on for several pages.[7]

Wood's target audience was Englishwomen. He noted, "Women readers [that is, Englishwomen] . . . may see their own happiness, if weighed in the woman's balance of these ruder Indians." He further claimed, "Since the English arrival, comparison [of labor tasks] hath made [Indian women] miserable."[8]

With the exception of helping to move their families' households, women in England labored in the fields, harvesting and weeding as did Native American women. However, the extent and the difficulty of women's agricultural labor in England had been increasingly minimized since the fourteenth century, when it acquired the new label of "housework." Women's labor in raising food crops became "gardening," whereas men's work became "husbandry" or farming.[9] Englishwomen's agricultural labor thus became categorized (in theory, but not always in practice) as subsistence work, with the level of effort minimized.[10] Ownership-creating labor implicitly referred to male, not female, toil.

English (male) colonists thus had several powerful motivations to avoid mentioning the female indigenous farmers of the New World. The dominant image of Native Americans would have to be identifiably male.

Because natives clearly subsisted on the terrain, English colonists would have to acknowledge that they performed *some* life-sustaining activity, albeit not at a level that would entitle them to ownership. The most popular sixteenth- and seventeenth-century English terms for male "non-laborer" or nonworker—*vagrant* and *vagabond*—implied that the offenders did no work at all. There was an activity, however, that could provide food, clothing, and shelter, but that did not entitle a breadwinner to own the land from which he obtained sustenance. Under English law, hunters did not necessarily own the land upon which they pursued game. Therefore Englishmen gradually came to characterize all Native Americans according to the male-dominated activity that did not allow its performers the right to own land: hunting.

The gendered political identity of "hunters" fixed natives as "nonowners" in the minds of English colonists, thereby allowing colonists to take over native lands in the name of "labor" or "farming." In characterizing Native American men as hunters, however, English colonists introduced an additional complication, for although hunting did not merit being called "work," there were forms of hunting that were denied to ordinary Englishmen. At the time of the conquest of the New World, English colonists' attitudes toward hunting comprised a mixture of disdain and jealousy.

Ambivalence Regarding Hunters

Sixteenth- and seventeenth-century Englishmen were torn between two conflicting hunting traditions. Medieval Saxon laws had allowed any citizen to hunt, often treating the activity as a kind of valuable public service that rid the countryside of boars and other dangerous animals.[11] After the Norman Conquest in 1066, however, certain types of hunting became a special privilege.

In traditional Norman society, hunting (particularly of large game) was a prerogative only of kings and nobles. Nobles had large tracts of land in their native Normandy reserved for their private use. But when they arrived in England, the victorious Normans encountered a society unfamiliar with their exclusionary practices. To introduce their custom of reserving land for elites' hunting, Normans had to resettle significant groups of Englishmen. Hundreds and even thousands of Englishmen and later Scotsmen were ejected from their homes to create hunting preserves, forests of fifteen to twenty thousand acres. The displaced launched protests in public and resented the displacement in private.[12]

The Normans introduced a second, even less popular, regulation that prohibited anyone but the king from hunting large animals. Persons who disobeyed this regulation could lose life or limb. The conquered English expressed their indignation at the novel restrictions and unprecedented severe penalties through popular legends about Robin Hood and his band of Merry Men.[13] More important, outrage over the new Norman rules centrally influenced the barons' uprising against King John, resulting in the signing of the Magna Carta (1215). This agreement put an end to the most drastic punishments for violating the king's hunting laws.[14]

Although resentment against the Normans' actions incited popular protest, the Norman tradition of reserving specific hunting grounds for the monarchs became English law. The Normans justified their actions by saying that kings had a right to hunt for amusement because of the great service they did their church and their country. Even the English legal great Sir Edward Coke called hunting a "royal pastime and [royalty's] lawful recreation."[15]

One of the frequent ironies of conquest is that at the same time defeated peoples resent the new constraints imposed by their conquerors, they often envy their conquerors' privileges in equal measure. Such envy can result in imitation. So it is not surprising that within a hundred years of conquest, English gentry, nobility, and ecclesiastics had reserved sections of their own estates as exclusive hunting zones. Only a few such "parks"—areas that enclosed semiwild creatures—existed before the Norman Conquest, but by 1200, hundreds of private hunting grounds had been created.[16]

Three hundred years later, the barons' revolt a distant memory, the

English upper classes again mimicked the Norman example. They prohibited the lower classes from hunting animals traditionally reserved for the nobility in Normandy—deer, hares, and rabbits—just as they themselves had once been prohibited from hunting animals set aside for the king.[17] By reserving such game exclusively for themselves, upper-crust Englishmen imposed on their social inferiors distinctions that the Normans had originally imposed on the English.

English aristocrats additionally began to reserve for themselves certain hunting techniques, such as hunting on horseback and using dogs. Owning a hunting horse required maintaining a very expensive non-farm-working animal. Practically speaking, hunting on horseback remained economically beyond the means of ordinary citizens. Not content to let monetary barriers exclude poorer people, English lords at the end of the eleventh century legislated against anyone other than themselves hunting on horseback.[18] The same lords forbade members of the lower classes to own hunting dogs as the breeds became increasingly popular among the nobles.[19]

Rationalizing his newfound aristocratic privileges, Edward, duke of York, described hunting as a means of avoiding idleness. "Now I will prove how a good hunter may not be idle," he wrote. "Early in the dawning of the day, he must be up for to go unto his quest . . . and in so doing he shall not be idle for he is always busy."[20] Privileged hunting thus allowed nobles to avoid laziness but did not constitute an activity—such as labor—that was inconsistent with aristocratic privilege.[21]

Finally, aristocrats and nobles began to adopt an elaborate set of rules and codes of behavior governing the hunt. This enabled them to keep out the merely uninformed as well as those of the wrong class.[22] Hunting became an important means of visibly demonstrating wealth and status; the elite owned horses, hunting dogs, and private game preserves (parks), and they demonstrated proper manners. The result was a sharply class-divided system of hunting. Aristocratic hunters provided meat for themselves and their families, but, more important, they demonstrated social superiority by appropriately performing the ritual itself.

In medieval England, therefore, class rather than gender defined hunting. There are well-known English paintings of titled women hunting, and it was a popular exercise among aristocratic and noble Englishwomen for centuries. Both Queens Mary and Elizabeth were celebrated hunters. Furthermore, the fifteenth-century noblewoman and nun Dame Juliana Berners wrote the first treatise showing how fishing could be transformed from a pedestrian activity engaged in by professional fisherman into a leisure ritual—sport fishing.[23] The class obsessions of hunting during the Middle Ages, however, were uniquely English.

Old World Juxtapositions

According to John Cummins, English writings on hunting "are all pervaded by the procedural and linguistic snobbery which excludes from consideration the lower social orders and their inglorious methods." This snobbery, Cummins notes, is absent even in French writings on the subject. "The French works, in contrast . . . address the needs not only of the courtier and the aristocratic landowner, but of the general rural population." In other parts of Europe, other codes and rules protected the local huntsman: "The royal authors of Spain and Portugal ignore the methods of the common man, but the local codes of law of Iberia reveal that not only the villager, but the townsman, too had his sport." Cummins notes that "in Germany one finds . . . an overall acceptance of the validity of the hunting aspirations of the lower classes of society."[24]

Other medieval European societies did not consider hunting to be an activity of social distinction. Even rules similar to those instituted in England did not have the same effects elsewhere in Europe. French rules restricting large-game hunting to aristocrats had been in place since the fourteenth and fifteenth centuries, and harsh penalties for poaching were instituted in France only early in the sixteenth century, to considerable protest.[25] But although hunting was becoming class-restricted, it was not perceived as a right of conquerors. Nor did the concern with class-based access to hunting remain paramount for long in France.

Forest (timber), rather than game, was the central concern of French leaders. From the fourteenth century on, Francophone forest legislation aimed to preserve timber rather hunting grounds.[26] Colbert rewrote the forest laws in 1669 to stress the preservation of wood, not animals.[27] The first official maps served to pinpoint wooded areas.[28]

As in France, from the fifteenth century on, English forests were being rapidly cut down. Timber was used for shipbuilding and home construction (half-timbered houses), and charcoal was used for smelting iron. By the middle of the sixteenth century the continued felling of timber, not poaching, posed the chief threat to forests.[29] The continued desires of aristocrats to create privately owned hunting preserves conflicted with the need for timber in ship and housing construction. Although English monarchs were still demanding private hunting grounds at the start of the time of New World occupation, this ambition was becoming increasingly difficult for lesser members of the nobility to realize.[30] In England, however, unlike in France, the social class distinctions attached to hunting remained as important as ever in law and culture, and the preservation of game rather than forests preoccupied English lawmakers.[31]

By the sixteenth and seventeenth centuries, the English elites' preoccupation with fixing and preserving certain kinds of hunting for kings, nobles, and aristocrats turned other forms of hunting into lower-class activities. In the years after the Norman Conquest, small game—fox, squirrel, and badger—was deemed harmful for deer, the object of royal privilege. Hunting small animals became regarded as extermination—ridding a region of pests potentially damaging to game animals, people, and crops. The Norman conquerors permitted Saxons and other members of lower social orders to exterminate nuisance animals.[32] Lower-class exterminators hunted pests on foot, using bows and arrows, techniques that the elites despised and that came to be associated with lower-class hunting.[33] King James I wrote, "Hunting, namely with running hounds . . . is the most honorable and noble sort thereof; for it is a thievish sort of hunting to shoot with guns and bows."[34] To seventeenth-century Englishmen, these hunting practices implied lower-class participation closely allied to criminal activity.

Hunting in England thus eventually divided into two categories: recreation and relaxation for the elite and subsistence (and pest removal) for the poor. In the New World, when English colonists classified Indians as "hunters," they were also invoking a set of social distinctions defined by hunting.

When Englishmen settled in the New World, they encountered hunting practices profoundly at odds with the sharply class-divided ones of their own society. Several Indian methods of hunting were identical to English aristocratic methods, whereas others resembled those characteristic of the poor and dispossessed. Some native practices, such as hunting deer, hares, and rabbits, and some native techniques, such as driving animals into cul-de-sacs and using dogs to sniff out prey, resembled those of Old World aristocrats. But other indigenous hunting methods resembled the practices of Old World subsistence hunters.

Natives often hunted using traps, as well as bows and arrows.[35] Such techniques and pursuit on foot resembled practices of the poorest and most despised Englishmen of the sixteenth and early seventeenth centuries, King James's "thievish sort of hunting." To seventeenth-century Englishmen, these hunting practices implied lower-class activities. Furthermore, Native Americans hunted for food.

The physical setting for native hunters reminded colonists of English parks, many of which were partially cleared in order to give horseback riders easier routes for chasing animals. Indians also often partially cleared the land by setting fire to the undergrowth of woods so "that they may not be hindered in hunting Venison, and Beares in the Winter season," wrote Edward Johnson. "[This action] makes them [the forests] thin of Timber in many places, like our Parkes in England."[36]

Natives of the northeastern woodlands chased or drove the animals into a river or into a palisade, the most aristocratic technique of hunting in medieval England and Scotland, performed principally by royalty and great nobles.[37] Furthermore, the Hurons of southern Ontario and the Mi'kmak on the eastern coast of what is now Canada also used dogs to hunt, a privilege available by law in England only to aristocrats.[38] Eastern-seaboard Indians hunted large animals as well as small game.[39] And only great lords devoted as much time to hunting as did America's native peoples of the northeastern woodlands.

Indians furthermore appeared free "to run over the wild grass," hunting whenever and wherever they pleased, unrestrained by systems of private parks or royal preserves. It seemed as though the entire continent was their hunting ground. Nor did there appear to be rules governing what they could hunt: every kind of game, from noble stags and hares to pesky raccoons, seemed theirs to pursue.

Many Englishmen (including Puritans) scoffed at the idea of natives owning their hunting territory like English kings. Nonnoble hunters with rights to hunt over vast territories sounded like a contradiction in terms.[40] Drawing upon the implicit irony of horseless savages dressed in the skins of animals cavorting as English aristocrats, Puritan theologian John Cotton mockingly underlined the differences between aristocrats and Indians, declaring, "We did not conceive that it is a just Title to so vast a Continent, to make no other improvement of millions of Acres in it, but only to burn it up for pastime."[41] "Pastime" was the king's legitimate privilege, and Cotton was underscoring the absurdity of New World natives enjoying royal privileges. "Millions of Acres" implied that natives held far greater lands for hunting than even the park-owning English kings and nobles. Private English parks (with their exclusive hunting rights) typically ran in the hundreds or thousands of acres, and even the king's hunting preserves only reached the tens of thousands. The absence of characteristics of English and French hunting forests—grazing animals, cut trees, stacked firewood, and occasionally residences—further confirmed colonists' impressions of the natives' unlimited hunting grounds.[42]

Natives did not engage in these activities on hunting grounds, with good reason. The northern half of the Americas lacked grazing animals, and northeastern Indians used given areas of land in rotation rather than simultaneously because they migrated seasonally. Collecting firewood, cutting timber, and constructing homes all were activities performed on hunting grounds, but in different years. To the natives' misfortune, however, the English did not take these factors into consideration.

Some scholars have argued that native hunting was "too close to certain English pastoral and aristocratic fantasies for Calvinists to tolerate" and that the Puritans objected to such "leisure" activities.[43] However, Puritans such as John Cotton respected and even defended English royal hunting privileges. But their defense of royal privilege was a means of denying native ownership of the land.

Under English law, the right to hunt on a piece of land did not customarily concede ownership of that land. But inspired by Norman tradition, kings and aristocrats had created private parks, allowing them to both own the terrain and control the right to hunt. When Roger Williams challenged the conventional wisdom among Puritan settlers that Indians were hunters and hence could not own their land, he specifically cited the king's ownership of large hunting preserves.[44] In response, Cotton and others recognized the legitimate landownership rights of certain recreational hunters, namely, kings and nobles. But they denied Indians the right to own land in the same way by repeatedly invoking the status differences between Englishmen and natives, denying the power of the analogy between Indians' dominion and English lords. Thus New World settlers, including Puritans, claimed that only their leaders were entitled to possess hunting grounds because they "possessed greater territories than other men, so they did greater service to church and commonwealth."[45]

Had Englishmen accepted Roger Williams's viewpoint that the natives were entitled to own the land on which they hunted, just as English nobles did, there would have been several negative consequences for settlers. According to English law and custom, colonists would have been trespassers and poachers upon land reserved exclusively for natives' hunting. Natives would have been legitimately entitled to expel and penalize the intruders (under English law). So Englishmen defined native hunting, despite all of its aristocratic characteristics, as an activity of the lower orders. Only the rights customarily associated with lower-class subsistence hunting in England would be accorded to Native Americans.

Hence in the New World indigenous peoples were permitted to hunt small game as a pest extermination service, as Saxons had once done for conquering Normans. Indigenous trapping was allowed because natives were ridding the landscape of vermin for European settlers and their agriculture.[46] Indeed, in the Virginia colonies, Indians were encouraged to perform this service by hunting wolves.

Settlers in the southern colonies also tried to curtail those activities that most closely resembled regal, or at the very least aristocratic, recreational privileges.[47] In a 1646 treaty with Necotowance in Virginia, the English claimed the land south of the York River as exclusive for their hunting. Indians could not enter the region (even to hunt nuisance animals) except on pain of death, much as Norman kings had introduced the death penalty for killing a stag on royal grounds.[48]

The death penalty was enforced. Settlers often appeared with guns when Indians arrived to hunt. If an Indian was shot, the law required only a colonist's unsupported oath that the Indian had been trespassing. In 1656, this law was amended somewhat: Indians "under English protection" were to be "corrected" rather than shot. But the Indians were required to obtain tickets of entry in order to fish, hunt birds, or gather berries.[49]

Thus in the southern colonies, Englishmen of ordinary means reinvented themselves as eleventh-century aristocrats aping Norman conquerors. They fixed their exclusive rights to hunt in a territory and simultaneously invented the Indians as poor (Saxon or subsistence) hunters whose social and political status prevented them from having rights to the hunting grounds. They also firmly established the right to hunt as the significant social dividing line between conquerors and conquered. The temptation to reproduce the rights of conquerors to hunt seems to have been irresistible.

By all accounts, the New World was richly timbered. It appeared to Englishmen an inviting and seemingly limitless forested hunting ground—a place where lesser aristocrats and even poor, socially marginalized Englishmen could live out fantasies of being noblemen, hunting in a way that was either impossible or fast disappearing for them in England.

Although the Puritans, like other English settlers, resented native men's freedom to roam and envied the natives' vast territories, their suspicion of leisure activities meant that they did not create exclusive hunting grounds for themselves. But like the Virginia colonists, they too banned natives from hunting large game.

Hostility toward native hunting in the English colonies was stirred up by yet another factor. Hunting in the Old World was restricted by class rather than gender. Hunting in the New World was restricted by gender, not class. It was the activity of men—and men alone. Hunting was a masculine ritual in the New World and an aristocratic one in the Old. The collision of a gender-based New World system with a class-stratified Old World one meant that English men saw all Indian men of the eastern seaboard as enjoying the privileges of the Old World aristocratic class. Despite the duke of York's assertion that noble hunters were avoiding idleness, other Englishmen saw hunting as a leisure activity. The result was a torrent of jealous accusations of masculine laziness based on the apparent recreational privileges of North American native men.

Englishmen George Percy in 1607 and John Smith in 1612 characterized native men as "idle." Percy wrote, "Women . . . doe all their drugerie. The men takes their pleasure in hunting."[50] Smith noted, "The men bestowe their times in fishing, hunting and wars. . . . the women be verie painfull [industrious] and the men often idle."[51] William Wood described native women as more "laborious than their lazy husbands."[52] Native men were simply perceived to be engaging in recreation (idle pleasure) while women worked.

Hunting was not work. It was not cultivation or laboring upon the land. The comparison drawn between native men's leisure activities and women's labor underlined the broader distinction between labor and recreation. Englishmen understood leisure to be a reward for labor or service, so in their eyes, native men were enjoying an undeserved recreational privilege.[53] Hence English colonists' efforts to restrict Indian hunting rights stemmed partly from the belief that Native American men were hunting recreationally without having labored.

Natives were thus simultaneously identified as subsistence hunters, in order to deny them the right to own hunting grounds, and as recreational hunters, to mock the lack of responsibility for farm labor that characterized New World men.

New World Juxtapositions

English, French, Dutch, and Portuguese colonists in the New World all confronted widely dispersed native settlements, often linked together in confederations and alliances, speaking a variety of sometimes related, sometimes quite different languages. But rather than being envious of the hunting and gathering societies or thrilled by the lush and abundant landscape, the Portuguese, for example, found both relatively worthless. "The king [João III] kept himself busy with the things of India," wrote his chronicler, "because they were of great importance. He dealt less with Brazil because profits [were not expected] . . . from trade with the people who were barbaric, changeable, and poor."[54] Without valuable commodities to trade, Brazil's people were of little interest.

French settlers similarly remarked upon the resemblance of Native American hunting to European aristocratic behavior. French traveler Gabriel Sagard described Huron men as "play[ing] the noblemen . . . and think[ing] only of hunting, fishing, and fighting."[55] Despite such similar observations, few Frenchmen envied natives' right to pursue game, for the French did not connect hunting with the prerogatives of conquerors or class-based humiliation.[56] Nor, despite new hunting constraints in the late fourteenth century, had ordinary Frenchmen experienced the kind of continual humiliation that English horseback hunters inflicted upon their inferiors to reinforce class divisions.[57] Consequently, French colonists failed to envy Indians and remained uninterested in resentfully creating hunting preserves for themselves.

The French colonists were attracted by the vast, rich forests of southeastern Canada, where they initially settled. Without a farm labor theory of property ownership, French settlers could easily respect woodland as a resource to be preserved rather than a site for their own recreation, regardless of the consequences. The French never directly challenged the ownership rights Algonquian-speaking peoples held over forested regions. Instead, they created the fur trade with the Indians and enabled the natives to retain their dominion over hunting grounds and their nomadic way of life.

Dutch and sometimes French settlers also noted the distinctly masculine cast of North American hunting, and occasionally also made derogatory remarks about such activities. A Dutch preacher to the Mohawks, Johannes Megapolensis, observed in 1644, "The men do nothing except hunt, fish, and wield war clubs against their foes."[58] In December 1624, Nicolaes van de Wassenaer, writing in the Netherlands, declared, "The men never labor except to provide some game."[59] Jesuit missionaries expressed similar thoughts. Pierre Biard, a French Jesuit missionary to Acadia in 1611, described how the "men concern themselves with nothing but the more laborious hunting and the waging of war."[60] But missing from Dutch and other Europeans' accounts is any resentment of masculine hunting. Only English writers appear to have been envious of native hunting, and this jealousy was rooted in the writers' own cultural history.

In Spanish America, the situation could hardly have been more different. Hunting enjoyed no special place of privilege; Spanish and Portuguese settlers held no conception of themselves as "farmers" or "laborers." They also believed themselves to have a legitimate right to confiscate different resources from native peoples. In the Iberian colonial world, it was buried mineral wealth, not land, that was popularly regarded as the rightful property of the colonizing nation.

4

Ownership of Mineral Riches and the Spanish

Need for Labor

> As a poor Indian once in the West Indies held out a piece of Gold saying *This is the Christians' God* so might I hold out a Turf of Earth and *say here is the God of many a poor New England man.*
>
> Cotton Mather, *Fair Weather,* 1692

Iberian settlers believed that all the valuable mineral reserves—gold, silver, emeralds, and diamonds—in the New World had become theirs once they had firmly established themselves. Whereas English colonists believed the *land* was rightfully theirs, Spanish and Portuguese colonists considered that *precious mineral deposits* belonged to them.[1] Like the conventions for pursuing landownership among English colonists, rules governing gold and silver deposits were profoundly familiar to and hence widely accepted among Iberian colonists. Thus the idea of collective ownership of precious mineral deposits remained popular among Iberians.

According to a long- and well-established Iberian tradition, members of the dominant religious faith collectively owned mineral reserves.[2] This tradition had no counterpart in England, in two important respects. First,

Englishmen would not have thought to separate ownership of surface and mineral deposits, as did Iberians. Under an Iberian tradition, the rules governing ownership, transfer, and inheritance of surface land remained entirely separate from those governing valuable minerals. Although Iberian law allowed a wide variety of local customs to regulate transfers of land, only a single tradition governed the use of valuable minerals.

Iberian tradition also diverged from English tradition in a second significant way. During the sixteenth century, the leaders of English society grew increasingly hostile toward collective property ownership. As the enclosure movement gained political momentum, it also increased the wealth of the largest private landowners. In Iberia, no parallel trend developed, so sixteenth-century Iberians lacked the hostility toward collective property that prevailed among their English contemporaries.

Sixteenth-century Spanish and Portuguese speakers, respectively, referred to the communally owned mineral reserves as *el subsuelo* and *o sobsolo*—in English, "the subsoil." However, there are good reasons for not using this word in English to refer to precious metals. The word *subsoil* came into English three hundred years after its equivalent was first used in the Spanish colonies. When it was adopted, it meant any layer of weathered material beneath the surface. This significance, which it retains today, has nothing in common with the shared Spanish and Portuguese understanding of "subsoil" as gold and silver owned separately from the surface land. Hence in this book I use phrases such as *valuable mineral deposits* to convey the meaning conveyed by the Spanish and Portuguese words *subsuelo* and *sobsolo*.

Origin of the Tradition of Mineral Wealth Ownership

The origin of the distinctive Iberian tradition governing the ownership of valuable mineral deposits lies in the peninsula's Islamic past. Muslims conquered nearly the entire Iberian Peninsula, except for a small northern section, early in the eighth century. They introduced a variety of novel economic practices, including the regulation of markets, customs, and tariffs; municipal control over weights and measures; and supervision of butchers.[3] But the custom they introduced that eventually had the greatest impact upon the acquisition of resources in the New World was their understanding of the ownership of valuable subterranean resources.

In many European regions precious metals were considered abandoned or undiscovered goods to which anyone could lay claim. In Islamic jurisprudence, however, buried precious stones and metals were called "treasure" (*rikaz* in Arabic). They were considered neither geological accidents nor abandoned goods. Rather, Muslims believed that God had planted or "embedded [them] firmly in the stomach [belly] of the earth."[4] Precious metals were therefore a gift from God, to be shared and used among his people.

The consequences of this understanding were many. First, the rules governing God-given objects could not be those governing the surface land. Only God-given rules could regulate what God had provided for his people from deep in the earth. Second, private people could not own such resources. It was unconscionable that any single individual, even a ruler, should claim as personal property that which God had given to all his people. Ownership of such minerals belonged permanently to the community of his people. They could belong only to Muslims, those who believed in Allah.

Finally, given that God had buried riches in the earth for believers, a significant portion of the profits from mining these resources was to be spent on the welfare of God's people. This portion was called the "fifth" (khums in Arabic), because classical Islamic tradition suggested that 20 percent of the profits be spent on God's people.[5] Those delegated by leaders to take charge of digging out the gold and silver often understated the total value of what they had mined in order to reduce the sums they would have to turn over, but they would neither question nor challenge the requirement of giving a fifth of the declared amount of gold or silver to their leaders for the community.

Differences among the Islamic traditions appeared principally in the identities of the religious leaders entitled to manage the mining of the mineral deposits as well as receive and redistribute the community's share of the resources. In the Shia branch of Islam, an exemplary religious leader (imam) or his representative was entitled to receive these funds, whereas in the larger Sunni branch, a leader combining political and religious functions (amir)—usually a caliph or sultan—would be entitled to them.[6] The Iberian Peninsula was under Sunni Islamic leadership, and hence an amir was charged with collecting and allocating one-fifth of the products of the gold and silver mines.

Within Sunni Islam there were four major schools of interpretation, some of which specified different leaders (amirs) as the recipients of these riches. In the legal school dominant on the Iberian Peninsula (Malikiite school), the traditional amir (commander of the faithful) had the right to receive the fifth that was owed the community. The commander of the faithful thus permanently regulated the redistribution of profits to the community throughout the majority of the regions of present-day Spain and Portugal.[7]

Muslims were pushed out of the Iberian Peninsula slowly, over the course of nearly four hundred years. Not until the eleventh century did any of the Christian kings make headway against their Islamic counterparts. And another four hundred years would pass before the last of the Muslim rulers were defeated. During the long, drawn-out process of supplanting Islamic lords, Christian rulers incorporated familiar Muslim economic customs into their own practices. Especially popular among subjects were Muslim regulations regarding the municipal oversight of weights and measures (to prevent cheating) and the close supervision of butchers (originally to assure that meat was prepared according to religious standards, but also to prevent food contamination).[8] These as well as several other commercial regulatory standards made as much sense under Christian as under Islamic rule.

Islamic rules regarding the ownership of buried minerals were gradually adopted throughout the Iberian Peninsula. Mid-thirteenth-century Castilian Christian kings were initially ambivalent about stewardship over mineral resources, but monarchs had accepted Islamic principles by the middle of the fourteenth century. As leaders of Christian believers, the Castilian kings from that period onward assumed the management of minerals. But, as under Islamic rule, the kings were merely the stewards of the mineral wealth. No king could transfer the mines to anyone other than his successor for any reason, including his own debts, because the property was not his, but his people's.[9]

Thus Christian Iberians by the fifteenth century adopted the idea that God had buried specific resources in the ground for his people. They also associated mineral ownership with a particular religious faith. When coming to the New World, they identified themselves as the people of God, just as Muslims had understood themselves as Allah's servants in Iberia. (As the natives of the New World were not Christian, Iberian settlers did not consider them to be people of God.) Thus despite Iberian kings' vaguely worded appeals to colonists to allow Native Americans to "benefit" from the minerals found in the New World, the colonists restricted natives' role to labor.[10] And the kings showed no interest in spending the share that was reserved for the community on aboriginal peoples. Because mineral wealth belonged to the people of God, Spanish and Portuguese colonists understood that as true believers they had a God-given right to the gold and silver of the New World.

Although Christians rarely if ever acknowledged the Islamic origin of this practice, Iberian Christian writers nonetheless employed the language of classic Islamic jurists to justify the colonists' stewardship of valuable mineral deposits in the New World.[11] Sixteenth-century Jesuit José de Acosta, author of one of the most widely read treatises on the New World, declared, "Metals, are . . . covered in the innards of the earth [en las entrañas de la tierra]." Acosta even directly adopted the traditional Islamic theological principle that God had buried gold and silver in the earth for his people, substituting the Christian God for Allah. "The creator buried such a diversity of metals in the cabinets and cellars of the earth."[12] The prominent seventeenth-century Iberian jurist Juan Solórzano Pereira justified Catholic monarchs' permanent and inalienable dominion over buried precious metals in the New World with exactly the same phrases as did classical Islamic jurisprudence. The metals were "material . . . from the innards of the earth [en las entrañas de la tierra]," a phrase precisely translating the Arabic *fi in batn al-ard*.[13] What had once been a theological principle had become firmly fixed as a legal and cultural one in the Spanish domination of the New World.

Furthermore, many Spanish Catholics considered that God had placed such wealth in the New World in order to attract Europeans, who would convert its people. Wrote Acosta:

> The Eternal Lord who wanted to enrich the lands of the world farthest away, and inhabited by less civil people, and there put the greatest abundance of mines that has ever been found so that with this [placement he] would invite men to look for such lands, and hold them, and be the means of their communicating their religion and worship of the true God to those who did not know him. . . . Thus we see that the lands of the Indies are more full of mines and riches than have been worked in the Christian religion in our times. Thus the Lord was making use of our pretensions for his sovereign ends.[14]

Although victorious Christians claimed collective ownership of mineral resources throughout Iberia, not all of the reconquering communities adopted the fifth as the share owed their rulers. Most claimed the customary fifth, but traditional Castilian monarchs in particular claimed that they deserved half of all the gold found in their region. The point was moot, however, as there were no new gold or silver deposits discovered in any of the territory Castilians retook from the Muslims. Therefore, when Spaniards arrived in the New World, not all of them shared the same tradition regarding the percentage of gold and silver owed the monarch.

When gold was discovered on the New World island of Hispaniola, the Castilian monarch demanded half, as was customary according to Castilian law. However, Iberians from all over the peninsula knew and shared the belief that the ruler should receive a fifth—the *quinto real*. And so the fifth became the law of the land in the New World. And in a remarkable reversal of Castilian tradition, in 1504 the fifth became law in Castile as well.[15]

For the next three hundred years, the kings and queens of Spain received from their subjects the royal fifth—the share to which they were entitled. The great treasure fleets that sailed the Spanish Main and excited the envy of pirates from all over Europe were bearing not just the private wealth of Spanish settlers, but also the royal fifth.

Islamic law also influenced Portuguese communities through a parallel process of Muslim conquest and Christian reconquest. In Portugal as well as Spain, valuable minerals belonged to the community of believers and their ruler. Private ownership was similarly inconceivable. Therefore, Portuguese men and women overseas, like Spaniards, assumed that such minerals belonged to them.[16] Portuguese colonists had less initial luck finding gold and silver in Brazil, and had to trek deep into the sparsely populated interior of what are now the states of São Paulo, Rio de Janeiro, Mato Grosso, and Minas Gerais to find treasure.[17]

When Portuguese subjects found gold and gems in the eighteenth century, two hundred years after the Spaniards did, they also assumed that they owned the minerals communally. With individual ownership of mines impossible, Portuguese settlers, like their Spanish counterparts, needed permission from crown officials to launch mining operations.[18] Once having secured royal permission to bring up minerals from beneath the surface, settlers held only a concession to work in the area. Hence the key to profits in both Iberian colonies lay in settlers' ability to mobilize natives to labor in the mines.

Mobilizing Labor: Encomiendas *and Other Oddities*

Spaniards found substantial amounts of gold in the very first places they arrived in the New World: a few small islands in the Caribbean, principally Jamaica and Hispaniola (the present-day Dominican Republic and Haiti). In order to pan the islands' streams for gold, Columbus and his sons assigned Indians to work for the Spanish settlers and threatened them if they failed to deliver sufficient quantities of gold. He called the practice of dividing up natives among the settlers "apportionment" (in Spanish, *repartimiento*).[19] Using natives in this fashion soon received royal approval.

In 1501, Queen Isabel ordered natives "to collect gold, and perform the other labors that We Order done."[20] She was unhappy leaving the right to assign labor in Columbus's hands, however, and she therefore instructed her official representative on Hispaniola to oversee this "forcing and compelling" of Indian labor so that "the gold therein is mined so that My Kingdoms and the residents . . . can make use of it [the gold]."[21]

These vague initial directives did little to stop private Spaniards from assigning native labor among themselves, and Isabel briefly contemplated stopping the practice altogether. Early in 1503, she sent Nicolás de Ovando, the first colonial governor, to halt the settlers' direct authority over Indian labor. But the outcry by colonists, accompanied by an immediate sharp drop in gold production (and hence in crown revenues), led Isabel to rescind her order only nine months later.[22] In December 1503 she adopted a different tactic, ordering that the Indians be *"forced and compelled to . . . gather and remove gold and other metals."*[23] She placed the apportionment of native labor under royal control, calling the practice a trusteeship, or *encomienda*.[24]

Encomienda was the first in a series of public institutions limiting Spanish settlers' autonomy in allocating natives for labor. Exactly how the term came to be used for this institution is steeped in controversy, but the word *encomendar* itself means "to entrust," to commend something to someone. Queen Isabel instructed Governor Ovando how he was to implement this policy: "A recognized person is to take charge of the place in our name, so that thus they [the Indians] be entrusted [commended]."[25] Isabel made it clear that her subjects could direct Indians to work but could not own them. Spaniards held the Indians in trust *for the crown*, "in our name."[26] Establishing a trusteeship of Native Americans in Spanish colonies gave colonists the right to use a quota of native labor, contingent upon royal approval.

Isabel stated that the principal purpose of this "trust" was to ensure that the natives were Christianized. Therefore, the settlers would be not merely exploiting the Indians, but bettering them. She gave no specifics regarding how settlers were to provide this religious instruction, so most Caribbean residents merely saw to it that the Lucayo who labored for them attended Sunday Mass.

Isabel further asserted that the trustee would ensure that "no evil or damage is done [to the Indians'] persons or their goods."[27] But asserting royal authority over the allocation of labor in no way mitigated the unrealistic expectations placed on the natives as a workforce. Isabel expected Spanish settlers to "see that the said Indians serve in the things which satisfy Our service," a cryptic expression referring to anything that benefit-ed the crown.[28] Among these things of royal service were such tasks as building warehouses and homes for the Spaniards, furnishing all the labor necessary to feed both the native community and the Spaniards, and "col-lecting" gold and other metals, as if there were no more effort to panning for gold than simply bending over to pick it up.[29] Queen Isabel defined the Indians' tedious and difficult panning and digging of gold as a legitimate royal service, to be performed under the supervision of a local Spaniard.

The queen initially placed Governor Ovando in charge of allocating natives among the Spaniards. He did not recruit the natives himself; rather, he delegated this task to indigenous Lucayo leaders, who in turn were required to choose the members of their community who would be required to serve the Spaniards.[30] After two or three years the governor could shift "trusteeship" of the Indian community to another Spaniard. The settlers, however, found this situation entirely unacceptable. The people of Jamaica and Hispaniola were hunter-gatherers, fishermen, and small-scale horticulturists whose traditional policies of lending labor assis-tance to neighbors were simple and relatively short-term. As a result, the communities and their leaders failed to meet the colonists' expectations of continuing regular labor—a response that the colonists described as a moral defect, "laziness."[31]

The colonists appealed to the crown, however, to transform their two- or three-year grants into a permanent right to a labor quota by casting themselves as defenders of the Indians. They claimed that short-term grants led to overworking the natives in order to maximize profits in a relatively short time, and that such consequences would be minimized with permanent trusteeships or quotas. An official inquiry into the difficul-ties of recruiting a regular labor force conducted by the Hieronymite friars concluded that the natives "lacked the capacity" to produce sufficient la-borers for Spanish needs.[32] The friars suggested creating Indian towns under Spanish administrators in order to concentrate native laborers in places more accessible to Spaniards, but the proposed changes were only sketchily implemented.[33]

But the Hieronymite commissioners agreed with the colonists about the abuse of native labor in the temporary labor quotas. Hence the crown was forced to accommodate the settlers' desire for permanent trustee-ships.[34] In practice (and later in law) these grants became hereditary, with Spaniards passing on Indian labor quotas to their spouses and children.[35] Thus by 1517 a charge (trusteeship) of a group of natives—a town, vil-lage, or tribe—gave Spanish settlers virtually unlimited control over the labor of a local community. Although a Spanish trustee could not actually own the Indians, he could claim their labor (and that of their descendants) for decades to come. Thus a temporary use right became a kind of property. Like all property rights, it was inheritable, monopolistic, and exclusive.[36] But several Spanish clerics, notably Bartolomé de Las Casas, objected to the *encomienda*, claiming that Spanish rights over native labor constituted a form of slavery.[37]

Slavery or Freedom?

Being held in trust (*encomienda*) was not the same thing as being a slave, although in some respects the differences were minor.[38] First, slavery usually signified ownership of an individual or a group of individuals, whereas *encomiendas* were trusteeships over the labor of a community. This was a technical distinction: a community's rather than an individual's labor was controlled.

Second, Spaniards could not permanently uproot any member of an "entrusted" native community and move him or her elsewhere, although they could "temporarily" transport natives for long-term labor in construction or mining. Third, the native communities assumed the costs of what economists today call "labor reproduction." Under such a system, all the expenses of housing, feeding, and clothing the laborers were borne by the Indian communities themselves.

A fourth distinction between *encomiendas* and slavery was honored more often in principle than in observance. According to rules governing trusteeships, Indians were supposed to be paid for their labor, a condition often ignored.[39] This requirement, however, also technically separated trusteeships from slavery, in which coerced labor goes uncompensated and there is no right even to claim wages.

Finally, and perhaps most important, trusteeships were deliberately constructed to be different from slavery because royal interests were at stake. Although Isabel was perfectly willing to coerce natives to mine gold, she drew the line at slavery because slavery was *private* ownership of labor, and she wanted to establish *public* control. The Indians were her subjects; hence Spanish settlers could only hold native labor quotas in trust from her or her descendants. The trusteeship could be transferred but not sold, because the *encomienda* was a grant from the queen, who had ultimate authority over the natives. Slavery involved outright ownership, which meant a right to buy and sell.

Isabel's ambition to eliminate private ownership of labor also led her and her successors to reject another form of private dominion, namely, serfdom. In 1503, Isabel declared that Indians were to be treated "as the free people they are, and *not as serfs*."[40] But given that serfdom meant being bound to the land, and therefore not transportable to the mines, Spanish settlers showed virtually no interest in making Indians serfs. In a massive self-congratulatory move, however, Isabel's grandson, Charles V, called royal prohibitions against serfdom "setting the Indians free."[41] "Freedom," however, meant only "freedom from" a European institution (serfdom) with which the natives were unfamiliar in the first place. Indians were not "free to" worship their traditional gods, reject Catholic definitions of kinship, or refuse Spanish coercion of their labor. Their only freedom was freedom *from* private ownership of their labor. Often in King Charles's decrees, he stated that Indians were to be placed "in freedom and trusteeship *[encomienda]*."[42]

The natives were thus said to be "free" to work for private Spaniards. Spaniards were "not to urge or to compel [i.e., as slaves] the said Indians to go to the gold mines . . . nor pearl fisheries . . . but if said Indians want to go or work of their will, we readily allow them [Spaniards] to use and benefit from them [Indians] as free persons."[43] The undeserved celebration of royal decrees on Indian "freedom" in this century seems to have overlooked what Spanish monarchs actually meant by *liberty*.[44] Natives' only path to freedom from royal demands was flight—deserting their original communities and kin.

Priests trying to convert the Indians had their own reasons for wanting the natives to be free. A Dominican friar first broached the subject in a fiery sermon whose central rhetorical question was "Are they [the natives] not men?" However, in demanding that Indians (as humans) be freed from Spanish labor quotas, Montesinos and the other Dominicans were seeking to subject the Indians to the friars' authority. They wanted the natives to have their labor obligations reduced so that they could spend more time with the priests who were converting them. But did the Indians want to be converted? That question was never asked. The "freedom" that the Dominican priests sought was for natives to be subject to spiritual domination.[45]

Using the rhetoric of native freedom furthermore allowed Dominican friars to believe that their own persuasive gifts had led the natives to adopt Catholicism. Converting a slave was far less satisfying than converting a person who was "free." But the natives were not really "free" to choose to become Catholics. If they practiced their old religion they could be tortured, executed, or enslaved. And on the frontiers of the Spanish empire, natives often escaped from the missions and then sought revenge upon mission priests for their abusive treatment in the name of furthering religious goals. In what are now Florida and New Mexico, it was Spanish troops who reestablished the missionaries' authority, not the friars themselves.[46]

Thus a contingent of priests opposed native slavery because its absence made it appear as though the natives were freer to adopt Spanish religion. But the priests as well as the settlers had coercive power over the natives to ensure that they adopted the Catholic religion, or at least observed its external forms. Priests and settlers alike thus established, in a way they found sufficiently satisfactory, that the natives were *choosing* Christianity, further proof of what they saw as God's entitling them to own the New World.

Trusteeships Revived, Then Retired

In 1521, Hernán Cortés successfully defeated the first major native empire in the Americas. As a longtime resident of Cuba, he was familiar with the trusteeships and the settlers' battles with the crown to secure permanent labor quotas. Shortly after his victory, the crown forbade future trusteeships.[47]

But the conqueror of the vast central Mexican plateau simply and neatly sidestepped the crown's prohibition against permanent labor quotas and handed out grants of Indian labor as compensation for military service or as rewards for pioneering settlers. By judiciously politicking the leaders of the Dominican and Franciscan religious orders (who had opposed trusteeships in the Caribbean), Cortés created enough public pressure to force the crown to withdraw its ban.[48] Faced with such a united front, in 1526 the crown attempted to divide the political interests of the clergy from those of the settlers by offering to place clergymen in charge of granting trusteeships over labor quotas. That effort also failed.[49] The independent-minded leaders of military expeditions in the Americas, ill disposed to defer to clerics, continued to hand out labor grants to their followers.[50]

Grants of native labor were attractive even in the many areas of the New World lacking gold, silver, or other precious metals. Although initially less lucrative, these areas could eventually yield considerable profits. Because owners of labor rights could use the labor for any purpose, they could and indeed did demand that natives produce baskets, blankets, and food and drink, which the owners would market and resell at a profit.[51] The revived trusteeships soon faced challenges from a different direction, however. As record numbers of Spanish subjects surged overseas in the wake of the conquests, competition for access to native labor increased dramatically. Newly arrived colonists demanded access to labor.[52] To accommodate the burgeoning number of new immigrants, Charles V finally succeeded in introducing a measure of royal authority over labor allocations. A bureaucrat called the "corrector" (in Spanish, *corregidor*) would assign temporary Indian workforces.[53] Thus Charles reprised a system his grandmother had attempted to establish on Hispaniola in 1503.[54] But even this move failed to halt the still-growing number of permanent labor trusteeships, which the monarchs had always regarded with suspicion. Charles V, no less than his grandparents, distrusted any institution that allowed wealthy subjects independent control over a large body of people, who could potentially be mobilized for rebellion. In 1542, after hearing extensive complaints about the settlers' abusive use of native labor from several of his advisers, Charles abruptly terminated all existing and future trusteeships and enslavement of the natives of the New World.[55]

The outright ban set forth in the decrees known as the New Laws failed catastrophically. They led to civil war in Peru, and to the north, in New Granada and New Spain, they were politely but firmly ignored. The crown backtracked, finally accepting that there was no way to abolish permanent trusteeships of Indian labor. All monarchs could do was to chip away at them, demanding that permanent trustees receive cash or goods instead of labor from native communities and limiting the inheritance of such privileges to three generations.[56]

The real pressure on these labor grants, however, came from the disastrous series of sixteenth-century epidemics that decimated the native population. By century's end, Indian communities had literally declined to one-tenth of their original size.[57] There were no longer Indians in sufficient numbers to mine, provide personal services, and manufacture large amounts of goods that could be profitably marketed elsewhere. Spaniards could no longer obtain wealth quickly simply by having access to Indian labor. Such labor could still be coerced, but competition among Spaniards for native workers meant that some, although not all, natives had greater leverage over their working conditions.

The Spanish crown further pressured trusteeships indirectly. Beginning in the 1520s, monarchs demanded that the natives pay their annual taxes to the crown in cash rather than in goods and services. The yearly royal demand for hard cash often forced natives to enter local wage labor markets and rotating labor pools. In effect, the need to pay tribute (annual taxes) impelled Indians to become wage laborers.[58]

Natives increasingly fled their original communities to escape their economic burdens, thus adding to the obligations upon those who remained. Their departures further contributed to the eventual disintegration and disappearance of many such communities, thus rendering useless grants of the labor of those communities. Spanish officials late in the sixteenth century reconfigured these near-deserted and quasi-decimated native communities, collapsing many into a single Spanish-style unit.[59] Still other natives escaped the sometimes erratic and occasionally overwhelming draft labor burdens by becoming directly dependent upon Spaniards as personal servants or laborers.[60]

As the realities of the demographic disaster and changes in access to labor became apparent, Spanish settlers increasingly came to depend upon other ways of acquiring wealth. Settlers had to build different methods of mobilizing indigenous labor, including wage labor, indebtedness, and direct coercion, practices that continued into the next century and beyond.[61] But the coercion of native labor, regardless of the form it took, nearly always appeared justified to the Spanish conquerors. It was the only way they could acquire the mineral riches of the Americas.

Juxtapositions

Believing that God had buried gold and silver for them, many Iberian settlers understood a connection between their finding gold and God's will for the New World. Although some Iberian leaders considered religious motives to be the only justification for overseas efforts, many more Iberians, including religious leaders, viewed religious and economic aims as fundamentally compatible.[62] Pursuing gold and God at the same time appeared entirely reasonable, and judging from the Iberians' successes, seemed (to them) to have been the correct way to proceed. As noted above, the sixteenth-century Jesuit José de Acosta wrote: "The Eternal Lord who wanted to enrich the lands of the world farthest away, and inhabited by less civil people, and there put the greatest abundance of mines that has ever been found. . . . Thus the Lord was making use of our pretensions for his sovereign ends."[63] Iberians could pursue economic ambitions and carry out the Lord's work at the same time.[64] As Bernal Díaz put it more colloquially, "We came to make Christians and to get rich."[65]

However, Englishmen understood economic and religious goals in the New World as fundamentally incompatible. The idea of "making Christians *and* becoming rich" at the same time was inconceivable. Because seventeenth-century Englishmen understood farming but not evangelizing as a believable motivation for overseas colonization, they viewed Iberian moral ambitions as mere cover. English colonists of the time accused Spaniards of hypocrisy, of "making religion their color when their aim was . . . but present profit."[66] Englishmen's aims were the same, but, to their way of thinking, they were presented less hypocritically.[67] As Rowland Watkins wrote, "[England's] merchants shall bring gold, and pearl, and spice, / to make this Garden rich as Paradise." Or in John Donne's words, "O my America! my new-found-land . . . My Myne of precious stones, My Emperie, / How blest am I in this discovering thee!"[68] Englishmen viewed their supposedly unvarnished greed for gold as a measure of their superiority over Spaniards.

But the reality was more complex. Iberian and British subjects had entirely different understandings of who owned mines and how they owned them. Sixteenth- and early-seventeenth-century Englishmen were permitted private ownership of below-ground minerals. Hence English colonists perceived the pursuit of wealth as a strictly individual ambition. But Iberians understood their ambition for gold and silver as a common goal, because as God's people they were entitled to all the land's mineral riches.

The English tradition split minerals between two separate private owners. On the one hand, English kings claimed to own gold and silver mines during the Middle Ages, but on the other, they often allowed landholders private tenure.[69] In 1338, a general patent allowed landowners to search for precious metals on their own estates, provided they pay a "round tax" to the king and bring the gold and silver to the mint to be coined.[70]

On other occasions, English kings claimed gold and silver mines as their royal property. But even these claims differed from those of the Iberian monarchs. Kings of Spain and Portugal did not own the mineral resources personally; rather, they acted as custodians for the people. But English kings claimed individual private property rights over such mines. As a result, British monarchs could transfer ownership of their mines to creditors in payment of debts, as Edward I did in 1299. Instead of an inalienable title for which the king was merely the guardian, English kings claimed practical, transferable rights to silver and gold mines.[71]

In the New World, English colonists frequently advocated private ownership and debated whether the crown should share in the revenues from mines, a dispute inconceivable in Iberian colonies.[72] Colonial governments permitted individual ownership of precious mineral resources in the New World. Individuals as well as groups of investors could own or share ownership in gold mines.[73] These shares, like any other commodity, could be bought and sold. To own underground gold and silver, therefore, Englishmen could purchase mines, shares in mines, or the surface land. Other minerals could be sold, transmitted, or inherited along with the surface land.

The Netherlands, like Spain and Portugal, prevented its colonists from privately owning mines in the New World, but for entirely different reasons. Neither the owner of the land (as in English law) nor the conquerors as a whole (as in Iberian law) could lay claim to precious metals in Dutch colonies. Rather, a colony's financial sponsor owned buried deposits of gold and silver.[74] Under Dutch law, individual proprietors (patroons) or joint-stock companies such as the West India Company could own mines if they had sponsored the expedition that settled the land. Dutch colonists failed to discover any substantial deposits of gold and silver in the New World. Had they done so, however, their forms of acquisition would have differed from those of both English and Iberian colonists.

Furthermore, in the Dutch colonies, discoverers of mineral deposits received special compensation. In return for locating precious metals and revealing their existence to the company (in the Netherlands) or to the commander (in New Netherland), a discoverer was entitled to a substantial reward—as much as 10 percent of a mine's proceeds for six years or even a lifetime.[75] This reward system was derived partly from Portuguese concepts of discovery and partly from German mining customs. Thus Dutch rights to own and to profit from mines were utterly distinct from those of any other European economic tradition.

An ancient Islamic tradition prohibited private Spanish subjects from owning mines of gold, silver, and emeralds. Ownership of the buried treasure belonged permanently and inalienably to the Spanish (and Portuguese) communities to be managed by their respective monarchs. To work a mining claim, a Spanish or Portuguese settler had to obtain a royal license.[76] To become rich off the mines, rivers, and oceans, Spanish and Portuguese subjects had to mobilize natives to perform the immensely hard, grinding labor of panning the surface of streams, of digging deep in the bowels of the earth, or of diving to the ocean floor in order to bring out the gold, silver, emeralds, or pearls. Therefore Indian labor, not land, was the key to riches in the Spanish-controlled New World in the years immediately following conquest. And when Portuguese settlers finally located enormous caches of gold and silver in the interior of Brazil two centuries after their arrival, mobilizing labor would be the key to riches there as well.

Access to a second valuable economic resource of the New World—fertile agricultural land—was also constrained by the crown's adoption of another economic rule derived from Islamic principles. How the crown successfully prevented colonists from seizing native lands is the result of another, equally complex, cultural history.

5

Tribute and Social Humiliation:

The Cost of Preserving Native Farmlands

Unlike English officials, who actively encouraged settlers to seize productive native land, Spanish colonial officials made such seizure difficult. Although some have attempted to claim moral superiority for the Spanish based on this, the origin of this policy lies less in a moral terrain than in the Spanish officials' economic and political interests in such communities.

After overwhelming the leaders of large native empires in the Americas, Spanish conquerors struck a deal with the survivors. If they would not resist the Spanish presence, the victors would allow them to retain their farmland. However, in exchange, these natives had to meet two conditions. First, Spanish officials imposed a tax they called tribute upon the adult men. The payment was often financially burdensome. Linked to this exaction was an intentionally humiliating set of behaviors that Native Americans had to perform in front of Spaniards. To this day in the Spanish language, taxes of all kinds—from customs duties to export and import tariffs, to sales taxes and assessments on industrial production—are most commonly called "tribute" (*tributo*).[1] But the word *tributo* in the Spanish-speaking world has always meant more than simply a way of raising revenue. It has signified rendering homage or handing over a token of admiration.

The second condition of the deal Spaniards struck was that these sedentary communities would be allowed their own leaders, subject to $\mathcal{Z}$ Spanish political and religious authority. Because there is no English political counterpart for these communities and hence no familiar English-language label for these groups, I will call them *subjugated* communities.[2] Although English leaders were unfamiliar with such customs, Iberian leaders were well acquainted with the practice of collecting demeaning tribute from the men of conquered communities in exchange for preserving farm ownership, a tradition stemming from centuries-old Islamic practices.

Tribute

Under traditional Islamic law, following a military defeat, able-bodied adult men of the conquered community who did not convert to Islam had to pay a per capita tax.[3] Muslims excluded those physically incapable of combat—the lame, the blind, the handicapped, and children. Muslim victors levied their poll tax according to the age at which the local men were traditionally mustered for combat. The payment was primarily intended to be a financial burden, but it was also meant to serve as a reminder of the men's military and social inferiority.

Under Islamic law, paying tribute was intended to be mortifying, as was explicitly laid out in the Qur'an. Surah 9:29 states, "Find those who believe not in Allah . . . nor who acknowledge the religion of truth . . . until they pay the poll-tax with willing submission and feel themselves subdued."[4] The Arabic word *fa'shaghirun* comes from the root *s-gh-r*, meaning "belittled" or "humbled."[5] Tribute payers on the Iberian Peninsula were required to pay the tax "with willing submission." Therefore poll taxes had to be paid *'an yadin*, literally "from the hand." Leaders of the Christian and Muslim communities had to collect the tax from their members and personally hand over their communities' tribute to Muslim rulers.[6] This was an intentionally public affront.[7]

This system of poll tax collection implicitly demanded well-ordered communities whose leaders could ensure compliance with Muslims' demands. Formal religious guidelines for collecting tribute did not explicitly mention the need for such structured communities; rather, most Islamic legal schools stated that poll tax should be paid by "people of the book," that is, adherents of scripture-based religions such as Christianity and Judaism. But according to Maliki jurisprudence (the Iberian and West African legal school), this tax could be collected from any community of unbelievers. Indeed, the most likely explanation for the broader Maliki requirement for poll tax payment is that Maliki Muslims encountered large animistic and pagan kingdoms in West Africa—in Mali and Ghana, for example[8]—each with complex internal hierarchies that allowed the levying of tribute.

Tribute payers everywhere were required to defer to Muslims, although this stipulation was not in the Qur'an. Although the exact form of respect depended on local custom, in Iberia, Christians and Jews were usually expected to bow their heads and give way to Muslims on the streets.[9] They were not to demonstrate physical superiority to Muslims in any way, including riding on horseback, which would have placed them physically above any Muslims on foot. Their houses, synagogues, and churches could not be taller than mosques. In all matters they were to demonstrate a generally respectful attitude toward Muslims.[10]

Iberian Christians and Jews were additionally often forbidden to dress more elegantly than Muslims. They could not wear silk clothes and gold jewelry in any public place, and they had to hide any evidence of financial superiority over Muslims.[11]

During their gradual series of victories over Muslims, Christians turned the tables. Beginning with the conquest of Toledo in 1085, Castilian monarchs imposed tribute payments and humiliations upon able-bodied adult Muslim (and Jewish) men defeated by Christian arms. The kings of Aragon and Navarre soon followed suit, and such payments became a part of all Christian victories up to and including their final triumph in Granada in 1492.[12]

Once formerly subservient Christians assumed the reigns of power, they exacted identical deference from the Muslims to whom they had once bowed, demanding that they give way on the streets, keep their buildings low, and wear deliberately plain clothing.[13] Similarly, they forbade Muslims the use of horses to ride, gold for ornamentation, and iron for defense.[14]

Before demanding tribute payment from Jews and Muslims, Christian overlords asked for and received ritual verbal confirmation that the taxes were identical to what they had once paid Muslim rulers.[15] Defeated Muslims were then required to engage in a degrading ceremony while paying what Castilian peace agreements called a *pecho* and what Aragonese pacts termed a *peyta*.

These words *pecho* and *peyta*, which meant simply "to pay," were regularly used in peace accords between Christians and Muslims to signify the tax paid by the defeated party. *Pecho* and *peyta* share a common Latin root with words in other Romance languages, a root signifying pacification, reconciliation, or restoring peace.[16] In conventional medieval Latin *pacare* signified conciliation, usually referring to an arrangement between equals.[17] Through their association with taxes, however, the words *pecho* and *peyta* quickly became identified with subservience and shame.[18]

Over time, *pecho* gained further degrading connotations. The word came to mean a fine paid by a wrongdoer, a penalty.[19] Eventually, it became even more broadly used to mean taxes paid not simply by Muslims, but by commoners. In time, the most crucial social division in medieval Spain—the separation between nobility (*hidalgos*) and commoners—became marked principally by the payment of (or exemption from) *pecho.* Thus tribute payment emerged as the central indicator of social inferiority in the Iberian kingdoms.[20]

Preserving Landownership in Agricultural Communities

Perhaps the most astute innovation of the early Islamic conquests was the *dhimma,* a pact of protection that encouraged defeated wealthy, often agricultural communities to accept rather than resist Islamic rule.[21] The *dhimma,* supposedly created in 637 by the Caliph Umar as a peace agreement with the Christians of Syria, was used by victorious Muslim armies who defeated Spaniards in 713.[22] The pact allowed those Iberians (Jewish and Christian alike) who abandoned combat to retain ownership of their farmlands and water resources.

The covenant did not require conversion to Islam. On the contrary, it allowed Jews and Christians in particular to retain their own religious practices, to worship in their traditional manners, to observe the feasts of their own faiths, and to select their own spiritual leaders.[23] Nor did these surrendering communities have a disrespectful name attached to them. In Arabic the members of these conquered, non-Muslim communities were called *ahl-dhimma*—literally, the "people of the pact or covenant."

This concession of religious independence and continued ownership of farmlands originally benefited both conquerors and defeated. The Arab victors often comprised a tiny mounted army that had conquered a well-armed, politically sophisticated, agriculturally advanced populace thousands of times larger than the conquering force.[24] In permitting well-established farming communities to continue their usual operations with little disruption, victorious Muslims provided economic incentives and tranquillity for themselves as well as for those whom they defeated.[25] But the Islamic pact did more. It also permitted Christians and Jews to transmit property according to the laws of their own communities. Contracts, sales, disputes over land boundaries, water rights, and similar issues whose resolution remained indispensable to the continued smooth operation of agriculture were to be settled according to the defeated communities' own customary laws and by their own chosen leaders.[26]

When Spanish Christian monarchs slowly began to oust their former rulers during the eleventh century, they defeated several large, wealthy Muslim communities. In addition to imposing the same tribute and humiliations that had been forced upon them, Christian monarchs instituted the same kind of landholding agreements that Muslims had previously set with Christians.[27] Defeated Muslim and Jewish communities were called by the Latinized version of the word *ahl-dhimma*: the word *aljama*, meaning in Arabic simply "community" or "congregation." These *aljamas* were guaranteed continued ownership of their surface lands and waters.

However, in these agreements the guarantee of landownership was given in exchange for a payment (tribute).[28] Whereas under Islamic tradition tribute was simply a sign of submission and the pact was a later development, Spanish Christians linked land title to tribute.[29] In subsequent centuries, Iberian Christian monarchs reached many similar agreements with large, prosperous Muslim and Jewish communities throughout the peninsula.[30]

As a result, the tradition of respecting the conquered community's rules regarding agricultural holdings became strongly ingrained throughout Iberia. Regardless of whether they lived in Valencia, Catalonia, Navarre, or Andalusia, all Spaniards were familiar with the pact of protection and the guarantees of landownership it offered conquered peoples. When occupying formerly Muslim lands, Christians often consulted elderly Muslims to settle boundary disputes among Christians, considering themselves bound by the traditions of those they displaced.[31]

Originally, Muslim and Jewish communities enjoyed autonomy when settling disputes over marriage, inheritance, and land. But as centuries passed, this self-rule was frequently threatened. Sometimes Jews and Muslims sought remedies in Christian courts when the results in their own were unsatisfactory. At other times, Christian officials intruded in Jewish and Muslim community affairs. The autonomy of Muslim communities, in particular, declined sharply two hundred years after their reconquest by Christians. By the fourteenth century, Muslim community leaders in some areas were sometimes little more than the king's official agents.[32]

Although the protection of Muslim (and Jewish) farmlands was far from automatic, an experiment abandoning this policy produced results that were wholly unsatisfactory to Iberian monarchs. During the fourteenth and fifteenth centuries, monarchs conquering Andalusia did away with the usual preservation of Muslim ownership. Intending to create a kingdom of small Christian proprietors, they permitted participants in the conquest of Andalusia to take productive terrain away from Muslim farmers. The policy failed totally. Using legal subterfuge, a small group of Christians carved out immense domains for themselves. As a result, in 1492, the year that Columbus left for the New World, Ferdinand and Isabel signed the final Castilian peace agreement, this time with the Muslims of Granada. Like the earlier agreements, it granted Muslims protection of their farmlands and the right to practice their religion in exchange for payment of tribute and accompanying forms of deference.[33]

New World Tribute

Three years after imposing exactly this levy on the defeated Muslims of Granada, Queen Isabel proposed a similar tax upon Indians in the New World. The Indians were subjects of the crown, she declared in 1501, and as such "are to pay us our tributes and rights [just] as we are paid by our subjects residing in our kingdoms and lordships." However, she did not have in mind the same taxes she required of her Christian subjects. Most Spanish Christians paid only indirect levies to the crown, whereas Indians were to pay direct per capita taxes, "each one, every year."[34]

Isabel's ambitions proved unrealizable in the short run. For the next twenty years, Spaniards encountered only nomadic farmers and hunter-gatherers in the circum-Caribbean region.[35] Such groups lacked the internal administrative structures necessary to collect funds. But the situation altered dramatically in 1519, when Hernán Cortés successfully landed a body of troops on the Yucatán peninsula. Cortés and his men encountered the Maya, the first heavily hierarchical native communities ever seen in the New World, then moved north to the equally hierarchical but wealthier Tlaxcalan and Aztec kingdoms. Spaniards for the first time had come into contact with highly structured native empires in the Americas.

Two years after Cortés's victory over the Aztecs, Isabel's grandson, Charles V, was able to implement successfully his grandmother's design for a per capita tribute.[36] Making the traditional Iberian-Islamic connection between tribute payment and military defeat, Charles V declared, "Indians who must be pacified [i.e., subdued by force of arms] into submitting and rendering obedience and vassalage [to us] [will] serve us and give tribute to recognize [our] lordship."[37] Spanish officials began levying per capita taxes upon militarily capable males between their teens and fifties, excluding the physically handicapped.[38] As in Spain, tribute was collected by authorities within the conquered community and paid in a specific place. Large native settlements were often placed in charge of collecting tribute from lesser ones.[39] As under earlier Islamic and Catholic Iberian regimes, tribute collectors had a right to imprison and whip the leaders of conquered peoples until payment was complete; this practice was often used in the New World.[40]

According to the leading political thinker of seventeenth-century Spain, Juan Solórzano Pereira, New World "tribute" was intended "to punish their [Indians'] faults."[41] The natives were required to atone for their earlier depravity by contributing to the costs of their being Christianized.[42] Like its predecessor taxes, Indian tribute was intentionally personal. Solórzano wrote: "[Tribute] does not take into consideration the estates, nor the charges on them, but is equally divided by head [count]. . . . Each Indian . . . *by his person* must pay the same quantity of money, wheat, hens, mantles, or corn, or other spices which are taxed."[43] But the tribute paid by Indians was not simply a tax. Nor had tribute ever been simply an economic payment in any of its previous Iberian, Islamic, or Christian forms. Tribute symbolized vassalage. Payments were declared to be in "recognition of lordship" or "superiority."[44] Tribute also indicated subjugation and military defeat.[45] Being Indian under Spanish domination in the New World meant continually being reminded of one's present conquered status by the payment of tribute.

This system of taxation and collection was subsequently introduced throughout the Americas wherever large, sophisticated native communities existed. It was established among the hundreds of communities along the backbone of the Andes, in highland Mexico, and in lowland Guatemala. Rather than calling these newly encountered communities *aljamas*, Spanish officials began to refer to them as the *república de indios* (literally "Indian republics"), the title by which they became known.[46] But to use the literal translation of "Indian republics" makes little sense. In English, a republic is a nonmonarchical form of government in which supreme power rests with elected representatives.[47] Although the leaders of the subservient native communities were elected and not hereditary leaders, they did not hold supreme power over their communities. That power rested with monarchs in Spain, to whom the natives were vassals ("subjects" in modern terms). Furthermore, communities' self-governance was limited to settling disputes among themselves. Spanish authorities adjudicated conflicts with Spaniards, and Catholic priests were additionally empowered to punish natives. Under Spanish domination, native communities were servile organizations,

politically and religiously subjugated to Iberians. One of the principal ongoing reminders of their subaltern status was the collection of tribute.

Just as Islamic law allowed flexibility in the actual amount of the poll
tax (tribute) collected, so too did the Spanish crown in the New World.
The exact amount each adult male was to pay depended upon his ability
to pay, but also upon the fiscal needs of the Spanish state.[48] Late in the sixteenth century, however, abrupt declines in tribute revenues (caused by
devastating epidemics) led to frequent complaints of abuse. Taxes began
to be levied on the blind and lame, those people traditionally exempted
for humanitarian reasons.[49] Even Spanish subjects began to dispute the tax
as abusive. In response to this challenge, which threatened a substantial
source of royal income, Hispanic monarchs abandoned the justification
that tribute collection continued long-standing Iberian practice.[50] Instead,
they asserted that they were merely carrying on native practices "so that
the Indians give and pay us [the crown] as they have before to their lords"
in Mexico.[51]

Querying natives about their practice of tribute also carried out a long-
standing Iberian tradition in which the defeated reassured the victors that
they were paying tribute that had always been paid. Royal officials in the
New World therefore carefully phrased their questions to selected Indian
informants using the identical language that Iberian Christians used when
addressing Muslim and Jewish tribute payers. Because Spanish officials
posed the questions in familiar terms, it did not matter that the expected
answers were untrue.

In Peru, for example, royal officials persuaded a carefully selected group
of indigenous leaders to swear (some fifty years after conquest) that the
Spanish/Islamic and Inca systems of tribute collection were identical.[52]
The fabrications of continuity successfully persuaded the crown's critics,
but, in fact, Spanish tribute in the New World was different from native
tribute in four different respects. First of all, Spanish New World tribute
was based, as was Muslim tribute, upon men of "fighting age." Yet such age
distinctions were unknown in the New World. The closest approximation
existed in Inca-dominated Peru, where status rather than age existed as a
category.[53] Second, many Indian communities did not necessarily pay
tribute to overlords. Tlaxcalans, whose society consisted of an egalitarian
confederation of regional communities, paid tribute to each other.[54] In
Peru, two different tribute systems used a complicated set of personal relationships and ecological zones to determine the amount of tribute owed.
Residents of the Aztec capital often paid tribute to places (palaces and
temples), not people.[55]

Third, Spaniards levied tribute on a per capita basis.[56] But this, too, was not an indigenous custom. As William Sanders observes, "The tribute collected by the Aztecs was not based upon a head count." He adds, "The relationship therefore between taxes and [total] population [was] an exceedingly tenuous one."[57] Prior to the arrival of Spanish conquerors, the community, not the individual, was responsible for producing the quantity of goods or services a community owed. In highland Mexico, for instance, communal tribute obligations ordinarily involved only a small portion of the population in the production of goods. "Commoners paid, but not all commoners. . . . Town assessments varied widely but many paid warrior suits, but 8 provinces did not."[58] Tetela did not pay tribute, only offering "gifts occasionally, battlefield captives."[59] Spanish tribute—like its Islamic predecessor—required all men to contribute, thus intentionally leveling all natives, reducing them all to a single category.[60]

Finally, the Spanish custom gendered the payment of tribute. In Native American "tribute" systems, it did not matter whether the products came from men's, women's, household, or communal labor. But Iberian tribute payments had originated as a form of punishment for men of fighting age, hence their initial masculine cast in the New World. This highly distinctive Iberian subordination of natives would be altered in the Americas, but only after several decades of financial pressure.

Although natives had been dying at extraordinarily high levels virtually since Spaniards first landed in the Caribbean, the continuing discoveries of vast new lands and large numbers of potential tribute payers kept adding to royal revenues even as tribute from previously contacted tribes and communities began to decline.[61] By the 1560s, however, there were no new large Indian empires to be discovered in the New World, and there were few large agricultural communities that had not been contacted. As a result, regal revenues from Native American communities were falling short of anticipated levels in the 1560s and 1570s. The crown responded by increasing the numbers of tributaries and adding new categories of tribute payers. In 1561 and 1562, the crown made explicit the demand that unmarried and widowed Indian men pay tribute.[62] The monarch then took the unprecedented step of requiring women to pay a poll tax equal to one-half of the tax on men.[63] But even these efforts did not produce sufficient income.

As wave after wave of devastating epidemics swept over the native population, Philip II required black and mulatto men and women to begin paying tribute. Royal motives were more nakedly financial in this instance, for tribute was paid by all blacks and mulattoes who "had farms and property," excluding the old, the poor, and children. The rationale for requiring blacks and mulattoes to pay tribute remained the traditional Islamic one: conquered peoples had to pay in order to "live in our dominions, and be maintained in peace." A further justification mirrored the rationalization created for Indian payment, namely, that blacks paid tribute in their African homelands.[64]

Both the original Islamic and derivative Christian tribute systems relied upon indigenous political structures to assemble and collect tribute. Blacks and mulattoes, however, had been torn from their communities and brought over to the New World as individual slaves. And although many re-created networks for themselves in Mexico and Peru, their ties did not establish the political organizational frameworks necessary for tribute exaction. As a result, the crown soon largely abandoned its efforts to collect tribute from blacks and mulattoes, the attempt merely signaling desperation to regain earlier levels of revenue.[65]

The unforeseen and dramatic decline in the native population also forced Spanish monarchs reluctantly to abandon collecting tribute from the native leaders themselves. Traditionally in Iberia, failure to produce such payments could mean a leader's imprisonment. But natives increasingly refused to assume the burden of leadership because it meant using force to extract sums from rapidly dwindling numbers of people increasingly unable to pay. Faced with losing the indispensable assistance they needed from indigenous governors, the monarchs allowed Indian leaders to plead an exemption from payment during their time in office and freed them from some petty humiliations. During their time in office indigenous leaders were addressed by the honorific *don* (equivalent to *seigneur* in French). And by century's end, native leaders were even permitted to ride horses for the duration of their stay in office.[66]

In the 1560s and 1570s, as the tax burdens upon survivors increased, many fled their traditional homelands. Pressure to come up with payment also pushed many natives out of their communities and into the labor market they worked to earn either the money or the goods they owed for the next round of tribute. Thus, despite policies protecting traditional landowners, tribute economically reoriented native communities.

Social Humiliations in the New World

Indians, like other conquered peoples, had to pay tribute in a ritual humiliation. Chiefs of the various regions were required to appear on specified days, at least twice a year, and personally hand over the tribute as an intended lesson in shame, inferiority, and military submission.[67] But the ritual of a per capita tax was not the only form of humility the victorious Spaniards expected from the Indians. The Spaniards also invoked prohibitions on native dress similar to those that had been customary in Iberia. They placed costly items of personal ornament—silk clothes, gold jewelry—off-limits for people they had defeated.[68] They also reserved the riding of horses as the exclusive prerogative of conquerors. Items of iron—including weapons and ordinary household implements—were also forbidden to natives. The Spaniards also required Indians to dress distinctively.[69] They had to register their difference from Spaniards by predominantly visual means. It should have been possible for a Spaniard to tell whether someone was Spanish or Indian simply by looking at hairstyle, clothing, or shoes. Initial prohibitions against natives wearing Hispanic clothing were only partially lifted for those performing heavy agricultural labor, permitting natives to dress in Spanish-style clothes made of coarse local materials.[70]

In the Americas, Spaniards required from the Indians those respectful behaviors that they had become accustomed to receiving from Spanish Muslims.[71] In their demeanor, Indians were to be "obedient, submissive, subdued, humble, servile, and yielding."[72] They were to give way to Spaniards on the streets and to indicate their subservience openly.

The other usual Iberian prohibitions were also introduced. Indians were forbidden to ride horseback and were initially prohibited from both herding animals and traveling on mules.[73] As the natives' numbers dropped precipitously, the bans on riding mules and herding animals were lifted, but not that on riding horseback.[74] Indians were not permitted to occupy a physically superior position to Spaniards. Only on the frontier—where few Spaniards could be found—and within the confines of Indian missions were natives occasionally permitted to ride horseback, not as a symbol of status, but in order to carry out their ranching duties on the Jesuit missions.[75]

Prohibitions against owning iron weapons were also carried over from the peninsula. Gunpowder weaponry was out of the question, but so too were swords, poniards, daggers, and knives, which had been ruled out in Spain.[76] Alongside the tradition of granting agricultural peoples protection of their lands in return for tribute and humiliation, the Iberian tradition of denying iron weapons to conquered peoples allowed Iberians to sustain the military victories they achieved over large, initially hostile populations.[77]

Native Americans soon grasped the nature of the dishonor that Spaniards imposed upon them. Understanding the intended insult implied by distinctions of dress and public display of deference, Indians of highland Mexico applied for exemptions from such demeaning laws. By 1597, fully a third of all Indian petitions made to the viceroy requested release from restrictive legislation on their appearance and conduct in public.[78]

Levying Islamic tribute (*jizya*) upon defeated peoples had historically required highly structured communities. All the communities previously subjected to payment of tribute were economically productive, usually practicing sedentary agriculture on a large scale. However, Spaniards did not encounter such large prosperous farming communities in the New World until several decades after Columbus first landed.

Protection of Native Lands

Invoking the Spanish tradition of protected communities, Charles V declared that Indians of the Americas were to retain their traditional surface lands and rights.[79] Unlike many other royal policies governing labor rights, the prohibitions on acquiring Indian lands met with little direct opposition.

The idea that defeated peoples resided in their own parallel communities was culturally familiar to Spaniards. Regardless of whether they came from Aragon or Castile, all Spaniards had grown up with quasi-independent Muslim and (prior to 1492) Jewish communities. Spaniards from all over the peninsula recognized a historically and culturally well-known practice in a similar although not identical situation. Thus Spaniards accepted, albeit sometimes with ill grace, natives' ownership of their traditional lands.

Spaniards have typically posed the self-flattering question, Why were so few of us able to defeat so many Indians? However, the real question is, and always has been, How were so few Spaniards able to hold on to those early victories, particularly over large, well-organized, and sophisticated empires? No small part of the answer lies in the ability of Spanish victors to give the defeated more to gain from rapid peace and resumption of traditional activities than from continuing warfare. This tactic, of course, was originally Islamic.

Therefore, the early Spanish settlers accepted terms dictated by the king for strategic reasons: to secure the acquiescence if not acceptance of the domination of a small military force over a large empire. Initial military superiority over the large New World empires was by no means secure. Indigenous armies had demonstrated repeatedly that they could mount attacks and sieges that could threaten or destroy Spaniards' tenuous military position. By allowing the natives to continue to own their lands, gather their crops, and raise their animals on the condition that they abandon their fight, conquerors provided the natives with a stake in accepting the Spanish presence rather than pursuing a war to the death.

But Charles V had an additional reason for invoking this culturally familiar model: if Spanish Christians were allowed to amass large landholdings, they could become a threat to royal authority. The direct prohibition against large landholdings in the wake of conquest had failed miserably in Andalusia in the century preceding the conquest of the New World. Faced with convincing evidence of the ineffectualness of direct royal prohibitions against sizable land purchases even in Granada after 1492, and on the heels of Cortés's own attempt at a land grab in Oaxaca, Ferdinand and Isabel's grandson understood the even greater futility of such measures thousands of miles away.[80] Under this Iberian custom of subjugated communities (both Muslim *dhimma* and Christian *aljamas*), land could be held communally, privately, or as a combination of the two. Local custom rather than the conquerors' norms governed requirements for landownership. And these rules carried over to the New World.

Furthermore, as under Iberian tradition in the treatment of subjugated communities, rules for transmitting property were determined by the defeated communities. When internal native disputes over ownership and transmission of property were brought before Spanish judges in the New World, the judges attempted to understand and to apply traditional native norms in their decisions.[81] Thus even the judicial structure was accustomed to following native rather than Spanish rules governing ownership and transmission of surface rights, even if the judges' understandings were imperfect.

In the New World, just as in Spain, this local autonomy often eroded over the centuries. Continual economic exchanges between the two communities ensured that both sides would become aware of the other's practices and adapt accordingly. Furthermore, economic disputes between protected peoples and conquerors were often resolved in the latter's tribunals.[82] Indians sometimes saw personal economic advantages in the conquerors' rules governing property and opted to appeal to the Spanish courts to resolve internal differences.

Similar undermining of native autonomy also occurred in the New World where powerful local Spaniards and regional royal bureaucrats often interfered with Indians' selection of their leaders.[83] But although practice often fell short of the ideal, Spanish custom conceded legitimacy to native traditions regarding property transmission, boundaries, and ownership.

The ideals of protection and respect for local inheritance and property transmission in the New World disintegrated far more rapidly than they had in Spain, for two central reasons. On the Iberian Peninsula, protecting the local communities' land rights had always been tied to protecting their religious independence. Muslim victors tolerated Christian and Jewish practices; Christians allowed Islamic and Hebrew services. But Ferdinand and Isabel abandoned religious toleration during the 1490s, forcing Jews and many Muslims to convert. In 1492, they first expelled Jews from the peninsula. And in 1498, certain that no military assistance for Muslims would be coming from North Africa, Isabel and Ferdinand seized a pretext to violate the treaty and forcibly convert the Muslim inhabitants of Granada, whose religious freedom they had sworn to protect.[84] Shortly thereafter, they exiled Islamic communities from Andalusia, Castile, and finally Navarre, leaving only a desperately needed but impoverished Muslim agricultural community in Aragon.[85]

In the New World, the Catholic kings and their successors followed the newly embraced policy of religious intolerance. Despite the monarchs' fine words about not forcing the natives of the New World to convert, it rapidly became clear that no religious practices other than Catholicism would be allowed in the Americas.[86] Indians under Spanish domination were forced to abandon their religious faith, with all of its spiritual sources of sustenance and familiar attitudes toward the natural and divine worlds.[87]

But as many scholars in the twentieth century have noted, religion is part of a cultural system that often has far broader implications than simply spiritual issues.[88] In demanding adherence to Christianity, Spanish conquerors unwittingly interfered with the economies of native communities. Particularly disrupting was the way mandatory Christianity imposed Western Europeans' ideas of kinship upon native communities.[89]

Throughout the world, kinship systems played and continue to play a crucial role in the circulation of economic goods.[90] Kinship ties determine whether a father or a mother's brother is the closest relative, thus fixing the order for passing on economic goods. The introduction of Western European ideas of patrilineal kinship in the New World, for example, prevented married Inca women from passing property on to their daughters.[91] Furthermore, in the Western kinship system, inheritance was defined as depending on something called "legitimacy," namely, the marital status of the parents at the time of a child's birth. Many New World native systems had no such requirement for inheritance, and introducing this concept disrupted traditional economic flows.[92]

The enforcement of conversion also disrupted kinship rules governing marriage alliances.[93] Daughters brought money or lands to a marriage, and when traditional alliances were forbidden by new Catholic rules prohibiting kin marriages, the underlying economic exchanges were disturbed as well. Although the rigid and extensive categories of prohibited kin for marriage were modified for the New World, the impact of the new rules was powerful nonetheless. For example, many American groups reckoned kinship only along the mother's or father's side; Western European kinship extended the definition of close kin to the mother's and father's sides, thus outlawing a great number of marriages.[94] Catholics also believed that assuming a ritual role (godparent) created a bond of kinship that prohibited marriage, thus again preventing a range of previously acceptable unions.[95]

A second, equally devastating pressure upon protection and respect for local inheritance and property transmission emerged in the New World.[96] Isolated for centuries from regular contact with people from other continents, natives throughout the Americas had immune systems that were unprepared for the onslaught of new diseases.[97] Measles, typhoid, and small-pox made their appearance with their human hosts, as did dysentery, cholera, and other diseases with their new animal hosts or vectors. The continuing stream of immigrants, constantly bringing new pathogens, ensured that even natives who failed to catch diseases from their neighbors would catch them from new European or African arrivals.[98] The range of diseases was so broad that it left no sector of the Indian communities immune. And as soon as a community recovered from one illness, another would sweep through, devastating already weakened community members.

The epidemic disaster caused immense disruption and even extermination of entire communities. When knowledgeable members of a community perished, traditional understandings of inheritance and economic customs died with them. And as the people with economic means died, the community and its economic life were devastated. Thus in the New World, epidemic disease destroyed knowledge of traditional customs as well as the people to observe them. As a result, the necessary reconstitution of agrarian communities along with the prescribed reorganization of kinship rules created even greater pressures for change in traditional economic practices.

Even when the first waves of massive deaths from epidemics left many native fields permanently vacant, royal officials were slow to accept Spanish claims to land. Spanish settlers could obtain land left vacant by the extermination of a community, a process that began in the 1560s when the first deaths left many native communities unable to farm.[99] But Spanish settlers who wanted to claim ownership to land had to observe a series of bureaucratic formalities. Acquiring even deserted Indian terrain was time-consuming and difficult. Only a royal official could formally grant title to a Spanish settler, and title obtained in such a fashion could not always be considered permanent. Merely renting Indian lands had to be officially arranged.[100]

Spanish title to land taken from Indians remained uncertain for lengthy periods of time. There was no time limit after which a community could not sue for payment or restitution, and no royal procedure that overrode native claims to a region. Even the periodic regularizations of question-able titles (called "land compositions") failed to invalidate Indians' rights to demand restitution of territory.[101] And during the colonial era, when Indians brought cases against Spaniards for encroachments on their lands, royal courts were usually sympathetic to the Indians. Historian Lesley Byrd Simpson writes that in "complaints of [Indian] pueblos against Spaniards encroaching on their communal lands—the Indians [were] in-variably given an *amparo* [protection]."[102]

Furthermore, the crown instituted a series of measures designed to pre-vent the abusive taking of land from native peoples. Although Indians were free to dispose of their land as they saw fit, they could not sell their land to a non-Indian without royal authorities intervening. Christian rulers had instituted a similar safeguard in thirteenth-century Aragon to preserve Muslim ownership of farms when Christians began forcibly and unfairly depriving Muslims of their productive lands.[103] Officials charged with preventing Spaniards from coercing Indians to sell their lands in-voked the same rationales in the New World.

Yet the price of native land tenure was a tax so burdensome that it forced thousands to abandon their ancestral lands and become laborers on the fringes of Spanish society—on farms, in mines, and on the streets of Spanish towns and cities. Spaniards regarded this poverty and margin-alization of Native Americans as beneficial because it provided them with a pool of near-desperate wage laborers. But the process destroyed the na-tives' traditional way of life, as well as their relations with friends, families, and members of their communities.

Furthermore, the subjugated communities were often under pressure from local clergy who monitored their religious practices for signs of idolatry or other indications of traditional religions. Priests could request the imprisonment, flogging, and execution of those who adhered to native rituals.[104] Catholic bishops also periodically appeared on inspection tours called "visits" (*visitas*) to investigate and punish all those suspected of in-voking earlier religious tradition.[105] As a result, Native Americans were sensitive to accusations that they had violated religious norms because such accusations would bring down the wrath of the Catholic Church. There was neither recourse nor appeal from the punishments of the church visits; religious liberty was not tolerated.

Nor can these communities be called preserved communities because they preserved the lives of the inhabitants. The lives of Native Americans were preserved from mass slaughter, but their religion, their ties of kinship, and their traditional relations were forever changed.

Juxtapositions

Only under Iberian, and particularly Spanish, colonization did natives retain their farms. Consequently, when Spaniards dispossessed indigenous peoples of their farmland, they avoided flaunting their actions. Public celebration could attract the unwanted attention of the authorities, who might well intervene—as they sometimes did—to restore the land to remaining indigenous inhabitants. By contrast, English colonists were able to tout their confiscation of land from native peoples openly, because to them seizing land was a culturally desirable and legitimate goal of colonization.

Furthermore, English colonists enjoyed the broadest leeway of all Europeans in achieving their culturally sanctioned objective. Of the three acceptable means of acquiring Indian land, only one—treaty—required official permission. All other European powers—Spain, Portugal, France, and the Netherlands—required government approval for taking over native farmlands.[106] Dutch settlers had to obtain formal permission from the officials of the Dutch West India Company before proceeding with a purchase.[107] Under both Spanish and Portuguese laws, two government organizations, the town council (chosen by local election) and the appointed royal regional head, had authority to grant land. In Spanish colonies, the royal official eventually became charged with full authority over land grants, whereas in the Portuguese colonies both officials retained the right to grant land, with predictable conflicts ensuing. However, far fewer conflicts over land emerged in Lusitanian colonies than in English ones because land title was a far less desirable colonial objective.

The Islamic practice of creating pacts with defeated farmers had been relatively little used in Portugal.[108] Much of Portugal had been a military frontier; only in the south did Muslims dominate large agricultural domains. As a result, victorious Portuguese Christian kings had created far fewer protected communities in northern Portugal than had their counterparts in Valencia, Aragon, Castile, and Navarre.[109] But Portuguese leaders in the New World created their own kind of subjugated communities. Because they never encountered the large sedentary civilizations needed for tribute and the pacts, however, Portuguese officials evolved their own version of this system—as I will explain in chapter 8.

One of the most obvious cultural differences between Spanish and English approaches to colonization was found in the governance of public decorum. Particularly distinctive were the incompatible rules regarding owning guns and iron weapons, wearing native dress, and riding horseback. Outside of the Iberian-dominated Americas, regulations against selling firearms to natives were often disregarded.[110] But in writing about the history of prohibitions, U.S. historians have assumed that the a "spirit of greed and lawlessness [prevailed]. . . . Profiteers who catered to it were to be *found in every colony*, totally oblivious to considerations of national policy or public welfare."[111] Although profiteering may well have existed everywhere, disregard for or prohibitions on gun sales did not exist in every colony. Regardless of the incentive to profit, Iberian settlers retained the deeply ingrained—originally Islamic—conviction that conquered peoples did not have a right to bear arms.[112] As a result, Spanish settlers rarely sold iron weapons or guns to Native Americans. Only societies lacking the cultural tradition of denying iron to defeated peoples could even consider flouting rules banning the sale of iron weapons.

Native dress was another area in which the English (as well as the French and Dutch colonists) differed from the Iberians. To these non-Spanish settlers, clothing was not a crucial sign of social distinction, as it was in the Spanish-controlled New World. At least half of the goods that English, French, and Dutch traders sold natives in the region now called the United States were items of clothing identical to those worn by the settlers themselves.[113] As the colonization of the New World began, distinctions in attire between servants and masters were starting to disappear in England.[114] The importance of distinctions in clothing declined even further in the New World. Because Englishmen relied upon a different cultural category—physical distance—to establish the boundary between themselves and natives, they never required distinctive dress of Indians.

Riding on horseback was a privilege to which only the victors were entitled in the Spanish New World. As Alexander von Humboldt would declare at the start of the nineteenth century, "A white [Spaniard] who rides barefooted on horseback thinks he belongs to the nobility of the country."[115] But the sense of superiority associated with riding horseback failed to appear in England. Recounts Conrad Heresbach, "As the proverb in England is, set a knave on horseback and you shall see him shoulder [insolently push] a Knight; for an Ape will be an Ape, though you clothe him in purple [kingly dress]."[116] Hunting on horseback was seen as a conqueror's privilege among English colonists, but merely riding a horse was not an honor.

Far from becoming a privilege to which only European settlers were entitled, riding on horseback became an integral part of the dominant English image of Native Americans. Even though Europeans introduced horses into the Americas, English colonists invoked horseback riding to symbolize the supposed "nomadic" and "hunting" lifestyle of Native Americans. Thus the image of the horseback-mounted plains warrior/hunter became widely popular in the nineteenth- and twentieth-century United States. Yet such a representation would have been considered an affront to Spanish status, demonstrating a superiority to which Indians were not entitled under Iberian dominion.

6

Cannibals: Iberia's Partial Truth

In 1992, at the Essex conference attended by many indigenous activists
from Spanish America, a prominent English historian, John Hemming,
gave a talk about the sixteenth-century peoples of Brazil.[1] When I politely
taxed him after the presentation with the fact that his extensive historical
description of the sixteenth-century coastal Tupis was missing an important dimension of their lives, namely, cannibalism, a Mapuche activist
from Argentina leaped to his feet. "You can't say that," he interrupted in a
raised voice, addressing me, not Hemming. "That's the excuse they always
use to attack us." As he continued to berate me for having raised the
subject, it became crystal clear why Hemming had omitted references to
cannibalism. Although four hundred years—or more—have passed since
Tupis practiced cannibalism, and thousands of miles and dozens of other
cultures separate Tupis from the Mapuche in present-day Argentina, the
mere mention of indigenous cannibalism in any region of South America
is still a sensitive political issue.

Such public defensiveness indicated that Hemming's omission of the
subject had likely not been accidental. But Hemming is far from alone in
his reticence to mention the topic. Such touchiness abounds in Spanish-
(and sometimes Portuguese-) language literature on aboriginal peoples in
the Americas—both within and outside of Latin America. Outsiders have

noted the extent of such omissions. Anthropologist Sherry Ortner, for example, recently observed that a well-regarded historian of the Maya conquest had omitted and downplayed references to Maya cannibalism in the years prior to conquest.[2] Literary critics of Spanish America sympathetic to aboriginal peoples carefully and repeatedly qualify their characterizations of "cannibal" practices. Some writers have even gone so far as to challenge the reality of cannibalism, even though few outside of Ibero-America and its scholars find such discounting credible.[3] Furthermore, to those who neither write on nor reside in Ibero-America, such touchiness appears excessive.

In contrast, the mention of historical Pawnee, Caddoan, or Iroquois cannibalism—all equally well-documented occurrences—draws little or no protest from English-speaking Native American activists.[4] Nor does mention of nineteenth-century cannibal practices among Pacific Islanders provoke such a response among contemporary Maori, Fijians, or Tongans.[5] Rather, all such reports of previous cannibalism are met with shrugs of indifference. The subject is historical, hence academic, and certainly not one that generates political heat, and especially not in the present day. In these regions of the contemporary world—all colonized by English rulers, incidentally—the issue of historic cannibalism remains politically insignificant. Such indifference is clearly not the case in Ibero-America.

War over Moral Standards

In the centuries preceding the conquest of the New World, intermittent warfare dominated the Iberian Peninsula. This warfare occasionally intensified into full-scale battles and then subsided into decades of border raiding between fixed lines of combat. These moments of relative quiet were originally named the "cold war," an expression more familiar for its later appropriation by the United States and Soviet Union.

During these often centuries-long intervals of cold war, hit-and-run raiders swooped down on pastures, often on horseback, carrying off crops and people. Alexandre Herculano described the "continual combat and repeated [twelfth century] raids in order to take away captives."[6] The organized incursions aimed not to strengthen the military position of either side, but, as Herculano declared, to obtain prisoners.

These episodic frontier raids rarely resulted in the loss of life, for prisoners from wealthy families could be held for ransom or captives could be sold as slaves to urban areas such as Cordoba. During labor shortages, leaders of Muslim towns were required to send specified numbers of Christian slaves every year to North Africa. The Muslim leaders of Alcácer (Al-Kassr al-Fetah) during the twelfth century, for example, had "to send a hundred Christian prisoners every year to the emperor of Morocco."[7] When Christians captured Alcácer in 1217, they enslaved all its inhabitants— approximately two thousand people.[8] And when Ferdinand captured Málaga in 1487, he similarly enslaved all of its inhabitants.

The unique characteristic of Iberian slavery was the religious distinction between slave and master. In the early Middle Ages, Anglo-Saxons often enslaved Welsh, Irish, and Scots, and Genoese and Venetians took Christian Greeks, residents of the Caucuses, and Balkan Peninsulans to sell as slaves in Italy and the South of France. In Iberia, however, slavery primarily occurred between Christians and Muslims.[9] It endured on the Christian/Muslim frontier for nearly eight hundred years, coming to an end only with the eventual cessation of hostilities in the fifteenth century. By then the pattern had been well-established: centrally organized raids by members of one faith resulted in the enslavement of members of the other faith, often to supply the labor needs of an empire.

Rarely were the inhabitants of conquered agricultural communities enslaved. In extreme circumstances Christians enslaved Muslims for violations of the dress code and for being unable to identify an employer.[10] Such incidents were relatively uncommon, however; border raids were the predominant source of slaves.

Both Christians and Muslims claimed their actions were morally inspired. Eighth-century Muslim conquerors had seen themselves as bringing a superior religion to the peninsula, hence Christians understood their eventual military rout of Muslims as vindicating their own religious superiority.[11]

Thus Iberians became accustomed to understanding their differences from their military opponents as ethical. These convictions began to be reflected in legal codes from the thirteenth century onward. Starting with the *Fuero real*, Spanish legal codes customarily opened with a profession of faith, such as "In the name of God, Amen" or "God is the beginning, the middle and the end of all things."[12] The placement of a credo at the start of a law code clearly signaled religion's centrality to the legal and political order.

But Muslims retained their own critiques of Christians. In addition to identifying the veneration that Catholics seemed to lavish upon images as idolatrous, Muslims firmly rejected the divinity of Christ. In Islam, Christ, like Mohammed, Abraham, and Moses, was one of the great prophets. Christians, however, insisted upon the duality of Christ as human and divine. Images of his crucifixion commemorated a type of human sacrifice and dominated their core religious ritual, the Mass. Islam had no such ritual, nor did it interpret Christ's death as a human sacrifice.

In constructing themselves as enjoying moral preeminence over Muslims (much as Muslims had earlier claimed ethical superiority over them), medieval Iberian Christians celebrated their own virtues in numerous anti-Islamic polemics. In particular, they portrayed Muslims as bloodthirsty tyrants who slaughtered innocent Christians for refusing to renounce their faith.[13] Although Christians were as guilty as Muslims of threatening unbelievers with death unless they converted, popular Catholic rhetoric labeled Muslims alone as perpetrators of such actions.[14]

Another favorite theme of Christian polemicists was Muslim sexual mores. Muslims' acceptance of multiple wives, hostility to lifelong chastity, and understanding of Paradise as a place of sexual delight greatly antagonized ascetic-minded Christians. Although the Qur'an does not tolerate homosexual relations, Iberian customs accepted them more readily than did other Islamic traditions.[15] Iberian Christians used this local leniency to identify Islam with homosexuality.

Finally, and with the least foundation in fact, Christian debaters labeled Muslims as both idolaters and heretics.[16] The Qur'an strictly prohibits the religious representation of humans. On the other hand, Catholic places of worship were frequently filled with all kinds of human representations—of saints, the Virgin Mary, and Jesus. In fact, medieval Catholicism—with its wood and plaster saints—was far closer to idolatry than Islam. Because Muslims accepted the New Testament as revealed by God, the Christian charge of heresy (deviation from an accepted orthodoxy) made Islam's acceptance of Christian holy texts appear as apostasy rather than the evaluations of an independent prophet and religion.

The War for Moral Standards Comes to the New World

By the time Iberians arrived in the New World, they firmly believed they were religiously superior to those they defeated. Portuguese and Spanish conquerors heaped moral opprobrium on the natives of the New World—calling them idolaters, heretics, pagans, and sodomites—thus continuing a long-established pattern of morally insulting their military adversaries.

Nearly all Spanish conquest narratives portray Iberians as engaged in a moral mission to eliminate "the ugly things" that Native Americans were doing; idolatry, cannibalism, sodomy, and human sacrifice were seen as particularly morally abhorrent.[17] But different Spanish narratives categorized such behavior as violating different types of norms. Some invoked philosophical standards, others religious or political norms. Although political leaders and royal advisers were cautious about exactly how they expressed Iberia's moral mission to the New World, few conquerors or colonists were so preoccupied.[18]

Formally educated Spanish scholars and leaders often termed cannibalism, idolatry, homosexuality, and human sacrifice "sins . . . against natural reason," using a category derived from medieval scholasticism.[19] Less formally prepared Spaniards occasionally used the more general language of moral turpitude ("sins"), whereas still others spoke of native conduct as transgressing public order ("crimes").[20] Finally, still others referred to native cannibalism and human sacrifices as peasant-like "coarseness" (*rudeza*). However they classified cannibalism, human sacrifice, idolatry, and sodomy—as immoral, criminal, or merely vulgar—ordinary Spaniards used examples of such behavior to justify conquering and ruling the natives to put an end to such conduct.[21]

The writings of the conquerors are replete with images of natives sinning, behaving crudely, and acting criminally, by Spanish standards. Wrote Gonzalo Fernández de Oviedo: "Natives are idolatrous, libidinous, and commit sodomy. . . . Their chief desire is to eat, drink, worship heathen idols, and commit bestial obscenities."[22] Cervantes de Salazar wrote in his *Chronicle of New Spain*, "They adored stones and animals . . . [and] sacrificed to them."[23] Another Spaniard wrote, "They adored the devil in his diverse forms and [worshipped] idols . . . in these Indies," keeping these "infernal images" everywhere.[24] Even Bernal Díaz del Castillo, who described his work *The True History of the Conquest of New Spain* as a demythologizing account, proclaimed the central significance of Iberia's moral mission to the New World.[25] And while loudly proclaiming the unfairness of accusing all natives of such actions, the imperial critic, Bartolomé de Las Casas, used words such as "contamination," "vice," "plague," and "evil" to describe practices in Native Americans that he did not similarly condemn in Europeans.[26]

Greeted at a Mayan temple by ten priests whose hair hung long and thick, "impenetrably matted and crusted with dried blood," Spaniards could not conceal their horror.[27] On several occasions during military conflicts, the Mexica at least appear to have understood the Spanish terror of human sacrifice, using this knowledge to demoralize the invaders. During the battle for Tenochtitlán, for example, the Mexica were careful to ritually slay Spanish captives in a place where their sacrifice would be fully visible from the Spanish encampment.[28]

Spaniards repeatedly and vociferously expressed fears that cannibalism was *everywhere*. The natives of the Desollado province of Nicaragua were "accustomed, that is it is nothing, to eat human flesh, it is sold in the markets," wrote Fernández de Oviedo. "The Caribs of these Islands, the people of New Spain, and the provinces of Nicaragua . . . Peru . . . Mainland . . . Quito, Popoyán and many other places customarily sacrifice humans and eat human flesh as in France and Spain and Italy they eat mutton and beef."[29] Although clearly exaggerating the prevalence of the activity,[30] such accounts suggest the depths of Spaniards' fears of ceremonial cannibalism on occasions that they did not understand and for motives with which they could not identify.

Spaniards frequently declared that they found ritual cannibalism unspeakable. Hernán Cortés reported that a member of his company found

> a native of Mexico, eating a piece of flesh of the body of an Indian he had killed when entering that town, and this Spaniard came to tell me of it, and I had the Indian burned in the presence of that lord, telling him the reason for such punishment, namely that he had killed and eaten one of his fellow men, which was forbidden by Your Majesty and which I, in your Royal name, had required and commanded them not to do. So I had him burned, for I wished to see no one killed.[31]

The obvious contradiction between "I had him burned" and "for I wished to see no one killed" indicates clearly that Cortés did not consider burning a native alive the same as killing a person. Nor did Cortés label his own actions as a human sacrifice.

Finally, Spaniards described male homosexuality as especially repugnant. Fernández de Oviedo claimed that just listening to Indians' unabashed descriptions of homosexual conduct made him feel mortified.[32] "They frequently committed the sin of sodomy which for its ugliness is called among the sins against nature," wrote Cervantes de Salazar.[33] Witnessing homosexual intercourse between natives usually unloosed a torrent of impassioned angry words. "Ugly, enormous abominations of these savage and bestial people. . . . In no province of the islands (Caribbean) or mainland (central and South America) that Christians have come across until now, have there not been sodomites."[34] Alvaro Núñez Cabeza de Vaca referred to the homosexuality he encountered in what is now the southeastern United States as "brutish and beastly," and Vasco de Balboa, discoverer of the Pacific Ocean, put forty native transvestites to death.[35]

While finding the practices themselves repugnant, Spaniards were equally horrified by the lack of prohibitions against such conduct. Possessing taboos meant feeling remorse or shame for cannibalism, human sacrifice, idolatry, or sodomy.[36] Indigenous peoples' failure to express contrition for these activities allowed Spaniards to consider themselves civilized merely by virtue of feeling ashamed, not necessarily by refraining from such behavior.[37]

Why idolatry, human sacrifice, cannibalism, and sodomy in particular drew expressions of outrage from Iberians cannot be understood through simple observation of native customs. But the tone and content of the Iberians' accusations become increasingly understandable when related to the image that Iberians had of themselves. Spanish colonizers, in the Americas as elsewhere, identified themselves as emissaries of a superior religion. Their antagonism toward male homosexuality continued a traditional theme of their anti-Islamic polemics. But another source of their hatred may have been their historic sensitivity to Muslim charges against their brand of Catholicism.

Idolatry, ritual commemoration of human sacrifice, and cannibalism all were suspiciously close to Catholic religious rituals. Sensitized by centuries of Muslim accusations of idolatry, Spaniards may have responded with rage when they came upon open worship of idols. Similarly susceptible to Muslim attacks on their ritual reenactment of a human sacrifice in the Mass, Spaniards were galled by witnessing actual ritual human sacrifice. The widespread Hispanic moral indifference to survival cannibalism on board ship contrasted sharply with Spaniards' responses to ceremonial cannibalism (especially in conjunction with human sacrifice).[38] Ritual cannibalism also came too close to one of their own religious rites—the transformation of the Eucharist into the body and blood of Christ.[39] In this respect, the "new" in the New World was less novelty than finding conduct in times and places and under circumstances unthinkable in the Old World.

A final explanation for the strength of Spanish antagonism toward cannibalism—real or imagined—among native peoples comes from the Spaniards' association of nonritual cannibalism with the conduct of animals. Carnivorous animals, such as dogs, wolves, and lions, do not cook their meat, but rather tear and eat it raw from the animals they have killed. To Spaniards, the occasional Native American practice of ceremonially eating parts of humans resembled the actions of animals. Cannibalism therefore threatened the culturally significant boundary between humans and animals that separated the Spaniards and the natives.

Native Perspectives on Human Sacrifice and Cannibalism

Contrary to Fernández de Oviedo's assertions, eating human flesh was usually ritualized to distinguish its status as a special, rather than an everyday, action. Two occasions led natives to eat the flesh of their fellow man: warfare and religious celebrations.[40]

The motives for American tribes who ingested human flesh after warfare ranged from revenge to the desire to assimilate the enemies' strength. The Iroquois would eat portions of an enemy's heart and his lips in hopes of acquiring his bravery or other virtues.[41] Huron, Mohawk, and Oneida tribes held feasts where the head of an enemy captive went into the kettle and was given first to the chiefs.[42] The coastal Tupi, who ate the flesh of their enemies as an act of vengeance, however, refused to touch any part of the head on similar occasions.[43]

In still other parts of the Americas, the belief prevailed that eating the flesh of an individual created the most intimate union possible with the deceased. In these instances America's natives understood ritual cannibalism as transcending the boundary between death and life, transforming dead beings into gods, or communing with the sacred.[44] In this form of cannibalism, the ashes of a deceased person were mixed with food. By ingesting ashes, individuals incorporated the substance and the spirit of the ancestors and thus partook of their good qualities: courage, vigor, or even psychic or magic powers.[45]

Spaniards neither grasped nor attempted to understand the complexity and variety of different motives for the rituals they lumped together under the heading of cannibalism. Nor did they understand their own conduct as cannibalistic. Using dogs to capture, maim, and kill aboriginal peoples, particularly in the Caribbean, in effect was employing animals as proxies for a terrifying form of ripping live humans to shreds. Yet while unleashing their dogs on native peoples, the conquerors never thought to label their own practices as surrogate cannibalism.

The accusation that natives were cannibals also generalized the practices of a few native groups to all. Some native groups, such as the northern Mexican Rarámuri (Tarahumara) and the Brazilian Bororo, had myths condemning cannibals.[46] Still other Native American groups had stronger prohibitions. Several groups would not eat the meat of animals that were carnivorous or ate human flesh. The Selk'nam of Tierra del Fuego, for example, refused to eat fox meat because foxes dug up human corpses.[47] The Waica of the Venezuelan Amazon refused to eat carnivorous birds and animals, although they would make exceptions for flesh-eating fish, such as the legendarily vicious piranha.[48]

Throughout the Americas, Europeans were as likely to encounter taboos against cannibalism as its ritual practice. Bartolomé de Las Casas observed: "It is not true, but a great falsehood and pernicious testimony raised by those who defame [the Indians] generally saying that all are contaminated by these vices [the sacrifice of innocents and eating of human flesh]. Because not everywhere or even in many places have they ever done so. . . . There are infinite peoples and great kingdoms where there has never been such contamination or plagues." He added later, "If in one area they eat human flesh, and in another they sacrifice the innocents, and in another contaminate themselves with the sin against nature, in many thousands of leagues none of these evils appears."[49] But Spanish conquerors appreciated none of the range of indigenous reasons for cannibalism. They understood such actions only through their own self-perception as the bearers of a superior morality and their own discomfort with moral attitudes they had long been criticized for holding.[50]

Portuguese America

Like their fellow Iberians, Portuguese colonists frequently attacked the aboriginal peoples on moral grounds. The most commonly used Portuguese word for Native American in the sixteenth and seventeenth centuries was *gentio*, a word signifying "Gentile" or "pagan." The word *Indian* initially appeared occasionally, becoming more common only during the seventeenth century.[51]

The Portuguese also attacked cannibalism, homosexuality, and human sacrifice. The prominent sixteenth-century Jesuit missionary Manuel da Nóbrega described the natives as always inclined to evil. In a letter dated August 10, 1549, he wrote: "This [cannibalism] is the most abominable thing there is among these people. They kill someone in a war, and bring him back in pieces and put him over the fire, and then eat him with the same solemnity and celebration."[52] He later remarked on their tendency even when Christianized to continue to celebrate victories by eating the flesh of their enemies.[53] A year and eight months after making that observation, he complained of the difficulty in getting the natives to stop having multiple wives, to stop killing, and to stop eating human flesh: "All of our task consists in getting them away from this. . . . Abandoning these customs appears rough."[54] Another of the early Jesuits in Brazil wrote to Ignatius Loyola that "these creatures . . . live almost in the manner of beasts . . . satiated in eating human flesh and wrapped up in that immorality"[55] A well-known contemporary Portuguese writer observed of the Jesuits, "One finds, in effect . . . black references to the cruelty . . . warlike propensities and cannibalistic contumacy of the Indians."[56]

Only on one minor area did the two groups of colonists separate. The

Portuguese could rarely detect idol worship among either the Tupi or the Gê (the two major linguistic groups of central Brazil) because they were unable to recognize the substances these people venerated.[57] Therefore, Portuguese settlers rarely characterized the aboriginal inhabitants of Brazil as idolatrous, resorting instead to labeling them heretics or pagans more often than did their Hispanic neighbors.[58]

Despite encountering aboriginal peoples who practiced greatly divergent religious faiths, used many different forms of agriculture, and inhabited highly distinct terrain, Spanish and Portuguese colonizers characterized the peoples of the Americas in remarkably similar ways. For example, inhabitants of the vast highland Aztec and Inca empires were tagged with the same labels as were the female-dominated farming Mapuche and Tupi.

Like English colonizers, the Spanish and Portuguese found purportedly uniform characteristics among aboriginal peoples. But in neither case did the unity originate with the natives. Rather, in both instances it began with conquerors, who shared a common history and hence a common interpretive framework—and who judged natives according to their own terms and found them lacking.

Right of Conquest, Right of Punishment

Many of the conquerors viewed themselves as pursuing a military right to bring the New World peoples to Christianity. In his official proclamation *Intra arcana* on May 2, 1539, Pope Paul III said, "We trust that . . . you will compel and with all zeal cause the barbarian nations to come to the knowledge of God . . . by force and arms, if needful, in order that their souls may partake of the heavenly kingdom."[59]

Iberian soldiers saw themselves as emissaries of a new morality, but theirs was often a murderous new morality. José de Acosta observed of his military predecessors, "Soldiers believed themselves to be rightful avengers of such crimes [against God]."[60] Wrote Bernal Díaz del Castillo: "In all the provinces of New Spain, there was not a filthier, more evil people of worse customs than those of the province of Pánuco. . . . They were punished with fire and sword two or three times."[61]

Native religious sites were particularly targeted for outbursts of destructive rage. "We climbed up [a temple] and flung [the idols] down and . . . the idols were smashed into pieces. They looked like horrid dragons, some like sheep, others half human, huge dogs, and evil likenesses. . . . And Cortés ordered that we take away the idols we had flung down to a place where they could never be seen again and burn them."[62] Spanish soldiers not only failed to respect sacred native sites, but they also frequently razed them. They leveled shrines where they had witnessed the scenes of idol worship, ceremonial human sacrifices, and cannibalism. They demolished depictions of native gods and the buildings in which they were worshipped, as if eliminating the physical settings would eradicate all memories of native worship.[63] In eviscerating native bodies, setting fires, and razing the scenes of worship or sacrifice, Spaniards believed that they were eliminating the traces of moral infamy.[64] Such actions are clearly not those of Crashaw's Englishmen who were "laughing in their sleeves" about a moral mission.

Destroying native religious sites also justified an economic objective. Under the rules of war prevailing on the Iberian Peninsula (and in many other parts of Europe), the victors had a right to plunder the defeated.[65] And while they were looting the tombs of children sacrificed to Inca gods and destroying golden altarpieces, Spanish conquerors were removing the precious metals for more pious uses.

No amount of punishment or property destruction inflicted on the natives could satisfy some Spaniards, however. Indians had sinned, openly, publicly, and shamelessly. A continuing form of punishment was needed.[66] They had to do penance, perform physical contrition by laboring for Spaniards. From ordinary soldiers to royal political advisers, Spaniards came to understand the harsh regimes of labor they instituted as punishment for the natives' moral transgressions.[67] Even the earliest arrivals in the New World adopted this perspective. Columbus declared that cannibals and other natives guilty of crimes would be given corporal punishment. In a position echoed by many others, the Caribbean settler Juan Ponce de León maintained that brutal Spanish work regimes legitimately castigated natives for their idolatry, cannibalism, and human sacrifice.[68] The classically trained humanist Juan Ginés Sepúlveda agreed that the "sins" of the natives could indeed justify drastic Spanish measures.[69]

The *encomienda*—the grant of labor created at the beginning of Spanish colonization of the New World—supposedly combined the moral end of religious training and the physical requirement of labor, even though the former was more likely to be neglected than the latter. Less credible Spanish defenders of forced labor argued that native communities operating on their own were actually already slaves to sin (i.e., their own religion) and were actually being freed from sin through their working for Christians.[70]

Although clerics frequently held themselves out as the protectors of native peoples against the harsh regimes of labor imposed by ordinary settlers, that virtuous self-portrait requires a few amendments. Many clerics benefited either individually or as a community from native labor and therefore failed to condemn the uses from which they profited.[71] Clerics also saw the punishing regimes of labor imposed upon Native Americans as a guarantee that the natives would lack future opportunities to conduct themselves immorally.

Avoiding the Near Occasion of Sin

Scores of clerics defended strict—even brutal—regimes of labor on grounds that without such work the natives would revert to idolatry. "They are inclined to many vices . . . none has the capacity to live in freedom, since that will give free rein to their vices," declared one friar.[72] King Ferdinand's preacher argued that the Indians lacked "the firmness to persevere in the faith and good customs [of the Spaniards]."[73] If left to their own devices, the litany proclaims, "I fear they will turn to their former rites and ceremonies."[74] Releasing natives from Spanish labor demands would provide them an opportunity to indulge their vices.[75] When asked, a leading Spanish settler observed candidly, "It is not convenient for them to be placed at liberty for they will revert to their savage life."[76] But not all Spaniards believed that such harsh measures were necessary.

Several prominent Spaniards believed that the regimes of labor were unfair. Those who did so argued that Spaniards had misread the moral makeup of the natives. Bartolomé de Las Casas, for example, described Indians as "unassuming, long-suffering, unassertive, and submissive . . . without malice or guile."[77] He believed it was not necessary to punish them with such harsh labor conditions because they could uphold Spanish moral standards without such measures.

Also, punishing a person with forced labor does not automatically imbue him with a sense of regret, let alone repentance. Spaniards did not insist that natives learn to draw a connection between the penance (labor) they were performing and what the Spaniards understood to be the original cause (moral infractions). Hence Spaniards' use of labor appears less like rehabilitation and more like punishment of (and revenge on) those whose primary offense was the apparent freedom to transgress Spaniards' own moral and ethical standards.

The fate of the natives served as a lesson for Spaniards as well. Abusive labor reminded Spaniards of the consequences should they ever decide to adopt native moral standards. They too would be subjected to identically brutal labor, therefore they were reluctant to assimilate into the Indian world.

Slavery

At times during the later years of American domination, Spanish and Portuguese monarchs appeared ill at ease with the enslavement of native peoples. Both often issued categorical statements that all Indians were "free," only to then nullify the statements with a series of qualifications or yank such pronouncements shortly after they were issued.[78] Such ambivalent attitudes frequently appeared during the seventeenth century. King Phillip III permitted enslaving Indians in Chile in 1608 and revoked the decree in 1610. His son Philip IV reinstated permission to enslave in 1625, then the queen regent revoked the decree in 1674.[79] It is not surprising that exceptions were granted for situations that had closely resembled the cold war slavery between Christian and Muslim Iberian empires.

Initially, the practice of enslaving native peoples was called "ransoming" (*rescate* in Spanish, *resgate* in Portuguese). The practice had been known by this name in prior centuries in Iberia.[80] Launching journeys to remote Caribbean islands or into the interior of Brazil, Iberian expeditionary leaders described themselves as searching to ransom hostages held by a pagan tribe, especially people whom the tribe had captured or held as slaves.[81]

To English speakers, this ransoming may have seemed a form of "purchase" because it involved paying money (or other valuable consideration) to the members of a tribe in order to obtain people. But Iberians never rationalized it as a purchase, because that category lacked legitimacy. However, the long tradition of ransoming captives on the peninsula— widely perceived as a charitable activity—was culturally acceptable. Hence Spanish colonists in the Caribbean and Portuguese colonists in the interior of Brazil justified their securing of Native American slave labor as rescuing natives from slavery at the hands of other aboriginal groups.

Colonists also discovered a moral objective that they could use to rationalize enslavement. Through most of the colonial era, natives could be enslaved, rather than merely forced to labor for Iberians, if they were charged with cannibalism.[82] Both Spanish and Portuguese monarchs consistently made exceptions for their general decrees of freedom if the natives were accused of eating human flesh.

Slavery and Cannibalism

Many Spanish and Portuguese monarchs were uneasy about permitting the enslavement of native peoples. In order to satisfy the rulers' consciences that they were justified in ordering slavery, petitioners had to employ the most persuasive grounds for securing royal permission. The most successful grounds customarily yoked together two entirely separate reasons for enslavement: cannibalism and military resistance to Iberian domination.[83]

Queen Isabel reserved slavery for those cannibals "who eat human flesh" and fought invading Iberians.[84] In 1503, she declared that the Spanish inhabitants of the Caribbean "had a license to war upon the Carib Indians who come to launch armed incursions against them and who eat human flesh. They may make slaves of those whom they capture."[85] The first Portuguese regulation, handed to Sousa in 1548, authorized slavery "provided that such Gentiles are in revolt and at war [against the Portuguese]."[86] So too did the second and third regulations, enacted in 1570, and another in 1587, which stated that "those who habitually attack the Portuguese" and eat Christians could be enslaved.[87]

Linking native cannibalism to military resistance allowed Iberian leaders to believe that they did in fact represent a new moral order. Thus they could satisfy themselves that indigenous resistance to Iberians' new morality could only have been motivated by a powerful moral attachment to a horrendously criminal activity—such as cannibalism. Thus the official authorizations for native slavery constantly slipped between "cannibalism," the Native Americans' supposed moral offense, and their resistance to Spanish or Portuguese conquest.[88]

More straightforward reasons for enslaving natives never succeeded. In 1509, King Ferdinand permitted slave raiding from other islands because of a shortage of Indians on Hispaniola.[89] But rationales based directly upon the need for labor never became widely accepted. Spaniards' visions of themselves as moral missionaries to the New World required that natives to be enslaved were "cannibals"—that is, those who militarily resisted rightful Spanish domination.

Juan Solórzano Pereira, author of the definitive synthesis of colonial legislation, observed that slavery was permitted for Caribes, cannibals, Chichimecas, and others who were said to be supremely fierce and barbarous, and who ate human flesh, or who had occasioned just motives for their punishment.[90] In all of the royal decrees, the "cannibals" were those who were vicious fighters and who launched armed incursions against Spaniards.

In the early years of conquest, rulers permitted the enslavement of native armies who had successfully fought Spanish domination. Cortés executed the lord and military leader of Tutupeque and sold the village's two hundred inhabitants into slavery for having burned twenty villages of Indians allied with the Spaniards. He accused the natives of treason, stating, as they had once "offered themselves as vassals of Your Highness, and have killed Spaniards, and done considerable damage, I have pronounced them slaves." On another occasion Cortés declared that he enslaved "natives who there were always engaged in warfare and rebellion . . . who killed said Spaniards, and rebelled against the service of Your Majesty, and all of whom eat human flesh." He added that he used their enslavement as a warning to other Indians who might be tempted to rebel.[91] The conqueror of the Yucatán Montejo enslaved two thousand Cupul Mayas in 1546–47.[92]

But for most of the colonial era, the tribes that were accused of cannibalism were technologically equipped to resist Spanish control. "Cannibals" were largely nomadic fighters who successfully fought against Spanish domination for an extended period of time. Thus the inhabitants of New World regions that continuously resisted Spanish rule were those whose inhabitants were most consistently labeled cannibals. These natives lived in the border regions of New Spain (northern Mexico), in Peru (the Charcas region), in coastal Venezuela, and in the provinces of what are now Argentina and Chile.[93] Natives impeding Spanish trade between Bogotá and Lima were also labeled cannibals.[94] Indians from the Peruvian province of Charcas who repeatedly invaded Spanish lands, "eating their captives roasted on barbecues" were to be enslaved like the "excessively fierce, barbarous [Chichimecas, Caribes] who eat human flesh, or have occasioned just motives for their punishment."[95]

Unlike English colonizers' decentralized attacks upon Indian communities, Spanish and Portuguese raiders had to seek and obtain official approval in advance of a raid. This pattern dated back to the frontier raiding on the Christian Muslim frontier. In the New World, Iberian colonists seeking to seize natives as slaves had to fulfill several formalities, including attestation to indigenous cannibalism.[96] Most critically, a raid required the approval of the duly constituted political authority of the region.[97] As the occasional rebel found out to his dismay, failure to obtain official sanction meant the confiscation and loss of any and all goods and people he had managed to seize.[98] The protocol for retaining Indians seized as slaves demanded that Spaniards label their captives as either cannibals or resistors, or both, or as having been freed from cannibals.

Portuguese Observations on Cannibalism

Like the Spanish, the Portuguese justified their brutality toward and enslavement of native communities as fitting chastisement for the latter's violation of what the Portuguese considered international moral standards. The best-known early story of such retribution occurred in 1556, when a Portuguese ship carrying the first bishop of Brazil, Pedro Fernandes Sardinha, and a high-ranking treasury official back to Portugal was shipwrecked not far from the coast of Bahia. Both the bishop and the treasury official managed to survive and reach the coast, only to be devoured by Tupi-speaking Caeté, whom the bishop had previously treated with great contempt. A vicious retaliatory expedition under Mem de Sá against the Caeté took place six years later. Although the actual reasons for the raid were likely more prosaic, inhabitants viewed the massacre as divine retribution. The seventeenth-century historian of Brazil Friar Vicente do Salvador wrote, "Thus God operated, so that afterwards, they [the Portuguese] left this Bahia to make war upon those gentiles and exacted vengeance from them."[99]

Kings from Dom Sebastião in 1570 to King João in 1808 permitted Indian slavery as a punishment for their cannibalism. King João added later that there was "no means of civilizing [such] barbarous people except . . . a harsh experience."[100]

Church leaders supported slavery of native peoples in Brazil even more vocally than did their counterparts in Hispanic America. Portuguese missionaries regarded slavery as a means of Christianizing the natives. "One can therefore neither expect nor obtain anything in all this land regarding the conversion of the Gentiles, without a great number of Christians coming here. If they fit themselves and their lives to the will of God, they subject the Indians to the yoke of slavery and oblige them to welcome the banner of Christ."[101] In arguing for a military expedition against the inhabitants of the backlands of São Paulo in January 1606, members of the town council argued:

> The Christian [Indian] neighbors are almost all finished off, but in the backlands are a multitude of them, and of many tribes who live the law of brute animals, eating one another. And if we bring them down in an orderly fashion so that they will become Christians, it will be a great benefit . . . that will redound for the good of the captaincy [the province] and in particular for the Gentiles in coming to the bosom of the Holy Mother Church."[102]

So widespread was the belief that Indians were cannibals to be chastised that merely affirming that natives were cannibals invariably resulted in colonial officials' approving their enslavement.[103]

In reinstating the rules regarding the slavery of native peoples, Portuguese kings sometimes broadened the moral grounds for enslavement beyond what Spanish rulers had permitted, yet remained within the framework of originally Iberian customs. In October 1653, the Portuguese monarch allowed slave raids against Indians for impeding roads or commerce, failing to pay tribute, refusing to obey calls to work for settlers or the crown, reverting to cannibalism after being Christianized, and impeding preaching of the Gospel.[104] In 1718, another monarch provided an equally broad list of offenses, reminiscent of those that some medieval Christian monarchs issued permitting the enslavement of Muslims in their domains: violation of dress codes, inability to identify a master, sexual misconduct. New World rules authorized enslaving those who "go naked, recognize neither king nor governor, do not live in the form or manner of a republic, trample the laws of nature, make no distinction between mothers and daughters in the satisfaction of their lust . . . [and] eat one another."[105]

But the more extensive list of offenses for which natives could be condemned to salvery also corresponded to the greater labor needs of Portuguese colonists. Because Portuguese settlers encountered no sedentary agricultural peoples, they occasionally broadened the traditional offenses for which slavery was the punishment in order to meet their labor needs.

Juxtaposition

Spanish and Portuguese colonists were not the only ones to encounter or anticipate encountering cannibalism, human sacrifice, idolatry, and sodomy in the New World. Dutch, French, and English colonists all reported these behaviors among New World inhabitants, but none responded to either the encounters or the information, as did Iberians, with the conclusion that they were to be emissaries of a new morality or that cannibals had to be enslaved.

The moral indignation and at times fury that leap off the pages of Spanish accounts are remarkably absent from most other European accounts. Dutch, French, and English responses to similar scenes (or anticipation of similar scenes) of idolatry, human sacrifice, and cannibalism ranged from ambivalence to fear. Also notably absent from other Europeans' accounts is Iberians' insistence that they must avenge themselves upon the natives or punish them for such activities. But while noting the cruelty inherent in indigenous cannibalism and human sacrifice, Perrot, Sagard, and Léry did not write about it, as did Spaniards, as an inherent moral evil to be ripped out of indigenous communities, forcibly if necessary.

As critic Frank Lestringant notes, French missionaries often reacted with a mixture of distaste and admiration for the code of honor and revenge that they understood cannibalism to represent.[106] Father Issac Jogues, the famous French evangelist in Canada, explained the motive of revenge behind the Iroquois's ritual sacrifice and cannibalization of members another Indian tribe as partly his fault, because he had tricked these natives into unknowingly delivering a message warning the French settlement of an attack. When the Iroquois realized his treachery, they were furious at Father Jogues for having tricked them. "If I had chanced to be in the village at the return of those warriors, fire, rage, and cruelty would have taken my life. . . . Another troop—coming back from Montreal . . . said that one of their men had been killed and two others wounded. Each one held me guilty of these adverse encounters; they were fairly mad with rage."[107]

Whereas Jogues understood the Iroquois's actions as a method of exacting revenge for something he had done, his counterparts among the honor-and-revenge-obsessed Spaniards were unable to take a similar view in their dealings with native peoples. Believing themselves the moral opposites of Native Americans, Spaniards were unable or unwilling to grasp any connection or similarity between their intentions and those of Native Americans.

Spanish observers also failed to understand their own role in provoking or instigating Native American responses. Whereas Jogues conscientiously noted that the natives' reaction was his own fault for having tricked them, Spanish accounts of native actions fail to convey any such sense of responsibility. Native torture of Spanish prisoners of war, for example, fails to appear as retaliation for Spanish brutality during the battle of Tenochtitlán; rather, it emerges in the accounts of Bernal Díaz del Castillo and Hernán Cortés as the natives' inherent immorality. Such denial of responsibility allowed Spaniards to justify their own violent outbursts unreservedly. Their claim to righteous anger rationalized their sweeping idols from pyramids and burning hundreds of books containing native religious and scientific information. Seeing in native actions only deep moral offense, Spanish colonists rationalized their own rage in a way that allowed them to punish natives through warfare and brutal labor. Portuguese accounts of native cannibalism were equally blind to the colonists' own responsibility for provoking such cannibalism and human sacrifice.

The responses of the Iberians' northern European counterparts to reports of cannibalism differ strikingly. Some of the best-known observations about indigenous cannibalism in the English- and French-speaking worlds resulted from the observations of the colonists who occupied the coast of Brazil (around present-day Rio de Janeiro) and who had plenty of opportunity to observe the ritual cannibalism of the Tupi people. Neither Jean Léry in his *History of a Voyage* nor Michel de Montaigne in his celebrated essay "Of Cannibals" indicted Native Americans for cannibalism. Instead, both men used the idea of cannibalism to reflect critically upon French moral standards. Léry, for example, readily acknowledged that Catholic Frenchmen savagely butchered and then ate the hearts and body fat of Protestant Frenchmen in 1572. And he further freely noted both his and his shipmates' impulses to ingest each other when famished on the return voyage to France.[108]

In his milder critique, Montaigne did not confront Frenchmen with evidence of their own cannibalism. Instead, he set up native cannibalism as a noble contrast to European greed: "If their [Brazilian Indians'] neighbors come from beyond the mountains to attack them and win the victory over them, the victor's gain is glory, and the advantage of having proved the superior in valor and prowess; for not otherwise do they give heed to the property of the vanquished."[109] But the acclaim lavished upon Montaigne's essay in the contemporary English- and French-speaking world has been noticeably absent in either Portugal or Portuguese America—where Montaigne's cannibals lived. Portuguese critics instead have largely dismissed Montaigne's essay as unjustifiably romantic. One modern Portuguese critic has written scathingly of Montaigne's portrait of the Tupi, "In contrast with Montaigne . . . there is not in the [sixteenth-century Portuguese] Jesuits [reports] the least tendency to gild or repress [the portrait of the Indians]."[110] Montaigne is a naive romantic; Jesuits are, as all those educated by them can attest, realists.

English colonists neither pointed out their own human flesh-eating practices nor used them as a means to critique European lust for riches. They also did not respond with moral outrage at the violation of sacred taboos. Rather, they most often expressed fear of being eaten themselves. Before setting out for the New World, William Bradford discussed the possibility of encountering cannibals with the members of his congregation who had heard of such activities. Unlike Frenchmen and like Spaniards, he reacted with horror to accounts of human sacrifice. The "savage people . . . being . . . merciless wher[e] they overcome; not being contente only to kill, and take away life, but delight to tormente men in the most bloodie manner that may be; fleaing [flaying] some alive with the shells of fishes, cutting of the members and joynts of others by peesmeale, and broiling on the coles [coals] . . . [and] other cruelties too horrible to be related."[111]

"Cruelties too horrible to be related" repeated a common theme of

Iberian accounts, the barbarity of native rituals and cannibalism in particular. But beyond repulsion, Bradford's response shared nothing with the responses of his Iberian counterparts. Unlike the Spanish and Portugese, both he and the colonists accompanying him feared primarily for their personal safety, dreading that they themselves would be eaten.[112] Anticipating terror among his fellow travelers, Bradford continued encouragingly: "Great difficulties . . . must be both enterprised and overcome with answerable courages. . . . It was granted the dangers were great, but not desperate; the difficulties were many, but not invincible." He intimated that they might be lucky. "Many of them [such occurrences were] likely, yet they were not certain; it might be sundry of the things feared might never befall."[113]

Although Bradford himself was a religious leader, he did not condemn natives for their cannibalism or accuse them of violating international moral standards. Nor did he use descriptions of native cannibalism to encourage his followers to seek revenge, to "punish with fire and sword," or to impose grueling labor upon indigenous peoples for their behavior. In other words, cannibalism threatened neither Bradford's nor his followers' political self-image. Outrage at a moral violation of sacred and immutable laws is very different from the fear of being eaten. And it was the fear of being eaten that would later make its way into such English children's tales as "Jack and the Beanstalk," in which the giant threatens to "grind your bones to make my bread."

Even in later years, English colonists failed to view the cannibalism of members of their own expeditionary forces as automatically demanding a retaliatory response, as did Spanish explorers. Captain James Cook, for example, knew that the Maori chieftain Kahura was responsible for the killing and eating of Captain Fureneaux's men at Grass Cove during his second voyage. But Cook, who had established that Kahura was responsible for the massacre, did not take revenge; rather, he trusted Kahura and continued to work with him.[114] By contrast, Portuguese colonists felt it was necessary to avenge the Caeté's deliberate ingestion of their high-ranking officials by exterminating the tribe as soon as an attack could be mounted.

Nor did Dutch settlers seek revenge against Native Americans for cannibalism. During a 1626 expedition against the Mohawks in the New York region, five Dutchmen were captured, resulting in the ritual cannibalism of one of them.[115] Compiling a report of the events of New World colonies to be published in Amsterdam, the physician Nicolaes van de Wassenaer wrote almost matter-of-factly about the captive:

The Maykans [Mohicans], going to war with the Maquaes [Mohawks], requested to be assisted by the commander of Fort Orange and six others.
Commander Krieckebeeck went up with them. . . . [They] were forced to
fly, and many were killed among whom were the commander and three of
his men. Among the latter was Tymen Bouwensz, whom they devoured,
after having well roasted him. The rest they burnt."[116]

Rather than responding with moral outrage or demands for revenge, the
Dutch settlers sent a representative to the Mohawks to inquire into the
deaths of the Dutch soldiers. "Some days after [the sacrifice] the worthy
Pieter Barentsen . . . visited them [the Mohawks]; they wished to excuse
their act, on the plea that they had never set themselves against the
whites, and asked the reason why the latter had meddled with them; other
wise they would not have shot them."[117] In other words, had Krieckebeeck
not intervened in an internal Indian matter, he never would have been
killed. No Dutch plans for revenge ensued, for the Dutch representatives
(and settlers) understood that they had been at fault in choosing sides.

Native customs themselves did not create political anxieties. Rather,
Spanish and Portuguese beliefs that they were entitled to conquer the
Americas in order to wipe out cannibalism, along with idolatry, human
sacrifice, and homosexuality, created an enduringly powerful moral censure of native peoples. And hundreds of years after the fact, as the
Mapuche activist charged at the Essex conference in 1992, cannibalism
among aboriginal peoples still is the central accusation used to deny
Central and South American natives access to their natural resources and
valuable goods, and even to order their use in forced regimes of labor.

But native cannibalism neither was nor is at issue. The real source of
the problem is the misuse of the label of cannibal to justify hundreds of
years of slavery. Only when this colonial connection between the labeling
of Native Americans and the denial of rights to their resources is severed
can the subject of aboriginal "moral" practices and beliefs be considered.

Looking to European society of the fifteenth and sixteenth centuries,
there is plenty of evidence of human sacrifice. The Inquisition in Spain
and Portugal burned people at the stake. Authorities throughout Europe
regularly engaged in public executions. In early medieval times, prisoners
of war in Germany were sacrificed to the gods.[118]

Nor can Europeans be exempted from the charge of cannibalism.
Englishmen and Frenchmen employed cannibalism on ship for survival;
Portuguese captains were also known to dispense orders for the ingestion
of particularly disobedient crew members.[119] French Catholics ate the

flesh of the Protestants they massacred outside Saint Bartholomew's Church in 1582, and fifteenth-century Swiss soldiers had to be specifically banned from ingesting the flesh of men they had defeated on the battlefield.[120]

European cannibalism—like European human sacrifice—was a fact, but the evidence never produced global condemnations of the people who engaged in such practices. Such condemnations, however, appeared explicitly and repeatedly in the indictments that one group of European colonizers, the Iberians, made about another group of people, Native Americans, over whom they exercised both political authority and economic control. These were colonial accusations.

Just as the English characterization of Native Americans as male hunters is only partly true, the Iberian characterization of Native Americans as cannibals is also a partial truth and a political fiction. Both labels were created by colonists to rationalize their taking Native Americans' resources—land for the English, labor for the Iberians.

7

Sustaining Political Identities: The Moral Boundary

between Natives and Colonizers

The partial fictions that Europeans created of native peoples contain two puzzles. First is that in the American colonies, categorical labels—*hunters* and *cannibals*—remained unchallenged by actual contact with the natives. Second is that the popularity of these labels endured throughout the colonial era.

The failure of concrete encounters to change partially fictitious images of colonized peoples has been partly addressed in another colonial situation. Edward Said, literary critic of nineteenth-century English and French images of Middle Easterners, first pointed out that Europeans' ideas about "Orientals" were unchanged by ongoing communication with actual people of the Orient. While unable to explain why even long-term face-to-face contact should have so utterly failed to alter specific portrayals, Said extensively illustrated that identifiable depictions in fact remained unchanged.[1]

The same process of persistent fictions prevailed earlier in the New World. Although real-life contact influenced settlers' conduct toward Indians, it never managed to shake the collective faith in the fundamental fictions. Finding the farming communities of natives in the southeastern and later southwestern United States never forced Englishmen to reconsider their representations of Indians as hunters, any more than exchanges with non-fleshing-eating natives undermined Iberians' depictions of indigenous cannibals. Critics' and historians' repeated exposures of the inaccuracy of these depictions have been equally ineffective in shaking enduring popular faith in their correctness.[2] When contradictory evidence uniformly and consistently fails to modify convictions, then other, more powerful factors must be motivating the believers. But were those other factors new, or had they long been present in Western European society?

The immediate past in Europe rarely provides examples of long-term stability in representations of others. Although neighboring communities frequently held uncomplimentary images of one another in the medieval era, these images waxed and waned with outbreaks of intense conflict. They rarely persisted in a stable form for hundreds of years.[3]

Permanence came from new sources of motives for overseas adventures—politics and economics. During the thousand years immediately preceding the conquest of America, European leaders frequently invoked the right to spread their religion in order to justify expanding into territories they did not have a right to inherit. Whether Charlemagne in Gaul, Eric IX in Finland, or Tarik in Iberia, medieval leaders claimed religion—whether Christianity or Islam—legitimated their conquest of distant lands.

But by the sixteenth century, religion was no longer an effective political rallying point throughout Europe. It retained its vigor in Iberia, but was much less central in other areas of Western Europe. Spanish and Portugese colonizers cherished their identity as "Christians." English colonists, on the other hand, valued their worth as "planters" (farmers), esteeming their own labor (and capital). Hence Christianity either became subordinate to political conceptions of religion or became displaced entirely, by other, more secular, motives.

The central participants in sixteenth- and seventeenth-century American colonization were far less like each other than the English and French colonizers who dominated eighteenth- and nineteenth-century efforts. Because of the Norman Conquest, French and English colonizers partly shared a political and legal vocabulary, making many of their concepts readily translatable from one language to the other. But the principal European actors in the Americas, English and Iberian colonists, did not, and their political and economic terms cannot be easily translated or comprehended from one language to another.

As a result, English and Iberian colonists treasured markedly dissimilar economic ambitions and understood their entitlement from strikingly different political perspectives. As I have noted, Spanish and Portuguese colonizers cherished their identity as "Christians," and English colonists valued their own worth as "planters." Iberians, who prized their self-identification as Christians, frequently depicted Native Americans as the opposite—pagans, idolaters, and, above all, "cannibals." English colonists, who cherished their self-image as "laborers" and capitalists, represented Indians as profoundly lacking in both endeavors. Natives had little or no fixed capital; they were nomadic and, above all, "hunters."[4]

But although political self-flattery explains the particular categories to which native peoples were assigned, the enduring sources of the representations lay elsewhere. The reasons for the enduring popularity of these colonial representations were simple. Nomads could lose their land under English rules, and idolaters and pagans could be deprived of their rights to minerals and labor under Iberian conventions. Long-term stability in each European colony's preferred economic objective explains most of the seeming permanence of certain representations. Englishmen pursued land throughout the colonial era, just as Iberians pursued labor. Thus at stake for colonizers in their sustaining specific images of others were enduring economic interests and their self-flattering political rationales.

In this explanation lies the reason for the long-term stability of the colonial fictions. Orientalism, like the colonial fictions of the New World, remained popular because of this enduring combination of political and economic self-interest. During the eighteenth and nineteenth centuries, English middle classes sustained self-images of thrifty, masculine, financially prudent investors, self-flattering traits that Max Weber astutely summarizes in *The Protestant Ethic and the Spirit of Capitalism*.[5] French middle classes elaborated similar images of themselves as civilized. Believing that they were the prudent, civilized, and rational investors allowed nineteenth-century British and French colonizers to consider that they merited the markets and raw materials of the Middle East and Asia far more than did those feckless, imprudent, spendthrift Middle Easterners. Thus Englishmen and Frenchmen persisted in seeing colonized Orientals as lacking prudence and economic rationality because such defects satisfactorily justified their own economic ends.

Settlers in the New World clung to such depictions centrally because they rationalized (in self-flattering ways) the continued pursuit of particular economic ends. It was simply more pleasant for colonizers to believe that they were legitimately entitled to use the resources they wanted because the current inhabitants either could not or should not do so than to attempt to consider less agreeable and less flattering alternatives. The combination of a politically satisfying self-image and an economic interest similarly served to perpetuate colonial fictions in the New World.

But these colonial representations have a final distinctive characteristic that separates them from other types of group identification. Many cultural identities have indistinct boundaries, but those differences that justify economic interests cannot be unclear. Those taking others' property needed to see a clearly defined boundary between themselves and the others to justify their seizing assets belonging to those others. If the line dividing the two were indistinguishable, then the colonizers' certainty about their right to seize resources might vanish, or at least become open to question. Consequently, in colonial situations, colonizers had to separate their respective identities clearly and unmistakably from those of the colonized. Although individuals might move from one category to another, the boundary between categories had to remain unambiguously drawn. Furthermore, that boundary had to be unassailable.

Despite their divergent political self-images and economic interests, Englishmen and Iberians used the same foundational tenets to draw the line between themselves and the Americas' natives. Not surprisingly, this principle was originally Christian, although it was interpreted differently by Englishmen and Iberians. The source of this unmistakably delineated boundary between Europeans and Indians was the originally Christian belief in the moral demarcation isolating humans from animals. Not surprisingly, however, both groups of colonizers interpreted the essence of human (as opposed to animal) status in culturally distinct terms connected to their own economic pursuits. For Iberians, to be fully human required Christianity; for Englishmen, it demanded "labor." We begin with Spaniards, for whom humanity was religious and, specifically, "Christian."

Iberians

It is often possible to understand something of how a people conceive of themselves by the names they use for themselves. The people that we today call "Spaniards," as well as those referred to as "Portuguese," the designations used throughout this book, are not the names by which they referred to themselves. Rather, "Spaniard" and "Portuguese" are the names that others applied to them. All Spanish and Portuguese colonists during their first hundred years in the New World called themselves simply "the Christians." If we were to use that designation today to refer to them, or if I were to use it in this book, the result would be confusing, for the Dutch, English, and

French also considered themselves Christians. But Portuguese and Spanish colonizers referred to themselves only as "the Christians," implying that others who used that name were perhaps not really followers of Christ.

Spanish and Portuguese understandings of themselves as "the Christians" lacked specific distinguishing content. There was no distinctive religious significance to Spanish faith—no specific creed or theological convictions that constituted Iberian Christianity as distinct from the allegiance of Catholics in France or England. Rather, the self-appellation of "Christian" originated when Iberian Catholics began distinguishing themselves from their fellow Iberians and political rivals, the Muslims. Since the twelfth century, both Christians and Muslims on the peninsula called themselves Iberians, and both Christians and Muslims called themselves Spaniards. Hence the name "Christian" referred to only one segment of Iberia's people. Although both Spanish and Portuguese colonists called themselves simply "the Christians," the two groups had evolved slightly different understandings of Christianity. The strictest definition of "Christians" appeared among Spaniards, who over the course of several centuries became intensely suspicious of moral contamination of their Catholicism.

Among Spaniards this conception of themselves as "the Christians" employed religion to define a political identity at the core of which was an idealized purity sustained by *resistance*.[6] One group of Spaniards (Christians) had initially used that identity to rationalize an extreme form of resistance (military struggle) against other Spaniards (Muslims) on the Iberian Peninsula. "Old Christianity," a label that gained popularity in fifteenth-century Spain, expressed the belief that recent converts to Christianity from other religions were untrustworthy. Old Christianity implied the moral superiority of those Christians who had lived among people from different faiths for centuries and had successfully resisted both entreaties and threats to join other religious communities. Therefore the essence of Old Christianity consisted of steadfastness in warding off efforts at conversion and conviction in the immaculate and uncontaminated nature of one's own faith.

Ferdinand and Isabel advanced this idea by deliberately encouraging the notion of a "Christian state"—that is, a political identity for Spain—constructed upon the self-concept of "Old Christians" as resisting efforts at conversion by non-Christians. The first political step in this process was to purify the nation. Ironically, Ferdinand and Isabel decreed exile for those non-Christians who had most firmly and steadfastly contested Christian efforts at conversion, the Jews. The capacity for resistance clearly defined only "Old Christians" positively, not others.

After the potential danger of contamination represented by Jews was ended by their forcible expulsion, Spanish Catholics during the sixteenth and seventeenth centuries continued to define themselves as the sole authentic Christians in Europe. As they understood it, they alone successfully resisted allowing heretics and apostates (i.e., Protestants) to practice on their terrain—unlike all other Europeans. French Catholics (whose monarch had briefly permitted religious toleration) were regarded with particular suspicion.[7]

This habit of referring to themselves (and their political identity) as "Christians" had thus become customary long before Spaniards arrived in the New World. On these shores, however, they also encountered people of different religions. Although the natives had a wide variety of beliefs— they might be idolaters, pagans, heathen, or infidels—they were all non-Christians.[8] All Iberians could thus persist in considering themselves "the Christians" and continue the traditional pattern overseas. Thus in referring to themselves as "the Christians," New World Spaniards were affirming their identity as the noncannibals, at least the not ritually literal cannibals.

Transferring a political distinction founded upon religion permitted Spanish conquerors to see an absolute moral distinction between themselves and those they conquered. Once the natives were conquered, however, Spaniards, like other European colonizers, did not preserve the boundary in its original form. In the first place, not only after settlement began, Spanish authorities insisted that all Indians were Spanish subjects. Thus, unlike the English, they did not consider Native Americans (until the twentieth century) to be members of foreign and therefore alien nations. Spaniards presumed that natives were subjects of the crown of Spain, an assumption that the crown ratified in repeated decisions and made into law in 1542. While removing this major formal political distinction between colonizers and the colonized, Spaniards sought to retain and transform the politico-moral dividing line.

After the conquest, and as natives were presumably (and at least nominally) Christianized, Spaniards continued to interpret their basic difference from the natives on the basis of religion. But Hispanic settlers could no longer call themselves *the* Christians, for natives, too, presumably shared their faith. The religious gulf between conqueror and conquered did not disappear, however; it simply took on a different form. Borrowing a traditional Catholic criterion created by the twelfth-century Dominican Thomas Aquinas, sixteenth-century Spaniards began referring to themselves as the "people of reason" (*gente de razón*). This concept stemmed from a distinction that Aquinas made between human beings and animals.[9]

Animals belonged in the category of beings who did not possess reason, and therefore could never be baptized. All humans possessed reason, and therefore all could be baptized. To Aquinas, anyone possessed of reason would become Christian.

Although all humans had reason, Aquinas had sought to distinguish those who could become fully Catholic from those who could accept but would never fully comprehend Catholicism, such as the mentally deficient, the insane, and juveniles.[10] Aquinas characterized such people as not fully attaining the use of reason. For Aquinas, this category functioned benevolently, for it meant that those without sufficient use of reason could not sin. Appropriating this distinction for colonial purposes, however, eliminated its charitable purpose as forgiveness for sin.

But it was into this category that Spaniards placed the newly converted natives of the New World. Spanish jurist and longtime Peruvian resident Juan de Matienzo put it best when he wrote that Indians were "participants in reason so as to sense it, but not to possess or follow it."[11] Thus the definition of Indians as "participants but not possessors of reason" became a standard that would prevent them from ever attaining equality with Spaniards. In establishing this standard, Iberians transformed Aquinas's moral distinction into a political category.

The moral distinction between people of reason (Spaniards) and people who were not quite reasonable (Indians) permeated numerous areas of everyday life during the colonial era. Parish priests throughout Spanish America created countless hundreds of rolls of parishioners' names in an effort to keep track of those who had received (and paid for receiving) the sacraments of confession and communion on an annual basis. Local clergy carefully noted the names and residences of those who had paid and those who had not, and they scrupulously kept two separate books: one whose title invariably bore the legend "People of Reason" and another just as invariably labeled "Indians." And although clear guidelines were lacking, blacks, mulattoes, and mestizos (those who were part Spanish, part Indian), in addition to Spaniards themselves, could unmistakably be found in the books labeled "People of Reason." Rarely were other groups labeled with racial categories before the final third of the seventeenth century, although names such as "John of Angola" and "Maria of Senegal" clearly indicated the origins of some as African, and other names bore witness to mixed ancestry.[12] Only Indians' names were kept in a separate book.

The concern with sustaining a moral difference between "the people of reason" and "Indians" featured in the parish records of even densely settled urban areas of Spanish America. Thus aboriginal peoples remained, in conception if not in labels on parish records, as those who had accepted Christianity but were not quite reasonable, and therefore were forever incapable of becoming fully Christian. Although this colonial distinction was far from Aquinas's original idea, it created a distinction that would separate conquerors from conquered indefinitely.[13] This boundary descended permanently in the final third of the sixteenth century, but not until after an initial period of welcome.

The Evolution of Iberian Religious Boundaries

The earliest missionaries were greatly impressed by the receptive ease with which natives greeted Christianity. To friars accustomed to working with Jews and Muslims who knew their scriptures and could provide a counter-argument for every argument they made, the New World's inhabitants appeared eager to convert. Their willingness to listen to preaching without arguing and their ready participation in Christian rituals, such as baptism, that both Jews and Muslims rejected led many of the earliest preachers to assume that the aboriginal inhabitants of the New World both understood and embraced Christianity enthusiastically. This perception—especially common among early Franciscan missionaries—initially led to their granting natives access to Latin and liturgical knowledge. But when the Indians' dexterity with Latin surpassed that of many Christian friars, the missionaries banned the Indians from learning the language. Because the Bible was not translated out of Latin until the eighteenth century, this prohibition denied them direct access to scriptures as well. Teaching other natives the faith in any but the most rudimentary form was forbidden from that time forward.

The priesthood was withheld from them as well because the friars feared that native practices would contaminate Christian beliefs, just as they feared the influences of Jewish converts on the Iberian Peninsula. As descendants of Hebrew converts rose to high ranks within the Church in Spain, "Old" Christians worried that many carried elements of Judaism into their teaching of Catholicism.[14] Similar fears of contamination with pagan elements led to the banning of native priests. As the famous seventeenth-century Franciscan Gerónimo de Mendieta declared, "Just as those converted from Judaism . . . should be prevented from joining religious orders, so also should Indians be barred."[15] Even mixed descendants of Indians and Spaniards had to receive special dispensation in order to study for the priesthood.[16] Therefore natives would remain at a permanent distance from "Christians," never permitted to understand their faith in depth, thus preserving the traditional barrier between the Christians and the not fully Christianized Indians.

Persistent Spanish concern with sustaining the moral boundaries between themselves and natives may appear surprising, particularly when military victories had long been assured. But Spaniards were less worried by military attacks than they were about the purity of their religious faith, for—even more than their Portuguese Iberian neighbors—Spaniards were preoccupied with immaculately maintaining their faith. Prohibitions against religious education, Latin, and the priesthood for Native Americans ensured that they would have no opportunity to contaminate any elements of the Catholic faith, because they would never be permitted to attain full knowledge or be completely in charge of teaching others about the faith.

As the sixteenth century drew to a close, prosecutions of Native Americans for their pagan religious practices gradually shifted away from the vigilante justice of conquistadors and their immediate successors. By the final third of the sixteenth century, the legal processes of a state had come to dominate enforcement of Iberian Catholicism's purity in the New World. Evidence of participation in pagan rituals had to be found and witnesses produced before Native Americans could be executed. By the close of the sixteenth century, Spanish priests and bishops, at the instigation of or in conjunction with political officials, instituted a legalistic judicial procedure resembling the Inquisition's in order to pursue continued allegations of religious deviation. And although Native Americans continued to be put to death for their aberrant religious practices, increasingly fewer met such a fate by the end of the following century.

The principal grounds for continuing suspicion of native peoples also shifted during this era. During the conquest, native cannibalism, human sacrifice, sodomy, and worship of idols justified brutality. But as prosecutions became more legalistic, the grounds became narrower, but for an unrelated reason. The quasi-inquisitorial proceedings against natives failed to look for homosexuality, but that did not mean that "the Christians" considered sodomy less of a crime against the state. Unlike elsewhere in sixteenth-century Western Europe, in Iberia homosexuality was automatically understood as politically treasonous because it was originally identified, wrongly, with Islam.[17]

Because toleration of male homosexuality was identified with Islam, homosexual relationships were regarded as the leading edge for the reintroduction of Islam through the middle of the seventeenth century.

During this period, homosexuals continued to be arrested and executed for treason. But sexual activities between men were not limited to the Native American population. Homosexuality also existed among Iberian settlers and their descendants, as well as between Spanish and native men. Sodomy remained a political crime, but it ceased being regarded as one by which conquerors could distinguish themselves from Native Americans. Hence it did not become the central subject of proceedings against Native Americans.

Accusations of cannibalism, frequently mentioned during the conquest of large native empires, also declined precipitously in these communities at the same time as the shift to bureaucratized prosecutions, but for a different reason. Under Iberian law codes, cannibalism was a valid reason for enslaving indigenous peoples. Postconquest, however, sedentary farmers were to be protected from slavery by their submission and reconstitution in the subjugated communities. Therefore no economic motivation existed to label them as "cannibals." Ironically, therefore, even though cannibalism had played a significant role in Aztec and Inca societies, accusations of cannibalism against these large sedentary communities virtually disappeared by the middle of the sixteenth century and remained absent for the rest of the colonial era. Accusations of eating human flesh were directed only against nomadic peoples (whether they were cannibals or not) because that was the excuse needed in order to enslave them.

The only accusations concerning sacrifice that targeted sedentary Indians after the mid-sixteenth century involved animal sacrifice, which had also figured in preconquest traditions but carried no specifically designated economic punishment. In the Andean area, Native Americans sacrificed animals—large beasts such as the llama and a smaller Andean guinea pig called a *cuy*—at religious rituals. Prosecutors in the quasi-inquisitorial proceedings against Native Americans paid extraordinarily close attention to stories of animal sacrifice—what had been sacrificed and how—largely because these stories concerned a politico-religious crime they could readily identify and prosecute among sedentary natives.

Idolatry was the major politico-religious crime of Native Americans in regions under Spanish colonial domination. It continued to be regarded as a serious crime because Catholicism was the religion of the state. Non-Catholic practices were treasonous. Their continued observance threatened the political integrity of the Iberian state, in addition to constituting a potential threat of contamination of Catholicism by pagan practices.[18] And as Irene Silverblatt notes, the campaigns against idolatry had the "obvious political motive" of forcing "the Indian into the reducciones—all the better to evangelize, to maintain political control, to facilitate the collection of tribute."[19]

Although Spanish fears of corruption of their Christian beliefs by both New World pagans and Jews eventually eased, that moderation did not occur until at least two centuries had passed. Persecutions of the Jewish "converts" came to an end only as the seventeenth century drew to a close; harassment of Indians in the New World eased either at the same time or shortly thereafter.[20] Concern with moral boundaries had not disappeared, but Spaniards no longer feared the adulteration of their faith to the same extent as before. Jews and New World pagans were no longer believed to be powerful enough to threaten profoundly the immaculateness of Spanish religious faith. Not surprisingly, the strength of Spaniards' convictions that their political identity was based upon religious purity began to fade at the same time their fears of New World paganism began to diminish. But this diminution signified an end only to the most brutal excesses and torture of Native Americans. Spaniards continued to consider Indians "not quite reasonable," withholding both the priesthood and knowledge of the scriptures from them. Natives continued to be denied access to the ecclesiastical rituals that would signify adulthood—confirmation (admission as an adult to Catholic practices)—and Holy Orders. And Spaniards in the New World would remain adamantly opposed to the admission of Indians to sainthood.[21]

Juxtaposition: Moral versus Physical Separation

Even at their height, Spaniards' fears of moral contamination by natives did not extend to maintaining a physical distance from them. Unlike Englishmen, Spaniards lived side by side with Native Americans. Spanish families settled in native towns, and native families resided in Spanish cities. Indians and colonists often wound up sharing the same residences, the same food, the same streets and alleys. Unlike their Iberian counterparts, English settlers rarely set themselves and their families down in the middle of Indian towns and villages. Rather, they tended to establish residences apart from natives and carefully organized their contacts with Native Americans around formal activities, such as trade and other structured forms of interaction.[22] Even so, these contacts were largely carried out by male colonists alone, and not by entire families.

Iberian colonists, however, never required that natives sustain an enduring physical separation from themselves as English settlers, who believed physical contact to be a source of contamination, were wont to do.

Mathew Hale wrote, "Where the Accessions [to a colony] are but thin and sparing, and scattered among the Natives of the Country where they come . . . it falls out that the very first Planters do soon degenerate in their Habits, Customs and Religion."[23] The Michigan territorial governor declared virtually identically in 1830, "A Barbarous people, depending for subsistence upon the scanty and precarious supplies furnished by the chase, cannot live in contact with a civilized community."[24] (That is to say, there is no economic motive for having them close, and, more than that, there is a fear of having them in close proximity.)

With their history of living in close contact with others of different faiths, the Spanish viewed the potential for contamination as far smaller. When Indians throughout the Americas began to flee their communities to avoid the burdens of tribute payment in the late 1570s, they often escaped to Spanish settlements, seeking work. Spaniards did not fear close physical contact with natives, only the polluting impact of their morality. After all, Christians on the Iberian Peninsula had spent centuries surrounded by people of other cultures without adopting their faiths. Their Christianity was, in itself, evidence of their ability to resist. All they demanded was that individuals harboring potentially polluting vices be properly identifiable by their dress and demeanor.

Spaniards had two additional reasons for not suspecting Indian migrants, as individuals or families, of harboring immoral beliefs or practices. Believing (and probably rightly so) that native communities sustained traditional (immoral) values, Spaniards understood natives' departure from their own societies to signify breaking the links that nourished traditional beliefs.[25] Therefore Spaniards did not fear homeless Indians among them and made no draconian efforts to prevent their moving freely about. Although such actions thwarted would-be tribute collectors from the natives' original communities, they did not profoundly threaten Spaniards' sense of security in the New World. Anglo-Saxon settlers' quasi-paranoid fears of *physical* insecurity regarding Indians were missing in Iberian colonists. Rather, many Iberians saw the natives' movement out of traditional communities as a benefit. Without a readily available source of income from their communities, Indians became a source of cheap, readily available labor for Spaniards, one that could eventually be assimilated economically (and often culturally) into the Spanish world and its labor markets.

Iberians' preoccupation with maintaining a moral boundary between themselves and those they conquered originated in a distinct cultural pattern on the Iberian Peninsula, as political opponents separated themselves into "Christians" and "Muslims." The colonial reaffirmation of this politicized concept of religion remade this distinction into a boundary between "people of reason" and not-quite-reasonable Indians. But this division permitted Spaniards to continue to deprive natives permanently of their ownership of buried gold and silver. Thus the most important distinction for Spaniards was that between the "reasonable" and the "quasi-reasonable" people, because that boundary secured the legitimate title to gold and silver. Through the seventeenth century, securing boundaries between African slaves and Spanish colonists was of secondary importance, because no sources of enormous wealth were at stake in such distinctions. Thus Spanish colonists in seventeenth-century Peru supported the canonization of black and mulatto saints at the same time they adamantly opposed the beatification of Native Americans and even mestizos.[26] Only the natives' continuing status as incapable of becoming fully Christian guaranteed Spaniards' permanent ownership of buried gold and silver (through their monarch), the major source of Iberian wealth. The economic source of the distinction meant that the most scrupulously defended boundary for the first two centuries of colonial rule was that between Christians and those not ever capable of attaining full Christian status.

Spaniards slightly shifted the location of the boundary between people of reason and those not quite reasonable as natives increasingly converted to Christianity. But Portuguese colonists continued to retain the original Iberian language, because they continued to find significant numbers of previously uncontacted groups throughout the colonial period (and even into the twentieth century).[27] Thus Portuguese colonists continued to sustain the boundary between themselves and the natives in terms of the differences between the Christians (people of reason) and the Gentiles, pagans, and idolaters (not-quite-reasonable people).[28]

Unchristianized natives were described as being "like beasts without knowledge of God" or as living "almost in the manner of beasts."[29] Manuel da Nóbrega, in an imaginary dialogue, had critics of the evangelization process declare that the natives "are like dogs in their eating and killing, and pigs in the vices and manner of treating each other. . . . They forget their upbringing like brute animals, and [are] more ungrateful than the sons of the snakes who eat their mothers." One of the faultfinders added, "I distrust [the idea] that these [people] are capable of baptism"[30] Even toward the end of the seventeenth century, missionaries were reflecting similar sentiments. Martinho de Nantes observed in 1671, "They [the Kariri] only have the shape of man and the actions of animals."[31] Elites in Portugal shared this attitude. In official Portuguese chronicles, Indians appear "barely as a kind of curious species of barbarous population, with-out ethical, social, or intellectual attributes [thus] leading the reader to the idea of [an Indian] 'natural humanity' different from their own."[32] Both Iberian nations thus retained the significance of their own humanity (rela-tive to the natives') based upon their possession of Christianity, a distinc-tion that allowed them to consider themselves entitled to use native labor in varying fashions.

The most striking contrast with the Anglo-Saxon colonial world cen-ters on the different ways in which the same moral boundary was re-created. To begin with, the natural resource that Englishmen believed they could legitimately covet and seize was native farmland.

English Counterpoint

Whereas Spanish conquerors self-identified as *"the* Christians," Englishmen self-identified as *"the* farmers," or, in the language of the seventeenth cen-tury, *"the* planters." These self-identifications are asymmetrical, as cultural categories invariably are.[33] Both self-images, however, reflected the self-flattering pictures that these different European colonizers wished to have of themselves. Whereas "Christianity" enjoyed an unmistakably divine origin, farming or planting had a similarly heavenly origin in the minds of Anglo-Saxon settlers.

Englishmen widely believed that farmland was entrusted to men by God, and that farming was given to them as man's mission on earth. "No travail more acceptable to God, than is the tilling of the ground."[34] Many sixteenth- and seventeenth-century English books described God as the First Farmer. John Milton in *Paradise Lost* described God as "the sovran Planter," and a Puritan favorite likewise declared, "God is the planter."[35] Another, using the popular term *husbandman* for "farmer," declared "God was the Originall, and first Husbandman, the pattern of all Husbandry."[36]

Englishmen initially preferred the word *planter* to describe a cultivator, because "farming" was originally linked to tax collection.[37] When it be-came associated with land use, *farmer* principally signified someone who rented or leased land for the purpose of cultivation.[38] These implications rendered *farmer* unsatisfactory for describing the process of overseas settle-ment during the sixteenth and early seventeenth centuries. But the word *planter,* with its originally neutral connotations of anyone who sets plants in the ground, was more than satisfactory.[39] The biological metaphor of a plant or an offshoot furthermore carried connotations of a natural rather than a political process.[40]

Thus English occupants of the New World referred to their earliest settlements as "plantations." During the sixteenth and seventeenth centuries, English colonists most frequently described themselves as planters. William Bradford's account of the Puritans' arrival and settlement is called a history of Plymouth plantation, and one of John Smith's writings is titled *Advertisements for the Unexperienced Planters of New-England* (1631).[41] Occasionally the word *colony* was used in conjunction with same metaphor. The Virginia Council observed: "A colony is therefore denominated, because they should be *Coloni*, the tillers of the earth and stewards of fertilitie."[42]

Over the course of the seventeenth century, the principal meaning of the word *plantation* shifted, coming to be associated with a particular kind of settlement—a coffee, cotton, indigo, sugar, or tobacco estate on which slaves or indentured servants performed the labor under English supervision.[43] But targeting aboriginal people as "lazy" while describing English colonizers as "laborious" for supervising others did not function credibly enough for plausible political rhetoric. Englishmen soon dropped the label of *planters* in favor of *farmers*, the civic identity they favored. Thus the word *planter* rapidly faded from widespread use during the eighteenth century.

Whereas Spaniards reinterpreted the boundary between "humans" and "not quite humans" in terms of their religion, Englishmen believed that the boundary between the "human" and the "not quite human" resided in the performance of a culturally specific form of labor. And although Englishmen understood something quite ethnically specific—namely, male farming—by the word *labor*, they nonetheless understood the boundary between "humans" and "nonhumans" to be constructed on the basis of "labor." For Englishmen, to labor was to be human, and not to labor was to be not quite human. In describing natives as *nonfarmers*, Englishmen conveyed the idea that aboriginal people were morally deficient based on a standard set by God. Where "nature being liberal to all without labour, necessity imposing no industry or travel [travail]," Walter Ralegh declared, there are "vicious countries," "full of vices."[44] Native men's failure to farm was fundamentally immoral, according to Ralegh, a profound breach of basic ethical principles.

Even more severely, and indeed even more frequently, Englishmen described natives' nonfarming as evidence that they did not even meet the standards for being human. To be human was to labor. As John Milton addressed God, thanking Him for showing that work was human: "Now Thou, that Adam in his vprightnesse, / (To shew, *that Labour doth to man belong*)."[45] Thus men who did not labor could not be truly human. And a long-established classical and Christian tradition had fixed the way of expressing the division between human and nonhuman life forms as the gulf separating man from beast. Thus a great many Englishmen would describe Indians as animals in this sense, as nonlaborers.

Frobisher said that the natives "live in Caves of earth, and hunt for their dinners or prey, even as the bear or other wild beasts do."[46] Cotton Mather referred to native homes as "kennels," and another Englishman compared them to a "den or hog stye."[47] Anglican preacher Robert Gray, in a sermon titled *A Good Speede to Virginia,* described natives, saying they "wander up and downe like beasts, and in manners and conditions differ very little from beasts," and Robert Johnson, in a 1609 publicity tract for the Virginia Company titled *Nova Britannia,* said they "lie up and down in troupes like heards of Deare in a Forrest."[48] Puritan Robert Cushman wrote that the natives "do but run over the grass, as do also the foxes and the wild beasts," and William Bradford expressed nearly identical sentiments, describing America as "being devoid of all civil inhabitants, there are only savage and brutish men, which range up and down, little otherwise that the beasts of the same."[49]

These expressions do not forthrightly state that natives *were* animals; rather, they describe one particular aspect of their behavior (constantly moving across the landscape) as *analogous* to the conduct of animals.[50] They hunt their dinners "*as* the bear," act "*like* beasts," "*like* herds of deer"; they "run over the grass *as* . . . foxes."[51] Natives were unmistakably human, but their failure to labor, identifiable by their dwelling in caves, hunting for their dinner, and constantly moving across the land in pursuit of game, meant that they behaved exactly like the animals they pursued. Just as Spaniards had frequently referred to certain aspects of Indian *behavior* as not human (i.e., their cannibalism and human sacrifice), so too did the Englishmen. But for Englishmen the gulf between men and beasts resided in an entirely different area. For them, farm labor separated those who were fully human from those who were not. Thus a profound and unbridgeable moral gap separated Englishmen from Indians.

Furthermore, this insurmountable ethical difference was understood by Englishmen of the time not as a particular cultural variation, but as a universal judgment. And for Englishmen no less than for Spaniards, universal principles could be found in the moral imperatives described in the Bible, and in their religious tradition. Perhaps the favorite and most often cited Bible verses for Englishmen came from Genesis.[52] English colonists quoted their own favorite passage, Genesis 1:28, as having an implicit colonial message: "Have dominion over the fish of the sea, over the birds in the sky and over the animals that move over the land." And because natives "run over the grass as . . . foxes," the biblical phrase "animals that move over the land" was usually understood to mean that Englishmen should rule over those people who behaved *like* animals.

But Englishmen, as fully human, never understood their power over those who were not (those people who behaved "as animals") to mean that Englishmen should directly subject Native Americans to English political and moral education in order to raise them to the status of full humanity (as did Spanish leaders). The secretary to the Spanish regent declared that the Indians needed, "just as a horse or beast does, to be directed and governed by Christians."[53] Englishmen did not interpret the Bible in this way. Rather, they understood Genesis 1:28 as signifying that natives (behaving as beasts) could not legitimately own *land*. "For God no sooner said . . . let us make Man after our image, but presently he adds his *Charter* of Supream Authority, And let him have dominion over the fish of the Sea, and over the fowls of the Air, and over the Cattel, and over all the Earth." And the phrase "dominion over . . . all the earth" was understood quite literally to mean ownership of the soil. In this fashion, English colonists—like others—interpreted biblical precepts as supporting culturally specific economic goals. William Symonds wrote, "Although the Lord hath given the earth to the children of men . . . the greater part of it [is] possessed wrongfully and usurped by wild beasts and unreasonable creatures or by brutish savages," and Anglican Robert Gray argued, "The earth was mine, God gave it [to] me, and by posteritie . . . and yet may [I] & take it not out of the hands of beasts and brutish savages which have no interest in it, because they participate rather of the nature of beasts then men."[54]

Like Spanish colonists, Englishmen perceived a fundamental moral gap between themselves and the natives, based upon the long-held Christian belief in a distinction between man and beast. But they conceived of that rift in a completely different way. Whereas Spaniards believed that reason (and the capacity for Christianity) distinguished men from animals, Englishmen seemed to believe that labor (and manual farm labor in particular) separated man from beast. And both groups' convictions were deeply rooted in their cultural systems and expressions of their religious traditions. For many Englishmen, farming was a mission from which man would never escape.

For people of many faiths paradise is a place of bliss, happiness, or delight. And in a great many traditions, Paradise is also a garden.[55] "What is Paradise?" asked popular seventeenth-century writer William Lawson, "but a Garden and Orchard of trees and hearbs."[56] According to popular sixteenth- and seventeenth-century English conceptions, however, Paradise was a place of either delightful labor or none at all.[57] One of Shakespeare's characters in *The Tempest* declares Paradise the one place where men do not have to work: "Without sweat or endeavor . . . / . . . Nature should bring forth, / Of its own kind, all foison, all abundance, / To feed my innocent people," declares Gonzalo.[58] His sentiments were echoed by scores of others.[59] As seventeenth-century essayist William Temple wrote, "Eden . . . was the state of innocence and pleasure; and . . . the life of husbandry and cities came after the fall, with guilt and with labor."[60] Walter Ralegh declared that "the abundant growing of palm-trees without the care and labour of man" could prove the location of Paradise.[61]

Equally popular among Englishmen was the viewpoint of Paradise as a place of labor—but not drudgery. In *Paradise Lost*, John Milton had Adam performing wholly enjoyable agricultural labor in Paradise before the fall: "With first approach of light, we must be ris'n, / And at our pleasant labor, to reform / You flow'ry arbors, yonder alleys green, / Our walk at noon, with branches overgrown, / That mock at our scant manuring."[62] Only after the fall did farming become "laborious, till day droop."[63] For royal apothecary John Parkinson, author of a widely read seventeenth-century gardening book, the Garden of Eden was one "wherein even in his innocency he [Adam] was to labour and spend his time."[64]

The frequent references to the New World as the Garden of Eden created unrealistic expectations in many of the original settlers, who thought that they would be able to acquire food effortlessly, or at least with only pleasant, enjoyable labor.[65] More important, however, this understanding of Paradise as having a fundamental relationship to farming reinforced the idea that farming was God-ordained. And it further sustained the conviction that labor (i.e., farming) was essential to humanity.

English colonists characterized natives as "beasts" not in the Iberian sense of lacking "reason," but in their own sense, as lacking "labor." If men had to labor in Paradise, then the conduct of the natives in the New World could not be fully human.[66] The injustice of mere mortal man—let alone "brutish savages"—being permitted to occupy Paradise was too much for many Englishmen to countenance. Indigenous peoples could not therefore possess the land because they did not farm.

Englishmen's belief that native hunting was not "labor" therefore conflicted not only with aristocratic ideas, but more profoundly with cultural ones at the core of Englishmen's civic identity. And those cultural convictions had a moral foundation. That ground, however, was not the "sins" that Spaniards saw, of idolatry, cannibalism, human sacrifice, and sodomy, but rather the refusal of native men to carry out the divinely ordained task of farming. God had given the earth to men to farm. Those who labored had a divinely inspired mission to take over the land from those who did not. As Robert Gray declared in 1609, "[We] may & take it out of the hands of beasts and brutish savages which have no interest in it, because they participate rather of the nature of beasts then men."[67] If the Indians did not labor, they could not possess the land, because only men labored. "Beasts" and those who participate in "the nature of beasts" did not. Farming (labor) constituted the firm moral boundary separating English settlers and natives.

As an enduring political (and ethical) identity for Englishmen, the self-image as "farmers" or "workers" resurfaced in English colonial experiences elsewhere, often manifesting profoundly regional expectations of temperate-zone farming. The practice of rising early in the morning and working until dusk, established in the mild temperatures of the British Isles, became the standard by which all other forms of labor were judged lacking.[68] Moving into increasingly disparate ecological zones, British settlers continued to judge other peoples' climate-appropriate work schedules by their own. Fishermen and farmers of equatorial regions, who quite sensibly worked from 3:00 A.M., when the weather was coolest, until 10:00 A.M., when the heat began to become unbearable, were judged "lazy" by Englishmen because they were sleeping in the midafternoon when the sun was at its hottest. Englishmen, regardless of where they traveled in the world, notoriously clung to their temperate-zone rhythms of work, because these were their standards by which labor (i.e., their civic virtue) was exercised. The perverse pride that "only mad dogs and Englishmen go out in the noonday sun" reflects the Englishmen's continued care to demonstrate the superiority of their work rhythms—they might be mad, but they would work when no one else would.[69]

Visual Forms of Distinction

Although a great deal of ink has been spilled in attempts to establish colonial rule as inevitably a form of racism, that effort seems misdirected. Racism accurately identifies a visually locatable boundary between two clusters of people that sustains the economic and political interests of the dominant one. Racism can be used and has been used to rationalize the requirement of one group to labor for another, to continue differentiated access to economic rewards, and to support an enduring sense of superiority in daily life. But racism is one form of visually recognizing (and therefore distinguishing) members of a dominant group in everyday life.

One of the crucial functions of any discriminatory category must be its ease of use in everyday existence. The colonizing or the dominant members of a society must be able to recognize members of the dominated group visually. Racism locates the signs of distinction in a set of visual identifiers founded upon specifically identifiable physical characteristics— skin color, hair texture, and the like. Therefore, although race is one form, it is not the only form of visual identification that enables members of a dominant group to recognize their distinction from those they control.

In colonizing different parts of the world, Europeans have not always used distinctive physical traits to separate themselves from those they have colonized. European colonists exoticized and romanticized Arabs in the Middle East, for example, but failed to develop a fundamentally physical definition of differences between the two groups. And in the New World, Europeans occasionally used "race" as a means of separating out aboriginal peoples from colonial immigrants—in the 1770s in Spanish America, or in the 1660s in Virginia.[70] But sustained use of "race" as the principal visible identifier of aboriginal status failed.[71]

Racism, the physical method of identification, served colonizers and their successors well when they introduced a requirement of labor (identifying the person with the body whose physical traits were required for labor). But colonial domination also required justifying other economic objectives—expropriation of natural resources—ends that may or may not have included labor. Hence the images of native peoples had to be created around specific aspects of their conduct that would readily legitimate (to disparate groups of colonizers) colonial economic and political aims. In the Americas, both Englishmen and Iberians created other visually based forms of identification to distinguish themselves readily from natives.

The visual forms of distinction differed according to the separate criteria of the colonizers. Iberians principally used dress and demeanor, whereas the English employed space and place of residence. Horseback riding was forbidden the natives of Spanish America, for horses were identified with superior social status. Distinct dress identifying the individual as indigenous was demanded in Spanish America. And the use of iron weapons, long identified in Iberia with the status of conquerors, was likewise forbidden. But among English colonists, the visual clues were different. Distinctive dress never became required of Indians; traders even sold natives clothes so that they could dress like settlers. Iron goods were never proscribed, only firearms, and then only ineffectually. Horseback riding was never prohibited; it became the principal identifier of native identity.

English colonists remained far more preoccupied with spatial boundaries than with dress and demeanor. Physical contact alone was believed to be potentially threatening, even to traders and diplomats who were in regular contact with Native Americans.[72] Visually gauging the space between colonists and natives seemed crucial. Geographic bounds and large physical distances were often established to separate settler and Indian societies, and the material preservation of boundary objects was strongly valued.

By borrowing a familiar group of Christian ideas—the absolute moral differentiation between man and animal—to differentiate themselves from natives, colonizers transformed a Christian category for economic and political ends. In the process, they fundamentally altered the underlying concept. They eliminated Christianity's most powerful means for overcoming its damage—namely, the narrative of redemption, the possibility of overcoming.[73] Although religious deliverance was possible, neither economic nor political liberation was possible as long as aboriginal peoples continued to exist as natives. Remaining as aboriginal peoples provided them no rights to land under English domination and no rights to mineral deposits under Iberian control. Colonizers thus based their claim for entitlement on an originally ethical distinction that was in fact justified not by their religious beliefs but by their distortion of those beliefs along specific cultural lines, in the service of political self-interest and the pursuit of material wealth.

Finally, critiques of the distorted images of Indians have not succeeded in changing minds simply because they have not addressed the two crucial considerations that were at stake: the legitimacy of the original (and subsequent) seizure of native resources and the continuing political legitimacy of the state originally authorizing the seizure of those resources. The "cannibal" label rationalized the continued enslavement of natives who refused to cooperate with Iberian labor demands during the colonial era. Similarly, the label of "hunter" justified both the original and ongoing English confiscation of native land. Because the need for Indian labor and land continued throughout the colonial period, these basic colonial fictions remained unchallenged.

The colonial fictions further remained in place because they mirrored the representational ideals that colonizers prized about themselves. Englishmen and Iberians cherished beliefs in a collective political uniqueness— the core of which set them apart from the natives. Englishmen prized their identity as sedentary farmers; Iberians treasured their status as devout Christians. To question colonial representations of Native Americans would be to challenge the colonizers' own cherished beliefs about their political identity.

But this identity also formed the basis of their convictions as to their superiority over Native Americans—especially the superiority that entitled separate European groups to claim specific New World resources. Englishmen believed that as "farmers" they were entitled to seize native land because the (male) natives were hunters unable to cultivate properly. Iberians similarly believed that they had a right to use native labor because otherwise the natives would backslide into immoral religious practices.

Crossing the political boundary invited retaliation. Natives who decisively demonstrated that they were as capable of the endeavors that colonizers understood as the core of their own cultural identity were rapidly denied the opportunity to pursue those activites in the future. Successful Cherokee cotton planters and Apalachee orchard growers were eliminated in Georgia and Florida, just as were Latin-speaking Nahua clergymen in Mexico City. Rather than reformulating their own understandings of themselves, colonizers eliminated any proof that natives could challenge the morally clear identity that they cherished about themselves. The result left political synecdoches and colonial fictions protecting colonizers' visions of themselves and firmly securing convictions of their entitlement to the wealth of the New World.

The final European colonizing power whose cultural operations have shaped the position of contemporary indigenous people is Portugal. The Native Americans in Brazil face many obstacles similar to those encountered in Spanish America, but with significant and important twists. It is to those differences, and then to the contrasts between English and Portuguese colonization of the Americas, that we now turn.

8

Indians in Portuguese America

Whereas English colonists expropriated Indian land overseas and Spaniards expropriated Indian labor, Portuguese colonists at first seized neither. Rather, their pattern, which was subsequently imitated successfully by Dutch and other European merchants, left the means of production in the hands of aboriginal inhabitants. This primarily mercantile model proved inordinately successful well into the nineteenth century in Africa and Asia, where local inhabitants had long been accustomed to producing goods for overseas markets.

When they arrived on American shores in 1500, the Portuguese simply wanted to bargain with the natives for the price of their goods and leave all the details of production in native hands. But this commercial mode had limited success in the New World. Lacking the infrastructure to cope with the new demands and devastated by the diseases that European traders brought with them, Native American societies found themselves subject to unprecedented and often intolerable pressures.

Nor was this commercial pattern any more satisfactory to Europeans. All three groups of Europeans who initially embarked upon this model it in the Americas eventually abandoned it. Dutch leadership simply refused more than minimal funding of the unprofitable North American colony in the 1630s. And although the French held on to their Canadian colony for strategic reasons (geopolitical competition with England), the settlement was unprofitable from the start. Only the Portuguese, in abandoning the trade model, successfully transformed their commercial empire into a large colonial one in which Europeans owned and managed the means of production.[1] In the New World, only two kinds of colonial policies were successful in the long run: the land-based empires of the English and the labor-based empires of the Spanish and eventually the Portuguese.

When forced to establish a permanent presence, largely to protect and fortify their trading posts against other marauding Europeans in the 1530s, Portuguese officials reluctantly ordered the settlement of the eastern rim of the South American continent. This terrain was profoundly under-populated, as was that encountered by the English in North America. Whereas mainland North America was inhabited by a mixture of nomadic and sedentary cultivators, eastern South America was inhabited entirely by nomadic cultivators and hunter-gatherers. But despite encountering both a terrain and a people that ideally fit the English rationales for con-quest (better even than North America)—a terrain that had in fact in-spired Thomas More's *Utopia*—Portuguese settlers never invoked any of the English colonists' terms or attitudes.

Rather than expelling aboriginal peoples from their land, Lusitanian settlers sought their labor. Portuguese reactions to the New World were far closer to those of Spaniards, with whom they shared an often common his-tory, a closely related language, and numerous similar cultural concepts.

As I have noted in preceding chapters, Portuguese and Spanish sub-jects believed that they shared ownership of all valuable mineral resources and that their officials managed such resources for them. Also as I have noted, Spanish and Portuguese colonists viewed the distinction between themselves and native peoples in terms of their identity as "Christians" and the natives' identity as pagans and idolaters. Both believed they had a right to punish Indians for their immoral conduct, cannibalism in par-ticular, through harsh regimes of labor. When encountering "cannibals," Lusitanians—like their Spanish neighbors—sought to capture such na-tives and make them slaves.

However, enslaving all natives was neither possible nor desirable. Under royal guidance, Portuguese colonists in the New World developed the Jesuit mission system, a distinct form of assimilating indigenous peoples to European norms of labor and conduct. But the missions' singu-lar success in Brazil led to the system's downfall and the eventual expulsion of the Jesuits.

Portugal's path to separate economic development began in the late

Middle Ages, following the end of Muslim rule. Its emergence as a commercial power during the fifteenth century provides the background for its transformation into a colonial empire in Brazil.

A Commercial Power

Over the course of the fifteenth century, as their navigators traveled steadily further down the West African coast, Portuguese monarchs found trade with the newly accessible regions increasingly profitable. Traders bought or traded for goods and in many regions deposited these goods at fortified local warehouses called *feitorias* (factories), where they could be safely stored until the next fleet came to transport the goods to Portugal.[2] Storehouses were usually situated on islands, where they were protected from attacks by ship by fortified walls and from land-launched attacks by the water separating them from the mainland. The king's taxes were customarily collected at these depots. Where the crown had not built fortified storage areas, goods were transported directly to giant government customs warehouses in Lisbon. The two most important of the Lisbon customhouses were the Casa da Mina (for West African goods) and the Casa da India (for South Asian goods).[3] These giant Lisbon storehouses received spices, clothing, porcelain, and precious stones from Africa and the Far East. Once customs duties were paid to the crown, the goods were shipped to all corners of Europe. By the first years of the sixteenth century, receipts from these customhouses represented 65–70 percent of the crown's annual revenue.

Thus at the financial heart of the Portuguese empire were the customhouses in Lisbon and elsewhere, taxing the flow of goods through a vast commercial web. The Portuguese crown was not interested in how the commodities were produced, under what conditions, or who harvested them. All these were matters to be handled by Portuguese settlers and/or traders in each of the various overseas locations.[4]

Monarchs sought to control only the purchasing and European marketing of overseas goods that had resale value in Western markets, ignoring or leaving to local merchants those goods without such value. In fact, Portuguese economic interests resembled those of the twentieth-century United Fruit Company, which in the 1950s controlled the purchase and European and North American distribution of only bananas from Central America.

Whereas private Portuguese subjects traded for silks, porcelain, coral, and shellac, the Portuguese monarchs traditionally monopolized the overseas sale and distribution of a continent's most valuable commodity.[5] For most of the sixteenth century, that commodity was pepper from India, making the region, as Salman Rushdie writes, "not so much sub-continent as sub-condiment."[6]

The only profitable commodity from Brazil for the first century of the colony's existence was the distinctive red dye taken from the heart of a tall tree known as brazilwood. It was long harvested in Asia for coloring fabrics sold on the Iberian Peninsula.[7] Thus the region's name, Brazil, stemmed from the only valuable resource it produced for the European market.[8] Consequently, the Portuguese king claimed a monopoly over its import to Europe.[9]

In addition to their own monopoly, Portuguese kings also granted other merchants separate monopolies on other marketable—usually slightly less lucrative—goods, usually other spices, such as cinnamon and nutmeg. Like the king's monopoly, these restraints governed only the purchasing and European marketing of goods.[10] Merchants holding a corner on particular commodities made a variety of different commercial and shipping arrangements with foreign traders, merchants, and princes overseas.

To defend these various monopolies, Portugal required a navy capable of enforcing the trade deals of the crown and its trading subjects.[11] Although their innovations in navigational knowledge gave the Portugese an initial advantage in accurately locating and returning to trade in foreign ports, their ability to defend their stores of goods from seaborne access with guns was equally significant. Superiority in weapons, battleship construction, and naval tactics gave the Portugese a continuing advantage over all their European and Asian competitors during the sixteenth century. These advances eventually changed the face of seaborne warfare as other Europeans emulated the Portuguese navy.[12] The combination of fortified storehouses and decisive superiority at sea kept potential economic competitors effectively at bay in both the Indian Ocean and Western Africa for more than a century. But these phenomenal maritime successes failed on the western edge of the South Atlantic.

Within four years of Portugal's first successful trip to Brazil, French competitors arrived on their shores. Trade across the South Atlantic did not have to pass through a narrow neck, such as the straits of Malacca in Southeast Asia, that could be effectively bottlenecked. The American coastline was long and the Atlantic shipping lanes broad. Plus there was no single place to station a fleet to effectively halt other European vessels sailing across the South Atlantic. In addition, Brazilian warehouses constructed to house newly cut brazilwood were often constructed onshore, usually near riverbanks, and hence were not as defensible as the island-based warehouses along the coasts of Africa and India. Therefore both indigenous peoples and marauding French visitors preyed upon them.[13]

To roust French pirates, the Portuguese had to resort to costly, often brutal tactics. (French sources invariably call these men "merchants," whereas Portuguese sources use only synonyms for "pirate.")[14] And the brazilwood trade, while lucrative, was not sufficiently profitable to justify continuing to launch such large, expensive naval operations.[15] The crown in 1530 reluctantly agreed to introduce settlers to occupy the region as a deterrent to would-be commercial interlopers. As Brazilian historian Carlos Malheiro Dias has noted, "The task the Crown gave to them [the lord proprietors] was less the settlement [of Brazil] than the defense and policing of the territories."[16]

King João III wanted men to organize and lead military operations to fend off the predominantly French pirates who were threatening his monopoly of the dyewood trade. Placing thirteen well-connected and preferably militarily experienced men in charge of such settlements seemed like an excellent idea. In return, these leaders, called "lord proprietors" (donatários), were given control over sizable chunks of New World territory, with the power to distribute land to those who served under them in military expeditions.

But these lord proprietors and their settlers had to have a source of revenue for themselves. Because brazilwood remained a royal monopoly, they looked for other sources of income. Finding nothing domestic of great economic value, colonists began cultivating imported plants such as sugar, imported animals such as cattle, and even native crops such as tobacco on a large scale. But doing so required a source of labor. Relying upon the shared Iberian understanding of themselves as "the Christians" and natives as pagan—often cannibal—tribes, Portuguese settlers began to look for natives as slave labor.[17] But the widespread native slavery that resulted was not without its problems.

Lusitanian settlers soon realized the foolishness of attempting to enslave local natives, who were, after all, far more familiar with the terrain and means of escape than the Portuguese were. To avoid the embarrassment of losing slaves, Portuguese settlers set their sights upon capturing natives farther and farther away from their own residences. In so doing, however, they often (and sometimes unknowingly) seized natives residing near other Portuguese settlements. When natives retaliated for the loss of their members, they attacked the nearby Portuguese, not the slavers, who had long since disappeared.[18] When these reprisals occasioned by slave raiders from another district destroyed several Portuguese settlements in the 1540s and threatened the existence of the remainder, the entire colony was placed in jeopardy, and the king intervened.

In 1548, King João III wrote:

> I have been informed that in said lands and populations of Brazil, there are some people who have ships and caravels and who travel in them from one captaincy to another . . . and who assault and rob the Gentiles that are at peace and deceitfully put them on said ships and for this the said Gentiles rise up and war against the Christians. And *this was the principal cause of the damages that up to now have been done [to the Christians].* [19]

He appointed the first governor-general, Tomé da Sousa, to regulate slaving expeditions and instructed him, "No person of what ever social standing and condition may rob/leap upon or make war on the Gentiles by land or by sea in their ships nor in others [ships] *without your [governor's] license or that of the captain of the district* in whose jurisdiction they are."[20] Furthermore, financial incentives were offered to anyone who notified royal officials of an illicit slave raid.[21]

The net effect of this requirement for permits was to turn slave raiders' attention away from the coasts where Europeans had settled and toward the interior where few, if any, Portuguese were to be found. Slave raiders shifted from sea-based attacks on native settlements to land-based ones. Embarking on lengthy expeditions into the interior of Brazil carrying flags (*bandeiras*) announcing their presence, these settlers searched for valuable agricultural products, minerals, and slaves—all potential sources of wealth.

Far from criticizing the long-distance hunting and gathering of native peoples, Portuguese colonists viewed indigenous skills in hunting, gathering, and exploration as highly desirable. Natives knew where marketable commodities, including cinnamon, vanilla, Brazil nuts, and occasionally gold and semiprecious stones could be found.[22] Indigenous groups could be used to locate and harvest these commercially marketable crops without substantial distortions in the original native patterns of collecting and gathering.

Native communities also had intimate knowledge of the topography of the land and the location of all their significant enemies. Thus by allying themselves with one particular native community, sometimes even marrying into the community and producing mixed-race offspring, the Portuguese assured themselves of a steady source of military collaborators. These allies were skilled in the tactics and strategies most successful in the terrain, and they were highly motivated to defeat the common enemies of their maternal and paternal families.

But neither these settlers nor the crown had any significant economic stake in the goods customarily harvested by native communities. Not even the dyewood harvested by the natives had been a traditional trade crop. American brazilwood trees were tall and difficult to cut, a task doubly challenging for the Tupi, who had only stone axes. Hence the precontact-era trees were felled rarely, and with great effort. To turn the cutting of trees into a profitable timber industry, the Portuguese, like their French competitors, had to persuade the natives to engage regularly in the arduous task of cutting lumber, even giving them iron axes to speed the process.[23]

Because the brazilwood trees were located in many different forests, Portuguese merchants harvesting dyewood trees employed Tupis from a particular community until all the local brazilwood trees were felled. Then the merchant traders simply moved on to another region and worked at persuading another community to fell the timbers. Therefore the brazilwood trade depended upon labor not from any particular native community but from a rotating series of native groups who happened to be residing near woods containing the dyewood trees.

Similar processes occurred with the collectors of vanilla and Brazil nuts. Vanilla is derived from the pod of a tropical climbing orchid native to northern Brazil and Central America. Brazil or Pará nuts are tricornered, high-fat, high-protein seeds from a giant tree indigenous to the Amazon. Guaraná, the fruit of an indigenous woody vine, yields a paste that when added to water produces a beverage with three times more caffeine than a cup of coffee. Natives used their traditional strategies to collect these tropical products, often on a larger scale than customary and in the company of Portuguese merchants specifically seeking these plants. Explorers protected these gathering activities (and the natives involved) in frontier zones. But once settlers invaded the region, merchant-explorers usually moved on to other areas to continue the process of gathering. Hence Portuguese monarchs (as well as both traders and settlers) lacked any significant financial interest in sustaining any particular native community over the long term.

The aim of Christianizing the natives, however, was too important politically to be neglected. And the institution of slavery was designed to punish communities, not convert them to Christianity. The Portuguese monarch needed a plan for converting natives without resorting to slavery. In 1548, he revived an earlier plan drawn up by the Hieronymites (a religious order) in neighboring Spain to instruct the natives and make use of their labor in the Caribbean.[24] In 1519 the Hieronymites had proposed—and halfheartedly attempted—to congregate hunter-gatherer and small-scale agricultural societies that were culturally and linguistically similar to those inhabiting large sections of Brazil.[25]

In embracing a similar program for Brazil, King João III placed some hunting and gathering communities under the supervision of a religious order. Like the "trustee" arrangements that Spanish officials had created with the *encomienda,* clerics were charged with the religious education of the aboriginal people to be placed under their supervision. As with the trust or *encomienda,* the priest-custodian had a right to receive labor services as part of the arrangement.[26]

King João III initially entrusted a single religious order, the politically powerful, independently run Jesuits, with the task of congregating these natives.[27] The Jesuits, perhaps alone among the possible missionary groups in Portugal, had both the financial and the political power to operate quasi-independently of the locally powerful landlords and merchants, who would have preferred simply to seize natives and use them as slaves.

Originally, the Jesuits congregated large numbers of natives on the outskirts of the large Portuguese settlements. This arrangement was a disaster. Concentrating native people lacking immunity to European diseases in a single locale increased the velocity at which diseases spread. The faster epidemics travel, the more often they leave the survivors weakened and unable to survive subsequent infections.[28] In the Caribbean, natives already living in close proximity to Spanish settlements were decimated by disease. Brazilian natives concentrated near Portuguese settlements suffered an identical fate.

Thus Jesuit congregations proved even more deadly to natives than had the halfhearted Spanish Hieronymite concentrations of natives in the Caribbean. In two years (1562–63), epidemics around Bahia killed one-half of the native population. To put these figures in perspective, let us remember that the Black Death in Western Europe killed one-third of the population over half a century, not two years.[29] After this initial disastrous experience, Jesuits were unable to sustain the self-congratulatory image held by Spanish cleric Bartolomé de Las Casas. He claimed that settlers' greed (rather than the mere presence of disease-bearing Spaniards) was causing the deaths of indigenous peoples.[30] But Las Casas could continue to promote his conviction that religious guardianship would prove beneficial to natives because his suggestion was only partially tested in the Caribbean.[31]

Following the devastation of original custodial missions near coastal urban centers, Jesuits moved toward the interior of the continent.[32] They refined and adapted their original policies for governing native communities into a system of mission villages (*aldeias* in Portuguese). Mission-settled Indians were infected with diseases carried by the Jesuits and their cattle, but they did not face the constant reintroduction of new diseases brought by recent arrivals.

The Jesuits were not the only Portuguese interested in the natives of the interior, however. Having been forced to redirect their search for slaves, flag-bearing *bandeirantes* ventured deep into the interior of Brazil. Both the Jesuits and the raiders sought to capture the natives for themselves, leading to frequent clashes between the two groups.[33] The crown was often unable to decide between Jesuits who wanted to Christianize the natives under the guise of protective "liberty" and colonists who were asking for slaves to work the land. When they lost such battles, the Jesuits moved inland in search of other aboriginal groups.[34]

In the process, the original proposal for congregating Caribbean natives became transformed into a novel policy of frontier pacification. Ecclesiastical missions gradually led Europeans into zones inhabited by Indians and frequently paved the way for the subsequent arrival of settlers. This enabled the Portuguese to occupy the vast interior of the South American continent.[35]

Moving farther and farther into the interior of Brazil, Jesuit missionaries encountered peoples of the Gê, Arawak, and Guaraní language groups, and they seized or enticed these different nomadic peoples into mission settlements. Sometimes the natives welcomed such missions as refuge against long-distance slave raiders. On other occasions they were coerced or seduced into joining by members of a friendly nearby tribe specially trained for that purpose. Unlike the British settlement of North America, in which armed (secular) settlers occupied regions and expelled the aboriginal inhabitants, these missions transformed the natives into sedentary farmers.[36]

But the missions frequently used coercion to change natives' agricultural practices. Inhabitants of the aboriginal communities of Brazil were entirely nomadic cultivators and hunters, but Portuguese religious guardians forced them to plow and weed sugar and tobacco fields and to herd cattle.[37] Failure to rise at a regular hour or to perform farm tasks in a particular order frequently led to whippings or a loss of rations.

Natives were required to adopt other changes connected to their Christianization. Western European Christian definitions of kinship set the guidelines for choosing marriage partners and defined to whom natives could leave their possessions. Just as in Spanish America, these alterations fundamentally restructured natives' status, roles, and rules for marriage and other relationships.

Using mission villages to convert natives left little of the original communities' customs intact. Brazil's Indians were required to adopt European dress, because their indigenous costumes failed to live up to missionaries' standards of decency. Their traditional leaders were replaced by Jesuits, and traditional authorities undercut. Even their language was altered, as Jesuits taught mission natives a simplified version of their language, one that made the Jesuits' task easier. But the most fundamentally destructive aspect of the Jesuit missions was their relocation of native peoples. In removing Indians from their traditional lands, Jesuits destroyed the material basis of these cultures.[38] Removed from the environment in which traditional cultural routines made sense, many other cultural behaviors and knowledge disappeared as well.

Jesuit missions' lengthy reeducation of the natives in the rhythms of sedentary agriculture eventually transformed a number of hunter-gatherers and nomadic cultivators into sedentary herders and farmers. Their success led other missionary orders—notably the Carmelites and Franciscans—to attempt to establish mission villages. Although several of these missions failed, there were notable successes (from the missionaries' point of view), particularly in the Amazon.[39]

But the Jesuits, the originators of the mission villages, were the most successful and the most profitable. In some regions of the country, notably the north, Jesuit missions using Indian labor were highly profitable exporters of cattle products and sugar. This economic success, however, excited considerable jealousy. Settlers held public protests against the Jesuits, who denied them access to Indians capable of laboring on farms and cattle ranches. They accused the Jesuits of hypocrisy, of selfishly exploiting the labor of the Indians whom they were presumably defending. When protests failed to achieve the desired results, Portuguese settlers took to raiding the missions for slave labor. They found a ready market and obtained high prices for mission-educated Indians because of their familiarity with agricultural labor.

By the second decade of the seventeenth century, settlers were convinced that they should be allowed to use Jesuit-trained laborers in their own agricultural and ranching operations without resorting to force. The level of settler protest increased until the crown was obliged to act. Beginning in 1609, the king insisted that mission villagers were obligated to work for settlers. Some of these newly proficient laborers, cowboys, and shepherds were to be allocated among the settlers from that time forward. Natives who formerly worked only for the missions had to be rotated out for work on the settlers' plantations and pastures. Natives were thus torn between two different sets of economic interests, the Jesuits' and the settlers', both of which for them, in the long run, were equally deadly.

Despite their formal rights of access, settlers in Brazil remained intensely jealous of the Jesuits' control over native labor. Their resentment was fueled by their observation that in otherwise economically marginal areas, such as the Amazon, the Jesuits were far more prosperous than the colonists, successfully producing hides and sugar for the international market.[40] Thinking that they would enjoy the same profits as the Jesuits once they had access to the same labor, these settlers clamored for the Jesuits' ouster. Their hostility united with anti-Jesuit sentiment sweeping Catholic Europe in the mid-eighteenth century and resulted in the order's expulsion from France, Spain, and Portugal, as well as their overseas colonies. Their early expulsion from Brazil in 1760 was hastened by the Jesuits' providing military help to the Guaranís, who were revolting against their transfer from Portuguese to Spanish control in 1750.[41]

Expelling the Jesuits from Brazil did not guarantee settlers a steady stream of sedentary laborers, for only the Jesuits had prepared practitioners of nomadic agriculture for the rigors of more sedentary farming. In 1760, upon their expulsion, the Jesuits' two-hundred-year-old training program for agricultural apprentices was turned over to an indifferent secular leadership called the "directorate of protected Indians." Secular directors were to allocate native labor for the hunting, canoeing, and gathering tasks for which settlers had always wanted native labor and knowledge. But lacking any long-term ambitions—such as conversion—that would have sustained the level of patience required to transform hunter-gatherers into farm laborers and herders, the directorate system swiftly failed. At the end of the eighteenth century, it was formally abolished and replaced with a similarly intentioned "model village" system that also swiftly faltered.[42]

In the middle of the nineteenth century, the Portuguese monarch, now based in Brazil, decided to school hunter-gatherers in farm and pastoral labor. Opting to combine secular leadership with long-term religious presence, the crown instituted state-run missions. But creating such missions where large numbers of uncontacted natives resided meant introducing the diseases to which isolated natives had always been vulnerable. Without a systematic approach to controlling and preventing the spread of disease, or even a system of replacing the natives who had died, illness wiped out those whom the government had been attempting to contact. As a result, this hybrid system collapsed at the end of the nineteenth century.[43]

Portuguese settlers cited natives' cannibalism as their rationale for enslaving natives. However, the excuse of cannibalism could not serve to rationalize settling natives in mission villages. Therefore the Portuguese missionaries characterized natives as primarily lacking religion and secondarily lacking recognizable government and identifiable political rules—characteristics that enabled them to employ natives as laborers while instructing them in Christianity.

One of the earliest missionaries to Brazil, Manuel da Nóbrega, declared that the Gentiles (Indians) lacked laws. He asserted that following laws and a chain of command were fundamental to individuals' being what he termed reasonable members of a civil society.[44] His complaints about the absence of clear-cut political rules among the natives of Brazil were repeated frequently over the next two centuries. In the seventeenth century, Diogo de Campos Moreno observed, "The true natural liberty of vassals . . . appears impossible in . . . Brazil . . . because the gentiles [Indians] appear so inconstant, incapable, and beyond authority."[45]

An even more popular Portuguese criticism was that the natives' languages were the reason for their lack of both a readily identifiable political hierarchy and a religious faith. Pêro de Magalhães de Gândavo stated: "The language of the Gentiles along the coast is the same. It lacks three letters. One does not find in it 'f' nor 'l' nor 'r' something worthy of astonishment because thus they have no faith nor law nor King and in thus live without justice or order [Não tem fé, nem lei, nem Rei]."[46] Gabriel Soares de Sousa exclaimed:

> They lack three letters of the alphabet, which are F, L, R. . . . They have no truth, no loyalty, and no one who does the right thing. And if they do not have L in their accent it is because they do not have any law to keep, nor precepts to govern themselves, and each one makes laws to suit themselves and their own wishes. Without laws among themselves, they do not have laws regarding others. And if they do not have R in their accent, it is because they do not have a king [*rei*] to rule them and whom they obey. They obey no one. The son does not obey the father, nor the father the son and each one lives according to his own will.[47]

These Portuguese critics were not entirely accurate, because none of the peoples they criticized had a written language. Therefore they lacked only the sounds represented by the letters *F, L,* and *R.* But citing such linguistic shortcomings allowed the Portuguese to attack native societies that were impeding their colonial ambitions. Portugese observers identified the lack of the *F* sound as indicating lack of faith, which meant that the peoples of eastern South America lacked a readily recognizable body of religious doctrine. Friars could not use arguments concerning native gods or forms of worship in persuading natives to convert. The deficit in the *L* sound, which Portuguese identified with the paucity of law, meant that they could not seek an economic deal with one member of the tribe and expect all the others to agree to an identical deal. Rather, they had to negotiate separately with different tribal members or families. Finally, the lack of the *R* sound, which they identified as a lack of a king (*rei*), meant that the Tupi group did not have a powerful political hierarchy capable of compelling followers to meet European demands.

By targeting these deficiencies in the natives' languages, Portuguese colonists in effect were complaining about the absence of particular customs among natives that had facilitated their expeditions to Africa and Asia, where Portuguese traders and colonists bypassed communities not producing marketable surpluses. In Brazil, the Portuguese had no such option. Constrained by an international agreement to a limited territory, colonists found the task of mobilizing natives to produce large surpluses far more arduous than that their countrymen had encountered outside the Americas.[48]

Juxtapositions

English criticisms of the North American peoples did not dwell on the natives' rules of law, religious faiths, or political hierarchies, nor did they target native languages. John Eliot noted that the eastern woodlands tribes used the letter sounds for *N* or *L* or *R*, but not all three. Roger Williams's extensive 1643 word list does not even mention the absent sounds.[49] Furthermore, neither Puritan drew any inferences about any specific native society's lack of "laws" because of the absence of *L* or absence of "respect" because of the lack of *R* sounds. Nor would later settlers denounce the prairie natives because their languages lacked the *F, V, Q,* and *K* sounds. Nor were the Northwest coast natives (Tlingit, Haida) criticized because their languages also lacked an *R* sound.[50] English colonists made relatively few observations on the sounds of native languages, and their observations, like those of the Puritans, were delivered neutrally—that is, without rendering a negative judgment about natives.

Nor did Spaniards note such distinctions. Yucatec Maya, the language of Cortés's female translator, Malinche, lacked the *R*, whereas Quiche, the language of highland Guatemala, lacked the *F.* In addition to lacking the

R, classical Nahua, the language of Aztec empire, also lacked the F and L.[51] All of these highly structured communities were able to provide Spaniards with the labor they needed, so Spanish colonists did not need to criticize language sounds to justify their goals.

Dictionaries of native languages were also rare in English colonies. At most, word lists contained limited vocabularies designed to facilitate contact or trade with native people.[52] By contrast, Iberian colonizers—Portuguese and Spanish alike—produced a veritable flood of dictionaries and grammar books. However, those Iberians who mastered native dialects were motivated by their ambitions to change natives' spiritual direction.

On the other hand, Portuguese settlers rarely, if ever, mentioned the gendered division of labor, the "lazy" men ("hunters") and farming women ("drudges"), that dominated English complaints about similar nomadic cultivators. Nor did they complain, as More did, that natives "wasted" their land.[53]

The terrain itself failed to inspire rapture among Portuguese colonists. There were neither paeans to uninhabited domains nor reverent portraits of untouched landscapes. Rather, virgin terrains were uninhabited and hence most often disparagingly dismissed as "deserted," that is, unpopulated and hence worthless. Only the prospect of gold, discovered in the interior of the state of Rio de Janeiro in the eighteenth century, could incite any enthusiasm for the terrain among Portuguese-speaking colonists.

Although Portuguese colonizers shared a common framework with Spaniards, using accusations of cannibalism among nomadic peoples to justify their enslavement and using labor to punish them, there were distinctive aspects to the Portuguese conception of the cultural boundary separating Europeans and natives. Spaniards permitted sedentary natives to own and inherit their traditional land in exchange for dressing as "Indians," paying tribute, and deferring publicly to Spaniards. But the Luso-American mission system preserved neither traditional native lands nor traditional inheritance rules. Hence natives in Portuguese America lost more land than did their counterparts in Spanish America because Jesuits, not native communities, held title to lands in indigenous areas.[54]

Furthermore, natives under Jesuit rule had to adopt Portuguese dress, because the clerics deemed the skimpy coverings of many aboriginal peoples too scandalous for public wear. Hence Luso-American natives were never strictly required to maintain traditional native dress, the readily visible indicator of distinction demanded by Spanish colonists.

Portuguese society and its leaders showed greater willingness to accept the racially mixed Catholic offspring of Iberian men and native women than did their counterparts in the Spanish-speaking world. In the second half of the eighteenth century, Spanish-American officials described unofficial rules requiring at least two generations to pass before offspring of native ancestry could be accepted as Spanish.[55] In Portuguese America this generational rule was far less salient. From the sixteenth century forward, the first racially mixed generation occupied politically, economically, and militarily influential positions in Brazil, albeit not without opposition.

Attitudes toward such racially mixed offspring even more strongly distinguished Portuguese from English colonists. The colonies of both groups had extensive geographic borders where many men served as intermediaries between European and native societies. Among the English colonists, however, many of these intermediaries were derogatorily called "Indian lovers," and their racially mixed offspring were marginalized from English society. The Portuguese crown, on the opposite side, consistently promoted marriage between the lower levels of Lusitanian society and native women, hoping to further native political and military allegiance to Portugal among the native communities.[56] But the sexual relationships that the crown promoted only enabled Portuguese men to have sexual dealings with native women. The possibility of sexual interaction between native men and Portuguese women did not enter into any discussion of interracial sex. Hence there was a tacit cultural acceptance of Portuguese men coercing native women into sexual relations. The acceptance of the offspring into Portuguese society depended largely upon the whim of the father.[57]

By contrast, English suspicion of racially mixed offspring appeared to reflect if not a taboo, at least a politically sensitive issue. Indeed, the earliest English bans on intermarriage between natives and colonists dated to the fourteenth-century statutes of Kilkenny, which prohibited marriage between English colonists and native Irish. These prohibitions were based on fears of political and military betrayal by the intermarried and their offspring.[58] In these statutes Englishmen seemed to interpret sexual relations with natives as a sign of likely political disloyalty. Accordingly, any racially mixed offspring were denied a place in English society.

In the New World, ambivalence rather than outright prohibition of such relationships prevailed. The Virginia colony passed laws in 1662 prohibiting Englishmen as well as Englishwomen from having sex with natives. But as Africans began to arrive in increasing numbers and natives physically receded from the edges of English colonial settlements, English colonial laws increasingly forbade interracial sex with blacks rather than Indians.

Some English colonists, as well as early national leaders such as Thomas Jefferson, remained attracted to a romantic myth of intermarriage with natives. The myth was portrayed in the popular Pocahontas legend, about an Indian girl who married an Englishman. In the frontier communities, however, hostility toward such unions prevailed over romance.[59]

In contrast, Portuguese officials deliberately recruited the offspring of Portuguese men and native women for military expeditions, slave raids against their maternal tribes' enemies, and scouting. Consequently, the offspring of Portuguese-Indian unions were accepted, albeit often with considerable jealousy, provided their military allegiance remained with Portugal and, of course, provided they did not commit the unpardonable sin of converting to native religions.[60]

Catholicism, even if only nominally adopted, and military loyalty when faced with other native or foreign attacks were of greater importance in the acceptance of racially mixed offspring than the natives' physical appearance or dress. And if Portuguese looks and religion were altered somewhat by racially mixed offspring, Lusitanian leaders remained certain that a European model of ideal religious rituals would be the standard.

The final clear distinction between Iberians and English colonizers lies in the categories of natives that the two groups enslaved. After the initial conquests, Iberians largely enslaved nomadic peoples, whereas English colonists principally enslaved sedentary natives. But the two were more similar than it would at first appear. Both Iberians and Englishmen enslaved the natives who represented the greatest obstacles to their respective economic interests. Iberians enslaved nomadic Indians who would not labor for them; Englishmen enslaved sedentary natives who would not abandon the land the English coveted.[61]

9

Fast Forward: The Impact of Independence

on Colonial Structures

Independence from Spain and England occurred roughly during the same period for most of North and South America, but the new citizens' attitudes toward their former colonizers differed strikingly. North of the tropic of Capricorn, independent Americans embraced the cultural traits—accents and social attitudes—of their former colonizers. South of this tropic, Americans initially rejected both. The key to the different attitudes toward their former overlords resides in the timing of the nations' independence.

By the time self-rule began, Spain, the dominant colonial power in the Americas during the sixteenth and seventeenth centuries, was gradually declining in power, wealth, and importance. As a result, leaders of the new Spanish-speaking nations rejected many traditional Iberian policies, including subjugated communities and their payment of tribute—the two central features of Native American life. By the eighteenth century, tribute was supplying a negligible amount of royal income, despite officials' herculean efforts to increase the contributions. Within a decade or two of independence, tribute collection ceased permanently, thus also terminating the rituals of humiliation to which Native Americans had been subject.[1]

The new attitudes toward native people reflected ideals of assimilation and the idea that natives and former colonists alike were to form the new Spanish-American nations.

By liberating subject native communities, however, newly independent Spanish-American nations also eliminated the historic protection of communally owned lands. Organized assaults began as large holders systematically confiscated communal lands through the end of the nineteenth century. Over time, these widespread private attacks on communal terrain became immensely unpopular. Nineteenth-century Spanish Americans found much to dislike about these seizures, including the loss of native traditions and the stranglehold wealthy landowners came to have on the economy. Virtually everywhere in Spanish-speaking America, restoring communal native ownership grew increasingly popular in the final decades of the nineteenth century, and by the start of the twentieth century traditional Indian ownership of surface land was restored throughout most of the former Ibero-America.[2]

One key colonial custom, however, survived independence substantially unaltered: the shared ownership of valuable minerals. Although guardianship passed from the crown to the nation, the fundamental principles remained unchanged. Laws governing ownership and exploration of mineral deposits remained separate from those governing surface land. The Hispanic community owned all valuable mineral deposits. Only communal ownership of petroleum was ever questioned.

Not long before independence, the Spanish monarch included petroleum products in the category of resources that belonged to the dominant community. However, under pressure from increasingly powerful landowners, two independent former Iberian colonies—Mexico and Brazil—briefly experimented with leaving petroleum in private hands.[3] But such private ownership quickly became politically unpopular, and public ownership was reinstated in the 1917 Mexican Constitution. In 1931 the president of Brazil, Getulio Vargas, reasserted federal control over the exploration of mineral resources in his country with the widely hailed slogan "The petroleum is ours."[4]

Whereas nineteenth-century Spanish Americans strove to eliminate vestiges of colonial policies, English-speaking U.S. citizens did not, in part because Britain was becoming unprecedentedly successful in its colonial endeavors. An international bit player in the competition for empires during the sixteenth and seventeenth centuries, Britain (followed by France) in the nineteenth century became the dominant world colonial power.

England and the Wider World

In the nineteenth century, England enjoyed a recently successful pattern of overseas colonization. New naval expertise allowed it to expand its colonial empire to corners of the globe nearly impossible to reach before. Innovations in shipbuilding and clock making made it possible for nineteenth-century Englishmen to dominate the maritime routes to the Americas and Asia that they had been unable to navigate—let alone control—at the dawn of the sixteenth century. As a result, Englishmen could colonize places as far away as Kenya in East Africa, India in South Asia, Australia, New Zealand, and much of Polynesia.

To each of these areas Englishmen brought the same cultural understandings of economic objectives and rationales for colonial rule as had prevailed earlier in the Americas. Land remained the principal objective of colonization, the rationale of occupying "waste land" was invoked to justify occupation, *waste* was identified with relatively unoccupied terrain, and ritualized hunting remained a central means of demonstrating superior status over indigenous inhabitants.

The traditional English preoccupation with land appeared overseas in places as diverse as densely packed India and more sparsely inhabited Polynesia. Unable to make sense of the traditional patterns of landownership in the Indian subcontinent, Englishmen perfected the science of land survey during the nineteenth century and successfully standardized property information.[5] Laws regulating property transfers were among the first pieces of colonial legislation Englishmen introduced on the subcontinent, and the 1891 Land Settlement Act had considerable impact on ownership patterns.

The British were equally preoccupied with land in the Pacific. In the Polynesian islands of Vanuatu, English colonists introduced their own land system, which favored physical occupation over title. In Fiji, British colonists also centralized the process of alienating natives from their land, using a system first established in Australia.[6]

English colonists frequently used their traditional American distinction between laborer and hunter to justify their new colonial occupation. English courts in nineteenth-century India consistently granted preference to farmers over hunters in adjudicating disputes between local litigants.[7] The greater moral legitimacy of farming over hunting was inserted into colonial laws in Australia (South Australian Constitution Act of 1834), India (Waste Lands Rule of 1863), and Uganda (during the establishment of the British protectorate in 1901).[8]

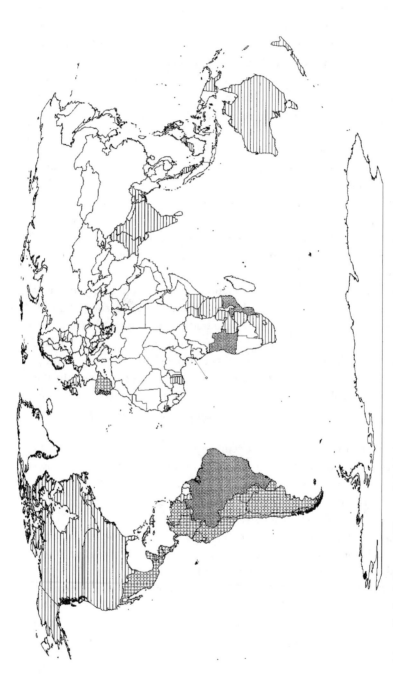

Map 2. England, Spain, and Portugal's legal systems in the wider world. The pattern of horizontal lines shows former colonies of England; the pattern of white diamonds represents former colonies of Spain; and the pattern of dense black dots shows former colonies of Portugal.

In nineteenth-century Africa, Englishmen also made derogatory statements about indigenous hunting. Eastern and southern Africa's nomadic peoples, who hunted for food, were classified as "wild" people who lived "upon the produce of their herds and by the chase and foray." Semipastoral groups were labeled "primitive" and "wild."[9] Nineteenth- and twentieth-century English courts in Australia held that aborigines neither tilled the soil nor enclosed their lands; hence they could not legitimately possess territory.[10] As in the Americas, these characterizations formed part of the rationale for English colonial authority: Englishmen "labored"—that is, they created ownership rights—whereas those whom they colonized did not.

Waste

In many places in Africa and Asia, English colonizers continued to use their classic sixteenth-century interpretation of "waste" land to justify nineteenth- and twentieth-century expropriation of native land. English colonists invoked the idea that they were making more profitable use of land than were the natives in India and Uganda.[11] In nineteenth-century Canada, the Hudson's Bay Company ordered, "All other [noncultivated, nonresidential] land [in British Columbia] is to be regarded as waste, and applicable to the purposes of colonization."[12] In 1953, the Maori Affairs Act declared that if native terrain was not being occupied or used, then it was "waste land" and could be expropriated by the government of New Zealand. A British Columbia trial court judge declared that land claimed by the Gitksan or Wet'suwet'en was unoccupied or vacant land.[13] Nineteenth- and twentieth-century Canadians, Australians, and New Zealanders accepted and used the sixteenth-century English definition of the term *waste land*: it meant that the natives were failing to populate the terrain sufficiently and were failing to make the most profitable and productive use of the land.[14] However, the English understanding that *waste* meant underpopulation was dramatically altered shortly before settlers arrived in Australia, a territory, like Brazil, inhabited entirely by hunter-gatherers.

An eminent legal scholar, William Blackstone, in 1765 transformed the traditional English understanding of *waste* into a colonial legal fiction that such land was unowned. He called this fiction *terra nullius* (literally, land of no one, land belonging to no one). However, Blackstone falsely implied that this cultural concept had a Latin origin.[15]

Blackstone actually took a late Roman law regarding hunted animals, which were not viewed as private property, and used it as a "source" to justify the English concept that relative underpopulation justified seizing land.[16] *Terra nullius* exaggerated the English proclivity to interpret unbounded, nonplowed, and sparsely settled areas as "waste" or "common" land by proclaiming that such land belonged to no one.[17]

Treaty

During the nineteenth century, treaties joined *terra nullius* as a popular colonists' rationale for, or means of acquiring, aboriginals' land.[18] Written documentation (treaties) became an increasingly popular means of acquiring aboriginals' land in both former and actual English colonies during the nineteenth century. That trend, begun in the Americas at the start of the eighteenth century, gained momentum during the nineteenth.[19] Much of the territory of Canada was acquired during the nineteenth century through a series of numbered treaties.[20] In New Zealand, Britain signed a written treaty in 1840 with the native Maoris.

One of the greatest differences among formerly English colonies concerns treaties, or written surrenders of native land. In Australia, no treaties were signed. In Canada and the United States, governments signed multiple written agreements, largely because they had to reach separate agreements with different tribes speaking multiple languages and having distinct leadership. Great Britain only had to sign a single treaty—that of Waitangi—in 1840, because the same people, the Maori, occupied both the North and South Island of New Zealand.

In addition to invoking underpopulation, underutilization, and treaties as they had in the Americas, nineteenth- and twentieth-century English colonists brought to new colonies their traditional understanding of large-game hunting as the social prerogative of colonizers.

English Hunting and Colonial Rule in Africa and Asia

In Africa, Englishmen re-created aristocratic hunting rituals to express social superiority. The highly structured and costly hunting ceremony Englishmen created in Africa was named a safari. For safaris, English colonial overlords—like Norman conquerors in eleventh-century England—reserved the largest game for themselves.[21] But in Kenya, Rhodesia, and South Africa, they pursued lions instead of deer.

Intricate social rituals were also re-created in India. The elephant replaced the horse, and the tiger substituted for the fox on raj safaris, highly staged and elaborate ceremonies of hunting. As in the aristocratic English past, sport hunting privileged class over gender. Englishwomen joined Englishmen on the African and South Asian safaris well into the twentieth century.

Sport hunting was another example of the British exporting their culture to newly colonized areas. Because independence only replaced English-speaking overlords born in Britain with those born in the Americas, the newly independent citizens of the United States took many cues from their former British overlords when dealing with aboriginal peoples. Sometimes these foundational British attitudes reappeared under different names—such as "frontier"—but faith in the cultural underpinnings of these rationales did not falter.

America and Britain's Wider Colonial World

The newly independent United States neither eliminated nor recast the basic fiscal and political structures governing aboriginal peoples. Instead, the basic trends of English colonial rule persisted and even paralleled those of the British during the nineteenth century, making continuities in the treatment of aboriginal people between colonial and national eras far more pronounced in the history of the United States. Leaders of the new nation continued the formerly English colonial practice of deriding natives for their communal landownership, categorizing them as men and as "hunters," and identifying their own practices as belonging to "history."

The identification of labor as God-given and riches the rightful result of "labor" survived the transition to independence. Francis Wayland, president of Brown University and a popular nineteenth-century author, wrote, "God has created man with physical and intellectual facilities, adapted to labor. . . . And . . . God has assigned to industry, rich and abundant rewards."[22] Wayland explained why possessing money (which he declared represented labor) justified depriving Native Americans of financial rewards: "The advantages which we enjoy over savage nations result principally from the possession of a greater amount of fixed capital; or, in other words, the permanent results of pre-exerted industry."[23]

In 1823, U.S. Supreme Court Chief Justice John Marshall also defined Indians as nonworkers, "fierce savages whose occupation was war, and whose subsistence was drawn chiefly from the forest."[24] Indians were thus formally classified as hunters or warriors, chasing animals or humans, their presence incompatible in either instance with farming and, far more important, incompatible with landownership. "The North American Indians could have acquired no proprietary interest in the vast tracts of territory which they wandered over; [or] . . . the land on which they hunted," declared Justice Marshall.[25]

Just like their nineteenth-century British counterparts overseas, U.S. officials also increasingly signed written agreements—treaties—to transfer land to the United States. The government initialed hundreds of treaties with aboriginal groups throughout the country.

While U.S. citizens continued using the same or even identical political rationales to expropriate land as British imperialists were employing in other parts of the globe, they also continued to believe the core colonial myth—that native Americans, and their way of life, were permanently part of an earlier period.

Vanishing into History

John Locke's statement that "in the beginning all the world was America" had relegated native peoples to the past. It placed their lives and land-ownership patterns into a narrative of English history. By transforming sixteenth-century English historical trends into the universal human past—the beginning of the *world*—Locke established the intellectual foundation of the legend of the vanishing Native American. Native Americans would disappear because their communal ownership of property represented an earlier stage of human development that could only and inevitably be replaced by individual possession and farming. Former president John Quincy Adams delivered a lecture in 1840 titled "The Progress of Society from the Hunter State to That of Civilization" in which he repeated this English narrative as "universal" history. He declared: "Man is first a hunter with no fixed habitation. His abode [is] the forest with its intricate mazes and dark caverns . . . then he becomes a shepherd and then a husbandman."[26]

The early works of national history carefully placed the Indian in the past. Works such as Jeremy Belknap's *History of New Hampshire*, Samuel Williams's *Natural and Civil History of Vermont*, Robert Proud's *History of Pennsylvania*, and Ezekiel Sanford's *History of the United States before the Revolution* all relegated natives to history.[27] As Roy Pearce has noted, the Indians belonged "in the American past and [were] socially and morally significant only as part of that past."[28]

The popular belief that native property would inevitably give way to English-style individual possession appeared in other statements as well. Senator Henry Dawes in 1883 said of America's natives, "They have got as far as they can go, because they own their land in common. . . . there is no enterprise to make your [Indian] home better than that of your neigh-bor's."[29] Although successful Cherokee planters had, in fact, proved the contrary true, U.S. citizens wanted to believe that communal property was incompatible with profit making, for this would mean that community ownership would inevitably give way to private holding. Both the fading of natives' forms of land tenure into "history" and their relatively small numbers remained enormously popular topics with American readers.

During the nineteenth and twentieth centuries, an immense literature on "vanishing" Indians flourished, confirming the rights of U.S. settlers to occupy the West because its original inhabitants were physically vanish-ing, making "a ground relatively uninhabited."[30] Even if disappearing natives were an illusion, they were an American reverie that extended beyond literature to both the law and language. In an 1823 case involving sedentary Cherokees, U.S. Supreme Court Chief Justice John Marshall declared that as more and more land was placed under cultivation, "the game fled into thicker and more unbroken forests, and the Indians fol-lowed."[31] The Michigan territorial governor in 1830 declared in terms vir-tually identical to Marshall's that "as the cultivated border approaches the haunts of the animals . . . they [Native Americans] recede and seek shelter in less accessible situations."[32] Thus the desire to have natives simply dis-appear into the forests or into other inaccessible places became expressed in these legal fantasies.[33]

In portraying the West, national officials depicted a scenic, uninhab-ited landscape. The word *waste* appeared frequently in U.S.-published textbooks and geographies in the 1830s and 1840s.[34] As historian Clyde Milner II notes, "Between 1840 and 1863 more than 700 prints of western scenes . . . appeared in government reports."[35] Millions of copies of these reports were printed. Thus in both words and images, the West was com-monly portrayed as containing large quantities of uninhabited land. Because the absence of people constituted traditional grounds (in English history) for seizing land, the visual representation of the West minus its peoples corresponded to one of the classic English-language meanings of *waste land.*

When presented with a land visually and verbally represented as "un-inhabited," U.S. colonizers established their claims by fencing, with or without the natives' consent.[36] Even when occupying regions where wood was rare and hedges would not grow, settlers in the United States found means by which they could reenact the reassuringly familiar English pat-tern of enclosing "common" or unfenced land, even though they argued with each other about whose responsibility it was to fence.[37] Barbed wire, which was invented in the 1870s, spread like wildfire through the American West because it allowed a culturally familiar and reassuring process to continue.[38]

During the nineteenth century, the word *frontier* in English acquired a new association. In all the other European languages in which a form of the word exists—French (*frontière*), Spanish (*frontera*), Portuguese (*fronteira*), and Italian (*frontiera*)—the term simply refers to a boundary or limit fronting on another territory.[39] British English shares this meaning of *frontier*. But during the nineteenth century in the United States and Australia, *frontier* came to mean a dividing line separating populated from relatively underpopulated regions.[40] As both societies proceeded with their slow, long-term dispossession of aboriginal peoples, their respective citizens began to use the word *frontier* to imply that they were occupying relatively uninhabited terrain. In nineteenth-century Australian and U.S. English the word *frontier* insinuated that the takeover of land on the other side of the frontier was legitimate because aboriginal or native territory was comparatively uninhabited. Thus in U.S. and Australian English the word *frontier* itself reflected English-speaking settlers' beliefs that they were entitled to take over relatively unpeopled land because in *their* cultural heritage such reasons were valid.[41] In New Zealand, the pioneer settlers' stories were retold in terms of a battle against the frontier environment, which shifted attention from the conquest of the Maori and focused on the conquest of nature.[42]

Scholarship in the postcolonial (independent) United States has not been exempt from the common cultural practice of equating *frontier* with population differences.[43] Because population differences are believed to justify occupation, U.S. scholars have (consciously or unconsciously) consistently underestimated Native American population densities in North America prior to European arrival.[44] The most famous scholarly example comes from the well-known historian Frederick Jackson Turner. When arguing that the American frontier no longer existed, Turner invoked the data most likely to convince U.S. readers of his position. He cited population densities measured by census tracts.[45] Thus his choice of facts— relative population—relied upon assumptions embedded in the culture and language he shared with those he was hoping to persuade. Only in formerly English colonial societies did settlers rationalize their land possession this way.[46]

Americans also regretted the loss of what they understood themselves to be destroying, the vanishing American commons. This paradoxical yearning for what they were exterminating, aptly termed "imperial nostalgia" by

Renato Rosaldo, became fashionable at the end of the nineteenth century just as the American public perceived the nation's "uninhabited" landscape to be disappearing.[47] Once a relatively insignificant political concern, conservation became enormously popular with the public. Middle-class Americans wanted to spend time in uninhabited spaces, sometimes seeking such activity in highly structured forms, such as scouting.[48] But in order for them to be able to experience the uninhabited landscape, it had to be re-created.

At the start of the twentieth century, the federal government transformed vast reaches of the western United States into a set of national commons.[49] Yellowstone became the first national park when a group of Montana tourists decided they wanted to secure a permanent pleasure ground.[50] The National Park Service and the National Forest Service (created in 1897 and 1916, respectively) were charged with preserving the all-but-lost commons as shared national possessions.[51] Neither the place nor the timing of these moves is coincidental. The government re-created great American commons in the West on the land where Americans once imagined natives held vast quantities of terrain in common, and at a time when the populace feared such land had disappeared.[52]

But imperial nostalgia does not lead, nor has it ever led, to reconsideration of the rights of those dispossessed from their commons. In 1998, the U.S. government continued to insist that the Shoshone Dann sisters not graze their animals in the commons, as had their parents and ancestors before them, because the commons can belong only to the federal (nonnative) government. Nostalgia fails to shake contemporary Americans' belief in their right to seize all open spaces. Even today this longing for the commons fails to alter beliefs that forbid natives to own their "commons," the fictive place to which they were assigned by the arrival of "history." Nostalgia only allows American citizens an outlet for their ambivalent sentiments about the loss of what they destroyed.

Modern Americans do not see the West today as teeming with "the invisible dead." They do not lament the time when natives "covered the land as the waves of a wind-ruffled sea cover its shell-paved floor." Nor do they sense, as Chief Seattle reportedly informed the settlers, that

> the very dust upon which you now stand responds more lovingly to [natives'] footsteps than yours, because it is rich with the blood of our ancestors. . . . [For] when your children's children think themselves alone in the field, the store, the shop, upon the highway, or in the silence of the pathless woods, they will not be alone. . . . At night when the streets of

your cities and villages are silent and you think them deserted, they will throng with the returning hosts that once filled them."[53]

Americans regret only what Englishmen regretted in England—the loss of shared common land. They regret the land, already stripped of people they do not wish to remember.

10

Continuities: Colonial Language and Images Today

In Africa and Asia, most decolonization occurred when native peoples led costly fights that forced Europeans to withdraw. In the Americas, however, the descendants of European colonizers led the independence movements. Had a similar anticolonial revolution occurred in India, it would have been the British Raj, not Gandhi, who led the revolt against English rule beginning in the 1920s.[1]

Nowhere in this hemisphere did Native American–led uprisings overthrow the descendants of Europeans. Nor were they likely to do so, for the aboriginal inhabitants were nearly extinguished by the arrival of Europeans. Even when their communities gradually began to recover after the first devastating hundred years, indigenous groups were forced to reconstitute themselves economically, culturally, and politically under the eagle eye of their colonial overlords. These twin factors have meant that where aboriginal populations were decimated, the postindependence status of native peoples differs markedly from that in regions of Africa and Asia where natives did not suffer such catastrophic population losses. The possibilities of reversing the colonial past have been virtually nonexistent in areas devastated by disease.

Athough descendants of conquerors made themselves politically independent of their European overseers in the Americas, they did not return the central valuable asset they or their predecessors had seized. Unlike African and Asian postindependence leaders, leaders of the United States did not return land to Native Americans, nor did Iberian leaders return mineral deposits to Indians. Rather, the leaders and the citizens of each of the independent American states continued to claim the same resources as had their colonial predecessors. Independence made it easier to abandon financially costly policies such as the collection of tribute in Spanish America, but newly independent settlers discarded neither the objectives nor the political traditions that had justified the colonizers' economic activities. Furthermore, they justified such seizures with the same political and legal language and partial fictions about natives as had their predecessors.

In former English and former Iberian colonies of the Americas, this continuation rested foremost on permanence in the language of politics and law. The political language of all these independent states was (and still is) that of the original colonizers, not the native inhabitants. Citizens of the United States realize their public discussions in English, not Algonquian or Dineh. Citizens of Mexico and Peru likewise carry out their political debates in Spanish, not Quechua or Nahua. The language of the courts in each of these nations also remains that of the colonizers. Decisions from the U.S. Supreme Court appear in English and those of the High Court of Argentina appear only in Spanish. Neither lawyers nor judges in either country question the cultural meanings that their words imply. Consequently, when using long-standing expressions about Native Americans, present-day lawyers, judges, and citizens, intentionally or not, often carry forward meanings created by the colonizers.

The Former English Colonies

In the English-speaking Americas, the most important long-term continuity resides in the meaning of the word *improvement*. English-speaking colonists used the term *improvement* to mean that their actions (unlike the Indians') increased the land's profit-making capacity. This usage exists today, and in contemporary U.S. courts it retains that meaning exclusively. A guide to basic U.S. legal categories declares, "Generally speaking, the word 'improvement' includes everything that permanently enhances the value of the premises."[2] U.S. courts use *improvement* only to mean "a valuable addition made to property," one that enhances its profits and its resale value.[3]

Contemporary American legal dictionaries also continue to define the means of achieving such profitability or *improvement* in terms that would have been familiar to the colonists—the expenditure of labor or capital on land. "Among the most common illustrations of such general improvements are . . . the clearing and draining of land—the preparation of land for building sites—the preparation of wild or raw land for agricultural purposes."[4] Fencing, which played a significant role in establishing claims to what is now the United States, still remains part of the legal definitions of improvement.[5]

Waste, a popular seventeenth-century word that described native land use, has new meanings in addition to its original significance. Although *waste* now also means "refuse" or "trash"—as it did not in the seventeenth century—the original core meanings of "unproductive" and "unprofitable" remain. Books about the "waste" or lack of profitable use for land appear throughout the popular and academic landscape. And the dispossession of native peoples because their land is "waste" still continues in the contemporary Americas.[6]

The concept that relatively underpopulated land equals "waste" land also remains popular. Only the most extreme reformulation of this idea— William Blackstone's fictitious *terra nullius*—has ever been abandoned by a former colony. In 1992, Australia's High Court decisively rejected this justification for the English takeover of aboriginal land. The growing world-wide popularity of aboriginal art made many contemporary Australians profoundly uncomfortable with Blackstone's claim that the land had no inhabitants capable of ownership. Acknowledging the prior existence of aborigines on the continent had become imperative.

Closely linked to the assumption that natives let land lie "waste" was cultural reasoning that justified occupation of the New World because Native Americans did not "labor." Such thinking persists. In the most recent writing on the subject of legal possession, Carol M. Rose declares, "The common law of first possession [i.e., English law] . . . *does* reward useful labor," adding that Indians had "never done acts on the land sufficient to establish property in it. That is to say, the Indians had never really taken those acts of possession that give rise to a property right."[7] Although her insight into contemporary U.S. law is accurate,[8] Rose's perception that natives did not perform "useful" labor relies upon highly culture-specific conceptions that have survived the passage of centuries. Natives were engaged in subsistence, feeding their families, and later occasionally producing trade goods for a European market. All of these certainly constituted "useful" labor. But, as Rose declares, these were not "acts on the land sufficient to establish property in it." Today, just as in sixteenth-century English legal culture, prominent lawyers argue that

Native Americans did not "labor"—that is to say, they did not "improve" the land. And this legal understanding of natives in the former English colonies of America also appears in the popular images of native peoples, which, like the words themselves, carry on representations accepted in colonial times. In the English-speaking Americas today, natives are still largely portrayed as hunters, warriors, environmental guardians, and/or spiritual guides. But none of these political identities is, according to English legal tradition, an occupation that performs labor on the land or makes profitable use of it.

If these political representations had no impact on the lives of contemporary native peoples, there would be little cause to describe them as continuing a colonial trauma, but these representations define codes of economic conduct to which native peoples must adhere. When the Goshute tribe of Utah wanted to lease part of their land for nuclear waste storage in 1998, government officials and conservationists called the proposal an "un-Indian like thing to do" and implored native peoples to be "keepers of the earth not protectors of its poisons."[9] When non-Indians charge Indians with doing "un-Indian things," they are using colonial language.

The Goshute were being told not to pursue a particular path of development that they wanted to pursue. The tribe is immensely poor, and few if any economic options exist for them, given that they have been effectively foreclosed from other options by their progressive exile. Seeking to store nuclear waste on their land was an act of economic desperation to which they had turned after other alternatives were closed off.

Native profit-making activities in the United States are rarely, if ever, allowed to develop. Natives are largely allowed timber only for their own use—consistent with their formal definition as minimal users of natural resources—in spite of the fact that logging constitutes the central source of income for many native communities.[10] Indians cannot contract to sell or to cut down timber on their lands without congressional approval. Commercial logging, as done by Menominees, must usually conform to an exceptionally high standard of sustainable harvesting.[11]

Similar and sometimes identical expressions and political identities for indigenous peoples appear in speeches and writings in other former English colonies. The Canadian Royal Commission on Aboriginal Peoples concluded in 1998: "Many Canadians know Aboriginal people only as noble environmentalists, angry warriors, or pitiful victims. A full picture of their humanity is simply not available."[12] In Australia as recently as the late 1990s, aborigines have been portrayed as peoples who cannot understand the economic gains that can be achieved by western economic development. The uses to which they intend to put their land, for instance, preserving sacred sites, resuming or continuing traditional hunting, fishing, and gathering . . . are not worthy when compared to the economic value of mining development, tourist resorts, and the continuation of . . . pastoral practices."[13]

The same cultural restrictions upon aboriginal peoples' economic conduct operate throughout the former English colonies. The failure of an aboriginal diver to prove that he or his family intended to eat rather than sell the abalone he had recovered led to his conviction for violating Australian fishing regulations.[14] The stiffest opposition that Maoris have encountered since the Waitangi tribunal recognized their traditional rights has been from the New Zealand Conservation Authority, which fears that Maori demands to have land restored to them on the South Island will result in the land's economic exploitation through logging rather than conservation. Hence Maori *iwi* or *hapu* must conform to expectations of natives as minimal users of the environment.[15] Although the Canadian High Court granted natives priority in fishing and hunting for subsistence and ceremonial purposes, the grant was conditional upon natives' meeting national conservation standards.[16]

In the United States, indigenous communities are sometimes only able to garner public political support for owning surface resources (land, water, and timber) by linking their aspirations to their historical ideological role in the English colonial world as hunter-gatherers—that is, as people making minimal economic use of the land. Local native activists in Hawaii in the 1980s had no success in fighting a potential geothermal development until they adopted the argument that they were protecting the only U.S. lowland tropical rain forest. In identifying Indians with nature, the U.S. public can covertly identify with Indian culture. They can be the active economic users of land, and as such they can comfortably wax nostalgic for the primitive wilderness.[17] They can long for an earlier epoch of pristine landscapes, unpolluted skies, clean water, and a world little used or untouched by humans, but from the comparatively safe domain of having been the active, profit-making improvers of that landscape. Political success in gaining land rights in the contemporary United States, Canada, Australia, and New Zealand therefore usually requires natives to conform to their original fictional colonial role. They must represent themselves politically in a way that satisfies the heirs to an English colonial system.

Most surprising, the partial fictions about Native Americans endure

amid increasing global self-consciousness about the negative consequences of colonialism. Citizens, lawyers, and public officials in contemporary English-speaking former colonies use colonial images of natives in
a wholly unself-conscious fashion. They do not deliberately intend to
make colonial statements or use colonial images, but they do so out of
tradition and habit. However, it is far more difficult to make English-
speaking Americans aware of the colonial implications of expressions and
images they use for natives than it would at first seem. In defining natives'
political identities, contemporary citizens secure a boundary that keeps
Indians morally on the opposite (and inferior) side.

The boundary separating productive profit seekers from mere environmental watchers has played and continues to play a crucial role in convincing U.S. citizens that they have priority over natives in profiting from
hunting, fishing, and logging. First colonial and later immigrants to the independent nations have insisted upon their superior rights over natives to
pursue the ground fish of the Atlantic's Great Banks for commercial purposes even when that activity has led to the near extinction of fish stocks
over a period of four hundred years. Timber companies have been able to
obtain public support for destroying forests by claiming that they are pursuing revenue and employment (labor), which natives did not (and were
not allowed to) do.

Even more important in English colonial thinking was agriculture,
where nineteenth- and twentieth-century settlers have ruthlessly enforced
their belief in their superior right to profitable farming. Whenever Indians
"began to produce and sell an agricultural surplus," remarks Russel Barsh,
colonists and citizens confiscated or used force to seize their farmland.[18]
By the 1920s, citizens had seized all the economically productive agricultural land in the continental United States, thus effectively preventing any
natives from engaging in profitable agricultural activities or competing
with other citizens in the future.

When these settlers used force to evict profitable native farmers, they
did not justify their actions by claiming superior military might. Rather,
when driving the Cherokees out of Georgia, for example, citizens said
that they were merely ejecting Indians who were pursuers of game, not
"users" of the land—"fierce savages whose occupation was war, and whose
subsistence was drawn chiefly from the forest."[19] Thus they could claim
that neither their greed nor their self-interest, nor even their malice, motivated their forcible eviction of Cherokees from their profitable agricultural, timber, and hunting terrain. Invoking the fiction of the natives' identity as "hunters" (nonworkers), nineteenth-century citizens made their

CURRENT FEAR of
UNEMPLOYMENT

self-seeking appear disinterested and their actions excusable. But their partial fictions only justified a national colonialism, the ongoing expropriation of indigenous peoples' resources by citizens of independent states.

The clearest evidence of nineteenth- and twentieth-century U.S. citizens' ongoing emotional investment in these colonial fictions has appeared in their reactions to natives who have transgressed the moral boundary laid down by colonists. When natives have acted as users of the land, profit seekers, and farmers—the identities that citizens believed were theirs alone—U.S. citizens have traditionally reacted, and continue to respond, with rage and violence. Nineteenth-century Americans shot the profit-making Cherokee cotton planters and burned their homes and possessions while the government that had sworn to protect them refused to lift a finger to do so. Neither the citizens nor the politicians claimed to be simply pursuing an economic interest. Rather, they maintained that they were merely taking what was theirs—but theirs by virtue of the political identity that *they* ascribed to the natives. The new citizens considered themselves alone as fully human, and therefore alone as fully entitled to exploit the economic advantages the New World had to offer. Cherokee farmers in the nineteenth century, like Apalache peach-tree growers in the seventeenth, were violating a presumably impassable moral boundary that kept Indians permanently inferior to citizens. By considering the natives as less than human, Anglo settlers could act as they wished toward the natives and not violate their own moral codes.

The emotional importance of retaining the boundary—and defining the natives as partially human—reappeared in occasionally violent late-twentieth-century responses to native fishing. At stake was not an economic interest but a neocolonial political image of citizens as "workers" and hence entitled to the traditional Anglo-colonial privilege of "recreation." From British Columbia to New Zealand's South Island, and including the American states of Michigan, New York, and Washington, the rights of natives to fish have been vociferously, sometimes violently, opposed by nonnatives who claim superior rights to "sport."[20] Even New Zealand's innovative approach to sharing the profits of commercial fishing with the Maoris has left access to recreational areas unresolved and open to conflict.[21]

U.S. courts in the second half of the twentieth century proved more willing to enforce the sections of signed written documents (treaties) allowing Native Americans to fish than any other aspects of these treaties.[22] (In 1993, the justices of the Supreme Court reaffirmed that official promises made in these treaties are upheld merely at the whim of Congress.)[23] Yet legal enforcement of even this seemingly minor right has provoked vociferous antagonism,[24] and state governments have sided with the sport fishermen against the courts. Just as nineteenth-century state governments refused to enforce decisions protecting the Cherokees from violent settlers, several 1970s-era state governments refused to protect Native Americans from attacks on their subsistence fishing. The U.S. Commission on Civil Rights observed, "The non-Indians of the State [of Washington] were refusing to accept the decision [allowing native fishing], and the State seemed unable or unwilling to stop illegal fishing [by whites]."[25]

Writes another observer of a conflict in Michigan: "Non-Indians want [fishing] dispute[s] resolved without reference to the past. Sport fishermen, in particular, seem to argue that placing a historical context on the debate is unfair. Indians and non-Indians alike are all 'native Americans' and all are citizens of the United States. Therefore, hunting and fishing laws should be applied equally to all."[26] But if Native Americans had the same rights as citizens, they would also have the same rights to own land, the same rights to sell or not sell their property, the same access to markets, and the same rights to pursue the profit-making occupations that would provide them with the right to "recreation." But they do not.

Natives do in fact fish for a valuable source of subsistence protein in waters that descendants of immigrants covet for sport. Sport fishermen remain convinced (regardless of the facts) that permitting natives to fish in such waters has the potential of limiting the amount of fish sport fishermen might catch, and thus they view natives' subsistence as competition for their sport. Sport fishermen's tremendous resistance of any limitation on their recreation—including any that may be caused by another group that barely ekes out a subsistence living—betrays an extraordinary degree of hostility to the mere presence of natives and their basic needs for food, clothing, and shelter. Just as the colonizers believed that their self-image of laborers and improvers granted them a superior right to expropriate a central means of native subsistence (land), the members of this modern neocolonial citizenry believe that their right to recreation (their due as "workers") justifies their right to take away others' means of subsistence. In the late twentieth century, however, these citizens sought fish instead of land, as their ancestors had already seized all the productive and potentially profitable terrain. Citizens' willingness to resort to violence (with the passive consent of state officials) when recreational fishing is potentially limited illuminates the powerful continuing emotional appeal of colonially invented convictions rooted in the partial fiction of natives who do not work.

Thus while citizens of the independent Anglo states of the Americas employed language and images of Native Americans that were familiar and therefore comforting, they were also sustaining a self-flattering understanding of the threats they were issuing against aboriginal peoples. They could comfort themselves that they were only acting in support of "Indians," but they were only acting in support of what they would acknowledge as "Indian"—the partially human, the native who could only act as the guardian or keeper of the earth.

The Plains Indian beloved of western movies, paintings, and children's games of cowboys and Indians is more than a genial cultural stereotype.[27] Like many other familiar aspects of contemporary culture, movies, images, and games reenact and thus reinforce colonial ideas and identities. National political representations are more powerfully remembered through everyday games and images than through official instruction.

Hunting remained the most traditional means of demonstrating Anglo-colonial superiority over natives through the first half of the twentieth century. But this tradition has evolved into two separate contemporary practices in the United States. The traditional sporting expression of class superiority, hunting with the hounds, flourishes both in contemporary England and along the eastern seaboard of the United States. The elaborate dress codes, hierarchized jacket colors, raiment of horses, and processional order are honored today in the elaborate social ritual of the fox-hunt. In these events, class is demonstrated through knowledge of the intricate social rules of conduct.[28] But these traditional class-based entitlements fail to generate political resentment among nonriders. Of far greater political sensitivity is the contemporary largely masculine attachment to hunting and fishing in the Americas.[29]

In the contemporary United States, traipsing on foot (rather than on horseback) through a forest in pursuit of game has become an identifiably masculine ritual, just as colonists misperceived native masculine privileges. "Huntin' 'n' fishin'," as such activities are colloquially known, are popularly believed today to provide significant male-bonding experiences.[30] Thus contemporary American hunters on foot ironically replicate gendered Native American conduct, whereas upper-class hunters on horseback replicate the neocolonial ritual in which both genders participated.[31]

A second Anglo-colonial political fiction also continues to prevent Native Americans from fully realizing their human potential. This representation depicts the prehistoric Indian, the native as representative of the primordial past. This powerful Anglo-political fiction appears innocently enough in the immensely popular television programs, movies, and popular fiction purporting to provide accounts of first contact. Tales of first encounters with previously unknown or hidden indigenous people remain well liked in English-language media. Yet such meetings only enthrall readers and viewers who share the same premise of the thrill of finding natives in an uncontaminated prehistoric state. Once that initial moment has passed, natives lose what English-language viewers see as their primal authenticity—and they become historicized. It is not surprising that such stories of encounters of first contact rarely guarantee similarly high ratings or sales among contemporary Spanish- and Portuguese-American audiences.

This distinctively English postcolonial insistence upon the prehistoric nature of natives has a darker side, however, for it forms the basis of the belief that a number of aboriginal customs belong to the past. This conviction surfaces in a variety of constraints placed upon native conduct by citizens of former English colonies. Natives whose conduct and advantages derive from the colonial era are often politically attacked (by non-native immigrants) as inauthentic. Thus a 1989 article by E. Allan Hanson showing that initial English colonization transformed traditional Maori cultural practices was hugely controversial in New Zealand.[32] Citizens of New Zealand insisted that only uncontaminated precontact behavior could be considered to constitute "real" Maori culture.

Some contemporary courts in post-English colonial societies have insisted that natives must retain the same material practices they had prior to the conquest and arrival of the English. In Canada, some courts have required natives to trade using techniques they employed when the English arrived. This distinction ensures that while other citizens' techniques will progress, natives' methods will remain frozen in historical time. Thus whereas English (settler) societies improve their technologies and places of fishing, as well as where and to whom they sell the fish, natives may not, because they must meet a standard of history that the settlers themselves cannot meet. This insistence by a dominant group that it has the right to set the terms of cultural authenticity for another group is another form of colonial language with significant ongoing economic consequences.

Finally, the fiction of the prehistoric Indian rationalizes prejudice toward Native American communal landholding. English colonizers misidentified collective land tenure as a part of the universal human past. Hence the U.S. popular press identifies returning either publicly or privately held lands to the natives as a return to the past. When a previously unknown treaty with Maine's Indians was uncovered, Frank Trippett wrote in *Time* magazine that returning land to Indians would result in an "unthinkable unraveling of society" and an "impossible rolling back of history."[33] In Trippett's sentence, "history" is a synonym for the precolonial conditions, identifying the appearance of the Anglo-colonists with the arrival of (written) history.

Demanding that present-day conduct conform to preconquest (or what are considered to be preconquest) characteristics denies native peoples the opportunity to progress or to participate in history. Thus "history" or progress can remain the sole prerogative of the political heirs to the English colonial tradition in Canada, the United States, and Australia, a different form of an impassable boundary that does not allow natives to participate in the activities of other humans.

Contemporary Spanish and Portuguese Americans, like their English-speaking counterparts, also use the language of the colonizers for their courts, legal decisions, and political debates. From Mexico in the north to Argentina in the south, Spanish is the language of political debate and discussion, the language of law codes and constitutions. Portuguese plays a similar role in contemporary Brazil. Thus Spanish and Portuguese Americans too invoke their embedded colonial assumptions in a similarly unself-conscious way, attacking the natives' morals, particularly by referring to either native religion or cannibalism.

The Former Iberian Colonies

In all but one of the contemporary Spanish- and Portuguese-language constitutions of the Americas, the word *subsoil* retains the significance it had in the sixteenth century. It means the valuable subterranean resources that are owned by the community—the nation—and administered by the government. And although more neutral terms such as *protected* or *secure communities*, or even native terms, have replaced the traditional colonial term *republic of Indians*, the concept of protected native communities remains intact.[34]

Many Spanish-American newspapers turn archaeological reports of cannibalism into front-page headlines. When a group of French archaeologists discovered a cave with Neanderthal bones showing evidence of cannibalism, the finding appeared in banner headlines in several leading Spanish-American newspapers.[35] By contrast, the same discoveries were sedately noted in the interior section labeled "Science" in the *New York Times*. When a team of Cuban archaeologists in 1997 discovered a cave in the province of Matanzas containing bones also showing evidence of ritual cannibalism, the news again made the front pages of Spanish-American newspapers.[36]

Contemporary Spanish-American news writers more frequently invoke "cannibalism" to express disgust with domestic political battles. An anonymous editorial writer characterized an attack on Honduran journalists in 1998 as cannibalism. "Never has the human eye seen such horrors," proclaimed one newspaper editorial, which continued with a vocabulary of outrage usually reserved in the English-speaking world for the public use of words associated with bathroom functions and sex. The accusations were called "coarse, rude," and a national disgrace.[37] In 1978, *Cannibal Holocaust* was even the title of a Spanish-language movie.[38]

Citizens of Spanish-speaking nations of the Americas closely scrutinize indigenous religious conduct when considering natives' political rights. Opponents frequently invoke traditional native customs that violate national ethical norms. Recently in Paraguay, for example, considerable public antagonism toward political rights for Guaranís emerged when it became known that some tribes practice infanticide and the killing of old people. When granted communal rights to their land, Guaraní communities were allowed only "to apply their customary norms in all that is compatible with the principles of public order."[39] "Public order" was widely understood to mean the moral values of the larger Hispanic society.

Modern Peruvians opposed to rights for Upper Amazon communities challenged the natives' use of different judicial penalties and standards. Physical mutilation was and is a common punishment for adultery in these communities (contrary to Peruvian law), and bad witchcraft merits death. (Witchcraft—good or bad—is not a criminal activity under modern Peruvian criminal codes.) Members of the larger society were unwilling to allow Indian communities to decide their own cases and assess their own punishments according to native moral codes. In the United States and other former English colonies, in contrast, issues of native witchcraft or infanticide rarely generate comparable widespread public indignation.[40] Native moral conduct is not understood in former English colonies as a reason for depriving indigenous peoples of economic assets.

An exceptional 1996 accord between Maya leaders and the government of Guatemala allowed Maya communities to preserve what were once sacred sites; this accord has aroused considerable public ire.[41] The most controversial of all the San Andrés accords between the Mexican government and the Zapatista rebels (January 1996) centered on the rights of the indigenous towns to protect their sacred sites and ceremonial centers and to use plants and animals that are considered sacred for ritual use. However, this right is qualified by the natives' willingness to conform to "constitutional guarantees and human rights," which can be undersood as the moral standards of the larger society.[42]

In Brazil, natives are reluctant to become full citizens in part because of the consequences they can suffer for taking part in some of their traditional religious practices. If emancipated, Indians would become Brazilian citizens, hence they would be subject to the full force of federal and state codes forbidding many of those practices (including polygamy, infanticide, and the use of hallucinogens).[43] Even with present-day guarantees of religious freedom, Indians traveling outside their territory have been arrested and punished for their religious practices. In 1978 a member of the Guajajara group, which uses marijuana for religious rites, was imprisoned and tortured for this usage when in a neighboring town.[44]

The failure of Brazilian native communities to observe national moral standards is considered an act of political disobedience. Whereas similar offenses in the former English colonial world are understood as criminal conduct, deserving of jail time, the Iberian world tends to see these offenses as political, not criminal. As a result, the military in Brazil is vocally opposed to the religious independence of native peoples in the northern regions of the country. Military authorities fear that the lack of adherence to national moral norms betrays a fundamental lack of political loyalty to the Brazilian nation. The rationales legitimate the military's intervention in the northern regions of Brazil.

But that same boundary is not the fundamental divide of the former English colonies. The U.S. and Canadian governments also banned some natives' religious ceremonies at the end of the nineteenth century. In 1883, the Indian Religious Crimes Code prohibited Native American ceremonial activity under pain of imprisonment and withholding of rations for up to ten days: medicine men "who shall resort to any artifice or device to keep the Indians of the reservation from adopting and following civilized habits and pursuits . . . for the first offensive shall be imprisoned for no less than ten days nor more than thirty days."[45] The following year the Canadian Indian Act made potlatch (a Northwest coast exchange ritual) illegal and participants subject to a misdemeanor and imprisonment for from two to six months; similar laws were introduced in 1895, 1914, and 1933.

All of these prohibitions were removed in the twentieth century as the material progress of the settler community increased, and as the national self-images in both countries increasingly centered on material prosperity.[46] The search for spiritualism to counter the dominant national identification with materialism has produced a resurgence in public interest (in Canada and the United States) in Native American religious beliefs and practices. Studies of native nature worship and "holy people" in the material world have surfaced.[47] But as anthropologist Alice Kehoe has noted, even academic studies of native shamanism use an aesthetic of Christian-influenced metaphysics that mirrors the observers' rather than the natives' society.[48]

Yet, as a result, it has been possible for native peoples in the United States and Canada to argue openly for the protection of sites sacred to their religions. The U.S. president has issued several orders protecting sites sacred to aboriginal groups, and the U.S. Congress passed an act in 1978 guaranteeing American Indians religious freedom.[49] Such rights are not always obtainable, particularly if they conflict with money-making (or potentially profitable) activities engaged in on a sacred site. Nonetheless, the political possibility for speaking openly about religious freedom exists.[50]

Furthermore, access to the priesthood or ministry, denied them in Ibero-America, has been allowed native Christian converts in the former English colonies. From 1865, when the Presbyterian Church ordained to the ministry John Renville, the first Dakota Indian so ordained, through 1932, when the church closed down the McBeth Mission School, nearly forty Dakotas, sixteen Nez Perces, a Makah, and a Spokane were ordained.[51]

Modern U.S. public inattention, or even the parodic New Age embrace of certain native beliefs, follows upon earlier decades of colonists' indifference to eliminating native witchcraft and other activities banned or harshly punished among Englishmen. Although at the end of the nineteenth century reformers succeeded in banning some indigenous customs, such as potlatch, the bans were soon lifted. Citizens of the contemporary United States likewise have shown only episodic interest in altering the natives' moral convictions because such indigenous customs neither threaten English justifications for seizing resources nor endanger a partial fiction about themselves. And the intermittent hostility toward (or jealousy of) apparent native religious freedoms appears to have always been balanced by an occasional curiosity or romanticization of such customs.[52] Although some Native American religious practices can and have been censored, such repression occurs almost stealthily. Unlike in Ibero-America, native retention of traditional religions threatens no significant economic or political interest in the United States and other former English colonies.

In a related vein, contemporary U.S. courts (and public opinion) have also been willing to tolerate Indians' gambling enterprises for similar reasons.[53] Gambling is conceived of as a recreational activity, and in both historic and present-day English use it is sometimes referred to as "gaming." Therefore even those Indians running successful multimillion-dollar casinos are still not engaging in economically productive "labor." Indians running casinos are not perceived to be pursuing an economically productive activity. But in this instance other Americans are able to benefit from the activities of Native Americans.

The partial Anglo fiction that Indians are "spiritual" and hence not engaged in profit making has no influence in formerly Spanish colonial societies. In fact, the opposite is more often the case. Several Mexican leaders criticized the economic demands raised in the Chiapas revolt because the community had failed to compete in coffee production following the dropping of protective barriers under the North American Free Trade Act.[54] That a native community would be attacked for its inability to meet the production demands of international competition is highly unlikely in the United States.

Continuities: Other Patterns of Indigenous Distinctiveness in the Americas

In former English and Iberian colonies, the visual, often physical, identifiers of native peoples as natives have remained in place. These forms of separation involve styles of dress, modes of speech, sounds of names, and places of residence—forms of cultural behavior that once reflected colonial differentiations.

Throughout Spanish America today indigenous peoples continue to be demarcated from other citizens by their dress: the bowler hats of Ayamara women in Bolivia and Peru and the embroidered blouses and braids of the Maya women in Guatemala distinguish them from other citizens. Although the natives rarely dress in the same kinds of clothes as their ancestors once did, they continue to identify themselves as Indians by their dress. Indians not identifiable by native dress in present-day Spanish America are marked off by their speech accents. They are also separated by their lack of educated speech and correct Spanish grammar.

In contrast, in the United States today, natives wear the same clothes as other citizens and speak in the same accents as others in their regions. Instead of dress or speech, where and with whom they reside identify a native visually. Native Americans live in segregated communities—called reservations—and in Native American urban ghettos.

Natives can most often be distinguished from nonnatives today in former English colonies by their names, which are often identified with parts of their spiritual heritage. Ben Nighthorse Campbell is a senator from Colorado; Honorable Tau Henare, Tariana Turia, and Parekura Horomia are Maori ministers in the New Zealand government. When Spaniards undertook the conquest of souls, on the other hand, they went about renaming their native subjects to make them *sound* Christian, even if they could not get them to *be* Christian. Without a political commitment to the conquest of souls, the English settlers and their successors allowed natives to keep their names.

Former English colonies have also retained many native names for places on the land. Thus the parts of the United States that were conquered by English settlers retain aboriginal names—Massachusetts, Connecticut, Nebraska, the Dakotas, and Seattle—even though the natives have long ceased to play a central role in these areas. Regions conquered by Spaniards largely have Christian names. Some of these names have become well-known since these places were incorporated into the United States. Our Lady of the Kingdom of the Angels, Nuestra Señora de los Reinos de los Angeles, is now simply known as L.A., and Silicon Valley resides in the basin of Saint Joseph (San José).

Patterns in speech, dress, names, and residences reproduce colonial forms of distinction for native peoples of the Americas. But, as with access to resources, the traits considered to be "indigenous" differ in Ibero- and Anglo-America. Iberians and Englishmen originally envisioned different economic goals in colonizing the New World, as well as different legitimate means of attaining those goals. Carried to the New World, these separate European-defined ambitions created Indians as people who could be dispossessed of either their land or their gold. But because economic aims were culturally constructed, they were embedded in broader cultural dynamics that did not evaporate simply because the nations of the New World became politically independent. Thus American revolutions for independence during the eighteenth and nineteenth centuries did little to alter the prevailing European cultural definitions of legitimate economic goals or acceptable means of achieving them.

This volume will close with an examination of how European cultural rules governing the pursuit of riches still constitute a legacy, largely unremarked, of the colonial era and how these principles continue to limit the resource rights of native peoples in the Americas.

Conclusion

No Perfect World: Contemporary Aboriginal Communities' Human and Resource Rights

From Australia to Brazil, and from Alaska to Patagonia, the economic beliefs and political languages of three small European states—Spain, England, and Portugal—continue to operate in often unacknowledged ways, dividing contemporary nations as well as aboriginal communities on issues as important as human rights and the claim to ownership of minerals and land. Nowhere is this division more obvious—and less acknowledged—than in the history of human rights. Not long ago, I was listening to a U.S. citizen introduce the history of human rights in international law. She started by talking about Grotius. In a corner of a room where we sat, Cubans, Panamanians, and Colombians were rapidly passing notes in Spanish. "What on earth is she talking about?" the notes read. "The history of human rights and international law began with Francisco Vitoria." They looked pityingly at the speaker and then shrugged their shoulders. The speaker was wrong.[1]

There was no cultural epiphany in that moment, any more than there usually is on such occasions. Spanish speakers know one version of this history, English speakers another. None of the significant Spanish-language histories of human rights or the intense debates in many contemporary Spanish-American countries have been translated or are even read in English. The same is true in reverse—none of the English (and nowadays German) books on human rights are read in Spanish.[2] As a result, there are two entirely separate approaches to a supposedly global subject. The two traditions operate in mutually exclusive communities, each wholly unfamiliar with the other. And the contemporary shape of human rights differs dramatically depending upon which of the two traditions one reads.

In the English-speaking world, the history of "human" rights appears as part of a broader history of individualism. As a result, English-language histories locate the origin of "human" rights in the eighteenth-century emergence of individual rights in northern European countries.[3] But Spanish- and Portuguese-language histories place the beginning much earlier (in the sixteenth century) and in a different place (the New World). Instead of starting with the declaration of men's political rights during the French Revolution, Spanish and Portuguese accounts begin with Francisco Vitoria's writing on victims of New World tribal wars and Bartolomé de Las Casas's pleas for native freedom.[4]

Whereas English-language histories stress the rise of the individual, Spanish- and Portuguese-language treatises often deal with the rights of communities, particularly those of different ethnic and religious orientations.[5] Their paradigm originated in the model of subjugated aboriginal communities. As a result, natives can far more easily appeal for communal rights in the Spanish- and Portuguese-speaking worlds than in the English-speaking ones. In the latter they must assert their rights as individuals rather than as tribes. This difference produces important consequences for native peoples today.

Throughout Spanish-speaking nations of the Americas, aboriginal peoples speak of their human rights in communal terms. In 1999 the United Nations Working Group on Indigenous Peoples heard from more than two hundred native communities the world over concerning their land rights. Speakers such as Aukin Wallmapu Ngulam from Chile described the loss of Mapuche soil as "contrary to the human rights" of his community.[6] His reference to human rights concerning land was not unique. Both governmental and aboriginal representatives from the former Iberian colonies of Ecuador, Guatemala, Chile, Bolivia, and Colombia similarly described native landownership at this 1999 meeting not as a political or economic concern, but as a human one.

On other occasions, native communities from Ibero-America have appealed to international organizations to assert their communally shared human rights. In 1997, when the U'wa of northeastern Colombia appealed a national decision allowing Occidental Petroleum to operate in their territory, they called Occidental's presence a threat to their ethnic, cultural, social, and economic identity. Such a threat to their way of life, they declared, violated their human rights as a community, therefore they asked the Inter-American Commission on Human Rights to intervene—and it did.[7]

The question of whether human rights belong to the U'wa as a community or as individuals raises important issues. Should Native Americans have rights in the contemporary world as societies or only as individuals? Should human rights operate on the basis of the rights of religious or ethnic groups or the rights of individuals? Who decides? And how do we reach international answers to these questions?

These two mutually exclusive histories also raise issues in the arena of international relations. According to English-language histories, individual human rights developed first; only later did they become a tool of international political critique. But Spanish-language histories include international criticism as an integral part of the history of human rights.

In characterizing their mission to the New World as a moral one, Iberians defined their right to intervene on the basis of a universally applicable set of moral principles. Although today we might be inclined to see these principles as Iberian cultural standards, conquistadors did not see their judgments in such relative terms.[8] In his 1538 legal lectures *On the Indies*, Francisco Vitoria declared that native leaders violated international standards when they conducted human sacrifices, which he defined as killing blameless individuals. Therefore Iberians had a right to intervene in the New World to protect the lives of the innocent.[9] Vitoria's argument for military intervention to defend the innocents has become one of the most popular doctrines of contemporary human rights. Yet in Vitoria's writing, "human rights" operated simultaneously as humanitarian gesture and as international political censure.

In accusing natives of violating human rights by practicing human sacrifice, Spanish conquerors were addressing what they considered to be international convictions. But anthropological studies have shown that humans do not universally share moral or political principles.[10] If nations are to avoid replicating colonial practices in the contemporary era, there must be international agreement on the meaning of human rights. Cultural differences must be negotiated, or we run the risk of repeating unilateral colonial decisions. More important, in order for an international consensus to emerge, the two traditions must read rather than dismiss each other. Until then, English, Spanish, and Portuguese speakers will remain convinced of each other's ignorance and foolishness. The concept of human rights must become more than competing visions and rival histories in which opposing sides neither read nor respect the other.

Natural Resources

This same lack of understanding continues to divide nations shaped by English and Iberian cultural assumptions. The ownership of natural resources provides an example. In the 1970s, the United Nations recognized that national, not international, policies define sovereignty over such resources.[11] Sovereignty is, as Stanley Hoffmann has rightly declared, a "slippery notion" dependent upon changing political and material circumstances.[12] But in many nations the original colonizing power fixed circumstances that now prevail among dozens of independent nation-states. In former English colonies throughout the globe, the nation retains permanent and uncontestable sovereignty over land, while in former Spanish and Portuguese colonies it preserves the same indisputable sovereignty over mineral deposits.

The consequences for the world's aboriginal peoples are significant. No international consensus exists regarding indigenous peoples' rights to own or to manage their resources. Therefore multinationals must negotiate for mineral and petroleum rights with aboriginals in Australia, but they do not need to consult with tribal leaders from Ecuador's eastern Amazonian rain forest before drilling for oil or prospecting for gold. The reasons stem not from contemporary political and economic distinctions but from the legacies of a long-ago past that continue to influence the present.

MINERALS

In 1963 in the Australian Northern Territories, a group of senior aboriginal men wrote a petition to the House of Representatives in Canberra in the Gumatj language claiming that an Australian government concession that gave 363 square kilometers of an aboriginal reserve to a French bauxite mining concern included land that contained sites sacred to aboriginal peoples.[13] Five years later, when mining had begun, the aboriginal representatives submitted a demand for compensation and for the right to be consulted regarding future mining contracts on their soil. Although their petition was initially turned down in the House of Representatives, in 1976 a law was passed (and amended in 1987) that secured aboriginal rights to compensation for mining activities in the Northern Territories.[14]

On the other side of the globe two decades later, another controversy erupted over indigenous peoples' rights to regulate mining. During the debates over the ratification of the 1988 Brazilian Constitution, the Indian Mission Council, a nongovernmental organization, proposed a prohibition on mining on Indian lands. The most controversial of all proposals regarding indigenous peoples, it was targeted by a sharp political attack orchestrated in the nation's four major newspapers. To ban mining (or suggest that Indians might be given the right to do so) was to undermine the sovereignty of the Brazilian state. Even making such a suggestion, the newspapers claimed, constituted bad faith. The proposal was swiftly withdrawn, and the final draft of the 1988 constitution (article 176) specifically excluded indigenous peoples from exercising any rights regarding mining activities in their territories. The regulation of mining remains solely in the hands of the Brazilian Congress, and only the national government can be paid for mining.[15]

It was politically impossible even to suggest that Indians should be consulted let alone paid for mining activities on their land in Brazil, but it was feasible both to discuss and to obtain compensation for aboriginal people in Australia.[16] In all of Canada, Australia, New Zealand, and the United States, native communities (or government officials representing them) can request compensation for mining conducted on their terrain.[17] In contrast, in former Iberian colonial states such an idea is unconscionable. These Iberian traditions regarding minerals also affect the wealth garnered from "black gold," or oil.

One of the great ironies of global geological history has left most of the world's oil and natural gas reserves beneath the surface of lands governed by legal principles of Islamic origin. In Saudi Arabia, Yemen, Iran, Iraq, Kuwait, Libya, United Arab Emirates, Qatar, Algeria, Indonesia, Ecuador, Mexico, Venezuela, Argentina, and Nigeria today, the people hold inalienable title to all petroleum resources.[18] And in most of these states the national government manages these resources for the community.[19] Sharing this Islamic tradition of communal ownership of mineral resources has made possible the only successful commodity consortium, the Organization of Petroleum Exporting Countries, or OPEC.

Venezuela created this highly successful multinational organization in 1960, but its success has been possible because both the many past and eleven current members of OPEC share not only a natural resource but also a common legal understanding of its ownership and management.[20] Even within modern Nigeria, many citizens remain indelibly convinced that oil is a gift from God to their nation or people.[21] Private ownership of petroleum resources is not only wrong but unthinkable. *Governments* alone can set national production levels and quotas without fear of private interference or competition.[22]

Yet the situation could not be more different in the regions colonized by England, where a hodgepodge of rules prevails. Whoever owns the surface land usually (but not always) owns the minerals.[23] As a result, individuals and corporations, as well as state and national governments, can own the petroleum beneath their land. The landowner usually sells the land or negotiates with international mining concerns for a portion of the profits. Frequently the mining companies hold more information about the resources than the owner and hence have the upper hand in negotiations.[24]

In an ironic twist, one twentieth-century U.S. judge defined oil in a way that allowed Native Americans the right to profit from it. After oil was discovered in the United States in the early twentieth century, lengthy debates about its legal status ensued. In 1934, a celebrated judge decided that natural gas behaved like wild animals (*ferae naturae*) and therefore was owned by the person who snared it.[25] Although controversial in legal circles, the definition of oil as a wild animal reinforced Texas and Oklahoma Indian communities' ownership of oil and natural gas. The laws of capture allowed Indians ("hunters") to ensnare petroleum.

However, aboriginal groups in former English colonies can neither own nor benefit significantly from their land.[26] They can regain lands that have been taken away only when it is understood that such lands will never be employed for profit. Only land that the natives will never use because they consider it sacred is ever returned in former English colonies.[27] The Taos Pueblos regained their sacred Blue Lake along with forty-eight thousand acres of the Carson National Forest—land already set aside for nonproductive use. In 1972 the U.S. president restored part of Mount Adams in Washington State to the Yakima Indians, but only because it was a place in which the Yakima would undertake no economic activity because it was sacred.[28] The Canadian province of British Columbia today allows native retention of "cultural heritage resources," meaning an "object, a site, or the location of a traditional society practice of historical cultural or archaeological significance to the Province, a community, or an aboriginal people."[29]

Just as in former Iberian colonies the nation owns mineral resources, in former English colonies the nation owns the land. Native people are entitled to reside upon but not own the land, a practice called "native" or "aboriginal" title.

Land

Aboriginal or "tribal" people are restricted to what is called "native title" in the United States, Australia, and New Zealand and "aboriginal title" in Canada.[30] The U.S. Supreme Court declared, "Aboriginal interest simply constitutes permission from the whites to occupy the land and . . . [is] not specifically recognized as ownership by Congress."[31] The Canadian Constitution Act of 1982 similarly defines aboriginal title as "the right to exclusive use and occupation of the land," but not ownership. The celebrated Australian Mabo case (1992) describes native title as preserving only "entitlement to use or enjoyment under the traditional law or custom."[32] In New Zealand a leading Maori chief, Nopera Panekareao, explained native title more poetically: "The shadow of the land passes to the Queen, but the substance remains with us."[33]

Claims of ownership of land are usually immediately denied throughout the former English colonies. When hereditary chiefs of the Gitksan or Wet'suwet'en from British Columbia in 1994 sought ownership of fifty-eight thousand square kilometers, the Canadian court transformed this claim into a request for aboriginal title.[34] But the right merely to use land severely limits how native people can earn a living, because in this legal tradition landownership is the key to raising capital. Denying Indians ownership actually eliminates their ability to use either the land or the valuable assets that it contains as collateral for loans for their own economic development.

When substantial quantities of highly profitable resources are discovered in native territories today, governments of former English colonies frequently rush to take the lands away. Thus they once again stifle native economic development. The Alaska Native Claims Settlement Act in 1971 extinguished Yup'ik and Inuit claims to aboriginal hunting, fishing, and land rights, thus clearing access to Prudhoe Bay and North Slope oil reserves.[35] In Canada, one-fourth of the remaining discovered petroleum and one-half of the country's estimated potential are located north of 60 degrees latitude. In order to obtain ownership of these hydrocarbon-rich parts of otherwise desolate tundra, the Canadian government agreed to create an indigenous Canadian province called Nunavut, meaning "Our Land." The Inuit now control only 770,000 square miles of ice and snow.[36]

In 1974, a previously undiscovered treaty signed by George Washington surfaced in Maine. This treaty granted half of the state to two tribes, the Passamaquoddy and the Penobscot. The U.S. government instantly and without any explanation reduced the acreage these two tribes could claim

from more than twelve million to three million, excluding from consideration both the populated coast and the valuable timber regions that George
Washington had granted the natives.[37] The Department of Justice was
able to do so because there exists a cultural and political consensus in the
United States that Native Americans are still not entitled to own any
highly profitable land. Instead of more than ten million acres of what had
become valuable timberland, the tribes received only three hundred thousand acres of "average quality timberland" plus the option to purchase an
additional two hundred thousand acres of such timberland at fair market
prices.[38]

Natives of former English colonies are rarely permitted to receive significant profits from income-producing resources. When they are allowed
to do so, there is usually a reason.[39] Because corporations control mining
and marketing of natural resources such as copper, zinc, and bauxite (for
aluminum), governments often remain at a distinct disadvantage in such
negotiations. Introducing into the negotiations another arm of the government that claims to represent native peoples (as in Canada and the
United States) or introducing the natives themselves (as in Australia and
New Zealand) provides national or provincial governments with a bargaining chip when they are negotiating payments with multinational corporations. In these negotiations governments customarily secure only a
nominal portion of mining revenues for native communities, and later
they fail to exercise reasonable care in seeing that natives receive what is
owed them.[40] In 1998 a federal court judge found that U.S. government
officials, including an internationally famous economist in charge of the
nation's treasury, were unable to account for two and a half billion dollars
in revenues owed Native Americans from oil and gas exploration in
Oklahoma.[41]

Aboriginal communities in former English colonies can occasionally
retain rights over resources when development will likely cause major environmental damage. Underneath Native American lands in the United
States, for example, are most of the country's uranium supplies. A coal
mine in Navajo territory requires enormous amounts of water to operate—and has polluted great regions of the desert. Uranium mining usually
also causes immense environmental damage, ensuring that the natives will
never again be able to use the land for profit.

A further constraint is that without legal ownership, natives lack the
freedom to sell their resources to the highest bidder.[42] Native peoples
cannot take advantage of the market in order to receive a fair price for
their land. From Jefferson to Carter, U.S. presidents have fixed arbitrary

figures—considerably less than fair market value—as compensation to natives seeking to sell their lands to the federal government.[43] Similarly, in 1994, the New Zealand government fixed the fiscal or settlement envelope of one billion N.Z. dollars to settle Maori land claims.

In most former English colonies, natives also cannot invoke standard legal requirements for consent to the sale of their land. Consent by verbal or written agreement, acquiescence, or other conduct must be present for binding real estate transactions under the law, but native consent is not required.

Natives' refusal to consent to the "sale" of their land is particularly apparent when the land has even a minimal or marginal economic value for ranching or farming. In the Nevada desert or the Dakota badlands, natives' repeatedly expressed desires to hold on to marginal pasture or agricultural land are usually unapologetically ignored. For more than a quarter of a century, the Western Shoshone have been struggling to hold on to their land—a battle they keep losing but refuse to give up. Their land is western scrub, arid and rough. The brush is prickly and hard to digest even for most animals. A large stretch of this desert nourishes just a few animals. But despite the land's lacking minerals or anything else of significant economic value, the U.S. government has steadfastly insisted since the 1970s that the Western Shoshone *may not keep* their marginal rangeland. Two Shoshone sisters have repeatedly taken their case all the way to the U.S. Supreme Court. In its most recent decision on the matter, the Court said unequivocally that holding on to their pastureland was not an option available to the Dann sisters.[44] The unwritten rule of former English colonies is that aboriginal people can retain only those lands lacking potential for farming or ranching.[45]

However, since 1975, one former English colony, New Zealand, has taken seriously present and past native consent to land transactions. Even so, the Maori cannot regain ownership of valuable land lost in earlier eras; they must settle for compensation. However, they can exercise authority (*rangatiratanga*) in managing some of the country's rivers, and they have a right of first refusal when traditional Maori terrain leased to others becomes available for purchase.[46]

The contrasts with the Iberian world are striking. In Spanish America, popular opinion widely holds that native communities are firmly entitled to own, not merely use, farmlands and pasturelands as well as other profitable resources (except, of course, for mineral deposits). Several national constitutions and presidential decrees throughout Spanish America in the 1980s and 1990s reinforced indigenous ownership of traditional lands. The

Indigenous Communities Statute of Paraguay (1981), the Peruvian Native Communities Act of 1974, and the Colombian Constitution of 1991 all recognize indigenous landownership. A series of ministerial resolutions in Bolivia in the 1990s, the 1994 Bolivian Constitution, and land grants in the 1980s by the Ecuadorian government all were passed with widespread public approval. Even the 1987 Philippine Constitution recognizes native ownership and not merely occupation. None of these governments assumes that natives are entitled only to unproductive or worthless land.

Among the most politically popular aims of the 1993 indigenous uprising in the southern Mexican province of Chiapas was the demand that owners of profitable farms return land to indigenous communities. "All poor-quality land in excess of 100 hectares and all good-quality land in excess of 50 hectares [approximately 124 acres] will . . . [be] taken away from [landowners, who] may remain as small landholders or join the cooperative farmers' movement, farming societies, or communal lands."[47] This demand was widely popular even with urban Mexicans.

Yet such moves are decidedly unpopular in the United States. The Maine congressional delegation on February 28, 1977, stated, "There is simply no equitable way of forcing a return of land which has been settled, developed and improved in good faith by Maine people for two centuries."[48] Claiming to have "settled, developed and improved" land constitutes neither a legally nor a culturally acceptable reason for refusing to return indigenous land in Ibero-America.

In Ibero-America, when documentation of a native claim to land is discovered, the current owners then must prove that they and other non-Indians acquired the land legitimately. Some national governments are even committed to helping natives recover written or pictorial evidence of old titles. The National Archives of Mexico, for example, has full-time staff fluent in native languages available who help Native Americans to find and identify documentary evidence of lands that they owned as recently as twenty years ago or as long ago as the sixteenth century.

Although the original Spanish covenant with subjugated communities applied only to agricultural communities, the tradition guaranteeing landownership has created a contemporary presumption in favor of such rights even in regions of mixed nomadic and sedentary peoples. Thus formerly nomadic communities on the periphery of Mexico, Chile, and Ecuador, for example, can rely upon a tradition that favors native communities' retaining their traditional lands. That is how the nomadic Mapuche have been able to obtain more than 185,000 acres in a recent settlement from the government of Chile and a larger amount from the government of Argentina.[49]

Native peoples in Brazil are neither entitled to own their mineral resources nor permitted to own their land. Although it would seem that Brazil's natives would have the worst of all possible worlds, this is not entirely true, because aboriginal peoples there are not entitled to own their lands for reasons different from those in the former English colonies. Not finding any large-scale agricultural communities during colonization, Portuguese officials never implemented the Iberian covenant protecting indigenous ownership. But Portuguese-speaking citizens did not question natives' holding potentially profitable terrain. Thus it was possible in the 1990s for lengthy political debates to take place concerning the natives' right to possess (but not own) profitable terrain in Brazil, debates that resulted in the 1993 restitution of exclusive land use rights for the Yanomami in the gold-bearing region of the Amazon basin. In Maine, no discussion was ever possible over the potential right of the Passamaquoddy and the Penobscot to occupy valuable timberland.

The dominant themes of historical studies of aboriginal peoples in these respective areas of the Americas continue to differ according to the nations' colonial past. Studies of aboriginal labor dominate the scholarly agenda in Ibero-America, yet just the opposite is true in Anglo-North America. Alice Littlefield and Martha C. Knack write, "Studies of North American Indian economic life have largely ignored the participation of indigenous people in wage labor, even though for over a century such participation has often been essential for the survival of Native individuals and communities."[50] The predominant topic in the study of aboriginal peoples and communities in Ibero-America concerns labor, whereas the equally central topic in Anglo scholarship is land. And the professional groups in the United States that study Latin America usually focus on the labor of aboriginal peoples as well.

Throughout the Americas, nationalists often assert that their countries' colonial and/or present-day treatment of natives was and/or is superior to others'. Not only are they vying for the dubious honor of proving the advantages of one colonial project over another, they are also unquestioningly assuming the validity of their own judgments about the proper path to riches. The belief that certain goods belonging to others can be expropriated while others remain untouchable rests on nothing more solid than historically and culturally constructed judgments about economics. Yet for modern nationalists, the only legitimate route to riches is their own;

objectives and methods remain as valid today as they were in the times of their ancestors.

Until citizens of former English colonies and Iberian colonies understand that national traditions still follow colonial ones, there will be no possibility for native peoples to overcome their still-colonial position within the nations of the Americas. Decolonization of the Americas requires that all persons living there no longer see each other as distorted reflections of themselves, but as fellow humans on this planet. For the indigenous peoples of the Americas and Australia, there was, and still is, no perfect world.

BUT THEN INTEGRATION
UNDER THE NATIONAL SCHEME
ENTAILS DANGER
FOREMOST CULTURAL EROSION
INCLUSION IN THE ECONOMY
IN WHOSE TERMS?
THE NATION DOESN'T TAKE WELL
TO EXCEPTIONS
      ↳ POLITICAL IMPLICATIONS

Map 3. Names of some American tribes.

Appendix

On the Names of Some North American

Aboriginal Peoples

Prior to European conquests, a majority of New World natives often referred to themselves as *people,* a word that separated them from other mammals. But those in frequent contact with other native groups called themselves by their technologies (flint makers, currency makers) or their locations (easterners). If relations with other communties were hostile, then the groups used derogatory names for their neighbors. English and French settlers often relied upon the first native peoples they encountered for the names of those groups' neighbors. If the tribes were friendly, the names the settlers were told were neutral or even respectful. If relations were hostile, the adjoining tribes wound up labeled by their rivals' favorite insults. Thus *Iroquois* is a favorite Algonquin insult, and *Sioux* is a hostile Chippewa term.

Abenaki called themselves Alnanbal, meaning "men." Neighboring Montagnais (Algonquin) called them "people of the dawn" or "easterners."

Algonkin may have come from the Micmac's *algoomeaking,* which translates roughly as "place of spearing fish from the bow of a canoe." Another possibility originates in the Maliseet word *allegonka,* which means either "allies" or "dancers." Of the two, "dancer" is the most likely.

Samuel de Champlain, who first used the term, might have mistaken for their tribal name what he was told while watching a combined Algonkin, Maliseet, and Montagnais victory dance in 1603.

Catawba means "river people," but they called themselves Iyeye (people) or Nieye (real people).

Cherokee comes from the Creek word *Chelokee,* meaning "people of a different speech." In their own language the Cherokee referred to themselves either as Aniyunwiya (or Anniyaya), "principal people," or the Keetoowah (or Anikituaghi, Anikituhwagi), "people of Kituhwa." Many today prefer Tsalagi.

Chippewa (also known as Ojibwe) call themselves Anishinabe (Anishinaubag, Neshnabek), meaning "original men," sometimes shortened to Shinob.

Creek is the English name for people living along the Ocheese Creek or Ocmulgee River.

Cuna call themselves Tule, which in their language means "men."

Delaware is the name of an early English settler (de la Warre). The "Delaware" called themselves Lenape, signifying either "original people" or "true men," because they and other Algonquin-speaking peoples believed that Lenape were the original Algonquin tribe.

Guaraní referred to themselves as Abá, that is, men.

Iroquois is an Algonquin insult, *Iroqu* (*Irinakhoiw*), meaning "rattlesnakes." The French added the Gallic suffix *–ois,* making the name Iroquois. The Iroquois call themselves Haudenosaunee, meaning "people of the long house."

Mi'kmac comes from a word from their own language meaning "allies."

Mohawk is from a derogatory Narragansett word, *Mohowaanuck* ("man eaters"). They referred to themselves as Kahniankehaka (Ganiengehaka), "people of the flint."

Montagnais comes from the French word meaning "mountaineers." They called themselves Neenoilno (perfect people) or Tshetsiuetineuerno (people of the north-northeast).

Narragansett is an English corruption of Nanhigganeuck, their actual name, meaning "people of the small point."

Pequot comes from the Algonquin slur *pekawatawog* or *pequttoog,* meaning "destroyers."

Pomo people created the common currency among California tribes. Their name comes from one of their two currencies, created from magnesite (a gray-white-buff mineral) that they called *po.*

Salish is the language of the Cowlitz, Chehalis, Shoalwater Bay, Quinault,

Twana, Puget Sound, Clallam, Squamish, and Lummi, and it means simply "people."

Sioux originated in a Chippewa insult—*Oceti Sakowin* or *Nadowe-is-iw*, meaning "little or treacherous snakes." The French corrupted the term to *Nadowessioux*, which the English, still later, shortened to Sioux. They call themselves Lakota and Dakota.

Tonkawa is another controversial name. One interpretation is that it comes from the Waco Indian word *Tonkaweya*, meaning "they all stay together." They called themselves Titskan-watich, which means "natives."

Tsimshian means "people inside the Skeena River."

Ute call themselves Noochew, "the People"

Notes

PREFACE

1 The version of Chief Seattle's remarks quoted here appeared in the *Seattle Sunday Star* on October 29, 1887, in a column by Dr. Henry A. Smith. For more on this speech, including criticism of its authorship, see note 53 in the notes to chapter 9.

2 Squanto was Pawtuxet; after his return from England, he was, like Malinche, living with a different tribe, Wampanoag.

3 The Plimouth Plantation organization has a wonderful Web site that provides a history of the holiday and an excellent account of its importance as a twentieth-century holiday about the colonial past at http://www.plimoth.org/library/thanksgiving/firstt.htm. The Plimouth Plantation organization notes that Theodore Roosevelt was the first president to connect Thanksgiving Day to the colonists in 1905, and the Pilgrims were not mentioned until Herbert Hoover's 1931 proclamation.

INTRODUCTION

1 The Zapatistas describe their opponent as "the power of money . . . [with] a new mask over its criminal face" and its goal as the "struggle for human values." Encuentro Intercontinental por la Humanidad y Contra el Neoliberalismo, *Zapatista Encuentro: Documents from the 1996 Encounter for Humanity and against Neoliberalism* (New York, 1998), 11, 14. Pro-indigenous human rights nongovernmental organizations in the United Nations, such as the Consejo Indio de Sudamerica, are predominantly from Spanish-speaking America.

2 Writes historian William Cronon, "There was one European perception that was undoubtedly accurate, and about it all visitors were agreed—the incredible abundance of New England plant and animal life, an abundance which, when compared with Europe, left more than one visitor dumbfounded." William Cronon, *Changes in the Land: Indians, Colonists, and the Ecology of New England* (New York, 1983), 22.

3 Widely read versions of the "pursuit of knowledge" interpretation include Anthony

Pagden, *The Fall of Natural Man: The American Indian and the Origins of Comparative Ethnology* (Cambridge, 1982); Tzvetan Todorov, *The Conquest of America: The Question of the Other,* trans. Richard Howard (New York, 1984).

4 The chronicler of King João III wrote that the king was preoccupied with India, but "he dealt less with Brazil because profits [were not expected] . . . from trade with the people who were barbaric, changeable, and poor." Francisco d'Andrada, *Chronica de el-rei João III* (Coimbra, Portugal, 1796), pt. 4, p. 130. See also Luís de Sousa, *Anais de D. João III,* 2 vols., ed. M. Rodrigues Lapa (Lisbon, 1938), 1:405.

5 George McClelland Foster, *Culture and Conquest: America's Spanish Heritage* (New York, 1960).

6 Emile Chénon, *Histoire générale du droit français public et privé des origines à 1815,* 2 vols. (Paris, 1926–29), 1:417. Jacques Bouineau provides comparative information on France and Scandinavia in his *Histoire des institutions Ier-XVe siècles* (Paris, 1994), 383–97.

7 Michel de Juglart and Benjamin Ippolito, *Traité de droit commerciale,* vol. 1, *Actes de commerce, commerçants, fonds de commerce,* 4th ed., ed. Emmanuel du Pontavice and Jacques Pupichot (Paris, 1988), 17ff., on the historical impact of maritime commerce and regulation of fairs.

8 Swedish laws were united in a general code under Eric (1319–65). In Norway there were four groups of customs, the North, West, Center, and Southeast. In the twelfth century these laws were reformulated by the *lagmadr,* and King Magnus Haakonsson (1263–89) produced a compilation of the laws. Iceland was a country of written law from the beginning, since writing was introduced in 1117. Scandi-. navia began the process in the twelfth century roughly the same time as did France. Ludovic Beauchet, *La loi d'Upland* (Paris, 1908), 398; Bouineau, *Histoire des institutions,* 398; Ludovic Beauchet, *Histoire de la propriété foncière en Suède* (Paris, 1904); Annette Hoff, *Lov og landskab ca. 900–1250* (Law and landscape, ca. 900–1250) (Odense, Denmark, 1998).

9 Law codes in medieval Europe were customarily composed in vernacular languages, not Latin. Many of them dealt principally with transfer and transmission of goods. See the Fuero Viejo de Castilla (twelfth century). The reintroduction of Roman law in some instances followed the revival of Roman law at Bologne University and began to be adopted irregularly in France during the thirteenth century. Jean-Louis Mestre, *Introduction historique au droit administratif français* (Paris, 1985), 111; Paul Ourliac and Jean-Louis Gazzaniga, *Histoire du droit privé français de l'an mil au code civil* (Paris, 1985), 131–35, 213–30, 232–34.

10 In principle, the subsoil belonged to the king, but in medieval France nothing disturbed the rights of the great lords until the early eighteenth century. Romuald Szramkiewicz, *Histoire du droit des affaires* (Paris, 1989), 86. Subsoil was the inalienable property of the crown of Castile from at least the fourteenth century onward. *Ordenamiento de alcalá* (1355), law 47, repeated in the *Nueva recopilación* (1567) as bk. 9, tit. 8, law 1. The *Siete partidas* have the rents from metal mines belonging to the crown (pt. 3, bk. 28, law 11). Codes appear in *Códigos antiguos de España,* vol. 1, ed. Marcelo Martínez Alcubilla (Madrid, 1885).

11 Conflating the quotidian and the correct creates the illusion of the primordial to which Partha Chatterjee refers in *The Nation and Its Fragments: Colonial and Postcolonial Histories* (Princeton, N.J., 1995), 5.

12 The category of international law emerged at this time as part of the effort to claim global privileges for European political and economic actions overseas. But even there, no agreement exists even today as to what the "universal" history is. Writers in Spanish and Portuguese invariably refer to the Iberian tradition of Francisco Vitoria, writers in English customarily refer to Hugo Grotius, and those in other languages sometimes opt for others. Alberico Gentili, the Italian Protestant refugee in Elizabethan England, is the third most commonly designated founder of international law, with supporters in both England and Italy. The two major exceptions to this rule have been Ernest Nys, *Etudes de droit international et de droit politique*, 2 vols. (Brussels, 1896–1901); and James Brown Scott, *The Spanish Origin of International Law* (Oxford, 1934). More typical are Spanish perspectives such as those of Camilo Barcia Trelles, *Francisco de Vitoria, fundador del derecho internacional moderno* (Valladolid, Spain, 1928); and Ramon Hernández, *Francisco de Vitoria: Vida y pensamiento internacionalista* (Madrid, 1995). Such perspectives contrast sharply with those of Henry Wheaton, *History of the Law of Nations in Europe and America: From the Earliest Times to the Treaty of Washington, 1842* (New York, 1845), frequently cited by the nineteenth-century U.S. Supreme Court. Popular modern English-language histories such as Arthur Nussbaum's *A Concise History of the Law of Nations*, rev. ed. (New York , 1962), and the textbooks of international law in U.S. law schools usually begin with Grotius. Starting historical narration with Grotius requires displacing the beginning of international law from the sixteenth to the seventeenth century. See Karl Mommsen, *Auf dem Wege zur Staatssouveranitat. Staatliche Grundbegriffe in Basler juristischen Doktordisputationen des 17. und 18. Jahrhunderts* (Bern, 1970). A typical Dutch title is Dirk Graaf van Hogendorp, *Commentatio de juris gentium studio in patria nostra, post Hugonem Grotium* (Amsterdam, 1856). On Alberico Gentili, the Italian-born Protestant who fled to England, see Aurelio Saffi, *Di Alberigo Gentili e del diritto delle genti* (Bologna, 1878); Gesina Hermina Johanna van der Molen, *Alberico Gentili and the Development of International Law: His Life, Work and Times* (Amsterdam, 1937). Although non–Spanish speakers often claim that the Spanish origin of international law is no longer credible, recent Spanish textbooks such as Juan Antonio Carrillo Salcedo's *El derecho internacional en perspectiva histórica* (Madrid, 1991) offer a very different outlook.

13 "Orientalism . . . *is* rather than expresses, a certain *will* or *intention* to understand, in some cases to control, manipulate, even to incorporate what is a manifestly different . . . world." Edward Said, *Orientalism* (New York, 1979), 12.

14 The "invention of tradition" literature is highly problematic for this reason as well. It relies upon the emotional trick of "demystifying" traditions that can be safely regarded as created. Therefore the literature addresses only traditions that create an emotional comfort zone, and does not address the more deeply rooted national traditions. Furthermore, it sanctions an undeserved smugness about the motives of others (preferably in the distant past) and allows denizens of the present to indulge the self-satisfied convictions of their own superiority to inhabitants of bygone eras. Yet the invention-of-tradition literature itself is a construction of the present— impelled by the intense anxieties of those living in the early twenty-first century who want to separate themselves from the horrors of the recent, and less easily relished, past by reassuring themselves that *they* are suitably distant. The classic statement of this approach is found in Eric Hobsbawm and Terence Ranger, eds., *The Invention of Tradition* (Cambridge, 1983).

15 Notable examples include Homi K. Bhabha, *The Location of Culture* (New York, 1994); Gayatri Chakravorty Spivak, *In Other Worlds: Essays in Cultural Politics* (New York, 1987); Sara Suleri, *The Rhetoric of English India* (Chicago, 1992). For an example of how such literature has come to be understood in the Latin American world, see Patricia Seed, "Colonial and Post-colonial Discourse," *Latin American Research Review* 26(1991): 181–200, and the debate that ensued—largely in literary studies—in *Latin American Research Review* 28(1993).

16 Some European diseases, such as tuberculosis, were introduced into Africa with devastating effects. But the kind of decimation that took place in the Americas—the reduction of entire populations by 90 percent in a hundred years—occurred neither in Africa nor in Asia.

17 See Noel Butlin, *Our Original Aggression: Aboriginal Populations of Southeastern Australia, 1788–1850* (Sydney, 1983); Oswald A. Bushnell, *The Gifts of Civilization: Germs and Genocide in Hawaii* (Honolulu, 1993); Russell Thornton, *American Indian Holocaust and Survival: A Population History since 1492* (Norman, Okla., 1987); Douglas Oliver, *The Pacific Islands* (Honolulu, 1989), 92 (regarding the decline in the Marianas population).

18 Peter Reich, "Western Courts and the Privatization of Hispanic Mineral Rights since 1850: An Alchemy of Title," *Columbia Journal of Environmental Law* 23 (1998): 57–88; Lewis A. Grossman, "John C. Fremont, Mariposa, and the Collision of Mexican and American Law," *Western Legal History* 6 (1993): 16–50; Kent McNeil, *Native Rights and the Boundaries of Rupert's Land and the North-Western Territory* (Saskatoon, 1982).

19 Although the word *pentimento* can mean "repentance," in art it can simply mean a change of mind that appears as layers of paint become semitransparent.

20 Another notable example is Titian's *Vendramin Family*. For a definition see also Jonathan Stephenson, "Pentimento," in *The Grove Dictionary of Art*, on-line at http://www.groveart.com/tdaonline/index.asp.

21 The reason for the neglect of the Pacific region is the absence of such resources. Noting the marginality of Pacific history, Robert Barofsky writes: "Part of the problem perhaps is that the region's resources have not been in particular high demand—compared to those of Asia and South America, for example. There has, as a result, not been a particular rush by outsiders to the region to understand its historical dynamics." Robert Barofsky, "An Invitation," in *Remembrance of Pacific Pasts: An Invitation to Remake History*, ed. Robert Barofsky (Honolulu, 2000), 25.

CHAPTER 1: OWNING LAND BY LABOR, MONEY, AND TREATY

1 William Searle Holdsworth, *An Historical Introduction to the Land Law* (1927; reprint, Darmstadt, Germany, 1977); 145.

2 S. F. C. Milsom, *Historical Foundations of the Common Law*, 2d ed. (Toronto, 1981), 3–4.

3 The "maintenance and advancement of Agriculture and tillage . . . was much favored in Law," wrote prominent seventeenth-century lawyer Edward Coke, *The First Part of the Institutes of the Laws of England*, 6th ed., 2 vols. (London, 1664), 2:86. See also Conrad Heresbach, *Foure Bookes of Husbandrie* (London, 1596), 5; William Lawson, *A New Orchard and Garden* (London, 1676), 56.

4 G. E. Aylmer, "The Meaning and Definition of 'Property' in Seventeenth-Century England," *Past and Present*, 86 (1980): 87–96.

5　Richard Hakluyt, *The Principal Navigations, Voyages, Traffiques and Discoveries of the English Nation Made by Sea or Over-Land to the Remote and Farthest Distant Quarters of the Earth at any Time Within the Compasse of These 1600 Yeeres*, 12 vols. (Glasgow, 1903–5), 8:18. Subsequent patents only expand the basic idea of space; for example, "lands, woods, soil, grounds, havens, ports, rivers, mines, minerals marshes, waters, fishings, commodities, and hereditaments" (Virginia, April 10, 1606), quoted in Alexander Brown, *The Genesis of the United States*, 2 vols. (1890; reprint, New York, 1964), 54. Further examples include "land, soyles, grounds, havens, ports, rivers, waters, fishing, mines and minerals" (Massachusetts, March 4, 1628), "soil, lands, fields woods, mountains, fens, lakes, rivers, bays and inlets" (Lord Baltimore, June 28, 1632), "lands, tenements, or heridements" (Connecticut, April 23, 1662), and "tract or part of land" (William Penn, February 28, 1681), all found in Samuel Lucas, *Charters of the Old English Colonies in America* (London, 1850), 32, 89, 48, 106.

6　Maryland's charter (1632) reads, "in fee simple or in fee tail or otherwise"; Connecticut's (1662) more fulsomely grants the right to "Lese [sic] grant, demise, alien bargain, sell, dispose of, as our other liege people of this our realm of England." Lucas, *Charters*, 89, 48.

7　Until 1677, it was unnecessary to prove the transfer of an estate by writing. Holdsworth, *Land Law*, 112.

8　Purchase was popular among individual settlers as a means of bypassing the town's land-granting capacity and acquiring land directly from the Indians. Neil Salisbury, *Manitou and Providence: Indians, Europeans, and the Making of New England, 1500–1643* (New York, 1982), 192–93. The first settlers gave the Indians of Paspahegh some copper to "purchase" the right of settlement, but later copper seems to have been used principally to trade for corn. *The Records of the Virginia Company of London*, 4 vols., ed. Susan Myra Kingsbury (Washington, D.C., 1906–35), 3:96, 99; *A True Declaration of the Estate of the Colonie in Virginia* (1610), in Peter Force, *Tracts and Other Papers Relating Principally to the Origin, Settlement, and Progress of the Colonies in North America, From the Discovery of the Country to the Year 1776*, 4 vols. (Washington, D.C., 1836–46), vol. 3, no. 1, p. 6; Emerson W. Baker, "'A Scratch with a Bear's Paw': Anglo-Indian Land Deeds in Early Maine," *Ethnohistory* 36 (1989): 235–56, esp. 245–46. Deeds, however, were relatively rare.

9　John Winthrop, *Winthrop's Conclusions for the Plantation in New England* (Boston, 1896), 6–7.

10　Abraham Lincoln, *Collected Works*, 9 vols. (New Brunswick, N.J., 1953), 2:352; Jonathan Charteris-Black, "'Still Waters Run Deep'—Proverbs about Speech and Silence: a Cross-Linguistic Perspective" *De Proverbio* 1, no. 2 (1995), on-line at http://info.utas.edu.au/docs/flonta/. Charteris-Black's Table E shows uses of similar proverbs in other languages are usually tied to specific tasks, such as eating. The English proverb is generic.

11　"Your Actions (without that I or any else speak of them) make you a lyar." Edward Herbert, *The Life and Reign of King Henry VIII* (1648; reprint, London, 1683), 230.

12　Harbottle Grimston, *The Third Part (Though First Publish't) of the Reports of Sr George Croke Knight: late one of the justices of the Court of Kings-Bench and formerly one of the justices of the Court of Common-Bench, of such select cases as were adjudged in the said courts during the first sixteen years of King Charles the First [1560–1642]* (London, 1669), 508.

13　John M. Lightwood, *Treatise on Possession of Land* (London, 1894); Frederick Pollock and Robert S. Wright, *Essay on Possession in the Common Law* (Oxford, 1888); William Searle Holdsworth, *A History of English Law*, 16 vols. (London, 1914–66), 7:459.

14 *Oxford English Dictionary*, 2d ed. (hereafter *OED*), s.v. "possession" (noun), definition 1d, dates the first cite from 1650: "Possession may be 11 points of the Law," Nathaniel West, *Discolliminium* (London, 1650).

15 During the fourteenth and fifteenth centuries, uses of the word *labor* included the *OED*'s definitions 1a, 3, 4, 5; s.v. "labor," 2d definitions 1, 2, 5, 6, 8, 9, 11, 12.

16 The synonymous use of *labor* and *farming* even appears in metaphorical statements such as Duncan's, in *Macbeth*, act 1, scene 4: "I have begun to plant thee, and will labour / To make thee full of growing."

17 John Locke, *Second Treatise of Government* (1690), in *Two Treatises of Government*, 2d ed., ed. Peter Laslett (Cambridge, 1967), sec. 32, 308; sec. 27, 306.

18 Robert Warden Lee, *An Introduction to Roman Dutch Law*, 2d ed. (Oxford, 1925), 257 n. 1, 258 n. 2.

19 Although non–English speakers often find such personification of capital contradictory or incomprehensible, it remains utterly familiar to English speakers, and hence they rarely question it. In sending the manuscript for this volume around to friends in other parts of the world, I was repeatedly told that this idea of capital as a form of labor was completely incomprehensible and that I would have to work harder to clarify it. Ironically, no native English speakers ever expressed such sentiments, even when I asked them directly, and told them about the doubts of my overseas colleagues. In Dutch, for example, medicine is the only inanimate object that "works."

20 Locke, *Second Treatise*, sec. 36, 310.

21 Ibid., sec. 36, 28; emphasis added.

22 On the legitimacy of expectations of money for labor, see, for example, *Two Gentlemen of Verona*, act 1, scene 1: "She . . . gave me . . . nothing for my labour." In 1349 the Statute of Laborers attempted to fix the rate of wages at which laborers should be compelled to work. Ebenezer Cobham Brewer, *The Dictionary of Phrase and Fable Giving the Derivation, Source, or Origin of Common Phrases, Allusions, and Words that have a Tale to Tell*, 2d ed. (Philadelphia, 1870). See also Neal Wood, *John Locke and Agrarian Capitalism* (Berkeley, Calif., 1984), 41, 87–88.

23 Ambrose Bierce, *The Devil's Dictionary* (New York, 1957), s.v. "labor."

24 David de Vries, *Korte historiael* (1655), trans. in *Narratives of New Netherland, 1609–1664*, ed. J. Franklin Jameson (New York, 1909), 203.

25 Adriaen Van Der Donck, Jacob van Couwenhoven, and Jan Everts Bout, *Vertoogh van Nieu Nederland* (The Hague, 1650), trans. in *Narratives of New Netherland, 1609–1664*, ed. J. Franklin Jameson (New York, 1909), 308.

26 Sharon V. Salinger, *"To Serve Well and Faithfully": Labor and Indentured Servants in Pennsylvania, 1682–1800* (Cambridge, 1987); James Curtis Ballagh, *White Servitude in the Colony of Virginia; a Study of the System of Indentured Labor in the American Colonies* (1895; reprint, New York, 1973). This same policy was adopted in other English colonies as well. Adrian Graves, *Cane and Labour: The Political Economy of the Queensland Sugar Industry, 1862–1906* (Edinburgh, 1993); Pieter Emmer and E. van den Boogaart, "Colonialism and Migration: An Overview," in *Colonialism and Migration: Indentured Labour before and after Slavery*, ed. Pieter Emmer and E. van den Boogaart (Dordrecht, Netherlands, 1986), 3–15; Biplab K. Majumdar, *Exportation of Indian Labourers* (Calcutta,

1994). In Virginia the "headright" system was created, granting fifty acres of available land to anyone who could prove he had paid the transportation of someone to America. William W. Hening, ed., *Statutes at Large: Being a Collection of all the Laws of Virginia, from the First Session of the Legislature in the Year 1619*, 18 vols. (Richmond, 1809–23), 3:304–6. The documents certifying these rights, formally termed Transportation Rights but commonly called headrights, were used as paper currency.

27 Estimates of the total number of "servants" transported by English colonists are found in Henry A. Gemery, "Markets of Migrants: English Indentured Servitude and Migration in the Seventeenth and Eighteenth Centuries," in *Colonialism and Migration: Indentured Labour before and after Slavery*, ed. Pieter Emmer and E. van den Boogaart (Dordrecht, Netherlands, 1986), 33–54. The contradiction between a person and a commodity in English thinking became one of the critical arguments for the abolition of slavery in Britain and the United States. However, in the Iberian world, slaves were not considered commodities. Although individuals could be sold, in the Iberian world they could self-purchase—that is, they had a right to buy their freedom. Thus they could not be commodities if they retained the right to purchase themselves.

28 Such obligations characterized many of the major New World empires. See Felipe Guaman Poma de Ayala, *Nueva coronica y buen gobierno* (Paris, 1936), 846, on kinship ties as sources of mutual assistance; see also James Lockart and Frances Berdan, *The Tlaxcalan Actas* (Salt Lake City, 1986), 23 *(coatequitl)*.

29 James Axtell, *Indians' New South: Cultural Change in the Colonial Southeast* (Baton Rouge La., 1997), 36–37; Amy Bushnell, "Ruling the 'Republic of Indians' in Seventeenth-Century Florida," in *Powhatan's Mantle: Indians in the Colonial Southeast*, ed. Peter H. Wood, Gregory A. Waselkov, and M. Thomas Hatley (Lincoln, Neb., 1989), 137–38.

30 "Any definition must be based on its functions: 1. Unit of account (abstract) 2. Common measure of value (abstract) 3. Medium of exchange (concrete) 4. Means of payment (concrete) 5. Standard for deferred payments (abstract) 6. Store of value (concrete)." Glyn Davies, *A History of Money: From Ancient Times to the Present Day* (Cardiff, Wales, 1994). A less developed definition appears in Pierre Vilar, *A History of Gold and Money, 1450–1920*, trans. Judith White (London, 1969), 19–20.

31 Locke, *Second Treatise*, sec. 41, 314–15. The idea that America would have kings of large and fruitful territories was a polemical exaggeration on Locke's part.

32 Anthony F. C. Wallace, "Political Organization and Land Tenure among the Northeastern Indians, 1600–1830," *Southwestern Journal of Anthropology* 13 (1957): 301–21, esp. 317; Anthony F. C. Wallace, "New Religion among the Delaware, 1600–1900," in *The Emergent Native Americans: A Reader in Culture Contact*, ed. Deward E. Walker Jr. (Boston, 1972), 344–61; George S. Snyderman, *Concepts of Land Ownership among the Iroquois and Their Neighbors* (Washington, D.C., 1951). Furthermore, many tribes held common title rather than individual ownership. And the idea that one could exchange money for land or that individuals "own" land in a Western European sense was in all likelihood a highly improbable notion. Wallace, "Political Organization," 311. English settlers were aware of the lack of European conceptions of property among Indian tribes as early as the 1820s. Loren C. Eiseley, "Land Tenure in the Northeast: A Note on the History of a Concept," *American Anthropologist* 49 (1947): 680–88; George Bird Grinnell, "Tenure of Land among the

Indians," *American Anthropologist* 9 (1907): 1–11. For examples of this in New Zealand, see Paul Moon, "The History of the Moutoa Gardens and Claims of Ownership," *Journal of the Polynesian Society* 105 (1996), 352–53.

33 George S. Snyderman, "Concepts of Land Ownership among the Iroquois and Their Neighbors," in *Symposium on Local Diversity in Iroquois Culture*, ed. William Fenton (Washington, D.C., 1951), 28. Some historians have argued that native peoples soon learned what Europeans understood by such contracts and manipulated them for their own purposes. Baker, "'A Scratch with a Bear's Paw,'" 235–56.

34 See Edward Johnson, *Johnson's Wonder-Working Providence 1628–1651* (1654), ed. J. Franklin Jameson (New York, 1937), 79.

35 An excellent account of such exchanges in New England is William A. Turnbaugh, "Assessing the Significance of European Goods in Seventeenth-Century Narragansett Society," in *Ethnohistory and Archaeology: Approaches to Postcontact Change in the Americas*, ed. J. Daniel Rogers and Samuel M. Wilson (New York: 1993), 133–60.

36 *Purchase* originally meant acquiring property by one's personal action, as distinct from inheritance. The *OED* cites Littleton's *Tenures* (1574) in definition 9, "Property acquired or obtained by one's own action or effort." Although today the word *purchase* is most commonly used in relation to the exchange of money for land, this used to be commonly called "bargain and sale." In a "bargain and sale," the purchaser paid, or promised to pay, money for land and in exchange received title. *OED*, s.v. "bargain," definition 6 (1641), cites John Rastell (d. 1536), *Termes de la Ley or, Certain difficult and Obscure Words and Terms of the Common and Statute Laws of England, Now in Use, Expounded and Explained* (London, 1641), 37: "By such a bargaine and sale lands may passe without livery of seisin, if the bargaine and sale bee by deed indented, sealed, and inrolled." In practice in the New World, the "bargain and sale" ritual occurred without enrollment, sometimes even with the encouragement of colonial leaders.

37 See the reference (dated 1050) in *Supplement to Ælfric's Gloss*, in Thomas Wright, *Anglo-Saxon and Old English Vocabularies*, 2d ed., ed. Richard Paul Wulcker (London, 1884), 180. The *OED* lists additional quotations from 1300, 1400, 1411, 1450, and 1475; see Gregory Clark, "Land Hunger: Land as a Commodity and as a Status Good, England, 1500–1910," *Explorations in Economic History* 35 (1998): 59–82, esp. 81.

38 John Smith, *Advertisements for the Unexperienced Planters of New-England* (1631), in *The Complete Works of Captain John Smith (1580–1631)*, 3 vols., ed. Philip L. Barbour (Chapel Hill, N.C., 1986), 3:276. Edward Waterhouse declared that the requirement for purchase of occupied Indian lands was an unnecessary nicety, rendered superfluous by the massacre of 1622. "Our hands, which before were tied with gentleness and fair usage, are now set at liberty by the treacherous violence of the savages." Edward Waterhouse, *A Declaration of the State of the Colony . . . and a Relation of the Barbarous Massacre* (1622), in *The Records of the Virginia Company*, 3: 556–57.

39 There is little evidence of widespread land "purchases" in Virginia after 1622. In Virginia, only a few scattered efforts were made to purchase territory from the natives. As mentioned in note 8, above, the first settlers gave Indians of Paspahegh some copper to "purchase" the right to land, but this was later referred to as "conquered or purchas'd" land; copper seems to have been used subsequently principally to trade for corn. *The Records of the Virginia Company*, 3:99. The company approved a

hundredweight of copper to trade for corn in 1618, but there is no record of its transport (3:96). See also *A True Declaration of the Estate . . . in Virginia*, vol. 3, no. 1, p. 6, on the copper for the Paspahegh Indians. Francis Jennings points out how little evidence of purchase exists for New England in *The Invasion of America: Indians, Colonialism, and the Cant of Conquest* (Chapel Hill, N.C., 1975), 128 ff.

40 William Strachey, *The Histories of Travell into Virginia Britania* (1612), ed. Louis B. Wright and Virginia Freund (London, 1953), 26. None of Hakluyt's writings mention purchase. See Richard Hakluyt, "Inducements," in *English Plans for North America the Roanoke Voyages, New England Ventures*, ed. David B. Quinn (New York, 1979), 61–69; Richard Hakluyt, "Discourse on Western Planting," in *The Original Writings and Correspondence of the Two Richard Hakluyts*, 2 vols., ed. E. G. R. Taylor (London, 1935), 2: 211–326. Salisbury sees the "purchases" of Massachusetts Bay as retroactive strategies justifying land already occupied; *Manitou and Providence*, 199–200. My objective here is to understand why "purchase" should be understood in this fashion.

41 Donald H. Kent, *History of Pennsylvania Purchases from the Indians* (New York, 1974), 9–10; Robert Ludlow's purchase of land from Indians in Fairfield, Connecticut, recorded in Herbert M. Sylvester, *Indian Wars of New England*, 3 vols. (Cleveland, 1910), 1:64; Roger Williams, *A Key into the Language* (1643), in *Complete Writings*, 7 vols. (New York, 1963), 1:120.

42 John Cotton, *Reply*, 27–28, 54–55, cited in Massachusetts Historical Society, *Proceedings* 12 (1873): 352–53; emphasis added.

43 To be legally binding as a contract in the contemporary United States, a promise must be exchanged for adequate consideration. State statutory and common (judge-made) law and private law mainly govern contracts. Private law includes principally the terms of the agreement between the parties who are exchanging promises.

44 On the gradual acquisition of land through purchases, see Jean M. O'Brien, *Dispossession by Degree: Indian Land and Identity in Natick, Massachusetts, 1650–1790* (Cambridge, 1997).

45 Quoted in Snyderman, *Concepts of Land Ownership*, 588–89.

46 U.S. historians have recently emphasized the trade between English colonists and natives, sometimes even arguing quite astonishingly that Englishmen uniquely brought trade to native peoples. This point of view may come as quite a surprise to anyone familiar with the extensive efforts of Spanish monarchs, beginning with Charles V (1500–1555), at monetarizing trade with native peoples (see chapter 4).

47 When natives could not meet wampum payments, they were obliged to sell their land. William De Forest, *History of the Indians of Connecticut* (Brighton, Mich., 1850), 245; Lynn Ceci, "Native Wampum," in *The Pequot in Southern New England* (Norman, Okla., 1987), 61.

48 Theodore Draper, "Treating the Indians" (1818), *Ethnohistory* 4 (1967): 210–17, esp. 213.

49 In the negotiations around Fort Pitt, the Missouri Osage and Illinois leaders noted that the French did not purchase land from the natives, and the English entered and assumed that they had acquired the land when they defeated the French. The natives noted that they had not. Again the Wabash River Indian groups pointed out to the English, "We tell you now the French never conquered, neither did they purchase a foot of our Country, nor have [they a right] to give it to you for we gave

them Liberty to settle for which they always rewarded us and treated us with great Civility." Quoted in William Corgham, "Journals," *Illinois Historical Collections* (journal of the Illinois State Historical Society), 11, 47–48 (Illinois State Historical Society), microform, F536.I18.

50 Cornelius Jaenen, "The Role of Gift-Giving in French-American Relations," in *Explorations in Canadian Economic History*, ed. Duncan Cameron (Ottawa, 1985), 231–50.

51 Johannes Megapolensis, "Een kort Onwterp vande Mahakvase Indianen" (August 1644), in *Beschrijving van Virginia, Nieuw Nederlandt, Nieuw Englandt*, comp. Joost Hartgers (Amsterdam, 1651), 176.

52 On the controversy over whether Verhulst or Minuit made the purchase, see the exchange in *De Halve Maen* between C. A. Weslager and Charles Gehring. C. A. Weslager, "Did Minuit Buy Manhattan from the Indians?" *De Halve Maen* 43 (1968): 5–6; Charles Gehring, "Peter Minuit's Purchase of Manhattan Island—New Evidence," *De Halve Maen* 55 (1980): 6ff. The New York Historical Society present- ed a good exhibit of the documents surrounding this story in the fall of 1999, demonstrating the brevity of the mention. Peter Schaghen's letter with the pur- chase, written November 7, 1626, is mostly about the fur trade. The letter may be viewed at the New Netherland Project's Web site at http://www.nnp.org/documents/ schagen_main.html.

53 Nicolaes van de Wassenaer, "Privileges and Exemptions for Patroons" (June 7, 1629), in *Historisch verhael alder ghedenck-Geschiedenisen die hier en daer in Europa*, trans. in *Narratives of New Netherland, 1609–1664*, ed. J. Franklin Jameson (New York, 1909), sec. 26, p. 95.

54 Van Der Donck et al., *Vertoogh*, 311.

55 De Vries, *Korte historiael*, 203; William Bradford, *Bradford's History of Plymouth Plantation 1606–1646*, ed. William T. Davis (New York, 1908), 302. Salisbury, *Manitou and Providence*, 204–9, suggests that a group of Indians seeking to contest the Pequot hegemony in the Connecticut River Valley approached Bradford and Winthrop of- fering to "sell" the Connecticut River Valley to them. Bradford accepted the offer, two years after the Dutch had acquired rights to the region through purchase from its longtime residents and two years after Dutch occupation of the region—thus suggesting an opportunistic use of "purchase."

56 Van Der Donck et al., *Vertoogh*, 308.

57 "Whosoever shall settle any colony . . . shall be obliged to satisfy the Indians for the land they settle upon." Van de Wassenaer, "Privileges and Exemptions," sec. 25, p. 95. Colonists were "above all to be careful . . . in trading or other business . . . to fulfill their promises to the Indians." See also Arnold J. F. Laer, ed., *Documents Relating to New Netherland, 1624–1626* (San Marino, Calif., 1924), 17; John R. Brodhead, ed., *Documents Relative to the Colonial History of New York*, 15 vols. (Albany, N.Y., 1853–57), 1:58.

58 James Sullivan, *A History of the District of Maine* (1795; reprint, Augusta, Me., 1970), chap. 7, details the problems arising from these disputes. For an extensive list of Puritan purchases, see Joel N. Eno, "The Puritans and Indian Lands," *Magazine of History, with Notes and Queries* 4 (1906): 274–81; Massachusetts Historical Society, *Proceedings* 12 (1873): 356. Controlling private purchase of indigenous land was one of the primary concerns of the English following the conquest of Canada. Derek G.

Smith, *Canadian Indians and the Law: Selected Documents, 1663–1972* (Toronto, 1975), 2–4.

59 In French, Spanish, and Portuguese, the word *treaty* comes from a root (*traiter* in French and *tratar* in Portuguese and Spanish) meaning to deal with other people.

60 The OED shows twelve uses of *treaty* as written document from 1382 to 1715.

61 The OED lists ninety-seven quotations containing the word *treaty* for the seventeenth century, nearly all of which deal with international alliances. There are only fourteen matches for the fifteenth century, four of which use an old spelling, *treatise* (*treatyse*). Theodor Meron acknowledges the fact that the word did not exist at the time, but then goes on to describe agreements between monarchs as if they were identical to the subsequent conception of treaties. He describes the mid-fifteenth-century English and French practices at roughly the time when the word first appeared with this meaning in English. Theodor Meron, "The Authority to Make Treaties in the Late Middle Ages," *American Journal of International Law* 89 (1995): 6 n. 45.

62 Nathaniel Morton, *New England's Memoriall* (1669), ed. Howard J. Hall (New York, 1937), 24.

63 The words are *tratar* (Spanish and Portuguese), *traiter* (French), and *trakteren* (Dutch). In Dutch, another commonly used word, *verdrag*, came from the word meaning to endure or tolerate.

64 *Coleção de tratados e concertos de pazes que o estado da Índia portuguesa fez com os reis e senhores com quem teve relações nas partes da Ásia e África Oriental desde o principio da conquista ate ao fim do século XVIII*, 14 vols., ed. Julio Firmino Judice Biker (Lisbon, 1881–87). Unfortunately, most historical scholarship in English remains ignorant of basic Portuguese texts such as this.

65 Treaties were often bilingual. See João de Sousa, *Documentos arabicos para a história portuguesa* (Lisbon, 1790), 166. Englishmen signed only one bilingual treaty with natives, with Maori in New Zealand in 1840.

66 Regarding these treaties, see Morton, *New England's Memoriall*. Dutch examples include Dutch East India Company (Verenigde Oost-Indische Compagnie, or VOC) treaties with the sultan of Kedah (Malay peninsula) in 1642, Aceh in 1650, Mataram in 1677, and Cheribon in 1681. There were other English treaties between the East India Company and the Mughal emperors or the rulers of Bengal in the early eighteenth century: Sulu (Manila, 1761) and Oudh (Fort William, 1788).

67 Treaties were used to extinguish aboriginal title legally in exchange for protection, goods, and money. See Kirke Kickingbird and Karen Ducheneaux, *One Hundred Million Acres* (New York, 1973); Francis P. Prucha, *American Indian Treaties: The History of a Political Anomaly* (Berkeley, Calif., 1994), 36–92. There were exceptions, such as the treaty of November 22, 1752, concluded at Halifax between Mi'kmak representatives and the governor of Nova Scotia. It was a peace treaty that guaranteed its indigenous signatories free hunting and fishing as well as free trading.

68 Reservations were established without treaties, but no treaty failed to require natives to surrender land.

69 "On several occasions, Seldon Kirk, long the venerable chairman of the tribal council and a man of great character, has insisted that on that eventful day at Council Grove soldiers from Fort Klamath under Captain Kelly fired at the feet of the

Indians, who then signed under duress." Theodore Stern, *The Klamath Tribe: A People and Their Reservation* (Seattle, 1965), 160.

70 Under contemporary English and American law, all title to land is held from the sovereign. Therefore private ownership in land depends upon establishing this principle. John E. Cribbet and Corwin W. Johnson state that personal property "clearly belongs to its producer. . . . [Land is] not produced by man. . . . He who controls the land does, in fact control the destiny of man. This monopoly, which we call private property in land, must come by a grant from the sovereign." John E. Cribbet and Corwin W. Johnson, *Principles of the Law of Property*, 3d ed. (Westbury, N.Y., 1989), 11. There is a slight twist on this principle in the New World because there were competing claims among Englishmen to exercise sovereignty. Therefore the crown claimed sovereignty, but in distinct regions local authorities claimed sovereignty as well. Some states claimed to succeed to the rights of the king after the American Revolution; others did not. Ibid., 39.

71 See Patricia Seed, *Ceremonies of Possession in Europe's Conquest of the New World, 1492–1640* (Cambridge,1995), chap. 1. Under Roman law, "there was a tendency to allow delivery of a document [a written instrument] . . . to operate as an actual [transfer of possession]. But these developments did not take place in England . . . [where] an actual livery . . . was required." Holdsworth, *Land Law*, 112–13.

72 "'The pipe never fails,' my people, the Cheyennes say. For the pipe is the great sacramental, the great sacred means that provides unity between the Creator and the people. Any treaty that was signed was a sacred agreement." Father Peter John Powell, "The Sacred Treaty," in *The Great Sioux Nation*, ed. Roxanne Dunbar Ortiz (San Francisco, 1977), 106.

73 Robert A. Williams Jr., *Linking Arms Together: American Indian Treaty Visions of Law and Peace, 1600–1800* (New York, 1997).

74 Although New Zealand and Canada in the 1970s and 1980s, respectively, declared such treaties to be enforceable, the justices of the U.S. Supreme Court have reaffirmed as recently as 1993 that the U.S. side of these treaties is upheld merely at the whim of Congress. The U.S. Constitution gives to the federal courts jurisdiction over "all Cases . . . arising under this Constitution, the Laws of the United States, and Treaties made, or which shall be made, under their Authority." U.S. Constitution, art. 3, sec. 2, cited by the U.S. Supreme Court, *South Dakota v. Bourland*, 508 U.S. 679 (1993). See also Blue Clark, *Lone Wolf v. Hitchcock: Treaty Rights and Indian Law at the End of the Nineteenth Century* (Lincoln, Neb., 1995).

75 See Franklin B. Hough, ed., *Proceedings of the Commissioners of Indian Affairs*, 2 vols. (Albany, N.Y., 1861), 1:355.

76 Letter to Governor George Clinton, January 27, 1790, in ibid., 1:360–61. Governor Clinton responded that the natives had said that they understood the terms at the time of the signing and that they were therefore stuck with the agreement (ibid., 1:366). However, Clinton's position relied upon an exotic and not commonly understood principle in Anglo-Saxon jurisprudence that gave no force of law to reliance on any verbal statements made at the time of signing (regardless of how misleading).

77 In law this principle is called the parole evidence rule. It states that verbal agreements are not binding, and then produces a series of exceptions. Unfortunately,

none of the exceptions includes accepting verbal agreements when dealing with cultures that prize the spoken word over the written word.

78 U.S. Bureau of Labor Statistics, *Analysis of the Census of Fatal Occupational Injuries Data* (Washington, D.C., 1999), table A-1; available on-line at http://stats.bls.gov/oshcfoi1.htm#1999.

79 Grotius objected principally to the idea of public or political ownership of sea-lanes. Because the Portuguese voyages had been organized and sponsored by the king rather than by merchants, the situation was different for Portugal than for the Netherlands chartered companies. Hugo Grotius, *De iure praedae commentarius: Commentary on the Law of Prize and Booty* (1604; reprint, Oxford, 1950).

80 A general charter for discovery granted by the States General in 1614 described to the States General the "diligence, labor, danger, and expense" of discovery, as well as the "outlays, trouble, and risk." A more specific charter granted several months later referred to "great expenses and damages by loss of ships and other dangers," simply as the result of an expenditure of money "at the cost of our own Nether-landers" and labor "due to our own efforts. . . . The country . . . was first discovered in the year of Our Lord 1609, by the ship *Half Moon* . . . at the expense of the char-tered East India Company. . . . it was first discovered . . . by Netherlanders, and at their cost." General Charter, March 27, 1614, and Grant of Exclusive Trade, October 11, 1614, both in Brodhead, *Colonial History of New York*, 1:5–6, 11.

81 Joost Hartgers, comp., *Beschrijving van Virginia, Nieuw Nederlandt, Nieuw Englandt* (Amsterdam, 1651), 14; Representation of the Assembly of the XIX to the States General, October 25, 1634, in Brodhead, *Colonial History of New York*, 1:94. Even dissident colonists used identical language: "The country . . . was first discovered in the year of Our Lord 1609 . . . at the expense of the chartered East India Company. . . . it was first discovered . . . by Netherlanders, and at their cost." Adriaen Van Der Donck, *Representation of New Netherland, concerning its Location, Productiveness, and Poor Condition*, trans. in *Narratives of New Netherland, 1609–1664*, ed. J. Franklin Jameson (New York, 1909), 293.

82 "Que este faça para esse efeito [ocupação] preparativos ou despesas publicamente conhecidas . . . e tido como ocupante . . . conforme responde Ulpiano . . . Bártolo n. 10, Ripa no. 49 à lei Quominus do tít. de fluminibus do *Digesto*." Seraphim de Freitas, *Do justo império asiático dos portugueses*, trans. Miguel Pinto de Meneses (Lisbon, 1983), chap. 8, para. 13, 1:227.

83 Duarte Pacheco Pereira, *Esmeraldo situ orbis*, trans. George H. T. Kimble (London, 1937), 141, 146, 152. See also D. João III, letter to his French ambassador João da Silvério, January 16, 1530, in M. E. Gomes de Carvalho, *D. João III e os franceses* (Lisbon, 1909), 182, 184. In these as in many Portuguese writings of the time, the discovery was attributed not to the private citizen who had actually embarked upon the voyage, but to the royal official who had subsidized and sanctioned the voyages of discovery. Prince Henry is characterized as the discoverer of the regions of West Africa even though he never traveled on any of these voyages. João de Barros, in *Ropica pnefma* (1532; reprint, Lisbon, 1983), mentions "the importance of the worlds the enlightened *kings of Portugal have discovered*" (emphasis added). The Dutch attrib-uted discoveries to the persons making the voyages.

84 Quoted in Sérgio Buarque de Holanda, *Raízes do Brasil* (São Paulo, 1998), 49.

85 Ibid., 50. "Those who already have used plows have lost everything," remarked a

Brazilian political leader in 1766. Quoted in ibid., 51, from *Documentos interessantes para a história e costumes de São Paulo*, vol. 23 (São Paulo, 1896), 3 ff. See also ibid., 66–70.

86 Sérgio Buarque de Holanda, *Visão do Paraíso*, 5th ed. (São Paulo, 1992), x–xi. The backwardness of agricultural societies has been the central theme in the construction of national identity in Brazil. The Brazilian literature on the subject is immense. Two important books are Joaquím Ponce Leal's *O conflito campo-cidade no Brasil: Os homens e as armas*, 2d. ed. (Belo Horizonte, Brazil, 1988); Roberto da Matta's *Brasileiro: Cidadão?* (São Paulo, 1992). The enormous debate over Gilberto Freyre's work in Brazil stems from Freyre's ambivalence toward (rather than straightforward rejection of) agricultural production. See Ricardo Benzaquen de Araujo, *Guerra e paz: Casa-Grande & Senzala e a obra de Gilberto Freyre nos anos 30* (Rio de Janeiro, 1994). See also Steven Topik, "Where is the Coffee? Coffee and Brazilian Identity," *Luso-Brazilian Review* 36 (1999): 87–92.

87 Cotton Mather, *Agricola; or, The Religious Husbandman: The Main Intentions of Religion, Served in the Business and Language of Husbandry* (Boston, 1717), 2.

88 Juan Ginés Sepúlveda, *Demócrates segundo o, De las justas causas de la guerra contra los indios*, ed. Angel Losada (Madrid, 1951).

89 William Blackstone, in *Commentaries on the Laws of England*, 4 vols. (London, 1790), claims the idea that consent must precede occupation is "a dispute that savours too much of nice and scholastic refinement" (bk. 2, chap. 1, sec. 8). However, according to the eminent Dutch jurist Hugo Grotius, occupation could not create title to land without the consent of the natives involved. Hugo Grotius, *Introduction to Dutch Jurisprudence*, trans. Charles Herbert (London, 1845), bk. 2, chap. 9, secs. 5–10, pp. 106–7.

CHAPTER 2: IMAGINING A WASTE LAND

1 Richard Hakluyt, *The Principal Navigations, Voyages, Traffiques and Discoveries of the English Nation Made by Sea or Over-Land to the Remote and Farthest Distant Quarters of the Earth at any Time Within the Compasse of These 1600 Yeeres*, 12 vols. (Glasgow, 1903–5), 8:18. See note 5 in the notes to chapter 1, above.

2 A frequently mentioned example is Walter Ralegh's description of Guayana as a country that "hath yet her maidenhead." Walter Ralegh, *The Discoverie of The Large, Rich, and Bewtiful Empyre of Guiana* (1596), ed. Neil L. Whitehead (Norman, Okla., 1997), 196. Earlier in the same text, Ralegh describes Charles V has having had the maidenhead of Peru (127), a statement that makes no sense in Spanish. Other texts showing the same usage include Henry Nash Smith, *Virgin Land: The American West as Symbol and Myth* (1950; reprint, Cambridge, Mass., 1978); Annette Kolodny, *The Land before Her: Fantasy and Experience of the American Frontiers, 1630–1860* (Chapel Hill, N.C., 1984).

3 Lydia Sigourney, quoted in Kolodny, *The Land before Her*, 7, 8–10.

4 Thomas More, *Utopia*, in *The Complete Works of St. Thomas More*, 15 vols., ed. Edward Surtz and J. H. Hexter (New Haven, Conn., 1965), 4:137; Thomas More, *Utopia* (1551), trans. Raphe Robinson (London, 1808), 2:47–48. Apologists for More have claimed that this part of *Utopia* is actually a critique of Swiss practice. However, given that More's language became widely used by sixteenth- and seventeenth-century Englishmen, his language is more likely descriptive rather than critical. See Alfred A. Cave, "Thomas More and the New World," *Albion* 23 (1991): 209–29.

5 In the 1808 version of *Utopia*, the words "void and vacant land" appear (bk. 2, chap. 5, p. 48). The version in the 1965 *Complete Works* uses the terms "idle and waste" (171).

6 "Fabula moderna he a Utopia de Thomaz Moro; mas nella quiz elle doutrinar os Inglezes como se havia de governar." João de Barros, *Asia* (Lisbon, 1777), dec. 3, pt. 1, prologue. (Unless otherwise noted, all translations are my own.) Conservative Spanish imperialist Juan Ginés Sepúlveda found this motivation outrageous. "What would happen if a prince, impelled . . . by the smallness or the poverty of his own domain . . . (acts) to seize their (other's) territory? That would not be war, but plain robbery," he declared. Juan Ginés Sepúlveda, *Demócrates segundo o, De las justas causas de la guerra contra los indios*, ed. Angel Losada (Madrid, 1951).

7 Colonial discourse theory has long recognized that prejudicial preconceptions fundamentally determine how colonizers experience and comprehend the people they dominate. Edward Said's contribution to this field, now more than twenty years old, demonstrates that academic knowledge about the colonized builds upon a self-contained and self-referential framework that then finds a body of "facts" that fit it. And as Said demonstrates quite well, prejudicial foundations determine what gets counted as a "fact" and what is ignored. Experience abroad neither altered nor placed into question any of the fundamental British or French presuppositions about the "Orient." Edward Said, *Orientalism* (New York, 1979).

8 *Oxford English Dictionary*, 2d ed. (hereafter *OED*), s.v. "waste" (noun), definition 1a (1200); "waste (adjective), definition 1 (1290). For the origins, see *OED* headings for "waste" and "land."

9 The word still has this meaning today. "Uncultivated and uninhabited or sparsely inhabited," *OED*, s.v. "waste"; "uncultivated or uninhabited," *Merriam Webster's New World Dictionary*, on-line, s.v. "waste."

10 The *OED* describes the word meaning in 1300 "of former places of habitation or cultivation, buildings, etc.: Devastated, ruinous. Obsolete." Another meaning, dating from 1338, is "to lie waste, to remain in an uncultivated or ruinous condition." Additional obsolete meanings include "of speech, thought, or action: Profitless, serving no purpose, idle, vain; (1303)" and "superfluous, needless (1380)." Interestingly, Hayden White, in "The Forms of Wildness: Archeology of an Idea," in *The Wild Man Within*, ed. Edward Dudley and Macmillan E. Novak (Pittsburgh, 1972), 3–38, basically explains the *English* conception of "wild."

11 *OED*, s.v. "waste" (noun), definition 2 (1377). It also signified a worthless expenditure or consumption of time or effort in vain: definition 5a (1297); definition 5e (1340–70).

12 *OED*, s.v. "waste," definition 1b (note translation). See also Edward Coke, *The First Part of the Institutes of the Laws of England, or a Commentary upon Littleton*, 5th ed., 5 vols. (London, 1656), vol. 1, bk. 1, chap. 7, sec. 67, pp. 52–54; Thomas Littleton, *Les tenures* (London, 1496); *Tenures in Englysshe* (London, n.d.). On use of Coke, see John Henry Thomas, *A Systematic Arrangement of Lord Coke's First Institute of the Laws of England on the Plan of Sir Matthew Hale's Analysis*, 1st American ed., from last London ed., 3 vols. (Philadelphia, 1827).

13 Henry R. Loyn, *Anglo-Saxon England and the Norman Conquest*, 2d ed. (New York, 1991), 161.

14 Conrad Heresbach, *Foure Bookes of Husbandrie* (London, 1596), 22v–23. This book was reprinted six times between 1586 and 1614.

15 See Dulcie Duke, *The Growth of a Medieval Town* (Cambridge, 1998); William Chester Jordan, *The Great Famine: Northern Europe in the Early Fourteenth Century* (Princeton, N.J., 1996), 27; Frances Gies and Joseph Gies, *Cathedral, Forge, and Waterwheel: Technology and Invention in the Middle Ages* (New York, 1995), 44 ff.

16 *OED*, s.v. "common," definition 1a (1300); definition 13d (noun): "In joint use or possession; to be held or enjoyed equally by a number of persons." John Wycliffe, *The Holy Bible Containing the Old and New Testaments*, ed. Josiah Forshall and Sir Frederic Madden (Oxford, 1850), Acts 2:44: "Alle men that bileuyden . . . hadden alle thing is comyn." Another meaning from 1400 is "patch of unenclosed or 'waste' land," which remains to represent that "the feofee could not plough, and manure his ground without beasts, and they could not be sustained with out pasture, and by consequence the tenant should have common in the wastes of the Lord for his beasts." Edward Coke, *The Second Part of the Institutes of the Laws of England*, 5th ed. (London, 1671), 2:83–88. *Common* was also defined as "a right or privilege which one or more persons have, to take or use some par or portion of that, which another person's lands, waters, woods, etc. produce . . . which being continued by usage is good, though there be no deed or instrument in writing to prove the original agreement. The most general and valuable kinds of common is that of pasture; which is a right of feeding one's beasts on another's land: for in those waste grounds which are called commons, the property of the soil is generally in the lord of the manor." William Cruise, *Digest of the Laws of England Respecting Real Property*, 5 vols. (New York, 1808), 3:92.

17 *OED*, s.v. "common": "To pastur commun þai laght þe land; Belonging equally to more than one; possessed or shared alike by both or all (the persons or things in question); of or belonging to the community at large, or to a community or corporation; public." Another meaning is "free to be used by every one, public" and "a common land or estate; the undivided land belonging to the members of a local community as a whole (1300)."

18 Loyn, *Anglo-Saxon England*, 167.

19 Heresbach, *Foure Bookes*, 111v.

20 Coke, *First Part of the Institutes*, 1:53.

21 See chapter 10, note 3, regarding a statistical analysis of the uses of the word *improvement* in all U.S. business and law publications.

22 *To improve* meaning "to invest money" was first used in 1292. By 1302, it signified the profitable cultivation of land by the owner and direct collection of customs by the king's officers. The word was an antonym for tax farming. Hence the profit in this case was to the royal treasury as well as the individual. This second meaning, however, soon disappeared, leaving only the individual profit-making landholder.

23 Hilton's thesis is that marginal arable land was being abandoned and the conversion to pasture was taking place before the enclosure. The number of tenants began to drop, and the landlord could enclose. Rodney Howard Hilton, *Class Conflict and the Crisis of Feudalism: Essays in Medieval Social History*, 2d ed. (London, 1990).

24 John Mason Lightwood, *Treatise on Possession of Land* (London, 1894), 13. The ready availability of information on English fencing practices (by contrast with the practices elsewhere in Europe noted by Wilbur Zelinsky) is one way of illustrating the importance of this practice. Wilbur Zelinsky, "Walls and Fences," *Landscape* 8 (1959): 14–20, esp. 15.

25 Charles Chenevis Trench, *The Poacher and the Squire: A History of Poaching and Game Preservation in England* (London, 1967), 38.

26 *OED*, s.v. "enclose," definition 2a. Shortly thereafter, a more generalized meaning of the word appeared: "surrounding an object on all sides," or framing an object; definitions 5a, 3a.

27 *OED* s.v. "enclose," definition 1a. For the previous use, see also definition 3a.

28 I include open-field cultivation under the category of cooperatively held terrain. Classic studies of this enclosure in this period are Gilbert Slater, *The English Peasantry and the Enclosure of Common Fields* (London, 1907); Richard H. Tawney, *The Agrarian Problem in the Sixteenth Century* (London, 1912); Edward C. Gonner, *Common Land and Inclosure* (1912; reprint, New York, 1966); J. L. Hammond and Barbara Hammond, *The Village Labourer* (1911; reprint, London, 1978); William Curtler, *The Enclosure and Redistribution of Land* (Oxford, 1920). See also J. A. Yelling, *Common Field and Enclosure in England 1450–1850* (London, 1977). Seventeenth-century works include Walter Blith, *The English Improver; or, A New Survey of Husbandry* (London, 1649); Adam Moore, *Bread for the Poor* (London, 1653).

29 *OED*, s.v. "enclose," definition 1b: "To fence in (waste or common) land with the intention of taking it into cultivation or, of appropriating it to individual owners." For the extent of and a legal definition of common lands in English law, see Gonner, *Common Land and Inclosure*, 43–70, 96–100.

30 The same meaning also dominates in Portuguese: "Pera que a terra se povoe e nao esteja tão deserta." Letter from Vasco Fernandes Coutinho, May 22, 1558, in *História da colonização portuguesa do Brasil*, 3 vols. (hereafter *HCPB*) (Pôrto Alegre, Brazil, 1921–27), 3:382. "Os indios o quemaram e roubaram pelo que este engenho ficou deserto." Letter from Jeronimo de Albuquerque to the king, August 28, 1555, also in *HCPB*, 3:381.

31 William Strachey, *The Histories of Travell into Virginia Britania* (1612), ed. Louis B. Wright and Virginia Freund (London, 1953), 25–26; Robert Gray, *A Good Speede to Virginia* (London, 1609). Sir William Alexander, in *An Encouragement to Colonies* (London, 1625), suggested the lands were practically barren.

32 Several New World societies had domesticated animals. Some Iroquois groups, for example, kept bears and fattened them like pigs before eating them. The Abenaki of Maine reportedly kept dogs and tame wolves. "Rosier's True Relation," in *Early English and French Voyages: Chiefly from Hakluyt, 1534–1608*, ed. Henry S. Burrage (New York, 1906), 377. The Incas of highland South America domesticated two animals, the llama and vicuña, both of which were raised for their wool and for use as pack animals. But none of the New World societies used animals for agriculture. More loamy soils and more hardy crops in the New World did not require such extensive preparation.

33 Samuel de Champlain, *The Voyages and Explorations of Samuel de Champlain*, trans. Annie N. Bourne (New York, 1904), bk. 2, chap. 4, 1:101–2. Champlain further observed that "in New France [which included land claimed by the French but occupied later by the English and Dutch], there are a great many savage peoples; some of whom are sedentary, fond of cultivating the soil, and having cities and villages enclosed within palisades; others are roving tribes which live by hunting and fishing, and have no knowledge of God" (1:4). Note the different emphasis. See also David Pietersz de Vries, *Korte historiael* (The Hague, 1911), 255–56.

34 Letter from Isaac Rasières to Blommaert (ca. 1628), in *Narratives of New Netherland, 1609–1664,* ed. J. Franklin Jameson (New York, 1909), 107, 113.

35 Emanuel Le Roy Ladurie calls the tendency to see communally held lands as historically prior or characteristic of "primitive" peoples as a contemporary myth. Emanuel Le Roy Ladurie, "Système de la coutume. Structures familiales et coutumes d'héritage en France au XVIe siècle," *Annales* (1972): 825–46.

36 John Locke, *Second Treatise of Government* (1690), in *Two Treatises of Government,* 2d ed., ed. Peter Laslett (Cambridge, 1967), sec. 26, 305. For a different analysis of the connection with colonialism, see James Tully, "Rediscovering America: The Two Treatises and Aboriginal Rights," in *An Approach to Political Philosophy: Locke in Contexts* (Cambridge, 1993). Beginning in the mid-fourteenth century, English landowners had begun to seize land held by tenants in common, shutting them out. Joan Thirsk, *Tudor Enclosures* (London, 1959); Yelling, *Common Field and Enclosure.*

37 In Hawaii, for example, a series of chiefs enjoyed a set of rights from a paramount chief for the use of land. Even these chiefs did not have the right to alienate land permanently. Linda S. Parker, *Native American Estate: The Struggle over Indian and Hawaiian Lands* (Honolulu, 1989), 189.

38 Gabriel Sagard, *The Long Journey to the Country of the Hurons* (Le grand voyage du pays des Hurons, situé en l'Amérique vers la mer douce) (1632; reprint, New York, 1978).

39 Walter Ralegh, "Fundamental Cause of Natural, Arbitrary, Necessary and Unnatural War," in *The Works of Sir Walter Ralegh, Kt,* 8 vols. (Oxford, 1829), 8:255. See also Alberico Gentili, *De iure belli libri tres,* 2 vols., trans. John Rolfe (Oxford, 1933), 2:80–81; John R. Brodhead, ed., *Documents Relative to the Colonial History of New York,* 15 vols. (Albany, N.Y., 1853–57), 1:128.

40 William Symonds, *Virginia: A Sermon Preached at White-Chappel* (April 1609), in Brown, *Genesis of the United States,* 288–89; Hakluyt, *The Principal Navigations,* 8:445; Richard Hakluyt, "Discourse on Western Planting," in *The Original Writings and Correspondence of the Two Richard Hakluyts,* 2 vols., ed. E. G. R. Taylor (London, 1935), 2:233–39.

41 Samuel Purchas, *Hakluytus Posthumous, or Purchas His Pilgrimes* . . . (Glasgow, 1906), 20:132. Sir William Alexander, in *An Encouragement to Colonies,* suggested the lands were practically barren and could be filled based on the injunction to go forth and multiply. Virtually identical sentiments came from the founder of the Plymouth colony; Bradford wrote of "those vast and unpeopled countries of America, which are fruitful and fit of habitation." William Bradford, *Bradford's History of Plymouth Plantation 1606–1646,* ed. William T. Davis (New York, 1908), 46–47.

42 Richard Eburne, *A Plaine Pathway to Plantations* (1624), ed. Louis B. Wright (Ithaca, N.Y., 1962), 32, 34 ff.

43 Francis Bacon, "Of Plantations," in *Essays (1625),* ed., Joseph Devey (New York, n.d.), 183.

44 Thomas More had called the right to settle waste land as a "law of nature," an allied concept.

45 Eburne, *A Plaine Pathway,* 32. Karen Kupperman analyzes this statement in "The Beehive as a Model for Colonial Design," in *America in the European Consciousness, 1493–1750* (Chapel Hill, N.C., 1995), 272–92. She points out the structured nature of this natural phenomenon.

46 Ralegh, "Fundamental Cause," 8:256; emphasis added.

47 In 1527, the population of Portugal was 1.4 million; Spain, 7 million; France, 14 million; Italy, 12 million; and Great Britain, only 4 million. Morocco had more than 6 million inhabitants. Vitorino Magalhaës Godinho, *Les découvertes XV-XVI: Une révolution des mentalités* (Paris, 1990), 62. Not only was England not overpopulated in absolute terms, it was not overpopulated in relative terms. In 1549, the Netherlands had roughly 3 million people and a total of 34,000 square miles (88.2 persons/square mile), whereas England, with 25 percent more people, had 50 percent more land area (51,000 square miles).

48 The only exception was Canada, and support for emigration to that destination lasted barely a decade. Jean Meyer, Jean Tarrade, Annie-Rey-Godzeiguer, and Jacques Thobie, *Histoire de la France coloniale: Des origines à 1914* (Paris, 1990), 17–18, 38, 80–81. Like many writers in a national tradition, the authors of this otherwise excellent volume generalize their own national attitudes to the rest of Europe. "Tous les états européens on eu peur de la *dépopulation* [All European states feared *depopulation*]," they write (17). The English did not. See also Séraphin Marion, *Relations des voyageurs français en Nouvelle France au XVII siècle* (Paris, 1923), 23; "Relation du Père Jamet," reproduced in Father Jouve, O.M., *Les Franciscains et le Canada* (Quebec, 1915), 157–65.

49 Pierre Pluchon, *Histoire de la colonisation française*, 2 vols. (Paris, 1991), 1:79, 81. By 1642, there were fewer than six thousand Frenchmen in the New World, of whom five thousand were in the Antilles (only three hundred in Canada). By the end of Mazarin's regime there were almost double that number (eleven thousand), of whom the majority were still located in the Antilles (seven thousand). On the resistance to settling in France and the high rates of return migration, see Peter N. Moogk, "Reluctant Exiles: Emigrants from France in Canada before 1760," *William and Mary Quarterly* (3d ser.) 46 (1989): 463–505.

50 Pluchon, *Colonisation française*, 1:58.

51 "Resolution of the States of Holland in regard to the Affairs of the West India Company," June 10, 1633, in Brodhead, *Colonial History of New York*, 1:65.

52 Letter from the "Councill and Company of the honourable Plantation in Virginia to the Lord mayor, Alderman and Companies of London," in Brown, *Genesis of the United States*, 252–53.

53 Gray, *A Good Speede to Virginia*.

54 Richard Hakluyt, "Preface to his Divers Voyages" (1582), in *The Original Writings and Correspondence of the Two Richard Hakluyts*, 2 vols., ed. E.G. R. Taylor (London, 1935), 1:176. See also Hakluyt, *Principal Navigations*, 8:445. Similar sentiments were expressed by George Johnson in a 1609 publicity tract for the Virginia Company titled *Nova Britannia*: "Unless we take measures to found new Colonies, the earth will not suffice to sustain the overwhelming number of human beings." Quoted in Brown, *Genesis of the United States*, 270.

55 Such sentiments (common in historical writing about England) have come to be known by the mechanical metaphor of the "escape valve" theory of emigration. In U.S. history a version of this became known as the Turner thesis. Smith, *Virgin Land*, 201–10. Such sentiments are uncommon in other languages.

56 Spoken by Emilia in *Othello*, act 4, scene 3 (1630). "A new Colony and plantation. . . . The Planters sustaine themselves by what God and Nature affords them for their labour upon the place." Giovanni Botero, *An Historicall Description of the Most*

Famous Kingdomes and Common-Weales in the Worlde (*Relationi universali*, pt. 2), trans. Robert Johnson (London, 1603), 641.

57 John Smith, *The Complete Works of Captain John Smith* (*1580–1631*), 3 vols., ed. Philip L. Barbour (Chapel Hill, N.C., 1986), 3:276–77. For a different perspective, see Jean de Léry, *History of a Voyage to the Land of Brazil, Otherwise Called America*, trans. Janet Whatley (Berkeley, Calif., 1990), 72. Léry did not see the soil as needing replenishing and did not share Smith's enthusiasm.

58 Strachey, *The Histories of Travell*, 8–10.

59 John Cotton, *Reply*, 27–28, 54–55, cited in Massachusetts Historical Society *Proceedings* 12 (1873): 352–53. "Where the land lay idle and vast, and none used it . . . so it is lawful to take a land which none useth and make use of it." R. C. (Robert Cushman), "Reasons and Considerations Touching the Lawfulness of Removing out of England and into the Parts of America" (1621), in *Mourt's Relation*, (Boston, 1865), 148.

60 Ralegh, "Fundamental Cause," 8:254. See also Gentili, *De iure belli libri tres*, 2:80–81.

61 John Winthrop, *Winthrop's Conclusions for the Plantation in New England*, (Boston, 1896), 6; John Winthrop, *The Journal of John Winthrop, 1630–1649*, ed. Richard S. Dunn, James Savage, and Laetitia Yeandle (Cambridge, Mass., 1996), 284; Strachey, *The Histories of Travell*, 8–10; Smith, *Complete Works*, 3:276–77. In postcolonial theory this explanation is most often referred to as supplying a lack. U.S. historian William Cronon considers Winthrop's and others' statements to be "little more than an ideology of conquest conveniently available to justify the occupation of another people's lands." William Cronon, *Changes in the Land: Indians, Colonists, and the Ecology of New England* (New York, 1983), 57. But in fact these same principles operate in contemporary modern American law, giving them not the status of a convenient ideology but a set of current practices. For a different but related critique, see Eric Cheyfitz, *The Poetics of Imperialism: Translation and Colonization from the Tempest to Tarzan* (New York, 1991), 56.

62 R. C., "Reasons and Considerations," 143–54.

63 Locke, *Second Treatise*, sec. 44, 317; emphasis added. Similar observations are found in Winthrop, *Winthrop's Conclusions*, 6.

64 "Areas within which crops grew were enclosed comparatively early." Grace Tabor, *Old-Fashioned Gardening* (New York, 1925), 186. When the English enclosed wider areas in the middle of the eighteenth century, they planted hedgerows made of bramble and sweetbrier instead of English hawthorn or quick. Only in the last quarter of the eighteenth century was pastureland enclosed. Ibid., 190–91.

65 Cronon, *Changes in the Land*, 130.

66 David Stephen Cohen, *The Dutch-American Farm* (New York, 1992), 77.

67 William Cronon, George Miles, and Jay Gitlin, "Becoming West: Toward a New Meaning for Western History," in *Under an Open Sky: Rethinking America's Western Past*, ed. William Cronon, George Miles, and Jay Gitlin (New York, 1992), 15.

68 Blith, *The English Improver*, 72.

69 Very little English-held land in the New World was held in common. By the early nineteenth century, there were only three such holdings in all of New England, at Plymouth, Cape Cod, and Salem. Slater, *The English Peasantry*, 183–86. Karen Ordahl Kupperman, in *Providence Island, 1630–1641: The other Puritan Colony* (Cambridge, 1993), argues that New England succeeded where Providence plantation did not

because the former settled for individual property rights in land. On large-scale landholding, see John Frederick Martin, *New England Profits in the Wilderness: Entrepreneurship and the Founding of New England Towns in the Seventeenth Century* (Chapel Hill, N.C., 1991).

70 Regarding Spanish practices, see chapter 5 of this volume; on the Portuguese, see chapter 8.

71 The tobacco grown in these colonies was imported from Bermuda, but a white flowering tobacco was native to the region. George A. West, *Tobacco, Pipes, and Smoking Customs of the American Indians* (Milwaukee, Wis., 1934), 61–62, 482; Gloria L. Main, *Tobacco Colony: Life in Early Maryland (1650–1720)* (Princeton, N.J., 1982); Vertrees J. Wyckoff, *Tobacco Regulation in Colonial Maryland* (Baltimore, 1936); Allan Kulikoff, *Tobacco and Slaves: The Development of Southern Cultures in the Chesapeake, 1680–1800* (Chapel Hill, N.C., 1986); Timothy Breen, *Tobacco Culture: The Mentality of the Great Tidewater Planters on the Eve of Revolution* (Princeton, N.J., 1985); Jacob Price, *Tobacco in Atlantic Trade: Chesapeake, London, Glasgow, 1675–1775* (Brookfield, Vt., 1995); John Smith, "Description of Virginia," in Purchas, *Hakluytus Posthumous*, 18:435–37; Thomas Hariot, "A Briefe and true report of the new found land of Virginia" (1588), in *The Roanoke Voyages*, 2 vols., ed. David B. Quinn (London, 1955), 1:341–44; Anthony F. C. Wallace, "Political Organization and Land Tenure among the Northeastern Indians, 1600–1830," *Southwestern Journal of Anthropology* 13 (1957): 301–21; Charles C. Willoughby, "The Virginia Indians in the Seventeenth Century," *American Anthropologist* 9 (1907): 82–84; Wilcomb E. Washburn, "The Moral and Legal Justifications for Dispossessing the Indians," in *Seventeenth-Century America: Essays in Colonial History*, ed. James Morton Smith (Chapel Hill, N.C., 1959), 23; James Axtell, *The European and the Indian: Essays in the Ethnohistory of Colonial North America* (New York, 1982), 292–95; R. Douglas Hurt, *Indian Agriculture in America: Prehistory to the Present* (Lawrence, Kans., 1987), 27–41. An excellent brief introduction to Iberian practices is William R. Fowler Jr., "The Living Pay for the Dead: Trade, Exploitation, and Social Change in Early Colonial Izalco, El Salvador," in *Ethnohistory and Archaeology: Approaches to Postcontact Change in the Americas*, ed. J. Daniel Rogers and Samuel M. Wilson (New York, 1993), 181–99.

72 For general versions of this critique, see Johannes Fabian, *Time and the Other: How Anthropology Makes Its Object* (New York, 1983). James Tully develops this idea in particular for Locke in *An Approach to Political Philosophy: Locke in Contexts* (Cambridge, 1993), 141–42.

73 Edward Burnett Tylor, in *Primitive Cultures: Researches into the Development of Mythology, Philosophy, Religion, Art, and Custom* (London, 1871), used this Lockean idea that "primitives" were merely at an earlier stage of human development that European cultures had long since passed.

74 Ralph B. Smith, *Land and Politics in the England of Henry VIII* (Oxford, 1970), 17–20, 160–64, 204; Joan Thirsk, "Enclosing and Engrossing," in *The Agrarian History of England and Wales*, vol. 4, *1500–1650*, ed. Joan Thirsk (Cambridge, 1967), 213–55. The first English efforts at coping with the effects of the enclosure movement were punitive. In 1495, wanderers were sentenced to be set in the stocks for three days before being returned home. The hysterical tenor of punitive legislation reached its height by the middle of the next century, as vagrants were ordered to be whipped, to have holes bored in their ears, and to be bound as slaves. When vindictive methods

failed, the English eventually mandated a welfare system for the unemployed called poor relief, and accompanied it with a regime of labor that included workhouses. Paul Slack, *Poverty and Policy in Tudor and Stuart England* (New York, 1988), 115, 118, 122–24, 126–28.

75 William Cronon et al., "Becoming West," 15. The identical idea reappears in many other places. See, for example, H. F. Raup, "The Fence in the Cultural Landscape," *Western Folklore* 6 (1947): 1; Eugene C. Mather and John F. Hart, "Fences and Farms," *Geographical Review* 44 (1954): 208–9.

76 *OED*, s.v. "improvement," definition 2b. See also Michael Turner, *Enclosures in Britain 1750–1830* (London, 1984); Thirsk, "Enclosing and Engrossing," 237.

77 Russel Barsh suggests that this attitude prevails today. He argues that the U.S. government has historically used confiscation and force against Indians when their agricultural productivity has been high. Using the Indians' resources for national purposes has not been cost-beneficial, however, because of what Indian administration and poverty have cost the federal government. Russel Lawrence Barsh, "Indian Resources and the National Economy: Business Cycles and Policy Cycles," in *Native Americans and Public Policy*, ed. Fremont J. Lyden and Lyman H. Legters (Pittsburgh, 1992), 213–16, 304–5.

78 In a letter to General Jeffrey Amherst dated July 13, 1763, Colonel Henry Bouquet suggested the distribution of blankets to "inoculate the Indians"; in his reply, dated July 16, 1763, Amherst approved this plan and encouraged Bouquet "to try Every other method that can serve to Extirpate this Execrable Race." These letters are contained in the British Manuscripts Project, a checklist of the microfilms prepared in England and Wales for the American Council of Learned Societies, 1941–45, compiled by Lester K. Born (New York, 1968), reel 34/40, item 305; reel 34/41, item 114. Pictures of the original are available on-line at http://www.nativeweb.org/pages/legal/amherst/lord_jeff.html.

79 Daniel Denton, *A Brief Description of New-York*, ed. Victor Paltsits (New York, 1937), 6–7.

80 In Ebenezer Hazard, *Historical Collections, Consisting of State Papers, and Other Authentic Documents; Intended as Materials for an History of the United States of America*, 2 vols. (Philadelphia, 1792–94), 1:105.

81 Winthrop, *Winthrop's Conclusions*, 7. Edward Johnson expressed similar sentiments in *Johnson's Wonder-Working Providence 1628–1651* (1654), ed. J. Franklin Jameson (New York, 1937), 41, 80: "The Indians . . . began to quarrell with them (the English) about their bounds of land . . . but the Lord put an end to this quarrell also, by smiting the Indians with a sore Disease. . . . Thus did the Lord allay their quarrelsone spirits, and made roome for the following part of his Army" (79–80).

82 "Real cédula a Hernán Cortés, 1523," in Diego de Encinas, *Cedulario indiano*, 4 vols. (1596; reprint, Madrid, 1945–46), 2:185.

83 Ibid., 2:186.

CHAPTER 3: GENDERING NATIVE AMERICANS

1 These natives were tropical horticulturalists whose lives revolved around garden cycles, and who moved when the soil was exhausted. William Keegan, *The People Who Discovered Columbus* (Gainesville, Fla., 1992), 145–47; Eric Williams, *From Columbus to Castro: The History of the Caribbean 1492–1969* (New York, 1970).

2 Serafim Leite, ed., *Cartas dos primeiros Jesuítas do Brasil*, 3 vols. (São Paulo, 1956–58); Andrés Pérez de Ribas, *History of the Triumphs of Our Holy Faith among the Most Barbarous and Fierce Peoples of the New World* (1645), trans. Daniel T. Reff, Maureen Ahern, and Richard K. Danford (Tucson, Ariz., 1999), bk. 1, chaps. 2, 3, pp. 87–93.

3 For discussion of eighteenth- and nineteenth-century U.S. images of the Indian, see Robert E. Berkhofer, *The White Man's Indian* (New York, 1979), esp. 138, 165–67. For a critique, see M. Annette Jaimes with Theresa Halsey, "American Indian Women," in *The State of Native America*, ed. M. Annette Jaimes (Boston, 1992), 311–44. Modern Americans know perfectly well that all Indians were and are not hunters—but that knowledge does not alter the predominant popular image of natives as hunters.

4 John Smith, *A Map of Virginia* (1612), in *The Complete Works of Captain John Smith (1580–1631)*, 3 vols., ed. Philip L. Barbour (Chapel Hill, N.C., 1986), 1:157; Francis Jennings, *The Invasion of America* (New York, 1976), 63; Nicolaes van de Wassenaer, *Historisch verhael alder ghedenck-Geschiedenisen die hier en daer in Europa* (Amsterdam, 1622–35), trans. in *Narratives of New Netherland, 1609–1664*, ed. J. Franklin Jameson (New York, 1909), 77. For similar observations by Pierre Biard, a French Jesuit missionary to Acadia in 1611, see Reuben G. Thwaites, ed., *The Jesuit Relations and Allied Documents*, 73 vols. (Cleveland, 1896–1901), 2:77, 79. See also Kathleen J. Bragdon, *Native People of Southern New England, 1500–1650* (Norman, Okla., 1996), 102–29; George R. Hamell, "Mythical Realities and European Contacts in the Northeast during the Sixteenth and Seventeenth Centuries," *Man in the Northeast* 33 (1987): 63–87. Only one-third of Cherokee men farmed the soil. Theda Perdue, *Cherokee Women: Gender and Culture Change, 1700–1835* (Lincoln, Neb., 1998).

5 James Axtell, *The Indian Peoples of Eastern America: A Documentary History of the Sexes* (New York, 1981), 112.

6 David D. Smits, "The 'Squaw Drudge': A Prime Index of Savagism," *Ethnohistory* 29 (1982): 281–306.

7 William Wood, *New England's Prospect*, ed. Alden T. Vaughn (Amherst, Mass., 1977), 112–13. See also Smits, "The 'Squaw Drudge,'" 281–306.

8 Wood, *New England's Prospect*, 115.

9 John Fitzherbert, *The Booke of Husbandry* (London, 1573); Samuel Hartlib, *His Legacie; or, an Enlargement of the Discourse of Husbandry* (London, 1651); Leonard Meager, *The Mystery of husbandry . . . in Bettering and Improving all Degrees of Land* (London, 1697). See also Bridget Hill, *Women, Work, and Sexual Politics in Eighteenth-Century England* (Oxford, 1989), 33–35; Michael Roberts, "Sickles and Scythes," *History Workshop Journal* 7 (1979): 3–28; Patricia Seed, "Did Men Steal Economics?" *Feminist Economics* (forthcoming).

10 For a history of this period, see my "Did Men Steal Economics?"

11 Some Saxon legislation may have restricted hunting to royals prior to the arrival of the Normans, but it was the conqueror who enforced the rules with a vengeance.

12 Charles Chenevix Trench, in *The Poacher and the Squire: A History of Poaching and Game Preservation in England* (London, 1967), 23, provides the figure of five hundred displaced families; Henry R. Loyn, in *Anglo-Saxon England and the Norman Conquest*, 2d ed. (New York, 1991), 378–79, suggests two thousand people. "Throughout our Middle Ages a *Forest was a place of deer, not necessarily a place of trees*," notes Oliver Rackham in *Trees and Woodland in the British Landscape* (London, 1976), 165–66; emphasis added. The Norman system was introduced (with modifications) into Scotland in the twelfth

century. In the fifteenth century, areas were declared waste and inhabitants were ejected to permit exclusive royal hunting. John M. Gilbert, *Hunting and Hunting Reserves in Medieval Scotland* (Edinburgh, 1979), 12, 20, 24–26, 93–95.

13 The new regulations were called "forest laws." *Forest* was a legal term meaning the place where forest laws operated—protecting the king's deer. "The laws of the forest . . . are differing from other judgments of the laws of the realm, and are subject unto the judgments of the King only, to determine at his will and pleasure." John Manwood, *Treatise of the Laws of the Forest* (London, 1665), chap. 24, p. 287. Forest laws were not necessarily tied to landownership. Rackham, *Trees and Woodland*, 166, 168; Trench, *The Poacher*, 16–32; Gilbert, *Hunting and Hunting Reserves*, 27, 190–91, 198 (regarding delegated rights in Scotland); Maurice H. Keen, *The Outlaws of Medieval Legend* (Toronto, 1961).

14 The 1215 charter restricted the king's forest to the bounds established by William the Conqueror. The revised version of the charter (1225) was accompanied by a charter of the forest that was far more extensive than that found in the original 1215 document. J. C. Holt, *Magna Carta*, 2d ed. (Cambridge, 1992), 37, 385–86, 512–17; William F. Swindler, *Magna Carta: Legend and Legacy* (Indianapolis, 1965), 112–13.

15 Quoted in Trench, *The Poacher*, 100. For a legal definition to this effect, see Manwood, *Laws of the Forest*, chap. 24, p. 487. See also George Hammersley, "The Revival of the Forest Laws under Charles I," *History* 45 (1960): 85–102.

16 Parks existed in the ninth century. The Domesday books record only thirty-one, belonging to the king, nobles, and bishops. John Cummins, *The Hound and the Hawk: The Art of Medieval Hunting* (London, 1988), 58; Rackham, *Trees and Woodland*, 151–53; Gilbert, *Hunting and Hunting Reserves*, 82–87, 221–22. This process did not occur in France until the fourteenth and fifteenth centuries. Michel Devèze, *La vie de la forêt française au XVIe siècle*, 2 vols. (Paris, 1961), 1:77–128, esp. 105.

17 Lesser game (other than deer, hares, or rabbits) was open for nonaristocratic hunting in France and Scotland. Gilbert, *Hunting and Hunting Reserves*, 38–39, 72–73. For discussion of the Norman reintroduction of the rabbit into England, see Elspeth M. Veale, "The Rabbit in England," *Agricultural History Review* 5 (1957): 85–90.

18 Loyn, *Anglo-Saxon England*, 380.

19 King Richard II declared that no one with less than "10 [pounds] a year income or 40s in landed property could keep hunting dogs, snares to catch deer, hares or rabbits since that was a gentleman's game." Gilbert, *Hunting and Hunting Reserves*, 38–39, 72–73.

20 Edward of Norwich, second duke of York (1373–1415), *The Master of Game*, ed. William Groham and F. Baillie Groham (New York, 1909), 6. This book is largely a translation of Gaston Phoebus's *Livre de chasse* (1389; reprint, Karlshawm, Sweden, 1971), 53–54. Hunting as an antidote to idleness was a commonplace, and Spanish writers described idleness as sin. Pedro Lopez de Ayala, chancellor of Castile, wrote that men "should avoid idleness, for it causes sin. . . . To avoid these evils, the sons of kings and princes . . . should go through the countryside for a few hours every day, taking fresh air and exercise." Quoted in Cummins, *The Hound and the Hawk*, 2.

21 The duke of York rationalized hunting as a military (cavalry) practice of attacking and maneuvering, following the Greek writer Xenophon. See John K. Anderson, *Ancient Greek Horsemanship* (Berkeley, Calif., 1961). But because this justification

excluded elite women, many of whom participated avidly in hunting, it was less satisfactory than the view that hunting served to help individuals avoid idleness.

22 The three basic styles of hunting were called "the drive," "the chase," and "par
force." Gilbert, *Hunting and Hunting Reserves*, 52–61. On the costs of mounting a hunt,
see 61–62; on "sport" see 73. On the food and social dimensions of hunting, see
Rackham, *Trees and Woodland*, 170. There were elaborate rituals for sounding the
horn, a hierarchy of animal parts assigned by social status, and specialized vocabulary for landscape features. For fuller descriptions, see Edward of Norwich, *The
Master of Game*; and the fourteenth-century poem by Sir Bertilak, "Sir Gawain and
the Green Knight," quoted in Cummins, *The Hound and the Hawk*, 53–54.

23 Dame Juliana Berners, *A Treatise on Fishing with an Angle* (1496), reproduced, with critical commentary by *Sports Illustrated* editors, in John McDonald, *The Origins of Angling*
(Garden City, N.Y., 1963). Regarding the controversy surrounding the authorship
of *A Treatise on Fishing*, see both the commentary in the McDonald volume and, more
recently, Lyla Foggia, *Reel Women: The World of Women Who Fish* (Hillsboro, Oreg.,
1995), chap. 1. The female authorship does not appear to have been questioned at
the time of the treatise's original publication. Charles Chenevix Trench, *A History of
Angling* (St. Albans, Eng., 1974).

24 Cummins, *The Hound and Hawk*, 234, 240.

25 Devèze, *La vie de la forêt*, 1:47, 105; 2:64–67, 70–73, 75–82.

26 Under the Carolingians, forest laws had protected game, but starting at the end of
the fourteenth century, the protection of forests began in earnest. Ibid., 1:58, 64,
67; 2:30, 44. By contrast, Oliver Rackham writes, "other countries have forestry
policies and laws . . . but in England, these were few and unimportant." *Trees and
Woodland*, 77.

27 Trench, *The Poacher*, 120.

28 The earliest French maps were drawn of forests. Chantilly and Périgord Forests
were mapped in the late fifteenth century, and a number of royal forests had been
mapped by the second half of the sixteenth century. The maps' central feature was
their careful identification of the location of timber wood. Roger J. P. Kain and
Elizabeth Baigent, *The Cadastral Map in the Service of the State* (Chicago, 1992), 210–12.

29 Trench reflects the conventional wisdom that the seventeenth century was the age
of destruction in *The Poacher*, 78, 90, 119. Rackham, in *Trees and Woodland*, 83–84, 97,
maintains that it was the eighteenth century. The process began in Scotland in the
fourteenth century, according to Gilbert, *Hunting and Hunting Reserves*, 237–39.

30 Fourteen years after the initial settlement of New England, Charles I attempted to
increase the amount of territory restricted exclusively for his own hunting, excluding his own nobility. Trench, *The Poacher*, 104–5.

31 The first edition of the *Dictionnaire de L'Académie française* (Paris, 1694), 473, defines
forest as "grande estenduë de pays couvert de bois de haute fustaye." The English
definition differs: "A forest is a certain territory of woody grounds and fruitful pastures, privileged for wild beasts and fowls of Forest, chase and warren, to rest and
abide in, in the safe protection of the king, for his princely delight and pleasure,
which territory of ground . . . is meted and bounded with unremovable marks,
meets and boundaries, either known by matter of record or else by prescription."
Manwood, *Treatise of the Laws*, chap. 12, pp. 40–41. See also Trench, *The Poacher*, 120.

32 The tradition of lower-class pest removal continued well into the nineteenth century,

and has even survived in present-day England. Trench, *The Poacher*, 38. In France and Scotland, hunting some small game (agricultural pests in particular) was regarded as free and open to everyone even during the period when aristocratic and noble restrictions were being put in place. Gilbert, *Hunting and Hunting Reserves*, 27–28, 232–33. Only a few small game animals in England were subject to exclusive hunting rights, called warrens. These included hares, rabbits, foxes, wild cats, partridges, and pheasants. Gilbert, *Hunting and Hunting Reserves*, 210–11; P. B. Munshce, *Gentlemen and Poachers: The English Game Laws, 1671–1831* (Cambridge, 1981), 3; Mark Bailey, "The Rabbit and the Medieval East Anglian Economy," *Agricultural History Review* 36 (1988): 1–20. After the end of the main foxhunting season in March/April in England today, "farmers who are losing lambs, piglets or poultry to a fox can call a hunt out, though this is a service, rather than a sport." Foxhunting fact file, BBC News, Saturday, November 29, 1997.

33 Trench, *The Poacher*, 74–75. The use of snares was another popular method considered to be only for common people. Lombard and Frankish laws described hunting with hounds; hunting with running hounds (par force hunting) was introduced into England from Europe. Gilbert, *Hunting and Hunting Reserves*, 57–61.

34 Quoted in Trench, *The Poacher*, 99.

35 Van de Wassenaer, *Historisch verhael*, 71; Howard S. Russell, *Indian New England before the Mayflower* (Hanover, N.H., 1980), 125–26; Karen Kupperman, *Settling with the Indians: The Meeting of English and Indian Culture* (Totowa, N.J., 1980), 88–89. They also hunted by driving large animals into enclosures and by trapping smaller prey.

36 Edward Johnson, *Johnson's Wonder-Working Providence 1628–1651* (1654), ed. J. Franklin Jameson (New York, 1937), 85.

37 David Pietersz de Vries, *Korte historiael* (The Hague, 1911), 257–58; Gilbert, *Hunting and Hunting Reserves*, 52–55.

38 Gabriel Sagard, *The Long Journey to the Country of the Hurons* (Le grand voyage du pays des Hurons, situé en l'Amérique ver la mer douce) (1632; reprint, New York, 1978), 222–28 (in English), 381–85 (in French); Mi'kmak from Nicholas Denys, *The Description and Natural History of the Coasts of North America (Acadia)* (1672; reprint, New York, 1968), quoted in James Axtell, *The Indian Peoples of Eastern America: A Documentary History of the Sexes* (New York, 1981), 116.

39 Van de Wassenaer, *Historisch verhael*, 71.

40 In "selling" land to the English, indigenous peoples could retain hunting rights because hunting was a right separable from landownership. On the separation of hunting from landownership, see Rackham, *Trees and Woodland*, 165–66. Hence deed conveyances of property to English settlers sometimes permitted Indians this use, when it was economically convenient to do so. Examples from Maine are discussed in Emerson W. Baker, "'A Scratch with a Bear's Paw': Anglo-Indian Land Deeds in Early Maine," *Ethnohistory* 36 (1989): 235–56, esp. 245–46.

41 John Cotton, *The Bloody Tenent Washed and Made White in the Blood of the Lamb . . . and a Reply to Mr. Williams* (1647; reprint, New York, 1972), 28.

42 Woodland was characteristically measured in terms of a form of pasturing called "pannage." Loyn, *Anglo-Saxon England*, 369–70; Rackham, *Trees and Woodland*, 155; Trench, *The Poacher*, 41, 43; Gilbert, *Hunting and Hunting Reserves*, 177–78. The use of forests for grazing characterized France and Scotland, but not the Iberian peninsula. Devèze, *La vie de la forêt*, 1:77–128; Gilbert, *Hunting and Hunting Reserves*, 26–28,

175–78, 260–62. Alfonso V's *Libro de Montaría* forbids cutting firewood in the hunting forest; text reproduced in Cummins, *The Hound and the Hawk*, app. 5.

43 William Cronon, *Changes in the Land: Indians, Colonists, and the Ecology of New England* (New York, 1983), 56. Catholic Thomas More is far more critical of English hunting practices in *Utopia* than is Puritan John Cotton. More calls hunting itself seeking "pleasure from the killing and mangling of a poor animal." Thomas More, *Utopia*, in *Complete Works of St. Thomas More*, 15 vols., ed. Edward Surtz and J. H. Hexter (New Haven, Conn., 1965), 4:171.

44 Roger Williams, later the founder of a Puritan settlement in Rhode Island, wrote a series of critical pamphlets beginning in the 1630s. The original treatise, now lost, and probably deliberately destroyed by its author, was drawn up between August 1631 and August 1633. See Massachusetts Historical Society, *Proceedings* 12 (1873): 341–43.

45 Cotton, *The Bloody Tenent Washed*, 28.

46 The tradition continues in England with what is called "terrier work," the use of small dogs to hunt out nuisance animals hiding underground or under rocks, and ferreting, a similar technique for chasing rabbits. Hunting deer on foot with a rifle is called stalking. These definitions are courtesy of the National Working Terrier Federation (U.K.).

47 At negotiations for the Treaty of Easton in 1758, Thomas King protested, "You claim all the wild creatures and will not let us come on your lands so much as to hunt after them . . . but those [animals] that are wild are still ours and should be common to both [Englishmen and natives]; for our nephews, when they sold the land, they did not propose to deprive themselves of hunting wild deer or using a single stick of Wood." Quoted in George S. Snyderman, "Concepts of Land Ownership among the Iroquois and Their Neighbors," in *Symposium on Local Diversity in Iroquois Culture*, ed. William Fenton (Washington, D.C., 1951).

48 William Waller Hening, *Statutes at Large*, 5 vols., 2d ed. (New York, 1823), 1:293–94. The original charters are silent on the subject of hunting rights, perhaps because under English law hunting rights were separable from landownership rights. Gilbert, *Hunting and Hunting Reserves*, 227–30. As a result, native hunting and fishing rights were originally created principally by "treaty," that is, by arrangements between settlers and natives in the New World. Arnold J. F. Laer, ed., *Documents Relating to New Netherland, 1624–1626* (San Marino, Calif., 1924), 10; van de Wassenaer, "Privileges and Exemptions," 91; Felix S. Cohen, *Handbook of Federal Indian Law* (Washington, D.C., 1942), 285–86. Not all "treaties" were so restrictive; Dutch regulations explicitly permitted hunting and fishing.

Regarding the Normans' imposition of forest laws in England, Blackstone accused the Normans of having constrained Saxon freedom to hunt, according to John MacKenzie, *The Empire of Nature: Hunting, Conservation, and British Imperialism* (Manchester, 1988), 13. However, a Saxon king forbade citizens from hunting on his reserves even before the conquest. Gilbert, *Hunting and Hunting Reserves*, 7, 11–12; Trench, *The Poacher*, 22–23, 25; Loyn, *Anglo-Saxon England*, 380. It appears to have been the harsh enforcement rather than the novel laws that most alienated the Saxons.

49 Hening, *Statutes at Large*, 1:410–15.

50 George Percy, "Observations gathered out of a Discourse of the Plantation of the

Southerne Colonie by the English, 1606," in *The Jamestown Voyages under the First Charter, 1606–1609*, 2 vols., ed. Philip L. Barbour (Cambridge, 1969), 1:141.

51 Smith, *A Map of Virginia*, 1:163.

52 Wood, *New England's Prospect*, 112.

53 Gervase Markham, *A Way to Get Wealth* (London, 1653), contains several sections titled "Farewell to husbandry" on the husbandman's recreation. "Gardening . . . I think ought to be applauded and encouraged in all countries . . . [as] a public service to one's country . . . which . . . improve[s] the earth." See also William Temple, *Works of Sir William Temple* (1690; reprint, London, 1814), 3:231.

54 Francisco d'Andrada, *Chronica de el-rei João III* (Coimbra, Portugal, 1796), pt. 4, p. 130. See also Luís de Sousa, *Anais de D. João III*, 2 vols., ed. M. Rodrigues Lapa (Lisbon, 1938), 1:405.

55 Sagard, *The Long Journey*, 96 (in English), 321 (in French).

56 Russel Bouchard, *Armes, chasse et trappage* (Quebec, 1987).

57 Charles V (1322–1328) allowed everyone to hunt for hares and rabbits, but in 1396, Charles VI prohibited nonnobles from hunting without permission. Cummins, *The Hound and the Hawk*, 247. In England, however, nonnobles could not even be granted permission to hunt.

58 Johannes Megapolensis, "Van de Mahakuase Indianen in Nieuw-Nederlandt . . . in 't jaer 1644," in *Beschrijvinge van Virginia, Nieuw Nederlandt, Nieuw Englandt*, comp. Joost Hartgers (Amsterdam, 1651), 46; a different English translation appears in *Narratives of New Netherland, 1609–1664*, ed. J. Franklin Jameson (New York, 1909), 174.

59 Van de Wassenaer, *Historisch verhael*, 77.

60 In Thwaites, *The Jesuit Relations*, 2:77, 79.

CHAPTER 4: OWNERSHIP OF MINERAL RICHES AND THE SPANISH NEED FOR LABOR

1 "Las minas y minerias . . . se tengan por . . . bienes pertenecientes a los Reyes . . . e incorporados por derecho y costumbre en su patrimonio y Corona Real, ahora se hallen y descubran en lugares publicos, ahora en tierras y posesiones de personas particulares." Juan Solórzano Pereira, *Política indiana*, 5 vols. (1648; reprint, Madrid, 1972), bk. 6, chap. 1, no. 17. See also *Recopilación de leyes de los reinos de las indias* (1681), 3 vols. (1791; reprint, Madrid, 1943), bk. 4, tit. 19, law 1 (1526, 1568); Mining Ordinance, for New Spain (Mexico), art. 1, disp. 22 (1783).

2 "La Corona deja sentado que el rescate del oro es negociación de su exclusiva competencia, . . . vigente en el derecho castellano bajomedieval refrendada en las Cortes de Briviesca de 1387." Antonio-Miguel Bernal, "Oro y plata de América," in *Tesoros de México: oro precolombino y plata virreinal* (Seville, 1997).

3 Arabic words that remain in Spanish from that time include *aduana* (customs), *alcalde* (mayor) *alguacil* (police), *almacén* (warehouse), and *arancel* (tariff). See Rafael Ureña y Smenjaud, *Historia de la literatura jurídica española*, 2d ed. (Madrid, 1906), 317.

4 The root *r-k-z* means precious minerals, buried treasures of the earth, positioned in place, embedded firmly, planted or fixed in the ground. Qudama B. Ja'far (d. 932) *Kitab al Kharaj*, ed. and trans. A. Ben Shemesh (Leiden, Netherlands, 1965), chap. 1, p. 24. Another term is *kabi'a* (pl. *kabaya*), a hidden, secret thing. *Kabi'a al ard* means that which is hidden in the earth, natural resources.

5 "And one-fifth of Rikaz (treasures buried before the Islamic era) is to be given to

the state." *Sahih Bukhari*, trans. M. Muhsin Khan, narrated Abu Huraira, vol. 9, bk. 83, no. 47. "Khumus is compulsory on Rikaz." *Sahih Bukhari*, trans. M. Muhsin Khan, narrated Abu Huraira, vol. 2, bk. 24, no. 575. (Both of the preceding translations are available on-line at http://www.usc.edu/dept/msa/fundamentals/hadithsunnah/bukhari/.) "Yahya related to me from Malik from Ibn Shibab from Said ibn al-Musayyab and from Abu Salama ibn Abd ar-Rahman from Abu Hurayra that the Messenger of Allah, may Allah bless him and grant him peace, said, 'There is a tax of a fifth on buried treasure.'" Malik's *Muwatta*, trans. 'A'isha 'Abdarahman at-Tarjumana and Ya'qub Johnson, bk. 17, no. 17.4.9 (available on-line at http://www.usc.edu/dept/msa/fundamentals/hadithsunnah/muwatta/017/mmt.html).

6 'Umar I (ruled 634–44) was the first Muslim leader to adopt the title of *amir* (*amir al Mu'minin*) or "commander of the faithful." In the tenth century, *amir* came to mean commander or leader of a variety of activities, and was customarily a title of the caliphs. The Shia tradition denied that the Omayad or Abbasid caliphs had a right to manage mineral riches, claiming that they could be managed only by an *imam*, of whom Muhammad had been the ninth. In Shia Islam today *ayatollahs* or respected religious leaders rather than the *amir* (who combines political and religious functions) claim permanent charge of all the precious metals underground. In the Sunni tradition, management rests with the *wali al-amir* (person in charge), usually the chief political leader.

7 The portion of the mine's profits were called the *khums* in Arabic and the *quinto* in Spanish.

8 John Henry Wigmore, *A General Survey of Events, Sources, Persons and Movements in Continental Legal History* (Boston, 1912), 604–6.

9 *Subsuelo* was the inalienable property of the crown of Castile from at least the fourteenth century onward. *Ordenamiento de alcalá* (1355), law 47, repeated in the *Nueva recopilación* (1567) as bk. 9, tit. 8, law 1. In earlier legislation the position of the mines was somewhat more ambiguous. The *Siete partidas* (Seville, 1491) have the rents from metal mines belonging to the crown (pt. 3, tit. 28, law 11), but grant ownership of gold, silver, and other precious metals found in placer mines to those who find them (pt. 3, tit. 28, law 5). All codes referred to appear in *Códigos antiguos de España*, vol. 1, ed. Marcelo Martínez Alcubilla (Madrid, 1885), with the exception of the laws for the New World, which are found in the *Recopilación*.

10 *Recopilación*, bk. 4, tit. 10, law 14 (1551, 1563, 1575).

11 *Las siete partidas del sabio rey Don Alonso el IX*, 4 vols., glossed by Gregorio López (Madrid, 1829–31), pt. 3, tit. 28, law 5, treasures laws 10, 11. See also Mining Ordinance for New Spain (Mexico), art. 1, disp. 22 (1783), extended to South America the following year.

12 José de Acosta, *Historia natural y moral de las Indias*, 2d ed. (Mexico City, 1940), chap. 1, p. 140; chap. 2, p. 141.

13 Solórzano, *Política indiana*, bk. 6, chap. 1, no. 15, uses this phrase and indicates the wide variety of political writers who adhered to this definition.

14 Acosta, *Historia natural*, chap. 2, pp. 142–43.

15 Solórzano, *Política indiana*, bk. 6, chap. 1, no. 17, p. 21. The last expedition for which the monarchy demanded a higher percentage was Vélez Mendoza's expedition to Española in 1502. For examples of the 20 percent, see the agreements signed with Diego Velázquez, Yucatán (1518); Rodrigo Bastidas, Sta. Marta (1524); Ldo.

Villalobos, Isla Margarita (1525); Montejo, Yucatán (1526); Pizarro, Perú (1524); Heredia, Tierra Firme (1532); Almagro, Mar del Sur (1534); and Sanabria, Río de la Plata (1540). The *quinto* was sometimes reduced in areas where little or nothing was anticipated, such as in Bermuda and Venezuela in the 1520s and in Argentina in the 1560s. *Recopilación*, bk. 8, tit. 10, law 1 (1504, 1572). The story of the reformulation of the Castilian law under pressure from overseas possessions is particularly ironic because Castilian law was formally the basis of New World law.

16 See *História da colonização portuguesa do Brasil*, 3 vols. (hereafter *HCPB*) (Pôrto Alegre, Brazil, 1921–27) 3:310, September 5, 1534, for the payment of the *quinto* on precious stones and metals. See also Basílio de Malghães, "Os bandeirantes e o reconhecimento do interior," in *História da colonização portuguesa no mundo*, ed. Antonio Baião, Hernani Cidade, and Manuel Murias (Lisbon, 1937–), 3:143–50, esp. 145. By contrast with the Spanish crown, the Portuguese king required that precious stones, pearls, gold, silver, coral, copper, tin, and lead be included in the *quinto*. *HCPB*, 3:312.

17 Roberto Amaral Lapa, *Economia colonial* (São Paulo, 1993, 15–138); Charles Boxer, *The Golden Age of Brazil, 1695–1750: Growing Pains of a Colonial Society* (Berkeley, Calif., 1962); David Davidson, "How the West Was Won: Indians and the State on the Matto Grosso Frontier," in *Colonial Roots of Modern Brazil*, ed. Dauril Alden (Berkeley, Calif., 1973), 61–106; Carlos Mattoso Filipe, "Colonização: A fixação dos colonos e o reconhecimento das riquezas brasileiras," in *Portugal no mundo*, vol. 3, ed. Luís de Albuquerque (Lisbon, 1990), 210–22; Sérgio Buarque de Holanda, "A mineração: Antecedentes luso-brasileiros," and "Metais e pedras preciosas," both in *História geral da civilização brasileira*, ed. Sérgio Buarque de Holanda (São Paulo, 1960), 2:228–58, 2:259–310; Augusto de Lima Jr., *A capitania das minas gerais (origem e formação)*, 3d ed. (Belo Horizonte, Brazil, 1965); Michel Morineau, *Incroyables gazettes et fabuleux métaux: Les Retours de trésors Américains d'aprés les gazettes hollandaises (XVI–XVIII siécles)* (Paris, 1985); Virgilio Noya Pinto, *O ouro brasileiro e o comércio anglo-português* (São Paulo, 1972); José Vicente Serrão, "O ciclo do ouro Brasileiro," in *Portugal no mundo*, vol. 5, ed. Luís de Albequerque (Lisbon, 1991), 272–85.

18 Part of the process of crown ownership was manifested in the requirements for official registration of the terrain in which one claimed to have a right to explore. The boundaries of metal mines are laid out in enormous detail in *HCPB*, 2:171–93, December 16, 1606.

19 The Caribbean *repartimiento* divided up labor, not land, and hence is not related to the division of lands in the Spanish reconquest beginning after 1085. Thomas Glick, *Islamic and Christian Spain in the Early Middle Ages* (Princeton, N.J., 1979), 99–100. Ferdinand legitimated this practice in 1509: "El adelantado, gobernador o pacificador, en quien esta facultada resida, reparta los indios entre los pobladores." *Recopilación*, bk. 6, tit. 8, law 1.

20 "Instrucción a Nicolás Ovando, September 16, 1501," in *Colección de documentos ineditos relativos al descubrimiento . . . en América y Oceanía* (hereafter *CDI*), 42 vols. (Madrid, 1864–84), 31:16.

21 *CDI*, 31:209–12.

22 The initial instructions forbidding coercion were written March 20 and March 29, 1503. The instructions rescinding those orders were issued December 20, 1503. Ibid., 31:156–74, 209–12.

23 Ibid., 31:210–11; emphasis added.

24 As noted above, the process of dividing up Indians among Spanish settlers was called *repartimiento;* the rights to use the labor were called *encomienda.* A still-valuable account is F. A. Kirkpatrick's "Repartimiento-Encomienda," *Hispanic American Historical Review* 19 (1939): 372–79.

25 *CDI,* 31:157.

26 Solórzano states this succintly: "Encomiendas . . . sean un derecho concedido por merced Real." *Política indiana,* bk. 3, chap. 3, nos. 1, 2. Charles V in 1526 also referred to this as "encomienda o tutela." *Colección de documentos inéditos relativos al descubrimiento, conquista y organización de las antiguas posesiones españolas de ultramar* (hereafter *CDU*), 25 vols. (Madrid, 1885–1932), 1:350.

27 *CDI,* 31:157.

28 Ibid. "It will be necessary for us to take advantage of the service of the Indians, compelling those who work." *CDI,* 31:16.

29 Indians were to "labor on their buildings . . . and prepare farms and food for the Christian citizens and residents." *CDI,* 31:210–11. Gold was present in placer deposits, alluvial deposits of sand or gravel containing particles of gold. Considerable effort was required to remove the sand and gravel.

30 Ibid., 31:211. In later years, Spaniards mixed free labor with an adaptation of traditional forms of work to coerce labor. Jeffrey A. Cole, *The Potosí Mita, 1573–1700: Compulsory Indian Labor in the Andes* (Stanford, Calif., 1985); Enrique Tandeter, *Coercion and Market: Silver Mining in Colonial Potosi, 1692–1826* (Albuquerque, N.M., 1993); Peter Bakewell, *Miners of the Red Mountain: Indian Labor in Potosi, 1545–1650* (Albuquerque, N.M., 1984); Valentín Abecia Baldivieso, *Mitayos de Potosí: en una economía sumergida* (Barcelona, 1988).

31 Some of their opinions are transcribed in Manuel Giménez Fernández, *Bartolomé de Las Casas, volúmen primero: Delgado de Cisneros para la reformación de las Indias (1516–1517)* (Seville, 1953), nn. 309–19. The comments of Judge Lucas Vásquez de Ayllón and Dominican friar Bernardo de Santo Domingo appear in their entirety in the same volume (573–600). An abbreviated account of the expedition in English is provided by Lewis Hanke, *The First Social Experiments in America* (Cambridge, Mass., 1935), 25–39.

32 "Carta de los padres jeronimos al Cardenal Cisneros, Jan. 20, 1517," in Manuel Serrano y Sanz, *Orígenes de la dominación española en América* (Madrid, 1918), 550–51.

33 Gímenez Fernández provides an outstanding history of this episode in *Bartolomé de Las Casas,* 363, 372–73, 637–48. See also Hanke, *The First Social Experiments,* 25–39; Serrano, *Orígenes de la dominación,* 339–450; Juan Pérez de Tudela Bueso, "Estudio preliminar," in Bartolomé de Las Casas, *Tratados de Fray Bartolomé de Las Casas,* transcription by Juan Pérez de Tudela Bueso, trans. Augustín Millares Carlo and Rafael Moreno (Mexico City, 1974), xlvii–lxxiv; Marcel Bataillon and André Saint-Liu, *Estudios sobre Bartolomé de Las Casas* (Catalonia, 1976), 10–14.

34 "Carta de los padres jeronimos," 550–51; Gímenez Fernández, *Bartolomé de Las Casas,* 372–73 (for Cisneros's response, see 363, 637–48); Lesley Byrd Simpson, *The Encomienda in New Spain,* 2d ed. (Berkeley, Calif., 1966), 39–55; Hanke, *The First Social Experiments.* In 1509, Ferdinand had unsuccessfully tried to limit the duration of ownership rights to two to three years. *CDI,* 31:439.

35 See *CDI,* 31:436–39 for "Real cédula a Diego Colón, Aug. 14, 1509," on the two- to three-year restriction.

36 The right to hold against others is Roman in origin (*erga omnes*). A subsequent medieval development included alienability. See Paul Ourliac and Jean-Lousi Gazzaniga, *Histoire du droit privé français de l'an mil au code civil* (Paris, 1985), 218–19. Solórzano carefully distinguishes the sense of the word *possession* of an *encomienda* from other senses of the word in *Política indiana*, bk. 3, chap. 3, nos. 4–17, pp. 24–26. He draws analogies to emphyteusis and usufruct, and concludes by describing *encomienda* as "natural" possession (i.e., physical appropriation) and "civil" possession, categories that did not exist in English laws of the time, but that resemble English understandings of usufruct. (bk. 3, chap. 14, nos. 30–32). By 1528, the crown succumbed to colonists' desire to enjoy trusteeship rights to Indian labor in perpetuity. "Instructions for the first Real Audiencia of Mexico, Dec. 1528, and October 8, 1529," in *CDU,* 9:386, 425, 427.

37 As late as the start of the nineteenth century, Alexander von Humboldt equated the *encomienda* with slavery. Alexander von Humboldt, *Political Essay on the Kingdom of New Spain*, 2 vols., trans. John Black (New York, 1811), 1:156.

38 David Brion Davis describes slavery as characterized by ownership of one individual by another; in slavery, the free will of the slave is constrained and labor and services are coerced rather than paid. David Brion Davis, *The Problem of Slavery in Western Culture* (Ithaca, N.Y., 1966).

39 *CDI,* 31:211.

40 Ibid.; emphasis added.

41 Sometimes the word *freedom* meant freedom from *encomienda*. A 1516 petition to the crown labeled the release of Indians from both *encomiendas* and slavery as "giving them their liberty." Relación del gobierno de los yndios" (1516), in Serrano, *Orígenes de la dominación,* 538–40. See also "Instrucciones a Puerto Rico, July 12, 1520," in *CDI,* 7:413. The crown sustained this position. See Diego de Encinas, *Cedulario indiano,* 4 vols. (1596; reprint, Madrid, 1945–46), 4:263 (1543); Serrano, *Orígenes de la dominación,* 605–07; *CDI,* 7:413–14 (1520). In other decrees, *encomienda* meant freedom.

42 *CDI,* 22:170 (1526), 235, 287, 373, 418, 442, 462, 487, 505, 524, 563 (1537). Although it is possible the crown meant these two as alternatives, the more likely formulation in that case would have been liberty or *encomienda*. Whether the crown viewed "*encomienda* and freedom" as alternatives or, more likely, as synonyms, it was clear that the *encomienda* was an institution separate from, and less harmful than, slavery.

43 See Richard Konetzke, ed., *Colección de documentos para la historia de la formación social de Hispanoamérica, 1493–1810,* 3 vols. (Madrid, 1953), 1:94; *CDI,* 1:450–55.

44 Lewis Hanke, *Aristotle and the American Indians* (Chicago, 1959); Lewis Hanke, *The Spanish Struggle for Justice in the Conquest of America* (Philadelphia, 1949).

45 A fuller statement of this argument appears in Patricia Seed, "'Are These Not Also Men?': The Indian's Humanity and Capacity for Spanish Civilization," *Journal of Latin American Studies* 25 (1993): 629–52. Father Manuel da Nóbrega asked the identical question in Bahia in 1556–57: "Estes tem alma como nós?" *Diálogo sobre a conversão do Gentio,* in *Cartas dos primeiros Jesuítas do Brasil,* 3 vols., ed. Serafim Leite (São Paulo, 1956–58), 2:234.

46 The Guale revolted against the Franciscans in 1597, the Apalachees in 1647, and the Timucuas and Apalachees in 1656. Robert Allen Matter, *Pre-Seminole Florida: Spanish Soldiers, Friars, and Indian Missions, 1513–1763* (New York, 1990), 43–44, 59–60.

47 Between 1520 and 1526, the crown strictly forbade trusteeships of Indians in newly conquered regions. *CDI*, 22:79–93, 98–106, 116–24; Encinas, *Cedulario indiano*, 2:185–86.

48 *CDI*, 12:213–15; Silvio Zavala, *La encomienda indiana*, 3rd ed. (Mexico, 1973), 40–50. In instituting the *encomienda*, Cortés renamed it a *deposito*, literally a "deposit," and incorporated the reform requirements given to Figueroa, that *encomenderos* reside in or near the Indian communities. Hernán Cortés, *Cartas de relación*, ed. Manuel Alcalá (México City, 1971), 3d letter; Cortés's ordinances in *CDI*, 26:135 ff. *CDI*, 36:163–64. The results of Cortés's politicking can be seen in Joaquín García Icazbalceta, *Colección de documentos para la historia de México*, 2 vols. (Mexico City, 1858–66), 2:545–53. See also "Provisiones a la Audiencia de México" (1528), in Encinas, *Cedulario indiano*, 2:187–89.

49 *CDI*, 22:153–79 (heirs of Villalobos for Margarita Island), 201–233 (Montejo for Yucatán), 360–83 (Alcazaba for southern Argentina), 406–33 (Alonso de Lugo for Santa Marta), 497–515 (Pizarro and Almagro); *CDI*, 23:8–33 (Cabeza de Vaca for Río de la Plata), 33–55 (Benalcazar for Popayán), 55–74 (Heredia for Cartagena), 74–97 (Gutíerrez for Veragua); *CDU*, 1:393 (Cuba).

50 Solórzano, *Política indiana*, bk. 3, chap. 3, no. 6, 2:23. In 1526 the crown complained that the *audiencia* of Hispaniola "sin comisión ni mandado nuestro se han entremetido y entremeten á hacer e hacen los repartimentos." *CDU*, 1:342. Ironically, the crown also wound up having to grant *encomiendas* to people who had fought for the royal position in Peru. Efrain Trelles Aréstegui, *Lucas Martínez Vegazo: Funcionamiento de una encomienda peruana inicial* (Lima, 1982), 83–85.

51 Trelles Aréstegui, *Lucas Martínez Vegazo*, 177. The collection of goods (rather than labor) from indigenous peoples was called "tribute," and that is the subject of the next chapter. For a recent history of the transition in Peru, see Susan Ramirez, *The World Turned Upside Down* (Stanford, Calif., 1996).

52 Sergio Navarrete Pellicer, "Las transformaciones de la economía indígena en Michoacán: siglo XVI," in *Agricultura indígena: Pasado y presente*, ed. Teresa Rojas Rabiela (Mexico City, 1990), 109–27.

53 Encinas, *Cedulario indiano*, 3:1; Solórzano, *Política indiana*, bk. 3, chap. 3, no. 6, 2:23; *CDU*, 1:342–44, 348–50.

54 *CDI*, 31:211.

55 Although Bartolomé de Las Casas is customarily credited with changing Charles's mind on this matter, it is perhaps equally probable that the letters from Franciscan Pieter van Gent (Pedro de Gante), possibly Charles's half-brother, made a bigger impression on the king. For some of Pieter's letters in English, see John Everaert, "The Conquest of the Soul," in *America: Bride of the Sun*, ed. Paul Vandenbroek (Antwerp, 1992), 59–68. A brief biography of Pieter appears in Benjamin de Troeyer, *Bio-bibliographia franciscana neerlandica saeculi XVI* (Nieuwkoop, Netherlands, 1969), 75–86.

56 The first law forbidding tribute payments with labor appeared in 1549. *Recopilación*, bk. 6, tit. 5, law 24 (repeated in 1633). Hunted goods and presents were banned as tribute in 1553 (bk. 6, tit. 5, law 26), and in 1612 the payment of tribute in money outright was welcomed (bk. 6, tit. 5, law 40). Further elaboration appears in Solórzano, *Política indiana*, bk. 2, chap. 2, no. 6; *Recopilación*, bk. 6, tit. 5, law 24, and bk. 6, tit. 12, laws 47, 49. Similar, but not identical, interpretations are found in Charles Gibson, *Spain in America* (New York, 1967), 60–62. Only Simpson appears

to date the effort to eliminate labor from 1542; see *The Encomienda in New Spain*, 140. The quantification enhanced the portability of profits, but also allowed the crown to demand a percentage. "Tasar a los indios en oro . . . de manera que S. M. pudiera tener provecho de los quintos del mismo." "Instrucción a Juan López de Cepeda (Dec. 15, 1570)," quoted in María Angeles Eugenio Martínez, *Tributo y trabajo de los indios en Nueva Granada* (Seville, 1977), 150. See also Enrique Semo, *The History of Capitalism in Mexico: Its Origins 1521–1763* (Austin, Tex., 1993).

Trustees often circumvented the rule limiting the inheritance of trusteeships by marrying, even on their deathbeds, very young spouses who would be considered the same "generation." Thus a trust could be held technically still in its first generation when, in fact, it had passed to another. Owing to such subterfuge, labor trusteeships did not entirely cease until the middle of the eighteenth century, by which time they were no longer the major source of wealth for Spaniards. Solórzano, *Política indiana*, bk. 3, chaps. 17–24.

57 Noble David Cook, *Demographic Collapse, Indian Peru, 1520–1620* (Cambridge, 1981); David Henige, *Numbers from Nowhere: The American Indian Contact Population Debate* (Norman, Okla., 1998). In addition to these books, there are several well-known articles on this topic, including Robert McCaa, "Spanish and Nahuatl Views on Smallpox and Demographic Catastrophe in Mexico," *Journal of Interdisciplinary History* 25 (1995): 397–426; Henry F. Dobyns, "Disease Transfer at Contact," *Annual Review of Anthropology* 22 (1993), 273–91; John Zambardino, "Mexican Population in the Sixteenth Century," *Journal of Interdisciplinary History* 11 (1980): 1–28.

58 Guillermo Lohman says that by the 1560s, finding mine workers had become more important to Spanish settlers than locating *encomiendas*. Guillermo Lohman, "Unas notas acerca de curiosos paralelismos y correspondencias entre cuatro documentos históricos sobre la época incaica," *Fénix: Revista de la Biblioteca Nacional,* 16 (1966): 174–97. Demanding tribute payments in cash to force natives to enter local wage labor markets was also common. By 1582, 50 percent of such payments had to be in cash. Cook, *Demographic Collapse,* 134; Ronald Escobedo Mansilla, *El tributo indígena en el Peru: Siglos XVI y XVII* (Pamplona, 1979); Nelida Bonaccorsi, *El trabajo obligatorio indigena en Chiapas, siglo XVI* (Mexico City, 1990).

59 See the extensive literature on the creation of *cabaceras* and *sujetos* in Peter Gerhard, *A Guide to the Historical Geography of New Spain* (Cambridge, 1972).

60 Silvio Zavala, *Fuentes para la historia del trabajo en México,* 8 vols. (Mexico City, 1939–45), 6:xxi–xxii, xxx–xxxi, xliv, 394–97, 616ff; Cook, *Demographic Collapse,* 138–39; Ann M. Wightman, *Indigenous Migration and Social Change: The Forasteros of Cuzco, 1520–1720* (Durham, N.C., 1990).

61 Juan Friede, "De la encomienda a la propriedad territorial," *Anuario Colombiano de Historia Social y de la Cultura* 4 (1969): 43.

62 "So color de religión / Van a buscar plata y oro / Del encubierto tesoro." Lope De Vega, *El Nuevo Mundo, descubierto por Cristóbal Colón,* in *Comedias,* vol. 7 (Madrid, 1994), jornada 1.

63 Acosta, *Historia natural,* chap. 2, pp. 142–43.

64 On the absence of such conflicts in Portuguese thinking, see the discussion in São Paulo, *Atas da câmara da cidade de São Paulo,* 72 vols. (São Paulo, 1914–), 2:497–500.

65 "Murieron . . . por servir a Dios y a Su Majestad, y dar luz a los que esteban en tinieblas, y también pro haber riquezas, que todos los hombres comúnmente

venimos a buscar." Bernal Díaz del Castillo, *Historia de la Conquista de Nueva España* (Mexico City, 1960), chap. 210, p. 584. There is, of course, the exception: "Es apariencia vana / querer mostrar que el principal intento / fue el extender la religión cristiana / siendo el puro interés su fundamento." Alonso Ercilla y Zúñiga, *La Araucana* (Madrid, 1993), 23:12–13.

66 John Smith, *Advertisements for the Unexperienced Planters of New-England* (1631), in *The Works of Captain John Smith*, 3 vols., ed. Philip L. Barbour (Chapel Hill, N.C., 1986), 3:272. See also William Crashaw (1572–1626), *A New-yeeres Gift to Virginia* (London, 1610).

67 Potential English colonists "make many excuses, and devise objections; but the fountaine of all is, because they may not have present profit." Crashaw, *A New-yeeres Gift*, n.p. See also Walter Ralegh, *The Discoverie of The Large and Bewtiful Empyre of Guiana* (1596), ed. Neil L. Whitehead (Norman, Okla., 1997); Louis B. Wright, *The Colonial Search for a Southern Eden* (New York, 1953), 8–19.

68 Rowland Watkins, "Faith," in *Flamma Sine Fumo; or, Poems without Fictions* (London, 1662), ll. 12–14; John Donne, "Elegy XIX," in *The Elegies* (Oxford, 1965), ll. 27–30.

69 "Nothing inconsistent with the notion that private property in mines accompanied ownership of the soil is to be found either in the notes of mineral property in the Doomsday Book or in the charters of the Anglo-Saxon kings." George Randall Lewis, *The Stanneries: A Study of the English Miner* (Cambridge, Mass., 1924), 75, 78.

70 Edward I's creditors were Florentine financiers. Ibid., 77, 192; J. H. Baker, *An Introduction to English Legal History*, 2d ed. (London, 1979), 317.

71 See Edmund Plowden, *Commentaries* (London, 1571), folios 313v, 315–315v; Thomas Bushell, *A Just and True Remonstrance of His Majesties Mines-Royall in the Principalitie of Wales* (London, 1641). Frederick Pollock and Robert S. Wright, in *An Essay on Possession in the Common Law* (Oxford, 1888), 42, point out how different English law on this subject was from the Roman law. See also William Searle Holdsworth, *A History of English Law*, 16 vols. (London, 1966), 7:485–88.

72 "Freeborn subjects of the Crown may have . . . full power of using their own endeavors to improve their own interests together with the revenues of the Crown." Payments to the king were between one-eighth and one-twelfth of the revenues realized. Thomas Houghton, *Royal Institutions: Being Proposals for Articles to Establish and Confirm Laws, Liberties and Customs of Silver and Gold Mines to All King's Subjects in such Parts of Africa and America Which Are Now (or Shall Be) Annexed to and Dependent on the Crown of England* (London, 1694), 86, 6–7. The royal grant to Lord Baltimore seeks the same amount the Spanish king received: "And We do by these presents . . . constitute him, the now Baron of Baltimore, and his heirs, the True and Absolute Lords and Proprietaries of the Region aforesaid . . . Yielding therefore, unto Us, our heirs and successors Two Indian Arrows of those parts, to be delivered at the said Castle of Windsor, every year, on Tuesday in Easter week; and also the fifth part of all Gold and Silver Ore which shall happen from time to time to be found within the aforesaid limits." *Archives of Maryland*, 73:21. (These archives are available on-line at http://www.mdarchives.state.md.us/.)

73 See "Payment by the Corporation of Dover for a share in a Venture to Virginia, 1610," in Alexander Brown, *The Genesis of the United States*, 2 vols. (1890; reprint, New York, 1964), 391–92. For a proposal to grant Englishmen private ownership, see Houghton, *Royal Institutions*, 86–87.

74 "Alle mineralen, nieuwe gevonden ofte noch te vinden minnen van goud, zilver, koper ofte enige andere metalen, als ook van gesteenten, diamanten, robijnen einde dergelijke, mitsgaders de peerlvisschereye sullen allen by die van de Comp. bearbeidt moeten worden." In Arnold J. F. Laer, ed., *Documents Relating to New Netherland, 1624–1626* (San Marino, Calif., 1924), 10. For ownership by the patroon, see Nicolaes van de Wassenaer, "Privileges and Exemptions for Patroons" (June 7, 1629), in *Historisch verhael alder ghedenck-Geschiedenisen die hier en daer in Europa*, trans. in *Narratives of New Netherland, 1609–1664*, ed. J. Franklin Jameson (New York, 1909), 95, sec. 24, p. 95.

75 Under the provisional regulations for Dutch settlement in the New World (1624), anyone who discovered gold, silver, copper, diamonds, rubies, or pearls was to be given one-tenth of the net proceeds of the mine for six years, beginning not with the date of discovery but with the date the company began to work the mine. The amount paid to the discoverer was to be net of the cost of exploiting the mine and the tools. Only the company would be allowed to work the mine. Laer, *Documents*, 10–13. The Spanish system, by contrast, permitted only private individuals to supervise work in the mines. The Dutch system of rewarding the finder developed from twelfth-century German mining tradition. For information on the German mining traditions (in English), see Lewis, *The Stanneries*, 70.

76 Solórzano, *Política indiana*, bk. 6, chap. 1, no. 17. For details of how mining claims were established in the sixteenth century, see Gonzalo Fernández de Oviedo, *Historia general y natural de las indias*, 5 vols, ed. Juan Pérez de Tudela Bueso (Madrid, 1959), bk. 3, chap. 8, 1:110. On Portuguese America, see the description of registration procedures in São Paulo, *Atas da câmara*, 2:71–93.

CHAPTER 5: TRIBUTE AND SOCIAL HUMILIATION

1 The modern *Enciclopedia universal ilustrada Europeo-Americana*, 10 vols. (Madrid, 1930–33), provides almost the same listing under the heading of "tributo" as does seventeenth-century political theorist Juan Solórzano Pereira (1575–1655) in the index he compiled for his *Política indiana*, 5 vols. (Madrid, 1972) 5:357–58.

2 Spanish uses the phrase *república de indios*, but the word *republic* came into English only at the start of the seventeenth century and developed an entirely different meaning. *Oxford English Dictionary*, 2d ed. (hereafter *OED*), s.v. "republic."

3 In Maliki jurisprudence all conquered males paid such tribute. In other schools of Islamic law, only Jews and Christians did so.

4 The full statement is as follows: "Find those who believe not in Allah nor in the last day [the day of Judgment] nor hold forbidden that which has been forbidden by Allah and his apostles nor acknowledge the religion of truth [Islam] even if they are the people of the book until they pay the poll-tax [*jizya*] with willing submission and feel themselves subdued [belittled]." Many contemporary exegetes make this struggle a personal one, but during the Golden Age of Islam in Iberia, the disgrace was public. All quotations from the Qur'an are from *Al-Qur'an*, trans. Ahmed Ali (Karachi, Pakistan, 1984).

5 Syed Muhammad Hasan-uz-Zaman, *The Economic Functions of the Early Islamic State* (Karachi, Pakistan, 1981), 70, also uses the related expression "being brought low." See also Bernard Lewis's transcriptions of the seventh-century peace terms in *Islam: From the Prophet Muhammad to the Capture of Constantinople*, vol. 1, *Politics and War* (New

York, 1987), 239–41. Later examples appear in Arthur S. Tritton, *The Caliphs and Their Non-Muslim Subjects* (London, 1938), 227.

6 Zaman, *The Economic Functions*, 70. See also Hanna E. Kassis, *A Concordance of the Qur'an* (Berkeley, Calif., 1983), 263: "Until they pay the tribute out of hand and have been humbled."

7 Sometimes paying tribute in a ritual humiliating fashion led individuals who had to pay the tax to abandon their religion. In Iran, the officers of the Iranian cavalry and some members of the Iranian aristocracy converted in order to avoid the ceremonial humiliation. Nehemia Levtzion, "Introduction," in *Conversion to Islam*, ed. Nehemia Levtzion (New York, 1978), 9.

8 Sundiata A. Djata, *The Banana Empire by the Niger: Kingdom, Jihad and Colonization 1712–1920* (Princeton, N.J., 1997), includes a brief account of the earlier history of this region.

9 Norman Stillman, *Jews of Arab Lands* (Philadelphia, 1979), 270.

10 *First Encyclopaedia of Islam* (1913–36; reprint, Leiden, Netherlands, 1987), s.v. "dhimma." For variation within Islam on the details, see Tritton, *The Caliphs*, 1–17, 114–26. Other deferential behavior was often expected. See Ali ibn Mohammed ibn Habib, el Mâwardi (d. 1058), *Akham al-sultaniyah wa-al-wilayat al-diniyah: Les statuts gouvernmenteaux*, trans. and annot. Emile Fagnan (Algiers, 1915), 299 ff.

11 Compare the complaints on Christian women's fine clothes in Mameluke, Egypt, and those against the silks of the blacks of New Spain. Stillman, *Jews of Arab Lands*, 271–72; Colin Palmer, *Slaves of the White God* (Cambridge, Mass., 1976).

12 Jean-Pierre Molnat, "Mudjares, cativos e libertos," in *Toledo, séculos XII–XIII: Musulmanos, cristãos e judeus: o saber e a tolerância*, ed. Louis Cardaillac, trans. Lucy Magalhães (Rio de Janeiro, 1992), 101–2. The architect of the policy, Sisnando Davídiz, was a native of Coimbra. Alexandre Herculano, *História de Portugal desde o começo da monarquia ate o fim do reinado de Alfonso III*, 4 vols., ed. José Mattoso (Amadora, 1980), 2:304 n. 37; Ramón Menéndez Pidal and E. García Gómez, "El conde Mozárabe Sisnado Davídiz y la política de Alfonso VI con los Taifas," *Al-Andalus* 12 (1947). 27–42. Iberian kings subsequently used these techniques in the cities of Sepúlveda (1076) and Cuenca (1177), and Jaime I employed them throughout Valencia. Robert I. Burns, *Jaume I i els valencians del seglo XIII* (Valencia, 1981), 1, 149–236; "Convenio hecho con los moros" (1352), in Mercedes García-Arenal and Beatrice Leroy, *Moros y judíos en Navarra en la baja edad media* (Madrid, 1984), 72. For a list of *pechas* to be paid by these Moors in 1234, see José María Lacarra, *Documentos para el estudio de la reconquista y repoblacion del valle del Ebro*, 2 vols. (Zaragoza, 1982–85), 2:98–100. For the Arago-Catalan world, see Felipe Fernández-Armesto, *Before Columbus* (London, 1987), 24–25.

13 On the dress requirements of Muslims in Aragon, see John Boswell, *The Royal Treasure: Muslim Communities under the Crown of Aragon in the Fourteenth Century* (New Haven, Conn., 1977), 331.

14 Distinctive dress was required initially of Jews but not of Muslims, because Muslim men in particular dressed differently owing to religious custom. *Las siete partidas* (Seville, 1491), pt. 7, tit. 24, law 11. On agreements with Aragon's Christian princes, see Boswell, *The Royal Treasure*, 272.

15 On Toledo, see Menéndez Pidal and García Gómez, "El conde Mozárabe Sisnado Davídiz," 27–42. Identical language appeared in the agreements with Muslims in

Sepúlveda (1076), Cuenca (1177), and Valencia. Lacarra, *Documentos*, 2:98–100; Burns, *Jaume I*, 1, 149–236; "Convenio hecho con los moros," 72.

16 *Thesaurus linguae Latinae*, 10 vols. (Leipzig, 1900–), 10:1, 11. *Pacífico* connotes reconciliation.

17 Juan Corominas and José Pascual, *Diccionario critico etimológico castellano e hispánico*, 5 vols. (Madrid, 1980–91), 4:337.

18 Contrast Jan Niermeyer, *Mediae latinitatis lexicon minus* (Leiden, Netherlands, 1976), 750, with the following: Corominas and Pascual, *Diccionario*, 4:337; Sebastian de Covarrubias, *Tesoro de la lengua castellana e española* (1611; reprint, Madrid, 1984). *Pecho por tierra* means to come with humility. Also contrast Paul Robert, *Dictionnaire alphabétique et analogique de la langue française* (Paris, 1985); and *OED*, s.v. "pacify," definitions 2c, 3.

19 In Aragon it was called *peyta*. Boswell, *The Royal Treasure*, 23–28. Covarrubias, in *Tesoro de la lengua castellana*, describes the Latin meaning of *pecho* as an agreement (*concierto*) because by means of the tribute or agreement, the punishment was satisfied. *Pecho* was a financial penalty imposed for a crime. *Pechar*, according to Corominas and Pascual's *Diccionario*, meant to pay *pecho*.

20 In the classic statement of the thirteenth-century Spanish laws known as the *Leyes de partida*, "Pechos or tribute are those [moneys] which are paid to the King as a sign of recognition of his dominion or lordship [*señorío*]." *Leyes de partida*, pt. 3, tit. 18, law 10, and the last law, which says, "Ca moneda es pecho que toma el Rey en su tierra apartadamente en señal de señorío conocido." In medieval Portugal, large portions of which were never subject to Muslim rule, a different set of exemptions distinguished the *fidalgo* (the noble) from the commoner. Rather than exemption from a personal tax, *fidalgos* sought immunity from royal jurisdiction and protection of their lands from royal land taxes. "Mas abusivamente todo o fidalgo foi considerando a imunidade das suas terras como privilégio inerente a sua condição." Marcello Caetano, *Lições de historia do direito português* (Coimbra, Portugal, 1962), 168.

21 *First Encyclopaedia of Islam*, s.v. "dhimma." On the origin of these protections in the actions of the Prophet, see Qudama B. Ja'far (d. 932), *Kitab al Kharaj*, ed. and trans. A. Ben Shemesh (Leiden, Netherlands, 1965), chap. 4, p. 30. For a brief history of the practice (rather than the theory), see Francesco Gabrieli, *Arabeschi e studi Islamici* (Naples, 1973), 25–36.

22 Similar agreements were signed with Goth leaders Theodomir and Tudmir in 713, and with the Christians of Mallorca and Minorca in 849.

23 The followers of scripture-based religions, such as Christianity and Judaism, were known as the "people of the book." Zoroastrianism is also sometimes included in this category.

24 This is a slightly different interpretation than the fourteenth-century Maghreb intellectual Ibn Khaldûn offered. In the *Muqaddimah* he suggested that tribally organized migratory peoples could easily acquire military superiority over settled peoples by capitalizing on the inherently stronger group feeling (*'asabiyyah*) that kinship organization provided. Ibn Khaldûn, *The Muqaddimah: An Introduction to History*, 3 vols., trans. Franz Rosenthal (Princeton, N.J., 1967).

25 Only aristocrats who had fought the invaders were deprived of their properties. Averroës (Ibn Rushd), *Jihad in Medieval and Modern Islam*, trans. Rudolph Peters (Leiden, Netherlands, 1977), 11; Stanley Payne, *A History of Spain and Portugal*,

2 vols. (Madison, Wis., 1973), 1:17; Antonio Dominguez Ortiz, *La sociedad española en el siglo XVII*, 2 vols. (Granada, 1992).

26 "In every sort of case, civil or criminal, you shall be judged by and according to the çuna [sunna] and not by the civil law or any other law or custom of the land." Quoted in Boswell, *The Royal Treasure*, 31. On Jews, see Yitzjak Baer, *A History of the Jews in Christian Spain*, 2 vols. (Philadelphia, 1961), 1:118–19. Muslims were to be governed by their own rules in Valencia. Robert Burns, *Islam under the Crusaders: Colonial Survival in the Thirteenth-Century Kingdom of Valencia* (Princeton, N.J., 1973), 102–3.

27 The imitation of Islamic tradition in this instance was often self-conscious. In the agreement signed in 1352 between the Moors of Cortés and the king of Navarre, the Moors became the tribute payers to the king of Navarre, according to those "privileges, agreements, treaties, and compositions said to be paid and passed in the times past between the Kings of said kingdom of Navarre and the Moors of the said town of Cortés. Said Charter, letter, privilege or compositions were in the archives and writings [*escritura*] of the said Chamber of Comptos where similar items and acts are held." Tomás Muñoz y Romero, ed., *Colección de fueros municipales y cartas pueblas de las [sic] reinos de Castilla, León, corona de Aragón y Navarra* (Madrid, 1847), 415–26 (Navarra).

28 The Spaniards called them *cartas pueblas* rather than *dhimmi* agreements, and they were used throughout the Iberian Peninsula from the eleventh through the thirteenth centuries. Robert Burns, *Muslims, Christians, and Jews in the Crusader Kingdom of Valencia* (Cambridge, 1984), 58–79, 248–83, 288–91; Jose M. Fonts Rius, ed., *Cartas de población y franquicia de Cataluña* (Madrid, 1969). Burns's comments on their "Roman" character center on only the novel rationalizations Christians created, not their content; see *Muslims, Christians, and Jews*, 54–58. Thus the thirteenth-century charters granted for the Alfandech valley differ from a *dhimmi* relationship only in the modification of the salt monopoly and the right to bear arms, which was accorded to these Muslims. All the other privileges are those of the Islamic *dhimma*. For examples of how such communities functioned, see Miguel Angel Motis Dolader, *Los judíos en Aragón en la edad media (siglos XIII–XV)* (Zaragoza, 1990); José Amador de los Ríos, *Historia social, política y religiosa de los judíos de España y Portugal*, 3 vols. (Madrid, 1984); Yom Tov Assis, *The Golden Age of Aragonese Jewry: Community and Society in the Crown of Aragon, 1213–1327* (Portland, Oreg., 1997). The explicit connection between tribute and retention of land rights is a Christian reinterpretation of the earlier Muslim pacts.

29 Boswell carefully calls the privileges of the Muslims under Christian rule in Aragon not "rights" but "concessions"; see *The Royal Treasure*, 261.

30 Charles Bishko, "The Spanish and Portuguese Reconquest, 1095–1492," in *A History of the Crusades*, vol. 3, *The Fourteenth and Fifteenth Centuries*, ed. Harry W. Hazard (Madison, Wis., 1975), 417.

31 Burns, *Muslims, Christians, and Jews*, 13.

32 Boswell, *The Royal Treasure*, 73; Donald J. Kagay, "The Essential Enemy: The Image of the Muslim as Adversary and Vassal in the Law and Literature of the Medieval Crown of Aragon," in *Western Views of Islam in Medieval and Early Modern Europe: Perception of Other*, ed. David R. Blanks and Michael Frassetto (New York, 1999), 119–36.

33 Ahmed ibn Mohammed al-Makkari (d. 1632), *The History of the Mohammedan Dynasties in Spain* (1843), 2 vols., trans. Pascual de Gayangos (New York, 1964), 2:388–89.

34 "Instrucción a Nicolás de Ovando, September 16, 1501," in *Colección de documentos ineditos relativos al descubrimiento . . . en América y Oceanía*, (hereafter *CDI*), 42 vols. (Madrid, 1864–84), 31:15–16. For the uniqueness of this requirement relative to other Spanish taxes, see José Miranda, *El tributo indígena en la Nueva España durante el siglo XVI* (Mexico City, 1952), 37.

35 The largest Spanish settlements were on Hispaniola, Puerto Rico, and Cuba. Only a few settled on the northern coast of Spanish America near pearl fisheries, surrounded by an inhospitable swampy landscape. The native communities on these islands and coastal Venezuela were small-scale cultivators, fishers, and hunters. They held only small amounts of fruitful agricultural terrain.

36 Isabel first connected tribute payment to crown vassal status in 1501 and repeated the statement in 1503. *CDI*, 22:79–93, 98–106, 116–24; Diego de Encinas, *Cedulario indiano*, 4 vols. (1596; reprint, Madrid, 1946), 2:185–86; Miranda, *El tributo indígena*, 40, 46–47,184–85. The crown was interested in levying these taxes as early as 1518, but as the Figueroa questionnaire indicated, had doubts about the potential for large agriculture-based settlements such as those upon which tribute in Spain rested. The complete Figueroa Interrogatory appears in Manuel Giménez Fernández, *Bartolomé de Las Casas, volúmen primero: Delgado de Cisneros para la reformación de las indias (1516–1517)* (Seville, 1953). On the attempt to use native structures, see Miranda, *El tributo indígena*, 45–93. Officials convened by Charles V in 1529 to study the legality of tribute agreed that Indians could pay "only those [charges] that such vassals paid in Spain." Solórzano, *Política indiana*, 1:102, 156. Columbus instituted a version of tribute requiring that every Indian male over fourteen years of age pay a fixed amount of gold ("a large belly-full of gold dust") every three months. Those who did not were put to death.

Sixteenth-century Spaniards were understandably reluctant to acknowledge the Islamic origin of their New World practices. As a result, Sebastian de Covarrubias invented an entirely new (and erroneous) etymology for the word *tribute* in his 1611 *Tesoro de la lengua castellana*. He claimed the word *tribute* came from Latin, where it meant both a group subject to head tax (tribe) and the taxes themselves. Unfortunately, "head tax" in Latin was *capitatio*, not *tribute*. Roman tribute was a fixed sum often levied on urban communities, where it was not dependent upon head counts. When levied on rural landowners, it taxed landholders according to the numbers of laborers they employed. Covarrubias was wrong about the origin being Latin, but he was right if you substitute Arabic for Latin. The Arabic word for tribute, *garama* (*gharam*), was also the same as that for the Arabic tribes subject to taxation (*al-gaba'il al gharima*). Reinhart Pieter Dozy, *Supplément aux dictionnaires arabes*, 2 vols. (Leiden, Netherlands,1881), 2:209. But asserting the Islamic origin of Christian political and religious practices has always been highly sensitive.

37 "Real cédula, June 26, 1523," repeated in the modified Ordenanzas of 1572 in Ord. 146, *Recopilación de leyes de los reinos de las Indias* (1681), 3 vols. (1791; reprint, Madrid, 1943), bk. 6, tit. 5, law 1.

38 *CDI*, 41:198; Woodrow Borah and Sherburne Cook, *Essays in Population History: Mexico and the Caribbean*, 3 vols. (Berkeley, Calif. 1971) 2:13, 78; Efrain Trelles Aréstegui, *Lucas Martínez Vegazo: Funcionamiento de una encomienda peruana inicial* (Lima, 1982), 145. Tribute payers in New Granada were men between the ages of fifteen or eighteen and fifty; women, children, and men who were physically handicapped

were excluded. María Angeles Eugenio Martínez, *Tributo y trabajo de los indios en Nueva Granada* (Seville, 1977), 185. A 1564 decision for the tropical regions set the lower age at 15. Martínez, *Tributo y trabajo*, 261. In 1578, the ages for tribute payers in New Spain were eighteen to fifty, but after the end of the sixteenth century the age at which payments began was twenty-five. Although the final quantities to be paid could be negotiated, the numbers of males fixed the framework. Miranda, *El tributo indígena*, 279–325, 332–41.

39 Miranda, *El tributo indígena*, 277.

40 Trelles Aréstegui, *Lucas Martínez Vegazo*, 180–81. In 1595 in Nazca (Peru) and in 1626 in Cayao Ayamara, leaders were imprisoned to force tribute payments. Noble David Cook, *Demographic Collapse, Indian Peru, 1520–1620* (Cambridge, 1981), 162, 228.

41 Solórzano, *Política indiana*, bk. 2, chap. 19, no. 21.

42 Tribute was considered compensation for the conquerors' having to teach the natives Christianity. Ibid. This rationale has also been used in Islam to justify *jizya*.

43 Ibid., bk. 2, chap. 19, no. 36; emphasis added.

44 "Instrucciones a Hernán Cortés, June 26, 1523," in *CDI*, 9:167; "Instrucciones a Ponce de León," in *CDI*, 9:24; "Instrucciones a Rodrigo de Figueroa, 1518," in *CDI*, 23:332; "Instrucciones a los frailes jerónimos, 1516," in *CDI*, 23:310.

45 Miranda, *El tributo indígena*, 180.

46 María de los Ángeles Frizzi, *El sol y la cruz: Los pueblos indios de Oaxaca colonial* (Mexico City, 1996).

47 *OED*, s.v. "republic," esp. definition 2a.

48 For figures on poll tax payments in Arabia under the Prophet, see S. M. Hasanuz Zaman, *Economic Functions of an Islamic State (The Early Experience)* (Leicester, 1991), 205–7. On Peru, see Karen Spalding, *Huarochirí: An Andean Society under Inca and Spanish Rule* (Stanford, Calif., 1984), 159–63, 217–19; Clara López Beltrán, *Estructura económica de una sociedad colonial: Charcas en el siglo XVII* (La Paz, 1988), 140–45.

49 Karen Dakin and Christopher Lutz, *Nuestro pesar: Nuestro aflición Tunetulinilz tucucua: Memorias en lengua náhuatl enviadas a Felipe II por indígenas del Valle de Guatemala hacia 1572* (Mexico City, 1996), 37, 73.

50 The rationale for continuing Spanish taxation policies was made official in 1529. Solórzano, *Política indiana*, 1:102, 156.

51 "Instrucciones que se dieron a Hernando Cortés, June 26, 1523," in *Colección de documentos para la historia de la formación social de Hispanoamérica, 1493–1810*, 3 vols., ed. Richard Konetzke (Madrid, 1953), 1:76; *CDI*, 23:358–59.

52 "Informáis y sepáis que servicio, tributo y vasallaje lleva . . . y si este . . . es de antigüedad, y que lo heredaran de sus pasados, y lo llevaran con su justo y derecho tributo, o si es impuesto tiránicamente." "Real cédula, Aug. 16, 1563," in *CDI*, 18:497. To show that tribute was legitimately imposed, the answer clearly had to be that it was merely continuing native traditions. An earlier questionnaire composed in 1559 for the kingdom of Peru asked the natives what tributes they paid to their lords, whether the taxes were based on land (*kharaj*) or head count (*jizya*), and whether they owed their lords "personal services" (code word for labor). The questions that the Spaniards consistently asked of indigenous communities were, at core, intended to show which of the Islamic categories of tribute the local system fit. John Murra, "'Nos Hacen Mucha Ventaja': The Early European Perception of

Andean Achievement," in *Transatlantic Encounters: Europeans and Andeans in the Sixteenth Century*, ed. Rolena Adorno and Kenneth Andrien (Berkeley, Calif., 1991), 80–81.

53 Cook, *Demographic Collapse*, 11, 45–48. Spanish bureaucrats and settlers experienced considerable difficulties in forcing their expectations of age sets to mesh with the status distinctions with which Incas and others were familiar.

54 James Lockhart, *The Nahuas after the Conquest* (Stanford, Calif., 1992), 14, 507 n. 69.

55 Susan Kellogg, *Law and the Transformation of Aztec Society* (Norman, Okla., 1995), 183.

56 "[Tribute] does not take into consideration the estates, nor the charges on them, but is equally divided by head [count]. . . . Each Indian . . . by his person must pay the same quantity of money, wheat, hens, mantles, or corn, or other spices which are taxed." Solórzano, *Política indiana*, bk. 2, chap. 19, no. 36.

57 Willam T. Sanders, "The Population of the Central Mexican Symbiotic Region, the Basin of Mexico, and the Teotihuacán Valley in the Sixteenth Century," in *The Native Population of the Americas in 1492*, 2d ed., ed. William M. Denevan (Madison, Wis., 1992), 113.

58 Ross Hassig, *Trade, Tribute, and Transportation: The Sixteenth-Century Political Economy of the Valley of Mexico* (Norman, Okla., 1985), 106–8.

59 The eastern tributary province provided luxury goods, precious metals, feathers, and stones. Frances F. Berdan, "Economic Alternatives under Imperial Rule: The Eastern Aztec Empire," in *Economies and Polities in the Aztec Realm*, ed. Margy G. Hodge and Michael E. Smith (Austin, Tex., 1994), 291–312, esp. 297, 300, 307.

60 In highland Mexico there were *teccallaec*, families of commoners assigned to support local officials, and *mayeques*, who tilled the private estates of the nobility. Borah and Cook, *Essays in Population History*, 1:18. None of these individuals paid tribute, nor did local caciques, nobles, or community officials. But after 1548, nearly all the regional exemptions were eliminated. In 1548 they were eliminated for Guatemala and Yucatán, followed by the *audiencia* of Guadalajara and, in 1570, the *audiencia* of Mexico. Ibid., 1:19–20.

61 "Instructions to Lic. Rodrigo Figueroa, December 9, 1518," in Manuel Serrano y Sanz, *Orígenes de la dominación española en América* (Madrid, 1918), 587–92. "Del intento que aquí se ha tenido . . . que es que los indios viven se conserven y multipliquen" (588).

62 *Recopilación* has single men at eighteen; bk. 6, tit. 5, law 7 (1578, 1618).

63 "How the *Jizya* Is to Be Collected and from Whom," in Stillman, *Jews of Arab Lands*, 159–60. Women remained tribute payers in Yucatán and New Spain for the next two hundred years. In 1785, shortly before its abolition, the Spanish crown reinstituted the Islamic system, requiring payments from all males ages fourteen to sixty. Borah and Cook, *Essays in Population History*, 2:10, 13.

64 *Recopilacion*, bk. 6, tit. 5, law 1 (1574, 1577); bk. 6, tit. 5, law 9, law 8 (adult offspring of blacks and Indians pay tribute; 1572, 1573); bk. 7, tit. 5, law 2.

65 Although the laws were never rescinded, in practice, most colonial officials abandoned the effort to collect tribute from blacks and mulattoes. Borah and Cook, *Essays in Population History*, 2:14.

66 "Real cédula 1572," in *Recopilacion*, bk. 6, tit. 5, law 18; Woodrow Borah, *Justice by Insurance: The General Indian Court of Colonial Mexico* (Berkeley, Calif., 1983), 53–54. On native leaders, see Charles Gibson, *Aztecs under Spanish Rule: A History of the Indians of the Valley of Mexico, 1519–1810* (Stanford, Calif., 1964); Spalding, *Huarochiri*; Nancy Farriss, *Maya Society under Colonial Rule: The Collective Enterprise of Survival* (Princeton,

N.J., 1984); Robert Haskett, *Indigenous Rulers: An Ethnohistory of Town Government in Colonial Cuernavaca* (Albuquerque, N.M., 1991).

67 Because those subject to Islamic rule did not (and were not allowed to) arm themselves, they were obligated to compensate the Islamic overlords for supplying military protection. Although it was a rationale of dubious value—imposing military control over a population and then demanding that the people pay the costs of their own domination—this unmistakably self-serving Islamic justification was copied by the Spaniards. Averroës, *Jihad*, 10; Zaman, *The Economic Functions*, 202. For some English-language examples, see Lewis, *Islam*, vol. 1, *Politics and War*, 234–41; Trelles Aréstegui, *Lucas Martínez Vegazo*, 177.

68 Alan Hunt, *Governance of the Consuming Passions: A History of Sumptuary Law* (New York 1996), provides a good overview of European laws. Additional details appear in Jacques Bouineau, *Histoire des institutions: Ier-XVe siècle* (Paris, 1994), 538.

69 Sumptuary laws also applied to blacks and mulattoes (free or slave), who, except for those married to Spaniards, were prohibited from wearing gold, pearls, or silk. Palmer, *Slaves of the White God*, 51. See also Hunt, *Governance of the Consuming Passions.*

70 On January 15, 1597, the viceroy allowed Indians to ride mules with saddles, spurs, and reins, and permitted them to own and use up to six pack animals, six yoke of oxen, and four milch cows. They could pasture up to three hundred sheep and fifty goats. They could use all mechanical trades, except those forbidden to them in the mines. The right to ride horses (with saddles and reins) was temporarily granted Indian caciques and governors during their terms of office. Borah, *Justice by Insurance*, 111.

71 Solórzano acknowledges the origin of these terms in the standards that Muslims set for the treatment of subjugated Christians; see *Política indiana*, 1:422, no. 23.

72 Solórzano uses these terms, along with "wretched," in ibid., 1:420, no. 10; 1:421, no. 1, 1:422, no. 31; 1:424. Legal consequences of such behavior were summary justice, little written documentation required, no "contentious" lawsuits, no ecclesiastical censure, no oath swearing.

73 *Recopilación*, bk. 6, tit. 1, law 22, December 17, 1551. It clearly took longer for horses to become accessible to the natives. The first law on this subject appears to have been issued July 19, 1565. Ibid., bk. 6, tit. 1, law 35.

74 Solórzano acknowledges the origin of these terms in the standards that Muslims set for the treatment of subjugated Christians; see *Política indiana*, 1:422, no. 23.

75 Juan Villegas, S.J., "La evangelización del indio de la Banda Oriental del Uruguay," in *Cristianismo y mundo colonial*, ed. Johannes Meier (Munich, 1995), 74–75.

76 "Law of Sept. 17, 1501" (repeated in 1536, 1551, 1563, 1566, 1567, 1570), in *Recopilación*, bk. 6, tit. 1, law 31. For discussion of the importance of this legislation to Spanish control over the Americas, see Patricia Seed, "The Conquest of America," in *Cambridge Illustrated History of Warfare*, ed. Geoffrey Parker (Cambridge, 1995). This accounts in part for the relative absence of iron materials in Spanish missions in California. See Douglas B. Bamforth, "Stone Tools, Steel Tools," in *Ethnohistory and Archeology*, ed. J. Daniel Rogers and Samuel M. Wilson (New York, 1993), 49–72.

77 The same tradition also prevailed in Portuguese America. See "Regimento a Tomé de Sousa, 1548," in *História da colonização portuguesa do Brasil*, 3 vols. (hereafter *HCPB*) (Pôrto Alegre, Brazil, 1921–27), 3:348; letter from Licenciado Manuel to the king, August 3, 1550, *HCPB*, 3:360.

78 See note 70 above.

79 This tradition was not Catholic. In medieval canon law there was little room for toleration of Muslims. A gloss on Gratian's (twelfth-century) *Decretum Gratiani emendatum
et notationibus illustratum: Una cum glossis, Gregorio XIII* (Venice, 1591) merely required
that Jews and Muslims be recognized as neighbors in the evangelical sense. No in-
human treatment was to be accorded them, and they should not be expelled from
their lands without cause. Normal Daniel, *Islam and the West* (Edinburgh, 1960),
115–16. Such statements clearly did not provide inalienable title to land.

80 José Enrique López de Coca, "El reino de Granada," in *Organización social del espacio en
la España medieval: La corona de Castilla en los siglos VIII a XV,* ed. José Angel García de
Cortázar et al. (Barcelona, 1985), 193–240, esp. 215–20. Ferdinand had successfully held on to traditional Muslim farmers in eastern Iberia through the traditional
measure of "protected communities."

81 See, generally, Kellogg, *Law and the Transformation.* For a slightly different perspective, see Borah, *Justice by Insurance.* As Borah notes, Indians were judicially subject to
the same laws as Jews and Muslims under the policies of 1476—local law was to be
enforced by Spanish judges unless it conflicted with Spanish law (16–17).

82 Boswell, *The Royal Treasure,* 133, 140. Lérida was the exception.

83 Anne Bos, *The Demise of the Caciques of Atlacomulco, Mexico, 1598–1821: A Reconstruction*
(Leiden, Netherlands, 1998).

84 Al-Makkari, *The History of the Mohammedan Dynasties,* 2:388–89. The capitulation of
the Muslims of Granada included provisions that "their laws should be preserved as
they were before, and that no one should judge them except by those same laws.
That their mosques . . . should remain as they were in the times of Islam. . . . That
no muzzein should be interrupted in the act of calling the people to prayer, and no
Muslim molested either in the performance of his daily devotions . . . or in any
other religious ceremony." Ibid.

85 Muslims were forced to convert or be exiled from Navarre in 1516. García-Arenal
and Leroy, *Moros y judíos en Navarra,* 64–65.

86 Corporal punishment of Indians for religious reasons was officially sanctioned in
1539. Slapping, hair pulling, and flogging were common. Inga Clendinnen, "Dis-
ciplining the Indians: Franciscan Ideology and Missionary Violence in Sixteenth-
Century Yucatán," *Past and Present* 94 (1982): 27–48, esp. 30–31, 43. A first-person
account by one who inflicted torture upon Indians as punishment for their religious
practices is Fray Diego de Landa, *Relación de las cosas de Yucatán* (1566; published,
Mexico City, 1994); Anthony Pagden provides an excellent English translation in
The Maya: Diego de Landa's Account of the Affairs of Yucatán (Chicago, 1975). See also
Mathew Restall, *Maya Conquistador* (Boston, 1998).

87 For a general understanding of this perspective from a contemporary Sioux writer,
see Vine Deloria Jr., *God Is Red: A Native View of Religion* (Golden, Colo., 1994).

88 For twentieth-century understandings of the range of conflicts between culture and
Christianity, see H. Richard Niebuhr, *Christ and Culture* (New York, 1951); George R.
Saunders, *Culture and Christianity: The Dialectics of Transformation* (New York, 1988);
Charles Scriven, *The Transformation of Culture: Christian Social Ethics after H. Richard
Niebuhr* (Scottsdale, Pa., 1988); Aylward Shorter, *Toward a Theology of Inculturation*
(London, 1988).

89 "But the aim of the preachers, of course, was not to conserve Indian culture: they

attempted to convert and to make the Indians enter into the Christian civilization of the faith." Alain Milhou, "Misión, represión, paternalismo e interiorización: Para un balance de un siglo de evangelización en Iberoamérica (1520–1620)," in *Los conquistados: 1492 y la población indígena de las Américas*, ed. Heraclio Bonilla (Bogotá, 1992), 284.

90 Jack Goody, *Comparative Studies in Kinship* (Stanford, Calif., 1969); Joan Thirsk and Edward P. Thompson, eds., *Family and Inheritance: Rural Society in Western Europe, 1200–1899* (Cambridge, 1976).

91 Irene Silverblatt, *Moon, Sun, and Witches: Gender Ideologies and Class in Inca and Colonial Peru* (Princeton, N.J., 1987), 220–21. See also Bernabé Cobo, *Historia del Nuevo Mundo*, 4 vols. (Seville, 1890–95), 3:167–68.

92 Even Spanish kinship terms differed fundamentally from those in Nahua and Tarascan languages, differences that were reflected in confession manuals and catechisms. Pierre Ragon, *Les Indiens de la découverte: Évangélisation, mariage et sexualité* (Paris, 1992), chap. 1. Charles Gibson writes, "In the sixteenth century, Spanish interests imbued it [legitimacy] with an ethical significance which it never lost." Charles Gibson, *The Inca Concept of Sovereignty and the Spanish Administration of Peru* (Austin, Tex., 1948), 25–26, 30–32. See also Floyd G. Lounsbury, "Some Aspects of the Inka Kinship System," in *Anthropological History of Andean Polities*, ed. John Murra, Nathan Wachtel, and Jacques Evel (Cambridge, 1986), 121–36.

93 Jack Goody, *The Development of the Family and Marriage in Europe* (Cambridge, 1983); Jack Goody, *The Oriental, the Ancient and the Primitive: Systems of Marriage and the Family in the Pre-Industrial Societies of Eurasia* (Cambridge, 1990); Daisy Rípodas Ardanaz, *El matrimonio en Indias, realidad social y regulación jurídica* (Buenos Aires, 1977), 103–10, 112–13, 132.

94 Rípodas Ardanaz, *El matrimonio en Indias*, 175. Silverblatt, in *Moon, Sun, and Witches*, notes that in the Andes a double descent system prevailed.

95 Mónica Patricia Martini, *El indio y los sacramentos en Hispanoamérica colonial* (Buenos Aires, 1993), 110–12, 232.

96 In Aragon, the crown had witnessed the impact of population loss on royal income, but nothing to compare with what happened in the New World. Boswell, *The Royal Treasure*, 23–28.

97 Regarding the effects of isolation or even semi-isolation on immune systems, see P. Jones, ed., *Health and Disease in Tribal Societies* (New York, 1977), 142. Suggestions that the diseases were themselves more virulent are found in Robert McCaa, "Spanish and Nahuatl Views on Smallpox and Demographic Catastrophe in Mexico," *Journal of Interdisciplinary History* 25 (1995): 397–426. Other perspectives are presented in Henry F. Dobyns, "Disease Transfer at Contact," *Annual Review of Anthropology* 22 (1993): 273–91; John Zambardino, "Mexican Population in the Sixteenth Century," *Journal of Interdisciplinary History* 11 (1980): 1–28.

98 Population thresholds to sustain some of the most devastating diseases were higher than the size of most communities. Ten million (the population of Taiwan) is not large enough to sustain rubella; five million (the population of London in 1906) was barely enough to sustain measles. Jones, *Health and Disease*, 109–13. Thus the most likely source of fresh pathogens was the immigrant population.

99 This transition has been discussed at length in many books on the subject. The trend began with François Chevalier's *Land and Society in Colonial Mexico*, trans. Alvin

Eustis (1952; reprint, Berkeley, Calif., 1963). See also Gibson, *Aztecs under Spanish Rule*; William B. Taylor, *Landlord and Peasant in Colonial Oaxaca* (Stanford, Calif., 1972).

100 Borah, *Justice by Insurance*, 46–47.

101 These were called *composiciones de tierra* in Spanish.

102 Lesley Byrd Simpson, unpublished field notes quoted in Borah, *Justice by Insurance*, 126.

103 Burns, *Islam under the Crusaders*, 108. Regarding Indians, see Solórzano, *Política indiana*, 1:429, no. 55; 1:427, nos. 42, 44. Prior to granting vacant land, the viceroy was to investigate that the land was not in use, that it was not claimed by anyone else, and that the grant was issued without prejudice to the right of a third party. Borah, *Justice by Insurance*, 140–41. Similarly, thirteenth-century Portuguese king Dinis formalized and centralized bureaucratic procedures by which a person had a right to request land that was lying fallow or unused in order to farm it. Virginia Rau, *Sesmarias medievais portuguesas*, 2d ed. (Lisbon, 1982), 142–44; for the laws, see 269–75.

104 Priests were not formally authorized to imprison, but they could call upon secular officials to arrest natives for flouting religious norms. For discussion of the complex relations between church and state, see Patricia Seed, *To Love, Honor, and Obey in Colonial Mexico: Conflicts over Marriage Choice, 1574–1821* (Stanford, Calif., 1989). The classic study of this topic is presented in Nancy Farriss, *Crown and Clergy in Colonial Mexico, 1759–1821: The Crisis of Ecclesiastical Privilege* (London, 1968).

105 Jose Antonio Bugarin, *Visita de las misiones del Nayarit 1768–1769*, ed. Jean Meyer (Mexico City, 1993); Jaime Martinez Companon and Baltasar Bujanda, *Trujillo del Peru* (Madrid, 1993).

106 John R. Brodhead, ed., *Documents Relative to the Colonial History of New York*, 15 vols. (Albany, N.Y., 1853–57), 1:58.

107 *Ecclesiastical Records, State of New York*, 7 vols. (Albany, N.Y., 1901), 1:49–68. Reverend Jonas Michaelis wrote to Adrianus Smotius on August 11, 1628, "The Mohicans have fled and their lands are unoccupied and are very fertile and pleasant. It grieves us that . . . there is no order from the Honorable Director to occupy the same." In J. Franklin Jameson, ed., *Narratives of New Netherland, 1609–1664* (New York, 1909), 131.

108 Herculano, *História de Portugal*, 2:436.

109 Only Jewish and Muslim residents of such cities as Lisbon, Almada, Palmela, and Alcácer had been subject to "pacts of protection" for long periods of time. Academia das Ciéncias de Lisboa, *Portugalia monumenta histórica . . . Leges et consuetudines*, 5 vols. (Lisbon, 1856–88), 1:396–97 (1209). They had to pay a per capita tax of seven maravedis every year, plus other costs. For a commentary on the subsequent fate of the Muslim community of Lisbon, see António Henrique de Oliveira Marques, *Novos ensaios de história medieval portuguesa* (Lisbon, 1988), 96–107. The agreement was entitled *carta de segurança e privilegios*.

110 Dutch regulations banning firearm sales to natives first appeared in 1639—long after trade had been established. The New England confederation forbade such sales in 1644. The Dutch leadership (States General investigating committee) abandoned efforts at enforcement in 1650. Allen W. Trelease, *Indian Affairs in Colonial New York: The Seventeenth Century* (Lincoln, Neb., 1997), 96–97, 100. Virginia prohibited sales of firearms to natives in 1637 and renewed the prohibition later.

William W. Hening, ed., *Statutes at Large: Being a Collection of all the Laws of Virginia, from the First Session of the Legislature in the Year 1619*, 18 vols. (Richmond, 1809–23), 1:222; William Hand Browne, ed., *Archives of Maryland*, vol. 1, *Proceedings and Acts of the General Assembly of Maryland, Han. 1637/38–September 1664* (Baltimore, 1883), 42–44.

111 Trelease, *Indian Affairs*, 94.

112 The origin of this prohibition in Islam is usually traced to Qur'an, Surah 57:25: "We send down Iron in which is (material for) mighty war, as well as many benefits for mankind."

113 One of the favorite sale items was a coarse woolen cloth called a duffel. See Arnold J. F. Laer, ed., *Documents Relating to New Netherland, 1624–1626* (San Marino, Calif., 1924), 223–32.

114 William Gouge, *Of Domesticall Duties, Eight Treatises* (London, 1622), 603.

115 Alexander von Humboldt, *Politcal Essay on the Kingdom of New Spain*, 2 vols., trans. John Black (New York, 1811), 1:185.

116 Conrad Heresbach, *Four Books of Husbandry* (1577; reprint, Amsterdam, 1971), 47. For similar proverbs, see Richard Puttenham and George Puttenham, *The Art of English Poesie* (1589), ed. Edward Arber (Westminster, 1893), 211.

CHAPTER 6: CANNIBALS

1 See John Hemming, *Amazon Frontier: The Defeat of the Brazilian Indians* (Cambridge, Mass., 1987); John Hemming, *Red Gold: The Conquest of the Brazilian Indians* (Cambridge, Mass., 1978).

2 Ortner, who is better known for her feminist writings, has worked extensively among the Nepalese. See Sherry Ortner, *Sherpas through Their Rituals* (Cambridge, 1978); Sherry Ortner, *High Religion: A Cultural and Political History of Sherpa Buddhism* (Princeton, N.J., 1989); Sherry Ortner, "Resistance and the Problem of Ethnographic Refusal," *Comparative Studies in Society and History* 37 (1995): 173–93. The historian she criticized is Inga Clendinnen, author of *Ambivalent Conquests: Maya and Spaniard in Yucatan, 1517–1570* (Cambridge, 1987).

3 William Arens, *The Man-Eating Myth: Anthropology and Anthropophagy* (New York, 1979), 139. In a recent revindication of his position, Arens claims that he is merely casting doubt on the subject. However, he fails to credit a single account—historical or contemporary—of cannibal practices, making his claim of mere skepticism appear disingenuous. Although I agree with his attack on the misuse of accusations of cannibalism, I believe that to deny its practice is counterproductive. See William Arens, "Rethinking Anthropophagy," in *Cannibalism and the Colonial World*, ed. Francis Barker, Peter Hulme, and Margaret Iversen (Cambridge, 1998), 39–62. There are also recent literary works that deal with the symbolic dimension of this subject in Western literature, such as Milad Doueihi, *A Perverse History of the Human Heart* (Cambridge, Mass., 1997); Maggie Kilgour, *From Communion to Cannibalism: An Anatomy of Metaphors of Incorporation* (Princeton, N.J., 1990). The charge of cannibalism among the Caribs is repeated in Roberto Cassá, *Los indios de las antillas* (Madrid, 1992), 166–68; regarding veneration of bones of the dead, 178.

4 On the Pawnee, see Ralph Linton, *Sacrifice to the Morning Star among the Skidi Pawnee* (Chicago, 1922); Richard P. Schaedel, "The Karankawa of the Texas Gulf Coast," *Southwestern Journal of Anthropology* 5 (1949): 129, 132; Robert S. Weddle, Mary Christine Morkovsky, and Patricia Galloway, eds., *La Salle, the Mississippi, and the Gulf:*

Three Primary Documents (College Station, Tex., 1987), 238, 249, 253, 272; Robert A. Ricklis, *The Karankawa Indians of Texas: An Ecological Study of Cultural Tradition and Change* (Austin, Tex., 1996).

5 Thomas Williams and James Calvert, *Fiji and the Fijians, and Missionary Labours among the Cannibals: Extended with Notices of Recent Events*, vol. 2, 2d ed. (London, 1852), 75; A. M. Hocart, "Early Fijians," *Journal of the Royal Anthropological Institute Great Britain and Ireland* 49 (1919): 42–51; Jan Critchett, *A Distant Field of Murder* (Melbourne, 1992).

6 Alexandre Herculano, *História de Portugal desde o começo da monarquia ate of fim do reinado de Afonso III*, 4 vols., ed. José Mattoso (Amadora, 1980), 2:256–57.

7 During the Muslim conquest of the Maghreb, an Arab leader demanded that the Berber Lawata tribes turn over a number of slaves as a condition of peace in 642 A.D. Slavery for prisoners of war does not occur in the Qur'an; Surahs 47:4 and 8:67–71 recommend mercy for captives. But in practice, the word for captive, *asir*, became synonymous with slave. (The most common word for slave is ʿ*abd*. See *Encyclopaedia of Islam*, 2d ed. [Leiden, Netherlands, 1960–] 1:31.) After conquering the Maghreb, Arabs frequently took to enslaving Berber tribespeople. One Arab provincial governor (*amir*) during the seventh century permitted his troops to raid Berber settlements and take captives—as many as one hundred thousand in one report—to be sold as slaves. Jamil M. Abun-Nasr, *A History of the Maghreb in the Islamic Period*, 3d ed. (Cambridge, 1987), 2, 34. For the practice elsewhere see Alfred Morabia, *Le Gihad dans l'Islam médiéval* (Paris, 1993), 104–5; *Histoire des musulmanes d'Espagne*, trans. R. Dozy and Emil Lévi-Provençal, 3 vols. (Leiden, Netherlands, 1932), 3:194–95; Herculano, *História de Portugal*, 2:256–57; Oliveira Martins, *História de Portugal*, 2d ed., 2 vols. (Lisbon, 1989), 1:86.

8 Herculano, *História de Portugal*, 2:269–70. On warfare as the source of slaves, see also Charles Verlinden, *L'esclavage dans l'Europe médiévale*, vol. 1, *Péninsule ibérique—France* (Brussels, 1955), 192–211.

9 Philippe Contamine, *War in the Middle Ages*, trans. Michael Jones (New York, 1998), 266, claims that this slavery was abolished in northern Europe. Charles Verlinden shows something quite different in *L'esclavage dans l'Europe médiévale* and in his "Medieval Slavery in Europe and Colonial America," in *The Beginnings of Modern Colonization*, trans. Yvonne Freccero (Ithaca, N.Y., 1970), 28–29. In the latter, he states: "Slavery is generally believed to have disappeared from most European countries at the end of Antiquity. . . . Slavery nevertheless . . . did exist in many European countries during the period between the fall of the Western Roman Empire and the time of the great discoveries" (26–27). See also Claude Larquié, "Captifs chrétiens et esclaves musulmans au xvii siècle une lecture comparative," in *Chrétiens et musulmans à la Renaissance: Actes du 37e colloque international du CESR (1994)*, ed. Bartolomé Bennassar and Robert Sauzet (Tours, 1995), 391–404.

10 John Boswell, *The Royal Treasure: Muslim Communities under the Crown of Aragon in the Fourteenth Century* (New Haven, Conn., 1977), 50–52.

11 Details are spelled out in Patricia Seed, *Ceremonies of Possession in Europe's Conquest of the New World, 1492–1640* (Cambridge, 1995), chap. 3. Twelfth-century commentators on Gratian such as Uguccione Da Pisa declared that the mere existence of infidels was an injury to Christians; see Uguccione, *Summa*, cap. 23, quaes. 8.c.11, cited by Frederick H. Russell, *The Just War in the Middle Ages* (Cambridge, 1975), 94. Theologian Robert of Courson considered any war of conquest justified by ecclesi-

astical authority to be a holy war or crusade. Uguccione, *Summa*, cap. 23, quaes. 8.c.11.

12 *Fuero real* (1255), bk. 1, tit. 1, **law** 1; *Ordenamiento de alcalá* (1386), preface; *Las siete partidas* (preface).

13 The best sources on Christian anti-Muslim polemics during the Middle Ages remain Norman Daniel, *Islam and the West: The Making of an Image* (Edinburgh, 1960); Benjamin Kedar, *Crusade and Mission: European Approaches toward the Muslims* (Princeton, N.J., 1984). Also useful are Michael Frasetto, "The Image of the Saracen as Heretic in the Sermons of Ademar of Chabannes," and John V. Tolan, "Muslims as Pagan Idolaters in Chronicles of the First Crusade," both in *Western Views of Islam in Medieval and Early Modern Europe: Perception of Other*, ed. David R. Blanks and Michael Frassetto (New York, 1999), 83–96, 97–117; John V. Tolan, ed., *Medieval Christian Perceptions of Islam: A Book of Essays* (New York, 1996).

14 Iberian Christians repeatedly threatened Jews with death unless they converted during the 1390s. Charlemagne is reported by several chronicles to have forced Franks to convert under threat of death. The polemical self-image of Christians as "peaceful" appears in Darío Cabanelas Rodríguez, *Juan de Segovia y el problema islámico* (Madrid, 1952).

15 Daniel, *Islam and the West*, 141. See also J. W. Wright Jr. and Everett K. Rowson, eds., *Homoeroticism in Classical Arabic Literature* (New York, 1997).

16 On Islam as a corruption of Christian teachings, see Daniel, *Islam and the West*, 188. On Islam as an invitation to sexual license, see Daniel, *Islam and the West*, 155–61; Kedar, *Crusade and Mission*, 86–89, 206–11. The charge of idolatry is, of course, totally inaccurate.

17 These are the four characteristics of native "moral" life mentioned most frequently and most intensely in Spanish narratives of conquest. Examples include Francisco Cervantes de Salazar, *Crónica de la Nueva España*, 2 vols., ed. Manuel Magallon (Madrid, 1971), bk. 1, chap. 16, p. 130; a letter to the king from the conquerors of Mexico in Bernal Díaz del Castillo, *Historia verdadera de la conquista de la Nueva España*, ed. Ramírez Cabañas (Mexico City, 1960), chap. 54, p. 92; José de Acosta, *De procuranda indorum salute* (Madrid, 1984), bk. 2, chap. 2; Juan de la Peña, *De bello contra insulanos* (Madrid, 1982), 215; Alan Stewart, *Close Readers: Humanism and Sodomy in Early Modern England* (Princeton, N.J., 1997); Jonathan Goldberg, *Sodometries* (Stanford, Calif., 1995). The association of sodomy and idolatry with abomination appears in thirteenth- and fourteenth-century English as well. See *Oxford English Dictionary*, 2d ed., s.v. "abomination," definitions 1, 3; s.v. "sodomy," definition 1. The political connection does not appear, however.

18 To the most highly educated clerics and Spanish political leaders the argument of native immoral practices was not acceptable as the sole grounds for conquest, because the Church at the Council of Constance (1415–16) had officially condemned John Wycliffe (1324–84) for a similar contention. Wycliffe had asserted that anyone in mortal sin could be deprived of political power. To protect their own political power against charges of illegality on moral grounds (because Church leaders were often obviously involved in major public sins), Church officials condemned Wycliffe's position as heretical. High-ranking Spanish political thinkers followed suit, because papal authority was one of the formal institutional pillars upon which official justification of the conquest of America rested. And the pope who made the

donation of the Americas to the crown of Spain was the infamous Rodrigo Borgia, father of Lucretia (the famous poisoner), also notorious for the crowds of prostitutes he entertained at the papal palace. The Church's condemnation of such arguments as heretical constituted mere bureaucratic self-protection, as did the Spanish government's insistence that the introduction of superior morality, rather than the condemnation of immoral behavior, was legitimate grounds for conquest. However, such technical details of bureaucratic self-protection mattered little outside government circles, and were ignored in fact by nearly all the colonists. Francisco de Victoria, *De indis et de iure belli relectiones*, ed. Ernest Nys (Buffalo, N.Y., 1995), relectio. 1, nos. 5–6: Peña, *De bello contra insulanos*, 212–21, 332–71; Acosta, *De procuranda indorum salute*, bk. 2, chap. 2, p. 265.

19 Juan Ginés Sepúlveda, quoted by Bartolomé de Las Casas, *Aquí se contiene una disputa o controversia* (Seville, 1552), in *Tratados de Fray Bartolomé de Las Casas*, transcription by Juan Pérez de Tudela Bueso, trans. Augustín Millares Carlo and Rafael Moreno (Mexico City, 1974), 319.

20 Sodomy had become punishable by death by 1255. *Fuero real*, bk. 4, tit. 9, law 2.

21 Spaniards popularly accused natives of these sins, as did the self-proclaimed "Inca" Garcilaso de la Vega. Garcilaso falsely asserted that Incas enforced taboos against homosexuality and idolatry in order to argue for Spanish support for Incas in their continuing political disputes with other indigenous groups. Garcilaso de la Vega, *Comentario real de las Incas*, vol. 133 (Madrid, 1960), 179 ff.

22 Gonzalo Fernández de Oviedo, *Historia general y natural de las indias*, 5 vols. (Madrid, 1959), bk. 3, chap. 3, vol. 1, p. 123.

23 Cervantes de Salazar, *Crónica de la Nueva España*: "Hacían tantas cosas contra toda ley natural, que aun has las bestias, con su natural instinto guardan, pues adoraban las piedras y animales que eran menos que ellos; sacrificaban a los que menos podían . . . frecuentaban el pecado de sodomía que entre los otros pecados por su fealdad se llama contra natura" (bk. 1, chap. 16, p. 130). See also Acosta, *De procuranda indorum salute*, bk. 2, chap. 2; Peña, *De bello contra insulanos*, 215.

24 Fernández de Oviedo, *Historia general*, bk. 3, chap. 3, vol. 1, p. 123.

25 Bernal Díaz del Castillo, *Historia de la conquista de Nueva España* (Mexico City, 1960), chap. 1; Mary Gaylord, "The True History of Early Modern Writing in Spanish: Some American Reflections," *Modern Language Quarterly* 57 (1996): 213–26.

26 Bartolomé de Las Casas, *Tratado comprobatorio*, in *Tratados*, 1177.

27 Clendinnen, *Ambivalent Conquests*, 10.

28 Fernández de Oviedo, *Historia general y natural*, bk. 42, chap. 11, 120:420. Bernal Díaz del Castillo makes the same statement about natives of Tizapancingo in *Historia verdadera*, chap. 51, p. 87.

29 Fernández de Oviedo, *Historia general y natural*, bk. 3, chap. 3, 117:122. Identical accusations occur in Amerigo Vespucci, *Mundus Novus* (Paris, 1503).

30 "Because not everywhere or even in many places have they ever done so . . . there are infinite peoples and great kingdoms where there has never been such contamination or plagues." Las Casas, *Tratado comprobatorio*, 1137, 1177. More recently, it has been suggested that cannibalism provided natives with a source of protein. However, Bernardo Ortiz de Montellano has noted that the timing of the sacrifices is not consistent with an explanation of hunger or protein shortages. The customary older explanation that the sacrifices involved giving thanks to the gods is more

consistent with the timing. Bernardo Ortiz de Montellano, *Aztec Medicine, Health, and Nutrition* (New Brunswick, N.J., 1990), 85–94.

31 Hernán Cortés, *Cartas de relación* (Mexico City, 1971), series "Sepan cuantos," 288. For excellent translations of Cortés's letters, see Hernán Cortés, *Letters from Mexico*, trans. Anthony Pagden (New Haven, Conn., 1986).

32 "No se podrían escuchar sin mucho asco y vergüenza." Fernández de Oviedo, *Historia general y natural*, bk. 3, chap. 6, 117:67. Angela Mendes de Almeida notes that the tone of discussion of sodomy in Portuguese confession manuals of this era is scandal and horror. Angela Mendes de Almeida, *O gosto do pecado: Casamento e sexualidade nos manuais de confessores dos séculos XVI e XVII* (Rio de Janeiro, 1992), 103.

33 Cervantes de Salazar, *Crónica de la Nueva España*, bk. 1, chap. 16, p. 130. See also Acosta, *De procuranda indorum salute*, bk. 2, chap. 2; Peña, *De bello contra insulanos*, 215. See note 23, above.

34 Fernández de Oviedo, *Historia general y natural*, bk. 3, chap. 6, 117:67. See also Vasco de Quiroga, "Información en derecho (1535)," in Paulino Castañeda Delgado, *Don Vasco de Quiroga y su información en derecho* (Madrid, 1974), 141–48.

35 Peter Martyr, *The Decades of The Newe Worlde or West India* (1516), trans. Richard Eden (London, 1966), 100.

36 Fernández de Oviedo, *Historia general y natural*, bk. 27, chap. 23, describes the punishment and shaming of soldiers in Veragua who took part in eating an Indian (vol. 119, p. 194).

37 Bartolomé de Las Casas, *Historia de las indias*, 2d ed., 3 vols., ed. Agustín Millares Carlo (Mexico City, 1965), bk. 3, chap. 8; Las Casas, *Aqui se contiene*, 323. For beliefs of the conquerors of Peru, see "Sobre las obligaciones de confesores, año 1560," reproduced in Antoine Tibesar, "Instructions for the Confessors of Conquistadores issued by the Archbishop of Lima in 1560," *The Americas* 3 (1947): 525. Alonso Ojeda views cannibalism as a just title; see Antonio M. Fabié, *Vida y escritos de Bartolomé de Las Casas*, 2 vols. (Madrid, 1879), 1:108. See also Sigmund Freud, *Totem and Taboo: Resemblances between the Psychic Lives of Savages and Neurotics*, trans. Abraham A. Brill (New York, 1931). Claude Lévi-Strauss engaged in a related attempt to discover whether the incest taboo was universal.

38 Survival cannibalism seems to have been a European rather than American phenomenon. Its best-known twentieth-century example occurred when a young Argentine soccer team was trapped without food for seventy-two days when their airplane crashed high in the Andes. Piers Paul Read popularized their story in *Alive: The Story of the Andes Survivors* (Philadelphia, 1974). The nineteenth century's version of the soccer players' tale can be found in Alfred W. Simpson, *Cannibalism and the Common Law: The Story of the Tragic Last Voyage of the Mignonette and the Strange Legal Proceedings to Which It Gave Rise* (Chicago, 1984).

39 The symbolic or real transformation of the Eucharist was a major point of Protestant-Catholic contention in sixteenth-century Europe. Frank Lestringant, *Le cannibal: Grandeur et décadence* (Paris, 1994), 35.

40 A more Freudian set of categories for cannibalism appears in Peggy Sanday, *Divine Hunger: Cannibalism as a Cultural System* (Cambridge, 1986).

41 Reuben G. Thwaites, ed., *The Jesuit Relations and Allied Documents*, 73 vols. (Cleveland, 1896–1901), vols. 51, 53.

42 Ibid., 10:181–83, 227–29; 26:19; 41:53; 50:63.

43 Jean de Léry, *History of a Voyage to the Land of Brazil, Otherwise Called America*, trans. Janet Whatley (Berkeley, Calif., 1990), 127.

44 These interpretations are offered, respectively, by Manuela Carneira da Cunha, *Os mortos e os outros: Uma analise do sistema funerário e da noção de pessoa entre os índios Kraho* (São Paulo, 1978); Edward Viveiros de Castro, *From the Enemy's Point of View: Humanity and Divinity in an Amazonian Society*, trans. Catherine V. Howard (Chicago, 1992); Florestan Fernandes, *A função social da guerra na sociedade Tupinamba*, 2d ed. (São Paulo, 1970); Ellen Basso, *The Last Cannibals: A South American Oral History* (Austin, Tex., 1995).

45 Viveiros de Castro, *From the Enemy's Point of View*. At least one contemporary anthropologist suggests that such practices occur in rural Taiwan: "Murder and cannibalism of elders may indicate that far from being a simple description of a now deplorable past, the story reflects people's deeply felt desires, desires that they would as soon not admit exist." Emily M. Ahern, *The Cult of the Dead in a Chinese Village* (Stanford, Calif., 1973), 207.

46 William L. Merrill, *Rarámuri Souls: Knowledge and Social Process in Northern Mexico* (Washington, D.C., 1988), 166. In these myths, the first inhabitants of the world, the Kapáche, were destroyed for their cannibalism and replaced with the ancestors of the Rarámuri. Zarko David Levak, "Kinship System and Social Structure of the Bororo of Pobojari " (Ph.D. diss., Yale University, 1974), 181.

47 Martin Gusinde, *Die Feuerland Indianer*, 2 vols., trans. Human Relations Area Files as *The Fireland Indians*, vol. 1, *The Selk'nam, on the Life and Thought of a Hunting People of the Great Island of Tierra del Fuego* (New Haven, Conn., 1931), 685. Also translated as *Los indios de Tierra del Fuego* (Buenos Aires, 1982).

48 James Barker Field, "Memoria sobre la cultura de los Guaika," *Boletín Indigenista Venezolano* 1 (1953): 433–89, trans. in Human Relations Area Files, *Memoir on the Culture of the Waica* (New Haven, Conn., 1953), 23.

49 Las Casas, *Tratado comprobatorio*, 1177.

50 Not all forms of cannibalism were regarded with equal horror. Spaniards, Frenchmen, and Portuguese engaged in casual cannibalism on board ship, devouring each other when hunger struck. Under European norms, this form of hunger cannibalism was accepted, whereas ritual cannibalism was not.

51 J. Mattoso Câmara Jr., *Dicionário de filologia e gramática*, 3d ed. (São Paulo, 1968), 171. For sixteenth-century usages, see São Paulo, *Atas da câmara da cidade de São Paulo*, 72 vols. (São Paulo, 1914–); *História da colonização portuguesa do Brasil*, 3 vols. (hereafter *HCPB*) (Pôrto Alegre, Brazil, 1921–27). *Indio* was sometimes used by priests as a first name and to describe some customs, but *gentio* predominated. See Serafim Leite, ed., *Cartas dos primeiros Jesuítas do Brasil*, 3 vols. (São Paulo, 1956–58); Serafim Leite, ed., *Cartas do Brasil e mais escritos do P. Manuel da Nóbrega* (Coimbra, Portugal, 1955).

52 In Leite, *Cartas do Brasil*, 48–49, August 10, 1549.

53 Ibid., January 6, 1550, 73.

54 Ibid., August 11, 1551, 86.

55 Antonio Blazquez, in a letter from Bahia, July 8, 1555, in Leite, *Cartas dos primeiros Jesuítas*, 2:252.

56 J. S. da Silva Dias, *Os descobrimentos e a problemática cultural do século XVI* (Coimbra, Portugal, 1973), 225. For similar observations from a contemporary Brazilian, see Laura de Mello e Souza, *El diablo em la tierra de Santa Cruz*, trans. Teresa Rodríguez Martínez (Madrid, 1993), 59–64.

57 "E, conquanto tivesse, alguma forma de culto aos deuses que havia, imaginado, era tão ridículo e vergonhoso o culto quanto as coisas que adoravam." Martinho de Nantes, *Relação de uma missão no rio São Francisco (1671)* (São Paulo, 1979), 4.

58 José da Fonseca, *Dicionário de Sinônimos* (Paris, 1871); José Pedro Machado, *Dicionário etimológico da lingua portuguesa,* 3d ed. (Lisbon, 1977). On the absence of idolatry, see Leite, *Cartas do Brasil,* 86, August 11, 1551. Treason and counterfeiting were included among the natives' offenses. Biblioteca Nacional, *Documentos históricos* (Rio de Janeiro, 1929); *HCPB,* 3:376. Pêro Magalhães de Gândavo, *Tratado da Província do Brasil* (1572; reprint, Rio de Janeiro, 1965), 187, 207–9, 211. Some of the documents in Leite, *Cartas dos primeiros Jesuítas,* instruct Indians not to eat human flesh (3:52, 57, 86–87, 91, 96–97, 135, 139–40, 239, 313) and to refrain from human sacrifice (3:259, 313). Instructions regarding sexual misconduct appear less frequently (3:315, 442).

59 "Barbaras nationes ad rerum omnium opificem et conditorem deum cognoscendum non solum edictus admonitionibusque, sed etiam armis et viribus (si opus ferit)." Text reproduced in Lewis Hanke, "Pope Paul III and the American Indians," *Harvard Theological Review* 30 (1937): 77. The right to punish natives for moral offenses was originally formulated by Pope Innocent IV (1200–1254), *Apparatus super V libros decretalium* (Venice, 1491), ratified by Giovanni da Legnano (d. 1383), *Tractatus de bello, de represaliis et de duello,* ed. Thomas Erskine Holland (Washington, D.C., 1917), and repeated in the popular French title by Honoré Bonet, *Arbre des batailles* (Paris, 1515). See Alfred Vanderpol, *La doctrine scolastique du droit de guerre* (Paris, 1919), 231. Similar ideas appear in Thomas Aquinas, *Summa theologica,* 21 vols., trans. Fathers of the English Dominican Province (London, 1912–25), secunda secundae, q. 10, art. 8.

60 Acosta called it "this popular belief"; see *De procuranda indorum salute,* bk. 2, chap. 2, pp. 263–65.

61 Díaz del Castillo, *Historia verdadera,* chap. 158, p. 385.

62 Ibid., chaps. 51–52, p. 88.

63 Cortés, *Cartas,* 2d letter, cited in Cristóbal de Molina and Cristóbal de Albornoz, *Fábulas y mitos de los incas,* ed. Henrique Urbano and Pierre Duviols (Madrid, 1989), 81.

64 Straightforward repulsion is apparent in the royal decrees. See *Colección de documentos ineditos relativos al descubrimiento . . . en América y Oceanía,* (hereafter *CDI*), 42 vols. (Madrid, 1864–84), 23:353 ff; *Colección de documentos inéditos relativos al descubrimiento, conquista y organización de las antiguas posesiones españolas de ultramar* (hereafter *CDU*), 25 vols. (Madrid, 1885–1932), 9:268–80.

65 For the right in England, see William Searle Holdsworth, *History of English Law,* 7th ed., 17 vols. (London, 1956–72), 7:481–84. For the principle in Catholic theology, see Aquinas, *Summa,* secunda secundae, q. 66, art. 8, ad. 2.

66 All non-Indians were subject to imprisonment by the Inquisition for blasphemy, idolatry, heresy, bigamy, polygamy, homosexuality, prostitution, pacts with the devil, and witchcraft. A superb study is Solange Alberro, *Inquisición y sociedad en México 1571–1700* (Mexico, 1988). See also Solange Alberro, *La actividad del santo oficio de la inquisición en Nueva España, 1571–1700* (Mexico City, 1981), esp. 86. The stated function of the Inquisition was to guard morality by protecting the "purity of the Catholic faith." Gustav Heningsen, *The Witches' Advocate: Basque Witchcraft and the Spanish Inquisition (1609–1614)* (Reno, Nev., 1980), 38. By contrast, prosecutions for sodomy in England were relatively infrequent, and many historians believe that

issues other than homosexuality were at the core of such trials. Cynthia Herrup, *A House in Gross Disorder: Sex, Law, and the 2nd Earl of Castlehaven* (New York, 1999).

67 Las Casas, *Aquí se contiene*, 323; Las Casas, *Historia de las indias*, bk. 3, chap. 8. On Peru, see "Sobre las obligaciones de confesores," 535. Michael Warner argues that the Puritan texts show an ambiguity about homosexuality. Michael Warner, "New English Sodom," in *Queering the Renaissance*, ed. Jonathan Goldberg (Durham, N.C., 1994), 330–58.

68 See Las Casas, *Historia de las indias*, bk. 3, chap. 8; Las Casas, *Aquí se contiene*, 323. On Peru, see "Sobre las obligaciones de confesores," 525.

69 Juan Ginés Sepúlveda, a longtime friend of one of the popes, was the only important Spanish political theorist who argued that idolatry and human sacrifice were deserving of punishment and that the pope authorized such punishment. Juan Ginés Sepúlveda, *Democrates segundo* (Madrid, 1951), 38–39, 41, 44, 45, 118. Prior to the conflicts between Charles V and the pope in the 1530s, one of King Ferdinand's preachers had argued for the *encomienda* as punishment for the worship of idols. Las Casas, *Historia de las indias*, bk. 3, chap. 12, 472–73. The canonist was Augustin de Anchona (1243–1328).

70 Las Casas, *Historia de las indias*, bk. 3, chap. 9, pp. 460–61.

71 Franciscan missionaries in the Caribbean benefited (to the Dominicans' dismay), and in Brazil the Jesuits did so as well. Patricia Seed, "'Are These Not Also Men?': The Indian's Humanity and Capacity for Spanish Civilization," *Journal of Latin American Studies* 25 (1993): 629–52; Dauril Alden, *The Making of an Enterprise: The Society of Jesus in Portugal, Its Empire, and Beyond, 1540–1750* (Stanford, Calif., 1996).

72 Fray Francisco Ruiz, Cardinal Cisneros's first secretary, so argued; *CDI*, 10:549–55. Ruiz was identified as the author of this statement by Manuel Giménez Fernández, *Bartolomé de las Casas, volúmen primero: Delgado de Cisneros para la reformación de las indias (1516–1517)* (Seville, 1953), 136 n. 406. The royal judge on Hispaniola said, "The Indians will return to their initial bestiality, and with even more preparation to offend God than before the island was discovered." Parecer de Lucas Vásquez de Ayllón, quoted in Giménez Fernández, *Bartolomé de las Casas*, 574. King Ferdinand's preacher's positions are described by Las Casas, *Historia de las indias*, bk. 3, chap. 9, p. 459. See also "Memorial de Fray Bernardino Manzanedo on the Indians of Puerto Rico," in Manuel Serrano, *Orígenes de la dominación española en América* (Madrid, 1918), 568; "Carta al emperador" (1555) in Toribio de Motolinia, *Historia de los indios de la Nueva España* (Mexico, 1990), 207; Tibesar, "Instructions for the Confessors," 529; Acosta, *De procuranda indorum salute*, bk. 2, chap. 18, pp. 377–79, and bk. 3, chap. 2, no. 4, p. 393.

73 Las Casas, *Historia de las indias*, bk. 3, chap. 9, p. 459.

74 "Memorial de Fray Bernardino Manzanedo," 568; Parecer de Lucas Vásquez de Ayllón, in Giménez Fernández, *Bartolomé de Las Casas*, 574; *CDI*, 10:549–55; Las Casas, *Historia de las indias*, bk. 3, chap.9, pp. 460–61.

75 See Giménez Fernández, *Bartolomé de Las Casas*, nn. 309–19; Lewis Hanke, *The First Social Experiments in America* (Cambridge, Mass., 1935), 25–39.

76 "No saberse regir e que habían menester tutores." Las Casas, *Historia de las indias*, bk. 3, chap. 8, p. 455. See also Serrano, *Orígenes de la dominación*, 538. Spanish settlers were responding to a question regarding whether "the Indians . . . are capable of living politically or ruling themselves." Giménez Fernández, *Bartolomé de Las Casas*,

185–90, 159. Slightly different versions of the entire interrogatory also appear in *CDI*, 11:258–76 and 23:310–31, esp. 330–31; *CDU*, 9:53–74; Giménez Fernández, *Bartolomé de Las Casas*, 177–205.

77 Bartolomé de Las Casas, *Brevísima relación de la destrucción de las indias* (1552), in *Tratados*, 15–17.

78 King Charles V of Spain proclaimed freedom of the Indians as the general policy in 1542, only to have his successors repeatedly grant exemptions to this rule. A Portuguese monarch issued such bans three times, only to withdraw them shortly thereafter. A general decree of freedom was issued in 1609, only to be canceled in two years, reinstated in 1680, nullified eight years later, revived in 1715, and over-ridden again just three years following.

79 The May 26, 1608, law allowed slavery, but the law of 1610 suspended it. It was re-instated in April 1625. Juan Solórzano Pereira, *Política indiana*, 5 vols. (Madrid, 1972), bk. 2, chap. 1, nos. 28–29, 1:139; bk. 3, tit. 4, law 9 (1523, 1528).

80 Sebastian de Covarrubias, *Tesoro de la lengua castellana o española* (1611; reprint, Madrid, 1984).

81 Demetrio Ramos, *Audacia, negocios y política en los viajes españoles descubrimiento y rescate* (Valladolid, Spain, 1981).

82 Beginning with the decrees of 1587, Portuguese monarchs employed the rationale that they were permitting ransoming of those who were about to be eaten. See "Lei, Feb. 24, 1587," and "Carta de Lei, Sept. 10, 1611," in Georg Thomas, *Die portugiesische Indianerpolitik in Brasilien 1500–1640* (Berlin, 1968), 201, 208–9.

83 Peter Hulme, *Colonial Encounters: Europe and the Native Caribbean, 1492–1797* (London, 1986), 16–22, 46–87; Lestringant, *Le cannibal*.

84 The regulation specifically referred to Caribbean residents, although it was often taken as a precedent for any enslavement for cannibalism. *Recopilación de leyes de los reinos de las indias* (1681), 3 vols. (1791; reprint, Madrid, 1943), bk. 6, tit. 2, law 13. Supposedly, no men over fourteen years old were to be enslaved. Richard Konetzke, ed., *Colección de documentos para la historia de la formación social de Hispanoamérica, 1493–1810*, 3 vols. (Madrid, 1953), vol. 1, no. 10, pp. 14–16; reiterated by Ferdinand after Isabel's death, no. 22, pp. 31–33.

85 In Konetzke, *Colección de documentos*, vol. 1, no. 10, pp. 14–16. Queen Isabel's list in-cluded resisting the Spanish invasion, fighting Indian allies of the Spanish, refusing to convert, worshiping idols, and cannibalism. Eventually, however, the list was narrowed down to cannibalism and resistance. The oft-cited role of Isabel in return-ing slaves captured by Columbus in 1495 is misleading. The instigator of the return was not the queen; rather, the bishop of Bajadoz rejected the sale of Indian slaves on a technicality. Isabel agreed with the bishop, and ordered the slaves returned, but then shortly thereafter set out the rules that permitted Indian slavery. See Konetzke, *Colección de documentos*, vol. 1, no. 10, pp. 14–16; "Carta al obispo de Baxadoz, April 13, 1495," in *CDI*, 30:335–36. Regarding the return of slaves to Hispaniola, see Angel Ortega, ed., *La rábida*, 2 vols. (Seville, 1926), 2:300.

86 "Regimento a Tomé da Sousa, 1548," in *HCPB*, 3:348.

87 "Lei, Feb. 24, 1587," 201.

88 This insight first appeared in Hulme, *Colonial Encounters*, chap. 1.

89 *CDI*, 31:438–39, 424, 429–430.

90 See Solórzano, *Política indiana*, bk. 2, chap. 1: "Tiene licencia para hacer guerra a los

Indios Caribes, que las va a infestar con mano armada, y comer carne humana, y puede hacer sus esclavos a as que cautivaren." Isabel's decree allowing slavery of cannibals appears in *CDI*, 31:196–200. See also Martín Fernández de Navarrete, *Colección de los viages y descubrimientos que hicieron por mar los españoles desde fines del siglo XV*, 5 vols. (Madrid, 1825–37), 2:415; *Recopilación*, bk. 6, tit. 2, law 13 (1569).

91 Cortés, *Cartas de relación*, series "Sepan cuantos," 2d letter, 88; 4th letter, 178, 195.

92 Robert S. Chamberlain, *The Conquest and Colonization of Yucatan 1517–1550* (Washington, D.C., 1948), 250–51.

93 Regal and viceregal declarations permitting slavery for cannibalism can be found in Phillip Powell, *Soldiers, Indians, and Silver: The Northward Advance of New Spain, 1550–1600* (Berkeley, Calif., 1969), 50–52, 63–64, 105–112, 197; Eduardo Arcilo Farias, *La doctrina de la justa guerra contra los indios en Venezuela* (Caracas, 1954); Eugene H. Korth, *Spanish Policy in Colonial Chile: The Struggle for Social Justice, 1535–1700* (Stanford, Calif., 1968), 85, 163–64, 178–81, 191–96; María Teresa Huerta Palacios, *Rebeliones indígenas de la época colonial* (Mexico, 1976), 79–102, esp. 92; Angel Barral, *Rebeliones indígenas* (Madrid, 1992).

94 Alvano Félix Bolaños, *Barbarie y canibalismo en la retórica colonial: Los indios pijaos de fray Pedro Simón* (Bogotá, 1994).

95 Solórzano, *Política indiana*, 1:136, 138–39.

96 Beginning with the royal Ordinance of 1569, notification had to be made to the governing body in Spain, the Council of the Indies, if indigenous people were enslaved.

97 Francisco Suarez, *De tripilici virtute*, t. 12, disp. 18, sec. 4; Domingo Bañez, *Decisiones de iure et iusticia* (Salamanca, 1584), 624, col. 533.

98 São Paulo, *Atas da câmara da cidade de São Paulo*, 72 vols., (São Paulo, 1914–), 2:47, 243.

99 "Assim o ouvia Deus, que depois se foi desta Bahia dar guerra aquela gentio e se tomou dele vingança." Frei Vicente do Salvador, *História do Brasil*, 3d ed., ed. Capistrano de Abreu and Rodolfo Garcia (São Paulo, 1931), chap. 3, bks. 3, 56. Following the Cunco Indians' killing of Spanish survivors of a shipwreck off the coast of Arauco in 1651, Spanish officials launched a bloody reprisal against the Cunco, selling the survivors as slaves. Korth, *Spanish Policy*, 179.

100 Thomas, *Die portugiesische Indianerpolitik*, 36 (March 20, 1570), 199 (Feb. 24, 1587), 201 (Sept. 10, 1611), 207; Humberto de Oliveira, comp., *Coletânea de leis, atos, e memórias referentes ao indígena brasileiro* (Rio de Janeiro, 1947), 67; Hemming, *Red Gold*, 92, 113.

101 Letter from Anchieta to Loyola, São Vicente, end of March 1555, in Leite, *Cartas dos primeiros Jesuítas*, 2:207. For additional examples of ecclesiastical support for slaving in Brazil, see Gândavo, *Tratado da Província do Brasil*, 125.

102 São Paulo, *Atas da câmara*, 2:497–500.

103 Antônio Vieira, "Informação sobre o modo com que foram tomados e sentenciados por cativos os índios do anno de 1655," in *Obras escolhidas*, 12 vols., ed. Antônio Sérgio and Herman Cidade (Lisbon, 1951–54), 5:72–135, esp. 40–54.

104 Portuguese legislation included the standard official Spanish pretext—preventing the teaching of Christianity—for only fifty years. (The Spanish justifications for slavery were expressed in the legal protocol called the Requirement.)

105 Boswell, *The Royal Treasure*, 50–52.

106 Lestringant writes convincingly of the complexities of French ambivalence toward

native cannibalism in *Le cannibal*. Of related interest is his *Le huguenot et le sauvage: L'Amérique et la controverse coloniale en France, au temps des guerres de religion (1555–1589)* (Paris, 1990).

107 Thwaites, *The Jesuit Relations*, 24:294–97.

108 Léry, *History of a Voyage*, 132, 212–13.

109 Michel de Montaigne, "Of Cannibals," in *The Essays of Michel de Montaigne*, 3 vols., trans. George B. Ives (New York, 1947), 1:282–83. See also Michel de Montaigne, *Essais de Michel de Montaigne*, 3 vols., ed. Andre Tournon (Paris, 1998), 1:352–53.

110 João Sebastião da Silva Dias, *Os descobrimentos e a problemática cultural do século XVI* (Coimbra, Portugal, 1973), 225. During the nineteenth century, romantic depictions of indigenous peoples appeared, for example, in the works of José de Alencar e Gonçalves Dias. But this literature was frequently associated with anti-Portuguese nationalism. Marga Graf, *Goncalves Dias und die Problematik des nationalen Dichters* (Rheinfelden, 1985).

111 William Bradford, *Of Plymouth Plantation, 1620–1647*, ed. Samuel Eliot Morison (New York, 1952), 84. See also William Bradford, *Bradford's History of Plymouth Plantation, 1606–1646*, ed. William T. Davis (New York, 1908), 45.

112 Fear for one's own safety also appears in a June 1715 entry in the *Diary of Cotton Mather*, 2 vols. (New York, 1957), 2:328–29; see also Cotton Mather, *Agricola or, The Religious Husbandman* (Boston, 1727), 87.

113 Bradford, *Of Plymouth Plantation*, 84; Bradford, *Bradford's History*, 45.

114 James Cook, *A Journal of a Voyage Round the World in H.M.S. Endeavour 1768–1771* (1771; reprint, New York, 1967), 69.

115 E. B. O' Callaghan, ed., *Documents Relative to the Colonial History of the State of New York: Procured in Holland, England and France*, 11 vols. (Cleveland, n.d.), 1:157, 167; John R. Brodhead, ed., *Documents Relative to the Colonial History of New York*, 15 vols. (Albany, N.Y., 1853–57), 1:245. See also J. Franklin Jameson, ed. *Narratives of New Netherland, 1609–1664* (New York, 1909), 84–85; Arnold J. F. Laer, ed., *Documents Relating to New Netherland, 1624–1626* (San Marino, Calif., 1924), 223–32.

116 Nicolaes van de Wassenaer, *Historisch verhael alder ghedenck-geschiedenisen die heir en daer in Europa*, 5 vols. (Amsterdam, 1622–35), 38v–39r.

117 Ibid.

118 Fritz Redlich, *De Praeda Militari: Looting and Booty 1500–1815* (Weisbaden, 1956), 29.

119 Bernardo Gomes de Brito, *The Tragic History of the Sea, 1589–1622*, trans. Charles Boxer (Cambridge, 1959), 225; Fernão Lopes de Castanheda, *História do descobrimento e conquista da Índia pelos portugueses*, 2 vols. (Porto, Portugal, 1979).

120 Redlich, *De Praeda Militari*, 3; Léry, *History of a Voyage*, 132.

CHAPTER 7: SUSTAINING POLITICAL IDENTITIES

1 Edward Said, *Orientalism* (New York, 1979).

2 James Axtell and Robert Berkhofer have been prominent in demystifying these images in the United States. James Axtell, *After Columbus: Essays in the Ethnohistory of Colonial North America* (New York, 1988); James Axtell, *Beyond 1492: Encounters in Colonial North America* (New York, 1992); Robert E. Berkhofer, *The White Man's Indian: Images of the American Indian, from Columbus to the Present* (New York, 1979). Less well-known but highly compelling is Cornel Pewewardy's "Commercial and Intellectual Exploitation of Native Peoples," *News from Indian Country; Ethnic News Watch*, January 1997, 17A.

3 See François Hartog, *The Mirror of Herodotus: The Representation of the Other in the Writing of History*, trans. Janet Lloyd (Berkeley, Calif., 1988).

4 The image of the native in popular U.S. culture "seems more like a Thanksgiving Day parade balloon-figure, blown up out of proportion and painted with artificial colors and cartoon designs. The non-Native people holding the ropes are marching in a display of cultural images far more reflective of themselves [non-Natives] than of the peoples such images claim to represent." Lee Irwin, "Themes in Native American Spirituality," *American Indian Quarterly* 20, nos. 3–4 (1996): 309. See also Homi K. Bhabha, "Signs Taken for Wonders," in *Location of Culture* (London, 1994), 108; Partha Chatterjee, *The Nation and Its Fragments: Colonial and Postcolonial Histories* (Princeton, N.J., 1995), 5.

5 Max Weber, *Die protestantische Ethik und der "Geist" des Kapitalismus* (Tubingen, 1904). Not surprisingly, this book has not been translated into Spanish or Portuguese, but is immensely popular in English.

6 See Patricia Seed, "The Key to the House," in *Home, Exile, Homeland: Film, Media, and the Politics of Place*, ed. Hamid Naficy (New York, 1998).

7 A French Catholic baker arrested by the Inquisition in Mexico City on suspicion of religious deviance was labeled a *gringo*, a kind of not-quite-Catholic.

8 "Al interior del mundo de las concepciones religiosas se acuñará el término 'infiel y su equivalente' gentil utilizados en contraposición a cristiano." Juan Villegas, S.J., "La evangelización del indio de la Banda Oriental del Uruguay," in *Cristianismo y mundo colonial*, ed. Johannes Meier (Munich, 1995), 74–75.

9 Aquinas's popularity in sixteenth-century Spain may have stemmed from his emphasis on the moral agent's attitude and intentions as well as the ends or goals of human activity. Both characterizations fit Hispanic political culture of that era. See Vernon J. Bourke, "Aquinas," in *Ethics in the History of Western Philosophy* (New York, 1989), 98–124.

10 "Homobruta animalia superexcedit in hoc quod habet ratio nem. . . . Ergo videtur quod, sicutbruta animalia no baptizantur . . . quod furiosi vel amentes carent usu rationis per accidens . . . non autem propter defectum animae rationalis, sicut bruta animalia." Thomas Aquinas, *Summa theologica*, 21 vols., trans. Fathers of the English Dominican Province (London, 1912–25), 3a, quest. 68, art. 12, 2, ad 2. A "barbarian" is one "in quantum ratione non regitur." *In omnes S. Pauli epistolas commentaria Super epistolam ad Romanos lectura*, chap. 5, lec. 5. For a more detailed treatment of this subject and its implications, see Patricia Seed, "'Are These Not Also Men?': The Indian's Humanity and Capacity for Spanish Civilization," *Journal of Latin American Studies* 25(1993): 629–52. And finally there were those who were never able to become Christians, the members of the animal kingdom. The intensely fought debates over the "humanity" of the New World natives only signified that Indians were capable of Christianization, and hence capable of being subjected to Catholic rule.

11 Juan de Matienzo, *Gobierno del Perú*, ed. Guillermo Lohman-Villena (1567; reprint, Lima, 1967), 17–18. See also Domingo Bañez, *Decisiones de iure et iusticia* (Venice, 1595), 79–80.

12 R. Douglas Cope, *The Limits of Racial Domination: Plebeian Society in Colonial Mexico City, 1660–1720* (Madison, Wis., 1994).

13 As evidence of its continuing power—Mexican scholar Roger Bartra interprets the "wild man" myth within this Hispanic framework, seeing natives as lacking the

rational control that characterized Spanish ideals. Roger Bartra, *Wild Men in the Looking Glass: The Mythic Origins of European Otherness*, trans. Carl T. Berrisford (Ann Arbor, Mich., 1994). See also Massimo Centini, *L'úomo selvaggio: Antropologia di un mito della montagna* (Turin, 2000).

14 Dauril Alden, *The Making of an Enterprise: The Society of Jesus in Portugal, Its Empire, and Beyond, 1540–1750* (Stanford, Calif., 1996), 257–58.

15 I am grateful to Judith Elkin for having pointed this out to me. See her "Imagining Idolatry: Missionaries, Indians, and Jews," in *Religion and the Authority of the Past*, ed. Tobin Siebers (Ann Arbor, University of Michigan Press, 1993).

16 In 1568, Philip II prohibited the ordination of mestizos, but in 1588 (under papal pressure) he changed the decree to prohibit only the ordination of illegitimate mestizos. Because most mestizos were illegitimate, this decree had the desired impact. Identical initial enthusiasm followed by refusal to admit natives occurred in Asia as well. See Alden, *The Making of an Enterprise*, 258–63. In the eighteenth century a few determined Asians succeeded in overcoming the barrier.

17 In Britain, *sodomite* was an epithet slung at the papists and the Jesuits. Homosexual relations largely remained out of public sight, carried out covertly in households and universities. Unlike in Iberia, in England sodomy was not also a political crime. Only one man, Christopher Marlowe, was accused of both homosexuality and treason; male homosexual conduct did not automatically imply treason, as it did in Iberian kingdoms. Alan Bray, *Homosexuality in Renaissance England* (London, 1982), 74; Valerie Traub, *Desire and Anxiety* (London, 1992), 106–13. In 1642, members of the Plymouth colony decided that homosexuality "was not capital by any express law of God," and judged sex with animals to be a far more serious offense. Robert F. Oaks, "'Things Too Fearful to Name:' Sodomy and Buggery in Seventeenth-Century New England," in *History of Homosexuality in Europe and America*, ed. Wayne R. Dynes and Stephen Donaldson (New York, 1992), 236–40. On the far harsher punishments of men for homosexual activities in Spain, see William Monter, "Sodomy: The Fateful Accident," also in the Dynes and Donaldson volume, 192–215; John Boswell, *Christianity, Social Tolerance, and Homosexuality* (Chicago, 1980), 174, 288–89; Josiah Blackmore and Gregory S. Hutcheson, *Queer Iberia: Sexualities, Cultures, and Crossings from the Middle Ages to the Renaissance* (Durham, N.C., 1999); Mary Elizabeth Perry, *Gender and Disorder in Early Modern Seville* (Princeton, N.J., 1990). For the more positive contemporary attitudes toward homosexual practices in North American native communities, see Louise Erdrich, *The Beet Queen* (New York, 1986); Sue-Ellen Jacobs, Wesley Thomas, and Sabine Lang, *Two-Spirit People: Native American Gender Identity, Sexuality, and Spirituality* (Urbana, Ill., 1997); Sabine Lang, *Men as Women, Women as Men: Changing Gender in Native American Cultures*, trans. John L. Vantine (Austin, Tex., 1998).

18 Pablo de Arriaga (1564–1622), *Extirpación de las idolatrías del Perú* (Buenos Aires, 1910); Pedro de Villagomez (1585–1671), *Exortaciones e instrucción acerca de las idolatrias de los indios del arzobispado de Lima* (Lima, 1919).

19 Irene Silverblatt, *Moon, Sun and Witches: Gender Ideologies and Class in Inca and Colonial Peru* (Princeton, N.J., 1987), 175.

20 George Kubler, "The Quechua in the Colonial World" in *Handbook of South American Indians*, 7 vols., ed. Julian Steward (Washington, D.C., 1946–59), maintains that the persecutions stopped in the Andes late in the seventeenth century. Nicholas

Griffiths, *The Cross and the Serpent* (Norman, Okla., 1996), 244–45, maintains that the persecutions did not end until the eighteenth century.

21 See Alice Wood, "The Discourse of Sanctity" (Ph.D. diss., Rice University, 1997). The same attitude toward ordination of racially mixed clerics appeared in Portuguese possessions as well. See Carlos Merces de Melo, S.J., *The Recruitment and Formation of the Native Clergy in India, 16th and 17th Century* (Lisbon, 1955).

22 Contemporary political ideologues of nationalism in the United States require asserting that English settlers had contact with Native Americans. However, historians of North America seem inclined to equate the highly attenuated forms of Anglo-Indian contact in North America with the constant daily interactions of Spanish America. Not only do such contacts differ in frequency, they differ in the range of permissible interactions.

23 Mathew Hale, *Primitive Origination of Mankind Considered and Examined According to the Light of Nature* (London, 1677), 197.

24 Lewis Cass, "Governor Cass on the Need for Removal," *North American Review* 30 (1830): 62–121.

25 See Ann Wightman, *Indigenous Migration and Social Change: The Forasteros of Cuzco* (Durham, N.C., 1990).

26 Wood, "The Discourse of Sanctity."

27 Among the groups discovered since 1974 have been the Araras, Paracana, Guaja, and Korubo. As of 1998, estimates of the number of groups remaining to be discovered ranged from thirty (according to the National Indian Foundation) to two or three (according to Elton da Luz Rohnelt, a miner and federal congressman from the Amazon-basin state of Roraima, Brazil). The boundary of the priesthood was also less firmly enforced in the Portuguese empire. In West Africa (Congo, São Tomé, Angola, and Cabo Verde), natives were admitted to the priesthood, but in Brazil and East Africa (Mozambique, Kenya) they were not. In India they were admitted only to the lower levels of the religious orders and could never become ordained Franciscans, Dominicans, Jesuits, or Augustinians. Charles Boxer, *Race Relations in the Portuguese Colonial Empire, 1415–1825* (Oxford, 1963), 56–57, 65–66, 117–18.

28 See Serafim Leite, ed., *Cartas dos primeiros Jesuítas do Brasil*, 3 vols. (São Paulo, 1956–58): "Estes gentios não tem rezois e são muito viciosos, tem a porta serrada para a fee naturalmente" (2:327). See also "A relação do frei Vitoriano Pimentel (1701)," reproduced in Manuel Maria Wermers, *O establecimento das missões camelitana no rio Negro e nos Solimões (1675–1711)* (Coimbra, Portugal, 1965), 24.

29 Letter of Padre Anchieta, August 15, 1554, and letter of Antonio Blazquez, July 8, 1555, both in Leite, *Cartas dos primeiros Jesuítas*, 2:82, 252.

30 *Diálogo sobre a conversão do Gentio*, in ibid., 2:321–22. On the tradition of applying animal names to humans between Christians and Muslims, see Benny Morris, "Hebron's History," *Tikkun* 9 (1994): "A Christian traveler reported from Hebron in the first half of the fourteenth century that 'Christian and Jewish people are regarded by them [Muslims] as dogs and they do not allow them to enter such a holy place'" (48).

31 Martinho de Nantes, *Relação de uma missão no rio São Francisco* (1671; reprint, São Paulo, 1979), 4.

32 Damião de Goes, quoted in João Sebastião da Silva Dias, *Os descobrimentos e a problematica cultural do século XVI* (Coimbra, Portugal, 1973), 221.

33 The demand for symmetry in such matters signals continuing self-absorption—the desire that other people be written about in ways that reflect one's own categories and interests, not theirs.

34 Edward Coke, *The First Part of the Institutes of the Laws of England*, 6th ed., 2 vols. (London, 1664) 2:86. See also Conrad Heresbach, *Foure Bookes of Husbandrie* (London, 1596), 5; William Lawson, *A New Orchard and Garden* (London, 1676), 56; Richard Eburne, *A Plaine Pathway to Plantations* (1624), ed. Louis B. Wright (Ithaca, N.Y., 1962), 41.

35 John Milton, *Paradise Lost*, ed. Alastair Fowler (London, 1998), bk. 4, l. 691; John Parkinson, *Paradisi in Sole Paradisus Terrstris* (London, 1629). Parkinson's book was owned by, among others, Increase and Cotton Mather. For discussion of the esteem in which they held this book, see Grace Tabor, *Old-Fashioned Gardening* (New York, 1925). For similar examples, see Thomas Cartwright, *A Confutation of The Rhemists Translation, Glosses and Annotations on the New Testament* (Leiden, Netherlands, 1618), 379; William Haller, *The Rise of Puritanism; or, The Way to the New Jerusalem as Set Forth in Pulpit and Press from Thomas Cartwright to John Lilburne and John Milton, 1570–1643* (1938; reprint, Philadephia, 1984). Harvard's copy of Parkinson's book comes from the library of John Hancock's grandfather.

36 Walter Blith, *The English Improver Improved* (London, 1653), 3–4.

37 *Oxford English Dictionary*, 2d ed. (hereafter *OED*), s.v. "farm," noun, definition 2, meanings 1–4 (from the thirteenth century onward) all share this meaning. *Farm* was used for tax farmers from 1385 on. The second definition of the verb form shows a similar historical pattern as well, with the widespread use of *to farm* as "to till" dating from the nineteenth century (definition 4).

38 The following sources are listed in *OED*, s.v. "farmer," definition 3: "One who rents land for the purpose of cultivation; = tenant farmer. Now chiefly as a contextual application of 5. 1487 Act 4 Hen. VII, c. 16 The Occupier and Fermer of them . . . to be discharged against his Lessor of the Rent. 1523 Fitzherb. Husb. (1523) Sect. 123 Though a man be but a farmer, and shall haue hys farme .xx. yeres. 1577 Harrison England ii. v. (1877) i. 133 The yeomen are for the most part farmers to gentlemen. 4. One who cultivates land for the owner; a bailiff, steward. Obs." See also in definition 2 the contrast between the dates for 4a (1382, 1526, 1579, 1580) and those for 5a (owner or tenant—1599, 1647, 1666, 1771).

39 *OED*, s.v. "plant," verb, meaning 1. "To insert, set, or place firmly, to fix in or on the ground"; definition 2, verb, "Beginning c. 1300 to settle (a person) in a place, establish as a settler or colonist"; verb form 3b.

40 "Now rare. 1362 Langl. Piers Plowman A. i. 137 Loue isþe leuest þing þat vr lord askeþ, And eke þe playnt [v. rr. plante, plaunte, plonte] of pees." *OED*, s.v. "plant," noun, meaning 1, definition 1c.

41 William Bradford, *Bradford's History of Plymouth Plantation 1606–1646*, ed. William T. Davis (New York, 1908); John Smith, *Advertisements for the Unexperienced Planters of New-England* (1631), in *The Complete Works of Captain John Smith (1580–1631)*, 3 vols., ed. Philip L. Barbour (Chapel Hill, N.C., 1986).

42 *A True Declaration of the Estate of the Colonie in Virginia* (1610), in Peter Force, *Tracts and Other Papers Relating Principally to the Origin, Settlement, and Progress of the Colonies in North America, From the Discovery of the Country to the Year 1776*, 4 vols. (Washington, D.C., 1836–46), vol. 3, no. 1, pp. 6, 15.

43 Originally utilized in the West Indies and the southern colonies of North America, the term later came to be used for the owner or manager of a tea or rubber plantation in Southeast Asia. *Macquarie Dictionary*, 3d ed., ed. Arthur Delbridge (Sydney, 1996), s.v. "planter."

44 Walter Ralegh, *History of the World*, bk. 1, chap. 3, in *The Works of Sir Walter Ralegh, Kt*, 8 vols. (Oxford, 1829), 2:89.

45 Milton, *Paradise Lost*, bk. 4, l. 691.

46 In Richard Hakluyt, *The Principal Navigations, Voyages, Traffiques and Discoveries of the English Nation Made by Sea or Over-Land to the Remote and Farthest Distant Quarters of the Earth at any Time Within the Compasse of These 1600 Yeeres*, 12 vols. (Glasgow, 1903–5), 7:5.

47 Cotton Mather, *Fair Weather* (Boston, 1692): "The Indians yet living in Hostility against us, after they had by a long silence and repose in their inaccessible Kennels" (88). George Thorpe in *The Records of the Virginia Company of London*, 4 vols., ed. Susan Myra Kingsbury (Washington, D.C., 1906–35), 3:552.

48 Robert Gray, *A Good Speede to Virginia* (London, 1609), n.p.; Robert Johnson, *Nova Britannia: Offering Most Excellent Fruites By Planting In Virginia* (London, 1609), 11.

49 R. C. (Robert Cushman), "Reasons and Considerations Touching the Lawfulness of Removing out of England and into the Parts of America" (1621), in *Mourt's Relation* (Boston, 1865), 148; Bradford, *Bradford's History* , 46–47. See also William Strachey, *The Histories of Travell into Virginia Britania* (1612), ed. Louis B. Wright and Virginia Freund (London, 1953), 24.

50 Compare this conclusion to Lewis Hanke's in his books *The Spanish Struggle for Justice in the Conquest of America* (Philadelphia, 1949) and *Aristotle and the American Indians: A Study in Race Prejudice in the Modern World* (London, 1959), among other places. I am critical of Hanke's presentation of both English and Spanish traditions regarding natives as "beasts." In claiming moral superiority for the Spanish tradition of proving the Indians' "humanity," Hanke exaggerates both sides. As his Spanish critics have pointed out, Spaniards rarely declared that Indians *were* beasts. Rather, they said that natives conducted themselves "like beasts." However, Hanke equally exaggerates the English position when he claims that Englishmen declared Indians *were* beasts. As the passages quoted show, Englishmen also described the natives as conducting themselves "like beasts," but did not state that the natives were animals. As I argue in the remainder of this chapter and in my article "'Are These Not Also Men?'" in providing an argument for superior Hispanic morality, Hanke ignores the political and economic interests at stake in both English and Spanish colonists' characterizations of native conduct as similar to animals. A sample of the earlier Iberian responses to Hanke's argument include Juan Pérez de Tudela Bueso, "Significado historico de la vida y escritos del padre Las Casas: Estudio preliminar" in *Obras escogidas de fray Bartolomé de Las Casas* (Madrid, 1957), ix–clxxxviii; Alberto María Carreño, "La irracionalidad de los indios," *Divulgación histórica* 1 (1940): 272–82, 328–39, 374–85; Edmundo O'Gorman, "La naturaleza bestial del indio," *Filosofía y letras* 1–2 (1941): 141–58, 305–15, esp. 305; Lino Gómez Canedo, "*Hombres* or bestias? (Nuevo examen critico de un viejo tópico)," *Estudios de historia novohispaña* (Mexico) 1 (1967): 29–51.

51 Cotton Mather described their language as "little more than is to be found among the very beavers upon the streams." Cotton Mather, *Magnalia Christi Americana; or, The Ecclesiastical History of New-England*, 2 vols. (Hartford, 1820), 1:505.

52 For a more extensive description of this phenomenon, see Patricia Seed, *Ceremonies of Possession in Europe's Conquest of the New World, 1492–1640* (Cambridge, 1995), chap. 1.

53 In Angel Ortega, ed., *La rábida*, 2 vols. (Seville, 1926), 2:306.

54 William Symonds, *Virginia: A Sermon Preached at White-Chappel, in the presence of many, honourable and worshipfull, the adventurers and planters for Virginia, 25 April, 1609* (London, 1609); Gray, *A Good Speede to Virginia*, n.p.

55 Paradise is a garden in both the Zoroastrian and the Islamic traditions.

56 Lawson, *A New Orchard and Garden*, 56. See also Parkinson, *Paradisi in Sole Paradisus Terrstris*; Ann Leighton, *Early American Gardens: For Meate or Medicine* (Boston, 1970), 148.

57 Lawson, *A New Orchard and Garden*, 56.

58 *The Tempest*, act 2, scene 1. It is often pointed out that the inspiration for this phrase was Ovid's *Metamorphoses*: "The fertile earth as yet was free, untoucht of spade or plough / And yet it yeelded of it selfe of every things inough . . . food / that on the earth by natures gift without their travell stoode" (1:115–16). But Ovid does not say "without sweat or endeavor," an alteration that is distinctly Shakespearean, and based upon the sixteenth-century English interpretation of using plows as "labor." The translation of Ovid used by Shakespeare (quoted above) contains several other culturally unique phrases. It mentions manure (1:125), an English word meaning both dung and labor—but employed only in England. It also mentions yoking oxen to plows (1:139–40), not a European practice prior to the ninth century. See W. H. D. Rouse, ed., *Shakespeare's Ovid Being Arthur Golding's Translation of the Metamorphoses* (Carbondale, Ill., 1961). "Manure" also appears in the translation by the first treasurer of the Virginia Company. Karl. K. Hulley and Stanley T. Vandersall, eds., *Ovid's Metamorphosis Anglicized, Mythologized, and Represented in Figures by George Sandys* (1632; reprint, Lincoln, Neb., 1970), 1:109. A recent translation says, "The earth itself without compulsion, untouched by the hoe, unfurrowed by any share, produced all things spontaneously and men were content with foods that grew without cultivation. . . . The earth, though untilled, produced corn too." *The Metamorphoses of Ovid*, trans. Mary M. Innes (Harmondsworth, Eng., 1955), 34.

59 See, for example, Guillaume Du Bartas, seigneur de Salluste (1544–90), *His Divine Weekes and Workes* (London, 1621), l. 102; Blith, *The English Improver Improved*, 5.

60 William Temple, *Works of Sir William Temple* (1690; reprint, London, 1814), 3:207.

61 Ralegh, *History of the World*, 2:127. Ralegh then went on to say that the New World was most definitely not Paradise: "The fearful and dangerous thunders and lightnings, the horrible and frequent earthquakes, the dangerous diseases, the multitude of venomous beasts and worms, with other inconveniences, and then thee will be found no comparison between the one [Paradise] and the other" (ibid.).

62 Milton, *Paradise Lost*, bk. 4, 624–28. John Martin Evans finds the necessity of cultivating the garden unusually stressed in *Paradise Lost*. See his *Milton's Imperial Epic: Paradise Lost and the Discourse of Colonialism* (Ithaca, N.Y., 1996), 80.

63 Milton, *Paradise Lost*, bk. 11, 179. See also Adam Moore, *Bread for the Poor* (London, 1653), 2.

64 John Parkinson, "To the Courteous Reader," in *Paridisi in Sole Paradisus Terrstris*, n.p. Regarding the popularity of the Parkinson volume, see note 34, above, as well as Blanche Henrey, *British Botanical and Horticultural Literature Before 1800*, 3 vols. (London, 1975), 1:79; Leighton, *Early American Gardens*, 148. According to Vivian R. Ludgate, *Gardens of the Colonists* (Washington, D.C., 1941), the title was also popular in

Virginia. Proponents of the Virginia colony declared, "Adam himselfe might not live in paradice without dressing the garden." *A True Declaration Of The Estate Of The Colonie In Virginia Published by advise and direction of the Councell of Virginia* (London, 1610), 15. Johnson, in *Nova Britannia*, writes of "that most wholesome profitable and pleasant work of planting in which it pleased God himself to set the first man and the most excellent creature Adam" (16–17).

65 John Hammond, *Leah and Rachel, Or, The Two Fruitfull Sisters Virginia and Mary-Land* (London, 1656), 10; William Wood, *New England's Prospect*, ed. Alden T. Vaughn (Amherst, Mass., 1977), 68.

66 In *Paradise Lost*, Adam describes labor as distinguishing humans from animals. Other creatures may "all day long / Rove idle unemployed / Man hath his daily work of body or mind / Appointed, which declares his Dignitie." Milton, *Paradise Lost*, bk. 4, 616–19.

67 Gray, *A Good Speede to Virginia*, n.p.

68 William Wilkie, *Epigoniad* (Edinburgh, 1757): "The stars descend; and soon the morning ray / Shall rouse us to the labors of the day" (bk. 7, 231).

69 The term *dog days*, applied to the period from early July to mid-August, arose from the pernicious qualities of the season, which were attributed to the "influence" of the Dog Star (Sirius), but it has long been popularly associated with the belief that it is during this season that dogs are most apt to run mad.

70 The introduction of racial identifiers during the seventeenth century—"red men"— failed to endure as the dominant category differentiating English colonists and native peoples. See Peter Hulme's illuminating account of this venture in *Colonial Encounters: Europe and the Native Caribbean, 1492–1797* (London, 1986).

71 For discussion of the use of "race" in mid-eighteenth-century Mexico, see Patricia Seed, *To Love, Honor, and Obey in Colonial Mexico: Conflicts over Marriage Choice, 1574–1821* (Stanford, Calif., 1988). On seventeenth-century Virginia, see Hulme, *Colonial Encounters*. The absence of clear-cut racial terminology in the Iberian Americas is also illustrated by the proliferation of terms. See Thomas M. Stephens, *Dictionary of Latin American Racial and Ethnic Terminology* (Gainesville, Fla., 1989), 13–367.

72 By contrast, Iberian colonial legislation was far more concerned with the pernicious impact of the colonists upon the Indians than vice versa. See *Fundación de Cusco y ordenanzas para su gobierno (1562)*, ed. Horacio Uteaga y Carlos Romero (Lima, 1926), 188, quoted in Jean-Pierre Tardieu, *Noirs et indiens au Pérou (XVIe-XVIIe siècles)* (Paris, 1990), 91–92.

73 The most significant effort to attempt to introduce a redemptory narrative into the political process appears in Frantz Fanon's conclusion to *Black Skins, White Masks*, trans. Charles Lam Markmann (New York, 1967). In his later works, however, Fanon abandoned this point of view, because, I believe, he found it impossible to use as the source of a satisfactory solution. Some U.S. writers have seen the possibility of religious salvation. Bernard Sheehan states: "Savagism placed no permanent impediment in the way of progress. Even when the Indian was portrayed in bestial terms there was still hope for his salvation." Bernard Sheehan, *Savagism and Civility: Indians and Englishmen in Colonial Virginia* (Cambridge, 1980), 6. But the more essential political uses of this moral category remain neglected in this formulation.

1 The French succeeded in turning their Caribbean islands into profit makers, but their possessions were small and success did not come until the eighteenth century.

2 In 1464, Afonso V gave Soeiro Mendes de Évora the Alcaidaria-mor, a castle on the island of Arguim. This was the first fortress constructed on the African coast (river of São João), where the Portuguese came to trade for gold, slaves, gum, and hides. In 1481 the fortress at Arguim was nearly finished and one at São Jorge da Mina was begun, finished by 1485. António Baião, Hernani Cidade, and Manuel Murias, eds., *História da expansão portuguesa no mundo*, 3 vols. (Lisbon, 1937–48), 1:363–65.

3 Ibid.

4 A critical perspective on this approach is provided by Luis Mendes de Vasconcelos, *O sitio de Lisboa* (1608), in *Antologia dos economistas portugueses*, ed. António Sergio (Lisbon, 1924), 62–63, 71–73, 77, 81. Mendes de Vasconcelos suggests that the Portuguese should have controlled the production of commodities instead of relying upon marketing for their profits. António Sergio, *Ensaios*, 8 vols. (Lisbon, 1928), 1:78–79.

5 Free trade prevailed from 1498 to 1504, with only a 5 percent custom duty imposed. From 1504 to 1506, the crown required merchants to sell all the goods they acquired overseas to the crown itself, which resold the goods and gave the merchant a percentage. In addition, the crown upped customs duties to 30 percent. In 1506 this general royal monopsony was abandoned in favor of a limited royal monopsony over the most valuable commodities of a region, leaving all other commodities open to Portuguese subjects. In 1520 the crown reserved for itself the trade in pepper, cloves, ginger, cinnamon, mace, nutmeg, sealing wax, shellac, silk, and borax, as well as gold, silver, copper, and coral. The crown operated its monopsony through agreements signed with merchants who would purchase the commodities overseas. From 1570 to 1576, the royal monopsony was abandoned on all foods except for pepper, which remained a royal monopoly. In 1576 the crown tried delegating acquisition to private companies, then reversed itself, allowing freedom of trade between 1581 and 1586 (except for silk, cinnamon, and pepper). The old monopoly system was reinstituted from 1598 to 1642, when free trade was established with the exception of cinnamon, which was in royal hands. In 1591 the Portuguese trade with the East declined by one-third, and again in the decade 1650 to 1660, when it nearly became extinct. Antonio Henrique de Oliveira Marques, *History of Portugal*, 2 vols. (New York, 1972), 1:258, 343–45; Kuzhippalli S. Mathews, *Portuguese Trade with India in the Sixteenth Century* (New Delhi, 1983), 99; James C. Boyajian, *Portuguese Trade in Asia under the Hapsburgs* (Baltimore, 1993). When settlement began in Brazil, the crown retained its monopsony over the purchase of brazilwood, relinquishing its earlier monopolies on slaves, spices, and drugs. *História da colonização portuguesa do Brasil*, 3 vols. (hereafter *HCPB*) (Pôrto Alegre, Brazil, 1921–27), 3:176.

6 Salman Rushdie, *The Moor's Last Sigh* (New York, 1995), 4–5. A state monopoly could be run directly by crown-appointed officials in ports or by special permission granted to individuals. Existence of a monopoly did not mean that others could not trade, but there were limits and controls on that trade. Thus military and civilian employees of the crown could trade in gold but had to submit it to customs control and have it minted in Lisbon. Oliveira Marques, *History of Portugal*, 1:257.

7 Letters from a medieval Jewish trader indicate that brazilwood was difficult to sell outside of Iberia. Shelomo Dov Goitein, *Letters of Medieval Jewish Traders* (Princeton, N.J., 1974), 133. See also Shelomo Dov Goitein, *A Mediterranean Society: The Jewish Communities of the Arab World as Portrayed in the Documents of the Cairo Geniza*, 6 vols. (Berkeley, Calif., 1967–93), 1:157; Bernardino José de Sousa, *O pau-brasil na história nacional* (São Paulo, 1978), 16.

8 The name comes "from love of brazilwood," according to Fernão Lopes de Castanheda, *História do descobrimento e conquista da Índia pelos portugueses*, 2 vols., (Porto, Portugal, 1979), bk. 1. For other quotations from sixteenth-century Portuguese writers, see Sousa, *O pau-brasil*, 53–55. Another less convincing explanation of the region's name appears in Luis Weckmann, *La herencia medieval del Brasil* (Mexico City, 1993), 29–40.

9 The king claimed a monopoly of brazilwood from Asia even before he claimed it in the Americas. José Ramos Coelho, ed., *Alguns documentos do arquivo nacional da torre do Tombo* (Lisbon, 1892), 33; Biblioteca Nacional (Brazil), *Documentos históricos*, 110 vols. (Rio de Janeiro, 1928–65), 13:85, 106–7, 114, 150–51, 197, 203, 216, 243; António Baião, "O comércio do pau Brasil," in *HCPB*, 2:317–47; Carlos Mattoso Filipe, "Primeiro contacto com terras brasileiras," in *Portugal no mundo*, vol. 3, ed. Luís de Albuquerque (Lisbon, 1990); Bernardino José de Sousa, *O Pau-Brasil no história nacional* (São Paulo, 1939).

10 This is the most frequently misunderstood part of the Portuguese commercial empire. Many scholars have erroneously invoked their own twentieth-century understandings of what a monopoly is and then criticized the Portuguese empire for failing to conform to a concept of monopoly (control of the means of production) that did not exist for another three hundred years.

11 Luis Ferreira Reis argues that the concept of "lord of navigation and commerce" was a right in fact (*jus in re*). Luis Filipe Ferreira Reis, "Estrutura política e administrativa do Estado da India no século XVI," in *Atas do II Seminário internacional de história Indo-Portuguesa*, ed. Luís Albuquerque and Inácio Guerreiro (Lisbon, 1985), 526. For a slightly different interpretation by a modern scholar wanting to see Portuguese colonialism as consensual, see Armando Gonçalves Pereira, "As consequencias ecónomicas dos descobrimentos e das conquistas," in *História da colonização portuguesa no mundo*, ed. Antonio Baião, Hernani Cidade, and Manuel Murias (Lisbon, 1937–), 3:65–82. An excellent guide to the literature is John E. Wills Jr., "Maritime Asia: The Interactive Emergence of European Domination," *American Historical Review* 98 (1993): 83–105.

12 Ramming and boarding continued to be the traditional mode of battle in inter-European struggles and in Mediterranean battles until the end of the sixteenth century. John Guilmartin, *Gunpowder and Galleys* (Princeton, N.J., 1979). Overseas, however, the newer Portuguese style of naval warfare became the rule.

13 *HCPB*, 2:59, 73; 3:287–91. There is some evidence, principally from Amerigo Vespucci, of a fortress warehouse being constructed in 1503 on an island off Cabo Frio. *HCPB*, 2:59–94, 333–34; report from Conde da Castanheira on Fazenda Real (1542), in appendix to Luís de Sousa (1555?–1632), *Anais de D. João III*, 2 vols., ed. M. Rodrigues Lapa (Lisbon, 1938), 1:261–62. Parmentier brothers from Dieppe, in *HCPB*, 3:288. Breton traders and ships from Marseille are also mentioned in *HCPB*, 3:290. See also Jean Léry, *History of a Voyage to the Land of Brazil, Otherwise Called*

America, trans. Janet Whatley (Berkeley, Calif., 1990), 100; HCPB, 2:59–94, 73, 333–34; HCPB, 3:287–91.

14 The Rouen, Dieppe, and Honfleur merchants were pirates, according to Portuguese sources. HCPB, 2:59–94, esp. 63, 68; Sousa, Anais de D. João III, 261–62.

15 Francisco d'Andrada, Chronica de el-rei João III (Coimbra, Portugal, 1796), pt. 4, p. 130; see also Sousa, Anais de D. João III, 405. The Cristovão Jacques expeditions to the coast of Brazil in 1516–19 and 1526–28 were very expensive.

16 Carlos Malheiro Dias, "Introduction," in HCPB, 3:xlvi. See "Carta de El-Rei a Martim Affonso de Sousa, Sept. 28, 1532," in Pêro Lopes de Souza, Diario da navegação (Lisbon, 1839), 81–83, esp. 82; Pêro de Magalhães de Gândavo, Tratado da província do Brasil (1570; reprint, Rio de Janeiro, 1965), 65.

17 Decree, April 28, 1688. Other official reasons for enslavement included a native's being a prisoner of tribal war and rebelling against political and religious officials. Rita Heloísa de Almeida, O diretório dos índos: Um projeto de "civilização" no Brasil do século XVIII (Brasilia, 1997), 156. But settlers rarely invoked these reasons.

18 On Bahia, see HCPB, 3:249; Gabriel Soares de Sousa (1540?–91), Tratado descritivo do Brasil em 1587, 5th ed. (São Paulo, 1987), 73–74. On Paraiba, see the letter from Pêro Góis, April 29, 1546, in HCPB, 3:240–41. French and Flemish ships also captured Indians on the north coast of South America, luring them onto ships on the pretense of trade but actually kidnapping them for sale in the Antilles. The natives responded by massacring all the European colonists. For a graphic story of this response, see Jean Hurault, Français et indiens en Guyane, 1604–1972 (Paris, 1972), 77.

19 "Regimento a Tomé de Sousa," in HCPB, 3:348.

20 Ibid. Alexander Marchant, in From Barter to Slavery (Baltimore, 1942), 82, misreads these royal orders to Sousa as a ban on slavery.

21 "Regimento a Tomé da Sousa," 3:347. The penalty for slaving without a license and causing these "annoyances" was flogging for a peon and a fine of twenty cruzados for a person of wealth. The fine was divided between the captives and the person who denounced the illegal slaving expedition.

22 Márcio Meira, Livro das canoas: Documentos para a história indígena da Amazônia (São Paulo, 1994).

23 Some of the iron tools—hatchets, wedges—made it easier to cut and trim the brazilwood logs. Others, such as iron barbs, knives, scissors, and mirrors were used for recreation and food. Léry, History of a Voyage, 99, 101–2.

24 The Hieronymite order, named for Saint Jerome, was formed in Spain and Italy in the fourteenth century through the amalgamation of several groups of hermits. The order's only significant role in the New World was on the island of Hispaniola (now the Dominican Republic and Haiti). The Escorial in Madrid and Belém near Lisbon are both Hieronymite monasteries. On the Hieronymites' plan, see Interrogatory in Colección de documentos inéditos relativos al descubrimiento . . . en América y Oceanía, (hereafter CDI), 42 vols. (Madrid, 1864–84), 11:258–76, 23:330–31, 34:201–29. See also Colección de documentos inéditos relativos al descubrimiento, conquista y organización de las antiguas posesiones españolas de ultramar, 25 vols. (Madrid, 1885–1932), 9.53–74; conclusions in "Carta de los padres jeronimos al Cardenal Cisneros" (January 20, 1517), in Manuel Serrano y Sanz, Orígenes de la dominación española en América (Madrid, 1918), 550–51. The best history of this episode is found in Manuel Giménez Fernández, Bartolomé de Las Casas, 2 vols. (Seville, 1953).

25 Neil L. Whitehead, "The Ancient Amerindian Polities of the Amazon, the Orinoco, and the Atlantic Coast: A Preliminary Analysis of Their Passage from Antiquity to Extinction," in *Amazonian Indians from Prehistory to the Present: Anthropological Perspectives*, ed. Anna Roosevelt (Tucson, 1994), 33–53; Jean-Baptiste Du Tertre, *Histoire general des Antilles habitées par les français*, 4 vols. (1667; reprint, Fort de France, 1978), 2:488. For commentaries by historians, see John Hemming, *Red Gold: The Conquest of the Brazilian Indians* (Cambridge, Mass., 1978), 51, 54, 55, 402; Philip B. Boucher, *Cannibal Encounters: Europeans and Island Caribs, 1492–1763* (Baltimore, 1992), 1–11, 35–36.

26 For explicit examples of such reasoning in Spanish legislation, see *CDI*, 12:213–15.

27 Dauril Alden, *The Making of an Enterprise: The Society of Jesus in Portugal, Its Empire, and Beyond, 1540–1750* (Stanford, Calif., 1996), 490–92.

28 Alfred Crosby, "Virgin Soil Epidemics as a Factor in the Aboriginal Depopulation in America," *William and Mary Quarterly* 33 (1976): 289–99, esp. 295; Marshall T. Newman, "Aboriginal New World Epidemiology and Medical Care, and the Impact of the Old World Disease Imports," *American Journal of Physical Anthropology* 45 (1976): 667–72.

29 Soares, *Tratado descritivo*, bk. 1, chap. 25. Anchieta reports that approximately forty thousand Indians were in Bahia before the start of the epidemic, and in 1585 only ten thousand remained. José de Anchieta, *Cartas*, 2d ed. (São Paulo, 1984), 377. See also Alain Milhou, "Misión, represión, paternalismo e interiorización: Para un balance de un siglo de evangelización en Iberoamérica (1520–1620)," in *Los conquistados: 1492 y la población indígena de las Américas*, ed. Heraclio Bonilla (Bogotá, 1992), 269–70; Darcy Ribeiro chamou-o, "Convívio e contaminação," in *Os índios e a civilização*, 4th ed. (Petrópolis, Brazil, 1970) . Even the epidemics devastating densely populated Mexico in the twenty-year period from 1560 to 1579 only killed 33 percent of the population.

30 "We are certain that our Spaniards, by their cruelties, and unspeakable acts have depopulated and desolated and they are today deserted, more than ten kingdoms bigger than all of Spain. . . . We provide as a very certain and true tale, that [the Indians] have died in those said forty years because of the said tyrannies, and hellish acts of the Christians, unjustly and tyrannically killing more than twelve million souls, men women, and children." Bartolomé de Las Casas, *Brevísima relación de la destrucción de las indias* (1552), in *Tratados de Fray Bartolomé de Las Casas*, transcription by Juan Pérez de Tudela Bueso, trans. Augustín Millares Carlo and Rafael Moreno (Mexico City, 1974), 8–10.

31 Las Casas proposed exactly the kind of concentration that would be shown to devastate natives in Brazil. He proposed to Regent Cisneros that the Indians be brought together to live in separate towns under their own chiefs, but supervised by Spaniards. *CDI*, 7:14–65, esp. 37–39. See also Giménez Fernández, *Bartolomé de Las Casas*, 126–27; for debate over alternatives, 129–43. Marcel Bataillon, in *Estudios sobre Bartolomé de Las Casas* (Barcelona, 1976), 77 n. 80, suggests that Las Casas's proposal was a commentary on Cisneros's instructions. On the Hieronymites' failure to investigate this possibility, see "Carta de los padres jeronimos al Cardenal Cisneros," 551.

32 Sérgio Buarque de Holanda, *Historia geral da civilização brasileira*, vol. 1, *A época colonial* (São Paulo, 1960), bk. 2, chap. 2, and bk. 3, chap. 4; Milhou, "Misión, represión," 269–70.

33 This violence was not a feature only of the eighteenth century. From 1628 to 1631 the *bandeirantes* destroyed the Jesuit missions of Guaira, Tapes, and Itatins.

34 Alcântara Machado, *Vida e morte do bandeirante* (São Paulo, 1978), 158–59. Paulistas succeeded in expelling the Jesuits.

35 I have recently examined a series of maps containing the Tordesillas division. The line clearly resides at what is now 60 degrees west longitude, and in fact grants Portugal most of the interior of Brazil, as well as Uruguay and part of what is now Argentina. The illustration is on-line at http://www.ruf.rice.edu/~feegi.

36 The establishment of Jesuit (and later Franciscan) mission villages in the frontiers of what are now the United States (Texas, Arizona, California) imitated this initiative, as did the French mission villages in Canada. Charles W. Polzer, *Rules and Precepts of the Jesuit Missions of Northwestern New Spain* (Tucson, 1976).

37 For a similarly intentioned understanding of Jesuit activities, see Alden, *The Making of an Enterprise*, 499–501.

38 Much of the writing on Jesuit missions does not criticize the cultural consequences of the forced relocation, introduction of Christian kinship, and other profoundly disruptive changes. Although the Jesuits' attitudes were admirable compared with those of the slave raiders, the Jesuits were not as devoted to the preservation of indigenous peoples as often appears in some secondary historical literature on the subject. Nor were they as horrifying as Brazilian writings of the 1930s suggest. For more balanced contemporary views, see ibid., 500–501; Manuela Carneiro da Cunha, *História dos índios no Brasil* (São Paulo, 1992).

39 Mercedarians were also briefly present in this region, and Carmelites moved into the Río Negro and Río Solimões after 1695. Mathias C. Kiemen, *The Indian Policy of Portual in the Amazon Region, 1614–1693* (Washington, D.C., 1954), 178. See also David G. Sweet, "A Rich Realm of Nature Destroyed: The Middle Amazon Valley, 1640–1750," 2 vols. (Ph.D. diss., University of Wisconsin–Madison, 1974).

40 The history of this jealousy is well-known in Brazil. See, for example, John Hemming, *Amazon Frontier: The Defeat of the Brazilian Indians* (Cambridge, Mass., 1987), 50–55, 447–51, 455, 458–59, 474–75; Alden, *The Making of an Enterprise.*

41 Sebastião José de Carvalho e Melo (1699–1782) expelled the Jesuits from Brazil in 1760. Kenneth Maxwell, *Pombal, Paradox of the Enlightenment* (Cambridge, 1995), 12–16, 20; Hemming, *Amazon Frontier*, 40–61. Opposition to the Jesuits in Brazil also stemmed from the resistance of the Guaraní to the rearrangements of the Treaty of Madrid. On the 1767 expulsion of Jesuits from Spanish America, see Magnus Morner, *The Expulsion of the Jesuits from Latin America* (New York, 1965).

42 The best history of this period is Almeida, *O diretório dos índos.* Hemming's interpretation of the events differs from Almeida's; see *Amazon Frontier*, 9–26, 40–80. See also Rodrigo Otávio, *Os selvagens americanos perante o direito* (São Paulo, 1946).

43 Hemming dwells upon the inability of the government to recruit directors as one of the causes (*Amazon Frontier*, 179, 254–67), but even the best-intentioned directors could not have stopped disease from devastating these communities in very short order.

44 Serafim Leite, ed., *Cartas dos primeiros Jesuítas do Brasil*, 3 vols. (São Paulo, 1956–58), 2:320–22.

45 Diogo de Campos Moreno, *Livro que dá razão do estado do Brasil* (Rio de Janeiro, 1968), 1.

46 Gândavo, *Tratado da província do Brasil*, passim.

47 Soares, *Tratado descritivo*, bk. 1.

48 They also correctly claimed a portion of eastern Canada. The current Canadian maritime province of Labrador is named for the first Portuguese colonist of the region. But the expedition to Canada was as disastrous as that of several Brazilian proprietorships. Having no trade goods as valuable as Brazilian dyewood, the Portuguese turned their backs on Canada by the 1530s.

49 Roger Williams, *A Key into the Language of America, 1643* (Menston, England, 1971).

50 See Joel Sherzer, "Areal Linguistics," in *Native Languages of the Americas*, 2 vols., ed. Thomas Sebeok (New York, 1976), 1:121–73. See also Harry Hoijer, "History of American Indian Linguistics," in the same volume.

51 See, in Norman A. McQuown, ed., *Linguistics*, vol. 5 of *Handbook of Native American Indians* (Austin, Tex., 1967), four chapters: Stanley Newman, "Classical Nahuatl," 181; Norman A. McQuown, "Classical Yucatec (Maya)," 203; Munro S. Edmonson, "Classical Quiche," 251; Velma B. Pickett, "Isthmus Zapotec," 292–93. Isthmus Zapotec has all three sounds. For general introduction to this subject, see Frank Parker and Kathryn Riley, *Linguistics for Non-Linguists: A Primer with Exercises*, 3d ed. (Boston, 1999); Steven Pinker, *The Language Instinct* (New York, 1994).

52 A list of contact languages in the Americas can be found in Lyle Campbell, *Historical Dictionary of Linguistics* (Oxford, 1997), 18–25. See also Edward G. Gray, *New World Babel: Languages and Nations in Early America* (Princeton, N.J., 1999).

53 See the stunningly different treatment of these issues in Soares, *Tratado descritivo*, chaps. 13, 68 (agriculture), 32 (hunter-gatherers), 39 (fishermen), 45 (legume crops and hunting), 63 (hunting and fishing); Fernão Cardim (d. 1625), *Tratado da terra e gente do Brasil* (São Paulo, 1980), 103; Gândavo, *Tratado da província do Brasil*, 97 (hunting), 118–19, 151–57 (wheat introduced but too costly compared to other similar cereals), 161–77 (local food). Magalhães de Gândavo composed his treatise ca. 1572. Only Soares de Sousa briefly mentions the gendered division of labor (311, 339).

54 Alden notes that the Jesuits claimed that it remained the natives' land; *The Making of an Enterprise*, 476. However, formal title was vested with the Society of Jesus and hence the contemporary chain of title for mission villages must be traced through the Society. See James Holston, "The Misrule of Law: Land and Usurpation in Brazil," *Comparative Studies in Society and History* 33 (1991): 695–725.

55 Nicolás Leon, *Las castas del México colonial o Nueva España* (Mexico, 1924); Patricia Seed, "Social Dimensions of Race, Mexico City 1752," *Hispanic American Historical Review* 62 (1982): 569–606.

56 This strategy was originally suggested for the Spanish Caribbean, but it met with less success there. See the edict of King Ferdinand in 1514 in Diego de Encinas, *Cedulario indiano*, 4 vols. (1596; reprint, Madrid, 1946), 4:27. On the Portuguese in Brazil, see Laura de Mello e Souza, *O diabo e a terra de Santa Cruz* (São Paulo, 1980), 64–67; Ronaldo Vainfas, *A heresia dos índios: Catolicismo e rebeldia no Brasil colonial* (São Paulo, 1995), 141–59.

57 In her study of Portuguese inheritance rules in nineteenth-century Brazil, Linda Lewin shows how such sentiments operated, as well as how they changed. Linda Lewin, *"Surprise Heirs": Illegitimacy, Inheritance Rights, and Public Power in the Formation of Imperial Brazil (1750–1889)* (Stanford, Calif., forthcoming).

58 Edmund Curtis, ed., *Irish Historical Documents 1172–1922* (London, 1943), 52–53.

59 Patrick Henry was another early national advocate of English-Indian marriages. John Smith invented the story of Pocahontas's rescue after her death and after she gained fame in London society. See Peter Hulme, *Colonial Encounters: Europe and the Native Caribbean, 1492–1797* (London, 1986); Pauline Strong, *Captive Selves, Captivating Others: The Politics and Poetics of Colonial American Captivity Narratives* (Boulder, Colo., 1999).

60 Leite, *Cartas dos primeiros Jesuítas,* 1:324–26, 525; 2:177–78.

61 "John Winthrop of Massachusetts Bay to William Bradford, Governor of Plymouth, May 28, 1637," in William Bradford, *Bradford's History of Plymouth Plantation 1606–1646,* ed. William T. Davis (New York, 1908), 342.

CHAPTER 9: FAST FORWARD

1 The decree of San Martín on August 27, 1821, abolished tribute, and his decree of March 30, 1824, ended the category of "Indian" for the modern states of Ecuador, Peru, and Bolivia. Bolívar decreed the end of tribute and made Indians equal in rights and obligations to other inhabitants of the state. Peru's 1828 constitution reiterated the equality. However, although tribute was abolished, a payment called the "contribution of the Indians," intended to pay the salaries of the authorities, did not disappear until June 5, 1854. Felipe de la Barra, *El indio peruano en las etapas de la conquista y frente a la republica* (Lima, 1948).

2 Lands were usually held as a concession from the state—much as land granted to conquered Indians was conceded by the crown. The grants did not entitle natives to contract with foreign powers, although they could contract with other citizens. *Resguardos* were reestablished in Colombia in the 1890s, as in several other South American states. Part of the popular support for Emiliano Zapata during Mexico's 1910 revolution stemmed partly from his attempt to reclaim traditionally native lands, and the new constitution after the revolution restored native communities' land rights.

3 In Mexico at the end of the nineteenth century, President Porfirio Diaz temporarily reversed national ownership of subterranean oil and gas. Mexico, *Proyecto del Código de mineria de la República Mexicana* (Mexico City, 1884), art. 10. John D. Wirth argues that Mexico's adoption of the nineteenth-century mining code was "inspired by the United States mining code"; Lorenzo Meyer claims it follows French example. John D. Wirth, ed., *Latin American Oil Companies and the Politics of Energy* (Lincoln, Neb., 1985), xxiv; Lorenzo Meyer, *Mexico and the United States: The Oil Controversy, 1917–1942,* trans. Muriel Vasconcellos (Austin, Tex., 1977), 24.

4 In the 1891 constitution of Brazil, which became independent from Portugal only in 1888–89, petroleum development was turned over to private landowners. The constitutional change responded to landholders who had resented the federal government's control over rights for oil and gas exploration. Mine ownership and the regulation of mining remained in public hands, but was turned over to state governments. Peter S. Smith, *Oil and Politics in Modern Brazil* (Toronto, 1976), 21, 58, 100–101, 169–70. In Portuguese, Getulio Vargas's phrase was "O petróleo e nosso."

5 Geodetic triangulation, invented by Englishmen in India, applied to land mathematical calculations developed by the Portuguese in the fifteenth century. A full account of this history appeared in the 1905 *Encyclopaedia Britannica* but had disappeared by the mid-twentieth-century editions of the same encyclopedia. See

Patricia Seed, "Taking Possession and Reading Texts: Establishing the Authority of Overseas Empires," *William and Mary Quarterly* 49 (1992):183–209; Matthew Edney, *Mapping an Empire: The Geographical Construction of British India, 1765–1843* (Chicago, 1997).

6 Codification was done under the Torrens system, but the result was the creation of orthodoxy about land that also relied upon codified lineage, clan, and tribe. Margaret Jolly, "Custom and the Way of the Land: Past and Present in Vanuatu and Fiji," in *Remembrance of Pacific Pasts: An Invitation to Remake History*, ed. Robert Barofsky (Honolulu, 2000), 340–57.

7 Frederick Pollock and Robert S. Wright, *An Essay on Possession in the Common Law* (Oxford, 1888), 31; Ranajit Guha, *A Rule of Property for Bengal* (Durham, N.C., 1995).

8 Henry B. Grigg, *A Manual of the Nilagri District in the Madras Presidency* (Madras, India, 1880), 342. When the British established the protectorate of Uganda, they affirmed: "Where the country is inhabited by settled natives they are to retain—as individuals or tribes—in their exclusive possession the land they actually occupy or cultivate. All forests and all waste land have become the property of His Majesty." *British Parliamentary Papers* (1901), 48:671, Africa no. 7. On Australia, see Henry Reynolds, *The Law of the Land* (Ringwood, Victoria, 1987), 32.

9 Richard F. Burton, *Zanzibar: City, Island, and Coast*, 2 vols. (London, 1872), 2:71–72.

10 Reynolds, *The Law of the Land*, 19. On June 18, 1829, the lieutenant governor of Western Australia proclaimed the right of English officials "to grant unoccupied lands." This quote comes from the preamble to the British Parliament's Swan River Act of 1829; see *Swan River Papers*, vol. 4, no.18. Relevant cases include *The State of Western Australia v. The Commonwealth, The Wororra Peoples and Anor v. The State of Western Australia*, and *Teddy Biljabu and Ors v. The State of Western Australia*. The Swan River Act allowed settlement "upon certain wild and unoccupied Lands on the Western Coast of New Holland." "Wild" signified uncultivated.

11 See note 7, above. See also Grigg, *A Manual of the Nilagri District* 342; Reynolds, *The Law of the Land*, 32. Trial court judges denied the claims of the Gitksan and Wet'suwet'en on these grounds, but the decisions were eventually overturned on appeal. *Delgamuukw v. British Columbia*, 3 (Canadian) *Supreme Court Reports* 1010 (1997).

12 Quoted in Paul Tennant, *Aboriginal Peoples and Politics: The Indian Land Question in British Columbia, 1849–1989* (Vancouver, 1990), 18.

13 See the report of the trial judge's decision (reversed) in *Delgamuukw v. British Columbia*.

14 This rationale was at the heart of the U.S. privatization of Indian lands under the Dawes Act of 1887, 23, 177–84.

15 William Blackstone, *Commentaries on the Laws of England*, 4 vols. (Oxford, 1765–69). The process of coining fine words out of Latin is an affectation that has been called a *cacozelia*. See "Silva Rhetoricae," on-line at http://humanities.byu.edu/rhetoric/silva.htm.

16 The Latin original that Blackstone cited as his authority is a text of Justinian dealing with hunted animals. The Latin original is *res nullius* ("a thing of no one"). But although land (*terra*) is a thing (*res*), all things (all *res*) are not lands (*terra*). And the "thing" to which Justinian's code refers is a deceased animal that has been hunted and thus can be acquired by anyone—a context that does not support Blackstone's interpretation. Furthermore, the first sentence of this section of Justinian's code (bk. 41) contradicts Blackstone's claim. It says that international titles (over foreign lands) must derive from the laws of nations in the first place, and the laws of cities

in the second. *The Digest of Justinian*, 4 vols., ed. Theodor Mommsen with Paul Krueger, trans. Alan Watson (Philadelphia, 1985), 4:487. Blackstone apparently invented etymologies freely—see the comments by John Kilty, *Land Holder's Assistant and Land Office Guide* (Baltimore, 1808), 24–25.

17 The concept was even espoused by Puritan John Cotton, who declared, "Vacuum Domicilium cedi occupanti." John Cotton, *Reply*, 27–28, 54–55, cited in Massachusetts Historical Society, *Proceedings* 12 (1873): 352–53.

18 David J. Wishart, *An Unspeakable Sadness: The Dispossession of the Nebraska Indians* (Lincoln, Neb., 1994); John W. Bennett and Seena B. Kohl, *Settling the Canadian-American West, 1890–1915: Pioneer Adaptation and Community Building* (Lincoln, Neb., 1995); Michael D. Green, *The Politics of Indian Removal: Creek Government and Society in Crisis* (Lincoln, Neb., 1982); Kenneth R. Philip, *Termination Revisited: American Indians on the Trail to Self-Determination, 1933–1953* (Lincoln, Neb., 1999).

19 Statute of Frauds, 1670, was the English legal decision requiring written documentation.

20 Eight of the numbered treaties were signed during the nineteenth century. *Indian Treaties and Surrenders: From 1680 to 1890*, vols. 1–2 (Ottawa, 1891).

21 John M. Mackenzie, "Chivalry, Social Darwinism, and Ritualized Killing: The Hunting Ethos in Central Africa up to 1914," in *Conservation in Africa: People, Policies and Practice*, ed. David Anderson and Richard Grove (Cambridge, 1990); John M. Mackenzie, *The Empire of Nature: Hunting, Conservation and British Imperialism* (Manchester, 1988), esp. 295–311; William K. Storey, "Big Cats and Imperialism: Lion and Tiger Hunting in Kenya and Northern India, 1898–1930," *Journal of World History* 2 (1991): 135–73; Brian Herne, *White Hunters: The Golden Age of African Safaris* (New York, 1999).

22 Francis Wayland, *Elements of Political Economy* (Boston, 1840), 111–12, 114.

23 Ibid., 41.

24 In Paul Francis Prucha, ed., *Documents of United States Indian Policy*, 2d ed. (Lincoln, Neb., 1990), 36–37.

25 *Johnson v. McIntosh*, 21 *U.S. Reports* 590–91 (1823). Also: "The lands occupied by each tribe were not used by them in such a manner as to prevent their being appropriated by a people of cultivators" (570).

26 Quoted in Roy Harvey Pearce, *The Savages of America: A Study of the Indian and the Idea of Civilization*, rev. ed. (Baltimore, 1965), 156–57.

27 Jeremy Belknap, *History of New Hampshire*, 3 vols. (Boston, 1813); Samuel Williams, *The Natural and Civil History of Vermont* (Walpole, N.H., 1794); Robert Proud, *The History of Pennsylvania*, 2 vols. (Philadelphia, 1797–98); Ezekiel Sanford, *History of the United States before the Revolution* (Philadelphia, 1819).

28 Pearce, *The Savages of America*, 161. For the reaction of nineteenth-century Native American writers to this point of view, see Cheryl Walker, *Indian Nation: Native American Literature and Nineteenth Century Nationalisms* (Durham, N.C., 1997).

29 Quoted in Angie Debo, *And Still the Waters Run: The Betrayal of the Five Civilized Tribes* (Princeton, N.J., 1940), 21–22.

30 Edward S. Curtis, *The Vanishing Race: Selections from Edward S. Curtis' The North American Indian*, ed. M. Gidley (Seattle, 1987); Zane Grey, *The Vanishing American* (New York, 1925); G. Harrison Orians, *The Cult of the Vanishing American: A Century View, 1834–1934* (Toledo, Ohio, 1934); Leslie A. Fiedler, *The Return of the Vanishing American* (New

York, 1968); Brian W. Dippie, *The Vanishing American: White Attitudes and U.S. Indian Policy* (Lawrence, Kans., 1982).

31 In Prucha, *Documents of United States Indian Policy*, 36–37.

32 See Lewis Cass, "Governor Cass on the Need for Removal," *North American Review* 30 (1830): 62–121. See also the work of Georgia's governor, William Lumpkin, *The Removal of the Cherokee Indians from Georgia* (New York, 1969), 83.

33 The fear of contamination by native people was also sometimes expressed. The Michigan territorial governor declared in 1830, "A Barbarous people, depending for subsistence upon the scanty and precarious supplies furnished by the chase, cannot live in contact with a civilized community." Cass, "Governor Cass," 64.

34 Martyn J. Bowden, "The Great American Desert and the American Frontier, 1800–1882," in *Anonymous Americans: Explorations in Nineteenth-Century Social History*, ed. Tamara K. Hareven (Englewood Cliffs, N.J., 1971), 51, Table 1. The language of agricultural fertility predominated from 1800 to 1824 (31 percent) and was followed by the language of disillusionment. From 1830 to 1845, 37.7 percent of all textbooks used the word *desert* or *waste*. After 1845, both *fertile* and *waste* were used with approximately the same frequency. See Tamara K. Hareven, "Anonymous Americans," in *Anonymous Americans: Explorations in Nineteenth-Century Social History*, ed. Tamara K. Hareven (Englewood Cliffs, N.J., 1971).

35 Clyde A. Milner II, "National Initiatives," in *The Oxford History of the American West*, ed. Clyde A. Milner II, Carol A. O'Connor, and Martha Sandweiss (New York, 1994), 160.

36 Although the government claimed it had a right to hand over land to *its* citizens through its own official acts, such as the Homestead Act, whether it had the authority to do so or had acquired authority from aboriginal peoples is open to question.

37 This argument is sometimes called the "stock versus range" debate. In an excellent study of the American West, Frieda Knobloch shows how settlers, whom she correctly labels "colonists," used trees, plows, grass, and weeds to take over the terrain. Frieda Knobloch, *The Culture of Wilderness: Agriculture as Colonization in the American West* (Chapel Hill, N.C., 1996).

38 Walter Prescott Webb, *The Great Plains* (1931; reprint, Lincoln, Neb., 1981), 280–318.

39 It has this same meaning in Dutch as well, even though the words, *grens* and *perk*, are not visually similar to English and the Romance languages. Patricia Nelson Limerick recognizes that the Spanish and English uses of the word differ, but she fails to grasp the uniqueness of the English uses. See Patricia Nelson Limerick, "The Adventure of the Frontier in the Twentieth Century," in *The Frontier in American Culture*, ed. James R. Grossman (Berkeley, Calif., 1994), 89–91. Another book whose contributors underestimate the impact of the linguistic differences is David J. Weber and Jane M. Rausch, eds., *Where Cultures Meet: Frontiers in Latin American History* (Wilmington, Del., 1997).

40 Oxford English Dictionary, 2d ed., s.v. "frontier": "That part of a country which forms the border of its settled or inhabited region." The OED notes that this usage is exclusive to the United States. Merriam Webster's Collegiate Dictionary, 10th ed., defines frontier as "a region that forms the margin of settled or developed territory." On the association with the right to settlement, see J. Norman Heard,

Handbook of the American Frontier: Four Centuries of Indian-White Relationships (Metuchen, N.J., 1987–98), 5 vols.

41 "That part of a newly settled country as the U.S. or Australia which is remote from closely peopled regions." *The Macquarie Dictionary*, 3d ed. (Sydney, 1996), s.v. "frontier." See also Reynolds, *The Law of the Land*. This meaning of *frontier* is notably absent in another Reynolds book, *The Other Side of the Frontier: Aboriginal Resistance to the European Invasion of Australia* (Queensland, 1981).

42 Jock Phillips, *A Man's Country? The Image of the Pakeha Male: A History* (Auckland, 1987).

43 The idea that the New World was a "vacant" land lived on in the histories of English North America and in the popular imagination. Henry Nash Smith, *Virgin Land: The American West as Symbol and Myth* (Cambridge, Mass., 1950); James H. Merrell, "Some Thoughts on Cultural Historians and American Indians," *William and Mary Quarterly* (3d ser.) 46 (1989): 94–119, esp. 98–99.

44 One indication that the subject has touched a cultural nerve is the vehemence and vitriol that occasionally characterize these debates. See Henry F. Dobyns, *Their Number Become Thinned: Native American Population Dynamics in Eastern North America* (Knoxville, Tenn., 1983); N. David Cook, *Born to Die: Disease and New World Conquest, 1492–1650* (Cambridge, 1998); David P. Henige, *Numbers from Nowhere: The American Indian Contact Population Debate* (Norman, Okla., 1998); Suzanne Austin Alchon, *Native Society and Disease in Colonial Ecuador* (Cambridge, 1991); Daniel Reff, *Disease, Depopulation, and Culture Change in Northwestern New Spain, 1518–1764* (Salt Lake City, 1991); Alfred W. Crosby, *The Columbian Exchange: Biological and Cultural Consequences of 1492* (Westport, Conn., 1972). U.S. audiences tend to prefer accepting disease mortality levels that minimize the precontact (i.e., preepidemic) population levels.

45 Frederick Jackson Turner, "The Significance of the Frontier in American History" (1893), in *History, Frontier, and Section: Three Essays* (Albuquerque, 1993); see also Frederick Jackson Turner, *Rereading Frederick Jackson Turner: "The Significance of the Frontier in American History" and Other Essays*, commentary by John Mack Faragher (New York, 1994).

46 A conventional interpretation of this event in the United States is found in David M. Potter, *People of Plenty: Economic Abundance and the American Character* (Chicago, 1954). Potter defines the problem using the language of "scarcity" and "abundance." However, given that *scarcity* referred to a culturally specific object—common land—it seems that it is the cultural perception of the resource rather than a generalized concept of "scarcity," which could mean people and land.

47 Renato Rosaldo, *Culture and Truth: The Remaking of Social Analysis* (Boston, 1993). To avoid the charge of nostalgia, the conservation movement also sought to introduce scientific principles for resource management and argued that the reason for the creation of forest reserves was to protect watershed. Samuel P. Hays, *Conservation and the Gospel of Efficiency: The Progressive Conservation Movement, 1890–1920* (Cambridge, 1959), 23.

48 Philip J. Deloria, *Playing Indian* (New Haven, Conn., 1998).

49 The U.S. government owns far more land in the western states than in the eastern states. Federal ownership ranges from slightly more than a quarter of New Mexico to nearly half of California, Arizona, and Wyoming. The U.S. government owns roughly two-thirds of Alaska, Utah, and Idaho as well as a whopping 85 percent of

Nevada. In the eastern states, federal landownership remains in the single digits, with the sole exception of Florida, where it reaches only 11 percent.

50 Wallace Stegner, *The American West as Living Space* (Ann Arbor, Mich., 1987), 38–39. An excellent recent history of the relationship between natives and parks in the United States is Robert H. Keller and Micahel F. Turek's *American Indians and National Parks* (Tucson, 1998).

51 National forests were established in an act of June 4, 1897; *U.S. Statutes* 30 (1897): 11; the national park system was created in an act of August 25, 1916. Desires for even more untrammeled space, which would be called "wilderness," were satisfied by the 1964 Wilderness Act, Public Law 88–577, *U.S. Code*, vol. 16, secs. 1131–36. The first national wildlife refuge was created in 1903.

52 Stephen Fox, *John Muir and His Legacy: The American Conservation Movement* (1981); Michael Cohen, *History of the Sierra Club, 1892–1970* (1988); Ethan Carr, *Wilderness by Design: Landscape Architecture and the National Park Service* (Lincoln, Neb., 1998).

53 The subsequent rewrite of Chief Seattle's speech by a Texas screenwriter eliminated the references to people and as a result became widely popular in the 1970s, 1980s, and 1990s. According to a recent study, the lament for the passing of a people was common in translated Indian speeches of the time. Albert Furtwangler, in *Answering Chief Seattle* (Seattle, 1997), points out that the speech delivered in the 1850s was a lament for the passing of a people, a theme that was common in translated versions of Indian oratory, so it might in fact have been what the listeners expected. See Crisca Bierwert, "Remembering Chief Seattle: Reversing Cultural Studies of a Vanishing Native American," *American Indian Quarterly* 22 (1998): 280–304. The version of Chief Seattle's speech quoted appeared in the *Seattle Sunday Star* on October 29, 1887, in a column by Dr. Henry A. Smith. For an interesting analysis of the depiction of Indians as ghosts, see Renee Louise Bergland, "Possession and Dispossession: Native American Ghosts and the Haunted National Imagination" (Ph.D. diss., Columbia University, 1997).

CHAPTER 10: CONTINUITIES

1 For discussion of other conservative dimensions of the American (i.e., U.S.) Revolution, see Woody Holton, *Forced Founders: Indians, Debtors, Slaves, and the Making of the American Revolution in Virginia* (Chapel Hill, N.C., 1999). My interpretation differs from the currently standard approaches exemplified by Richard Graham, *Independence in Latin America: A Comparative Approach*, 2d ed. (New York, 1994); and Lester Langley, *The Americas in the Age of Revolution, 1750–1850* (New Haven, Conn., 1996).

2 *American Jurisprudence*, 2d ed., 83 vols. (St. Paul, Minn., 1962), 41:292–93. See also Daniel Oran, *Oran's Dictionary of the Law*, 2d ed. (St. Paul, Minn., 1991). "Work and labor bestowed on the land" signal what even contemporary U.S. magistrates understand as the means to "improvement." *Words and Phrases* (St. Paul, Minn., 1959), 20:511.

3 Using the years 1993 and 1994, I studied all the cases available in the Lexis database. There were 267 mentions of "improvement" in legal reports and cases in the United States in those two years. All of the cases used the same criteria—using labor and capital to increase profit and affixing objects that permanently enhanced the value of the land. There were no exceptions.

4 *American Jurisprudence,* 41:292–93. See also notes 1 and 2, above.

5 For the similarity of seventeenth- and twentieth-century conceptions, compare Walter Blith, *The English Improver; or, A New Survey of Husbandry* (London, 1649), 2–3, with the contemporary *Words and Phrases,* 20:491, 493–95, 501, 511.

6 The phrase is still used today: "Nos peuples ont toujours été et continue d être spoli sur l'ensemble de nos territoires sous couvert des dispositions spéciales ou décrets régissant le domaine privé de l'Etat sur les terres 'soi-disante' vacantes." Chef coutumier de Kourou Wayanas de l'intérieur de la Guyane française, seventeenth session, U.N. Working Group on Indigenous Peoples, Geneva, July 26–30, 1999.

7 Carol M. Rose, "Possession as the Origin of Property," *University of Chicago Law Review* 52 (1985): 82, 86. See also William Blackstone, *Commentaries on the Laws of England,* 4 vols. (Oxford, 1765–69), vol. 2, sec. 9, 258, and sec. 7 on how cultivation establishes title.

8 "Aboriginal rights to land in the contemporary United States simply constitutes permission from the whites to occupy the land and . . . [is] not specifically recognized as ownership by Congress." *Tee-Hit-Ton Indians v. U.S.,* 348 U.S. 272–95 (1955).

9 Unnamed critics quoted in Timothy Egan, "New Prosperity Brings New Conflict to Indian Country," *New York Times,* March 8, 1998, A1.

10 Only 1 percent of the commercial timber in the United States is on Indian land, although it provides from 25 to 100 percent of all the income for fifty-seven reservations and 80 percent of the income for eleven of those reservations. See Monroe Edwin Price and Robert N. Clinton, eds., *Law and the American Indian: Readings, Notes, and Cases,* 2d ed. (Charlottesville, Va., 1983), 729–30.

11 Felix S. Cohen, *Handbook of Federal Indian Law* (Washington, D.C., 1942), 313–16. The inability of Indians to profit from timber was fixed in 1873 by Chief Justice Chase in *United States v. Cook.* Indians could cut timber only to improve agriculture, not to make a profit. Petra Shattuck and Jill Norgren, *Partial Justice: Federal Indian Law in a Liberal Constitutional System* (Providence, R.I., 1991), 54–55. The exception is the profit-making Navajo Forest Products Industry, whose environmental policies closely resemble those of Peabody Coal in the same region. Similar restrictions in Brazil are founded on legal incapacity, the inability to make contracts without state intervention. In the United States the constraint operates for very different reasons.

12 Royal Commission on Aboriginal Peoples, "Gathering Strength," in *People to People, Nation to Nation* (Ottawa, 1996). This chapter is available on-line at http://www. inac.gc.ca/ch/rcap/rpt/gs_e.html.

13 Jennifer Nielsen, "Images of the Aboriginal: Echoes from the Past," *Australian Feminist Law Journal* 11 (1998): 104. The debates Nielsen discusses are those surrounding the Native Title Act (1993) and the Wik debates.

14 In *Mason v. Tritton and Anor,* the High Court held: "There is no evidence that the defendant either intended to consume the abalone himself or to make them available for consumption by the immediate members of his family or to exchange them for other food. Accordingly I am not satisfied that the defendant has established as a matter of fact that he was exercising a customary right to fish for abalone on 9 October 1991." Text available on-line at http://www.arts.uwa.edu.au/anthropwww/mason.txt, judge 2, at p. 18. For the law, see Native Title Act (1993), sec. 211, 2a.

15 *Iwi* and *hapu* are separate Maori forms of organization based on descent from a common ancestor. *Iwi* consist of individuals tracing descent (in the maternal or paternal

line) from a single occupant of one of the original canoes settling Aotearoa. *Hapu,* also descent groups, are usually sited in a particular village and control the farming land. Of the surviving indigenous forests, 4.9 million hectares are crown owned and 1.3 million hectares are privately owned. Most of the crown forests are on fully protected conservation land (except for 150,000 hectares set aside for timber production on the West Coast). Most of the private indigenous forests are unprotected from conversion to other land uses, but timber production from them is subject to the sustainable management provisions of the Forests Act of 1949 (except 60,000 hectares set aside for economic purposes under the South Island Landless Maoris Act of 1906, the management regime for which is currently under negotiation). Ministry for the Environment, *The State of New Zealand's Environment* (Auckland, 1997).

16 *Sparrow v. Queen,* 1 (Canadian) *Supreme Court Reports* 1075 (1990). To be fair to Canadian authorities, they have more readily accepted comanagement of migratory wildlife and fish with native communities than have authorities in Australia and the United States, where such claims to comanage have been fiercely contested and native participation as equals nearly always rejected. Communities in Quebec and the Arctic have comanaged migratory wildlife and fisheries since the mid-1980s, prior to the decision in *Sparrow v. Queen.* Comanagement was fixed in both the Inuvialuit Final Agreement and the revised 1993 Nunavut Land Claims Agreement. Evelyn Pinkerton, ed., *Co-operative Management of Local Fisheries* (Vancouver, 1989), 209–27. See also Nunavut Planning Commission material on-line at http://npc.nunavut.ca. In 1992 the Department of Fisheries and Oceans, which manages fisheries in the Atlantic Provinces, British Columbia, Quebec, and the Territories, began a seven-year program to integrate aboriginal communities into fisheries management. For the preference given native hunting, see the decision in *Badger v. Queen,* 1 (Canadian) *Supreme Court Reports* 771 (April 1996); Tracy Campbell, "Co-management of Aboriginal Resources," *Information North* 22, no. 1 (1996); Fikret Berkes and Peter George, "Co-Management," *Alternatives* 18 (1992): 12–18. Lockouts by holders of pastoral leases were common in Australia in 1998 to prevent aboriginal peoples from gaining access. In the United States, the Mille Lacs Band sought the right to manage hunting and fishing on its own ceded territory, but negotiated agreements have been rejected by the Minnesota legislature. See *Mille Lacs Band v. Minnesota,* 97 Sup. Ct. 1337 (1999); *U.S. v. David Sohappy, Sr., et al., Sohappy v. Smith,* and *U.S. v. Oregon,* 302 F. Supp. 899 (1969); Institute for Natural Progress, "In Usual and Accustomed Places: Contemporary American Indian Fishing Rights Struggles," in *The State of Native America,* ed. M. Annette Jaimes (Boston, 1992), 226; Great Lakes Indian Fish and Wildlife Commission, *A Guide to Understanding Chippewa Treaty Rights* (Odanah, Wis., 1995). A good means of contrasting Canadian and U.S. "comanagement" is to read both the "Memorandum of Understanding between Federally Recognized Tribes of Washington State and the State of Washington, July 12, 1989," and the Inuvialuit Final Agreement (1984).

17 For examples of such uses of language in a recent court case, see E. Richard Hart, ed., *Zuni and the Courts: A Struggle for Sovereign Land Rights* (Lawrence, Kans., 1995), 138, 142.

18 Russel Barsh, "Indian Resources and the National Economy: Business Cycles and Policy Cycles," in *Native Americans and Public Policy,* ed. Fremont J. Lyden and Lyman H. Legters (Pittsburgh, 1992), 304–5. For further examples, see Daniel H. Usner Jr.,

American Indians in the Lower Mississippi Valley: Social and Economic Histories (Lincoln, Neb., 1998); Daniel H. Usner Jr., *Indians, Settlers, and Slaves in a Frontier Exchange Economy: The Lower Mississippi Valley before 1783* (Chapel Hill, N.C., 1992); Patricia Galloway, *Choctaw Genesis, 1500–1700* (Lincoln, Neb., 1995); Claudio Saunt, *A New Order of Things: Property, Power, and the Transformation of the Creek Indians, 1733–1816* (New York, 1999).

19 In Francis Paul Prucha, ed., *Documents of United States Indian Policy*, 2d ed. (Lincoln, Neb., 1990), 36–37.

20 Karen Ferguson, "Indian Fishing Rights: Aftermath of the Fox Decision and the Year 2000," *American Indian Law Review* 23 (1998): 97ff.; U.S. Commission on Civil Rights, *Indian Tribes: A Continuing Quest for Survival* (Washington, D.C., 1981). For a report on the violence against the Ashinabé of northern Wisconsin from 1987 to 1990, see Institute for Natural Progress, "In Usual and Accustomed Places," 233–35. Similar opposition had appeared in Washington (state) in the 1970s after the *Boldt* decision. The "steelhead salmon" is, in fact, a trout. Off the coast of New Brunswick (Canada) in 1999, nonnatives destroyed native lobster traps in Miramichi Bay and damaged fishing plants back on shore. Details appeared in the *Globe and Mail*, October 4, 1999.

21 The innovation lies in the final settlement of native fishing claims in 1993. According to my calculations, Maori receive roughly 27 percent of all the profits made from commercial fishing off New Zealand's shores as their share of treaty claims (including their share of profits from the Sealord Corporation). In July 1995, Hawera (N.Z.) court judge P. J. Toomey rejected a claim by a Maori fisherman that customary rights to fish took precedence over others' right to do so, and the appeal has been upheld.

22 See note 16, above. New Zealand and Canada, in the 1970s and 1980s, respectively, declared such treaties to be enforceable.

23 The U.S. Constitution gives to the federal courts jurisdiction over "all Cases . . . arising under this Constitution, the Laws of the United States, and Treaties made, or which shall be made, under their Authority." U.S. Constitution, art. 3, sec. 2, cited by the U.S. Supreme Court, *South Dakota v. Bourland*, 508 U.S. 679 (1993). See also Blue Clark, *Lone Wolf v. Hitchcock: Treaty Rights and Indian Law at the End of the Nineteenth Century* (Lincoln, Neb., 1995).

24 "Non-Indian fisherman . . . sense that they had been wronged by it [the *Boldt* decision] and the protesters claimed that they had lost income as a result." Ferguson, "Indian Fishing Rights," 73.

25 U.S. Commission on Civil Rights, *Indian Tribes*, 73–74, 82.

26 Ferguson, "Indian Fishing Rights," n. 19.

27 "Many turn-of-the-century artists—Russell, Remington, Sharp—and even many of today's cowboy artists have ignored the deprivation of Indian communities on the nation's reservations in favor of a nostalgic return to former Plains lifeways." Patricia Trenton and Patrick T. Houlihan, *Native Americans: Five Centuries of Changing Images* (New York, 1989), 137. See also Jacquelyn Kilpatrick, *Celluloid Indians: Native Americans and Film* (Lincoln, Neb., 1999); Robert E. Berkhofer, *The White Man's Indian: Images of the American Indian, from Columbus to the Present* (New York, 1979), 138, 165–67. S. Rodriquez observes that the face-painted, bonneted, and buckskin-clad "chief" was popularized in paintings commissioned by the Atchison, Topeka &

Santa Fe Railway in the 1900s. S. Rodriquez, "Art, Tourism, and Race Relations in Taos: Toward a Sociology of the Art Colony," *Journal of Anthropological Research* 45 (1989): 77.

28 Foxhunting began in the nineteenth century, replacing deer hunting as the sport of aristocrats. David C. Itzkowitz, *Peculiar Privilege: A Social History of English Foxhunting, 1753–1885* (Hassocks, Eng., 1977).

29 In June 1996, the U.S. Supreme Court let stand a lower court ruling prohibiting Indians from hunting on unoccupied land (i.e., Bighorn National Forest in northern Wyoming) without a license. The 10th U.S. Circuit Court cited an 1896 Supreme Court decision that treaties with natives guaranteeing such rights were "temporary and precarious." *Crow Tribe of Indians v. Repsis*, 73 F.3d 982, 986 (1995); *Ward v. Race Horse*, 163 U.S. 505 (1896). The rights to fish are sometimes less contested in areas such as Alaska, where the fishers are women.

30 Stuart A. Marks, *Southern Hunting in Black and White: Nature, History, and Ritual in a Carolina Community* (Princeton, N.J., 1991), 79–80. The male bonding part of the ritual was admired by early-twentieth-century romanticists such as the Tamany societies. On these groups, see Philip J. Deloria, *Playing Indian* (New Haven, Conn., 1998), 203 n. 25. For the antiromantic perspective, see Jan E. Dizzard, *Going Wild: Hunting, Animal Rights, and the Contested Meaning of Nature* (Amherst, Mass., 1994), 112–30.

31 A slightly different perspective on the origin of the gender recoding suggests that it resulted from attempts to copy the increasing masculinization in nineteenth-century English society. See John M. Mackenzie, *The Empire of Nature: Hunting, Conservation and British Imperialism* (Manchester, 1988), 42–53.

32 E. Allan Hanson, "The Making of the Maori Cultural Invention and Its Logic," *American Anthropologist* 91 (1989): 890–902.

33 Even the article title screams, "Should We Give the U.S. Back to the Indians?" *Time*, April 11, 1977, 5.

34 They are called *resguardas, ejidos,* or simply *comunidades.* The Constitution of Argentina, art. 75, inciso 17, includes among the powers of Congress, "reconocer la personería jurídica de sus comunidades, y la posesión y propiedad comunitarias de las tierras que tradicionalmente ocupan."

35 For example, *Clarín* (Buenos Aires).

36 "Revelan aborígenes cubanos practicaron el canibalismo," *La Prensa* (Honduras), June 7, 1999. Cannibalism has made front-page news in San José, Costa Rica, as well, in *La Nación*, Apr.16, 1998. See also "Caníbales ancestrales," *La Nación*, October 3, 1999. North Korean cannibalism has made front-page news in similar fashion in Spanish-American newspapers. See "Diario habla de canibalismo en Norcorea," *La Nación*, April 16, 1998. Similar responses appeared in *Inchalá* (Noticias del Uruguay), no. 55 (1999).

37 The entire section is quite explicit: "un enfrentamiento plagado de grosería, rencor y falta de ingenio que debiera ser una vergüenza . . . jamás el ojo humano contempló tanto horror." "Alto al canibalismo," *La Prensa* (Honduras), June 9, 1999.

38 The film is *Holocausto caníbal* (1978), directed by Ruggero Deodato.

39 Esther Prieto, "Derecho consuetudinario indígena en la legislación paraguaya (siglo XX)," in *Entre la ley y la costumbre: El derecho consuetudinario indígena en América Latina*, ed. Rudolfo Stavenhagen and Diego Iturralde (San José, Costa Rica, 1990), 327. See

also María Magdalena Gómez Rivera, "Las cuentas pendientes de la diversidad jurídica: El caso de las expulsiones de indígenas por supuestos motivos religiosos en Chiapas, México," in *Pueblos indígenas ante el derecho,* ed. Victoria Chenaut and María Teresa Sierra (Mexico City, 1995), 193–220.

40 Francisco Ballon Aguirre, "Sistema jurídico peruana y positivismo," in *Entre la ley y la costumbre: El derecho consuetudinario indígena en América Latina,* ed. Rudolfo Stavenhagen and Diego Iturralde (San José, Costa Rica, 1990), 128–39. A recent overview of the relationship between Peruvian and native law is Joanna Drzewieniecki, "Indigenous People, Law, and Politics in Peru" (paper presented at the annual meeting of the Latin American Studies Society, 1995). The Seneca tribe's killing of a Seneca woman for witchcraft in early-nineteenth-century New York neither created public uproar nor resulted in punishment for the native executioner. Sidney L. Harring, *Crow Dog's Case: American Indian Sovereignty, Tribal Law, and United States Law in the Nineteenth Century* (Cambridge, 1994), 37–38. In subsequent U.S. cases, federal intervention has resulted from the killing of witches, not from aversion to the idea of witchcraft. Harring, *Crow Dog's Case,* 240–47.

41 "Maya Renaissance in Guatemala Turns Political," *New York Times,* August 12, 1996.

42 The accords allowed indigenous communities "to obtain the recognition of their internal normative systems for regulation and sanctions, *insofar as they are not contrary to constitutional guarantees and human rights*" (emphasis added). San Andres Accords, January 18, 1996, sec. 6b.

43 Alcida Rita Ramos, "Indian Rights and Indian Policy in Brazil Today" (Occasional Paper 28, 1979, University of Glasgow Institute of Latin American Studies), 5.

44 Ibid., 6.

45 Quoted in Alvin Josephy, *Now That the Buffalo's Gone* (New York, 1982), 85. See also Prucha, *Documents of United States Indian Policy,* 160–61.

46 The prohibitions were repealed in the Canadian Indian Act of 1951, which removed government control of the display of culture.

47 Joseph Epes Brown, in *Animals of the Soul: Sacred Animals of the Ogala Sioux* (Rockport, Mass., 1992), discusses the idea that animals represent spirits. Accounts of the "holy people" in the material world appear in Trudy Griffin-Peirce's *Earth Is My Mother, Sky Is My Father: Space, Time, and Astronomy in Navajo Sandpainting* (Albuquerque, N.M., 1992).

48 Alice Kehoe, "Themes in Native American Spirituality," in "To Hear the Eagles Cry: Contemporary Themes in Native American Spirituality" (special issue), ed. Lee Irwin, *American Indian Quarterly* 20 (1996): 309–18. This article is an excellent example of how "academic discourse creates its own paradigms" that often appropriate and distort (through inappropriate labeling) the actual practices and beliefs of diverse native peoples.

49 U.S. Executive Order 96–05–24, "On Protection of Indian Sacred Sites" (May 24, 1996); American Indian Religious Freedom Act (1978). Another bill that has been proposed is the Native American Free Exercise of Religion Act (Senate 1021).

50 The Lakota and Tsistsistas unsuccessfully battled the South Dakota state government over their contention that Bear Butte, a Lakota holy ground, should not be open to tourists. *Fools Crow v. Gullet,* 706 F.2d 856 (1983). An excellent collection of articles on the subject of native religious freedom is John Wunder, ed., *Native American Cultural and Religious Freedoms* (New York, 1996).

51 Bonnie Sue Lewis, "The Creation of Christian Indians: The Rise of Native Clergy and Their Congregations in the Presbyterian Church" (Ph.D. diss., University of Washington, 1997). Other histories of missions include Henry Warner Bowden, *American Indians and Christian Missions: Studies in Cultural Conflict* (Chicago, 1981); John Gilmary Shea, *History of the Catholic Missions among the Indian Tribes of the United States, 1529–1854* (New York, 1854).

52 This aloofness was jarred only slightly during the 1880s, when the U.S. public found native punishments for Indian-on-Indian crimes insufficiently harsh. Congress insisted that murder, manslaughter, rape, assault with intent to kill, arson, burglary, and larceny between Indians had to be punished more severely in the 1885 Major Crimes Act. The effect of the law in the succeeding years, however, was minimal. See Harring, *Crow Dog's Case*, 100–141, 170–71.

53 An excellent study of Indian gaming is Libra Rose Hilde, "Gambling with Sovereignty" (Senior honors thesis, University of California, Berkeley, 1991). See also the Indian Gaming Regulatory Act of 1988, *U.S. Code*, vol. 25, secs. 2701–21.

54 For a general commentary on these attitudes, see Maria Eugenia Modena, "Autonomía, territorialidad y comunidad indígena: La nueva legislación agraria en México," in *Pueblos indígenas ante el derecho*, ed. Victoria Chenaut and María Teresa Sierra (Mexico City, 1995), 231–59.

CONCLUSION

1 For these listeners, raising the issue in discussion afterward and confronting the speaker with evidence of such professional incompetence would have been unnecessarily humiliating. Hence their pitying looks and shrugs.

2 The category of international law emerged in an effort to claim global privileges for European political and economic actions overseas. But no agreement existed among European nations as to what global privileges they had. Writers in Spanish and Portuguese invariably refer to the Iberian tradition of Francisco Vitoria, writers in English customarily refer to Hugo Grotius, and writers in other languages agree with neither point of view. Alberico Gentili, the Italian Protestant refugee in Elizabethan England, is the third most commonly designated founder of international law, with supporters in both England and Italy. The two major exceptions to this rule have been Ernest Nys, *Etudes de droit international et de droit politique*, 2 vols. (Brussels, 1896–1901); and James Brown Scott, *The Spanish Origin of International Law* (Oxford, 1934). More typical are Spanish perspectives such as those of Camilo Barcia Trelles, *Francisco de Vitoria, fundador del derecho internacional moderno* (Valladolid, 1928); and Ramón Hernández, *Francisco de Vitoria: Vida y pensamiento internacionalista* (Madrid, 1995). Such perspectives contrast sharply with those of Henry Wheaton, whose *History of the Law of Nations in Europe and America: From the Earliest Times to the Treaty of Washington, 1842* (New York, 1845) was frequently cited by the nineteenth-century U.S. Supreme Court. Popular modern English-language histories such as Arthur Nussbaum's *A Concise History of the Law of Nations*, rev. ed. (New York, 1962), and the textbooks of international law in U.S. law schools usually begin with Grotius. Starting historical narration with Grotius requires displacing the beginning of international law from the sixteenth to the seventeenth century. See Karl Mommsen, *Auf dem Wege zur Staatssouveranitat. Staatliche Grundbegriffe in Basler juristischen Doktordisputationen des 17. und 18. Jahrhunderts* (Bern, 1970). A typical Dutch title is Dirk

Graaf van Hogendorp, *Commentatio de juris gentium studio in patria nostra, post Hugonem Grotium* (Amsterdam, 1856). On Alberico Gentili, the Italian-born Protestant who fled to England, see Aurelio Saffi, *Di Alberigo Gentili e del diritto delle genti* (Bologna, 1878); Gesina Hermina Johanna van der Molen, *Alberico Gentili and the Development of International Law: His Life, Work and Times* (Amsterdam, 1937). Although people who do not speak Spanish often claim that the Spanish origin of international law is no longer credible, recent Spanish textbooks such as Juan Antonio Carrillo Salcedo's *El derecho internacional en perspectiva histórica* (Madrid, 1991) offer a very different outlook. The Spanish editions of Vitoria's lectures have subtitles such as "Liberty of the Indian" and "Magna Carta of the Indians," and a recent German publication has the subtitle "Folk Rights, Politics, and Church." Interestingly enough, the U.S. Library of Congress has classified the German edition under civil—that is to say political—rights, not human rights. Luciano Pereña and José María Pérez Prendes, eds., *Relectio de Indis: o, Libertad de los indios* (Madrid, 1967); Luciano Pereña and José María Pérez Prendes, eds., *Relectio de Indis: Carta magna de los indios* (Madrid, 1989); Ulrich Horst, Heinz Gerhard Justenhoven, and Joachim Stuben, eds. *Vorlesunge: Volkerrecht, Politik, Kirche,* 2 vols. (Stuttgart, 1997). Note that the most common translation for French and English concepts of human rights in contemporary German is *Menschenrechte,* but in the volume edited by Horst et al., Vitoria's understanding is referred to as *Volkerrecht.*

3 Michel Vovelle, Jean Imbert, Gerard Chianea, and Robert Chagny, eds., *Les droits de l'homme et la conquête des libertés: Des lumières aux révolutions de 1848: Actes du colloque de Grenoble-Vizille 1986* (Grenoble, 1988); Lynn Hunt, ed., *The French Revolution and Human Rights: A Brief Documentary History* (Boston, 1996); Philippe Ardant, ed., *Les textes sur les droits de l'homme,* 2d ed. (Paris, 1993); Stephen F. Englehart and John Allphin Moore Jr., eds., *Three Beginnings: Revolution, Rights, and the Liberal State: Comparative Perspectives on the English, American, and French Revolutions* (New York, 1994); Ludger Kuhnhardt, *Die Universalität der Menschenrechte: Studie zur ideengeschichtlichen Bestimmung eines politischen Schlüsselbegriffs* (Munich, 1987); Walter Laqueur and Barry Rubin, eds., *The Human Rights Reader,* rev. ed. (New York, 1990).

4 Bartolomé de las Casas, *De regia potestate,* ed. Luciano Pereña et al. (Madrid, 1969); Mauricio Beuchot, *Los fundamentos de los derechos humanos en Bartolomé de las Casas* (Barcelona, 1994); Antonio Linares Maza, *Bartolomé de Las Casas, un andaluz en el Nuevo Mundo: Desagravio psiquiatrico al primer anticolonialista, precursor de los derechos humanos* (Malaga, 1993); Antonio Agundez y Fernández, *La doctrina jurídica de Gregorio López en la defensa de los derechos humanos de los indios* (Badajoz, Spain, 1992); Ramón Hernández, *Un español ante la ONU* (Madrid, 1977).

5 Cleber Mesquita dos Santos, *Os direitos humanos: o Brasil e o direito de um povo* (São Paulo, 1998); Mauricio Beuchot, *Derechos humanos: Historia y filosofia* (Lima, 1999); Comision Andina de Juristas, *Seguridad ciudadana y derechos humanos* (Lima, 1999); Ministerio de Justicia y del Derecho, *Derechos humanos* (Bogotá, 1998); José Antonio de la Torre Rangel, *El derecho a tener derechos: Ensayos sobre los derechos humanos en Mexico* (Mexico City, 1998); Secretaria de Estado de Relaciones Exteriores, *Derechos humanos: Recopilación de tratados, leyes, decretos, reglamentos y resoluciones vigentes en la Republica Dominicana* (Santo Domingo, 1998); German Jose Campos Bidart, *Derecho internacional, derechos humanos y derecho comunitario* (Buenos Aires, 1998).

6 Consejo de Todas las Tierras Mapuche, seventeenth session, U.N. Working Group on Indigenous Peoples, Geneva, July 26–30, 1999.

7 The Inter-American Commission on Human Rights is a subgroup of the Organization of American States. On the recent use of international forums by indigenous communities, see Alison Brysk, *From Tribal Village to Global Village* (Stanford, Calif., 2000); Lydia van de Fliert, ed., *Indigenous Peoples and International Organizations* (Nottingham, Eng., 1994).

8 The relative rarity of charges concerning moral principles in the writings of other European colonizers is notable. For an exception, see Robert Gray, *A Good Speede to Virginia* (London, 1609), who wrote that there was a "report" that in Virginia "the people are savage and incredibly rude, they worship the divell, offer their young children in sacrifice unto him" (n.p.) Earlier, he referred to the natives as idolatrous. French historian Frank Lestringant, *Le cannibale: Grandeur et décadence* (Paris, 1994), sees an almost entirely different list among the French: incest, infanticide, and cannibalism (67). The conquistadors perceived natives as committing unprecedented wrongdoing and as lacking fundamental human values of "piety," "kindness," and "humanity." Gonzalo Fernández de Oviedo, *Historia general y natural de las indias,* ed. Juan Pérez de Tudela Bueso, 5 vols. (Madrid, 1959), bk. 40, chap. 11, vol. 4, p. 420; Vasco de Quiroga, "Información en derecho" (1535), in Paulino Castañeda Delgado, *Don Vasco de Quiroga y su información en derecho* (Madrid, 1974), 141–48.

9 Francisco Vitoria established the principle of an international (read Spanish) right to intervene in defense of the innocent. Francisco de Vitoria, *De indis et de iure belli relectiones,* ed. Ernest Nys (Buffalo, N.Y., 1995), bk. 3, sec. 15.

10 Donald E. Brown, *Human Universals* (New York, 1991).

11 Newly independent African and Asian states successfully argued in the 1970s for national control in order to prevent former colonial masters from continuing to claim ownership of resources when they were evicted. But in the Americas, where indigenous peoples did not overthrow their colonial rulers, the situation was different. National control over natural resources kept indigenous peoples from claiming ownership of natural resources. An excellent history attributing this principle to anticolonial movements is Nico Schrijver, *Sovereignty over Natural Resources: Balancing Rights and Duties* (Cambridge, 1997). See also Kamal Hossain and Subrata Roy S. Chowdhury, eds., *Permanent Sovereignty over Natural Resources in International Law* (New York, 1984); Gerhard Brehme, *Souveranität der jungen National-staaten uber Naturreichtumer* (Berlin, 1967), 71, 266; Ian Brownlie, "Legal Status of Natural Resources in International Law," in *Principles of Public International Law,* 4th ed. (Oxford, 1990), 287; General Assembly Resolutions 626 (1952), 837 (1954), 1314 (1958), all reprinted in *United Nations Resolutions: General Assembly,* ed. Dusan J. Djononvich (New York, 1973–74), 4:106, 5:137, 7:121. For reflection on the United Nations debates of the 1970s that declared permanent national sovereignty over natural resources, see George Elian, *The Principle of Sovereignty over Natural Resources,* trans. Andre Bantas (Alphen aan den Rijn, 1979), 83–139.

12 Stanley Hoffmann, "Foreword," in Sohail H. Hashmi, *State Sovereignty: Change and Persistence in International Relations* (University Park, Pa., 1997), vii. Slightly different but largely similar lines of argument appear in Thomas J. Biersteker and Cynthia Weber, eds., *State Sovereignty as Social Construct* (Cambridge, 1996).

13 L. R. Hiatt, "Aboriginal Land Tenure and Contemporary Claims in Australia," in *We*

Are There: Politics of Aboriginal Land Tenures, ed. Edwin N. Wilmsen (Berkeley, Calif., 1989), 100–101.

14 Aboriginal Land Rights (Northern Territory) Act, pt. I, sec. 3, "Traditional Aboriginal Owners." On the regulation of mining in aboriginal areas, see pt. 4, secs. 44–48D, of the act. This information is available on-line at http:www.austlii.edu.au/au//legis/cth/consol_act/alrta1976444/.

15 Mining or hydroelectric projects must be approved by the Brazilian Congress rather than by indigenous communities. Constituçáo republica federativa do Brasil, art. 231, 3. Manuela Carneiro da Cunha, "El concepto de derecho consuetudinario y los derechos indígenas en la nueva constitución de Brazil," in *Entre la ley y la costumbre: El derecho consuetudinario indígena em América Latina*, ed. Rudolfo Stavenhagen and Diego Iturralde (Mexico City, 1990), 299–313, esp. 304–6, 309; Constituçáo republica federativa do Brasil, art. 176.

16 The Native Title Act of 1993 provides parties holding native title the right to negotiate with the government and the mining company about any proposal for mining, including exploration. See section 51 of the act, which may be viewed on-line at http://www.austlii.edu.au/cgi-bin/disp.pl/au/legis/cth/consol_act/nta1993147/. See also "Procedures under the Right to Negotiate System" (paper issued by the National Native Title Tribunal, June 7, 1995), on-line at http://www.arts.uwa.edu.au/anthropwww/negotiat.htm. For the Northern Territories legislation, see the Aboriginal Land Rights (Northern Territory) Act, pt. 7, sec. 69.

17 Native communities can negotiate directly with multinationals in New Zealand and Australia; government officials represent these communities in Canada and the United States. In Canada, First Nations are entitled to full economic benefits from metallic minerals only on reserves created before 1930 in Alberta, Saskatchewan, Manitoba, Yukon, and the Northwest Territories. In other areas the resources belong to the crown or the province. Natives still are entitled to lesser economic benefits in British Columbia; in reserves created after 1930 in Alberta, Saskatchewan, and Manitoba under the Natural Resources Transfer Agreement (Constitution Act, 1930); in Ontario; in Quebec (where the province claims mineral rights); in Nova Scotia; in New Brunswick; in Newfoundland; and on Prince Edward Island.

18 John D. Martz, *Politics and Petroleum in Ecuador* (New Brunswick, N.J., 1987); Jonathan C. Brown and Alan Knight, eds., *The Mexican Petroleum Industry in the Twentieth Century* (Austin, Tex., 1992); Gustavo Coronel, *The Nationalization of the Venezuelan Oil Industry: From Technocratic Success to Political Failure* (Lexington, Mass., 1983); Luis Vallenilla, *Oil, the Making of a New Economic Order: Venezuelan Oil and OPEC* (New York, 1975).

19 In Argentina, the provinces and national government own the resource. Carl E. Solberg, *Oil and Nationalism in Argentina: A History* (Stanford, Calif., 1979).

20 The eleven OPEC members are Saudi Arabia, Iraq, Kuwait, United Arab Emirates, Iran, Venezuela, Libya, Nigeria, Algeria, Indonesia, and Qatar. All of these members, save Nigeria, which has a modified version of this idea (see note 21, below), share the same political perspective on subsoil ownership. Furthermore, of the next five largest non-OPEC oil producers—Mexico, Norway, Egypt, Oman, and Yemen—only Norway does not share the Islamic heritage regarding subsoil ownership. In Iran the mullahs claim that the *imam* owns the resources. Former OPEC

member Ecuador, which withdrew from the organization in 1992, shared this assessment, but Gabon, which resigned in June 1996, did not.

21 This is the case in Nigeria, where the leadership is Muslim and the oil fields are located in the Christian regions of the country.

22 The World Bank still operates under a profound misunderstanding regarding the nature of mining claims in Spanish America. In 1996 it called for an implementation of "a clear and effective legal framework," but used Anglo-Saxon legal criteria, insisting that the concession holder be *"able to transfer the title to any eligible third party, and that he is permitted to mortgage the title to raise finance or other purposes"*! Such a proposal is unacceptable where the oil and petroleum are national property. *World Bank, A Mining Strategy for Latin America and the Caribbean* (Technical Paper 345, Industry and Mining Division, Industry and Energy Department) (Washington, D.C., 1996), executive summary.

23 The exceptions are the areas of the southwestern United States conquered or purchased from Mexico. In those areas (under the influence of Mexican and originally Islamic law) the separate sale of surface and mineral rights has become possible.

24 The 1872 mining law that still governs such transactions in the United States says that "all valuable mineral deposits in lands belonging to the United States . . . are hereby declared to be free and open to exploration and purchase." *U.S. Code*, title 20, sec. 22.

25 Commissioner Osso Stanley of the Court of Appeals in *Hammonds v. Central Kentucky Natural Gas Co.*, 75 S.W.2d 204 (1934).

26 Hiatt, "Aboriginal Land Tenure"; Henry Reynolds, *The Law of the Land* (Ringwood, Victoria, 1987); Paul Tennant, *Aboriginal Peoples and Politics: The Indian Land Question in British Columbia, 1849–1989* (Vancouver, 1990); Claudia Orange, *Treaty of Waitangi* (Wellington, 1987); Hugh Kawharu, ed., *Waitangi: Maori and Pakeha Perspectives* (Auckland, 1989). Indians could not even sue to regain lands until the twentieth century, and even then only during a twenty-five-year period. Petra Shattuck and Jill Norgren, *Partial Justice: Federal Indian Law in a Liberal Constitutional System* (Providence, R.I., 1991), 141–43.

27 The set-aside for hunting and fishing by the James Bay Cree also ensures the continuance of a sacred relationship. See Adam Tanner, *Bringing Home Animals: Religious Ideology and Mode of Production of the Mistassini Cree Hunters* (London, 1979).

28 Donald Worcester, *Under Western Skies: Nature and History in the American West* (New York, 1992), 147–48.

29 Forest Act, British Columbia, pt. 1, "Cultural Heritage Resource." This legislation originally passed in 1994.

30 Aboriginal title encompasses the right to exclusive use and occupation of the land—not ownership of the land. Canadian Constitution Act, 1982, sec. 35(1). Aboriginal title in Canada was created by the Royal Proclamation of 1763, the common law that recognizes occupation as proof of possession. *Delgamuukw v. British Columbia* 3 (Canadian) *Supreme Court Reports* 1010 (1997).

31 *Tee-Hit-Ton Indians v. U.S.*, 348 U.S. 272–95, (1955).

32 Canadian Constitution Act, 1982, sec. 35(1). The statement is by Deane Gaudron and J. J. Gaudron to Mabo (no. 2) in *Commonwealth Law Reports* 175 (1992): 109–10. The Native Title Act (1993) does not state so clearly that no ownership is meant.

Even the dissenter from the decision, J. Dawson, considered "native title, where it exists, is a form of permissive occupancy at the will of the Crown."

33 "Ko te atakau o te whenua i riro i a te Kuini, ko te tinana o te whenua i waiho ki nga Maori." Waitangi Tribunal Reports, Muriwhenua Fisheries Claim (1988), 10.3.3, Legal Perspectives of the Maori Context (h) citing Shortland to Hobson, May 6, 1840, CO 209/7. The Tribunal Report continues, "The natives kept to themselves what Vattel calls the 'useful domain' while they yielded to the Crown of England the 'high domain.'" Victoria University Law Review 14 (1984): 227, 240.

34 The land represented territories claimed by the seventy-one houses representing all of the Wet'suwet'en people, and all but twelve of the Gitksan houses. The Nisq'a recently received a fee simple title in a landmark British Columbia case.

35 Joseph G. Jorgensen, Oil Age Eskimos (Berkeley, Calif., 1990); Gary C. Anders, "A Critical Analysis of the Alaska Native Land Claims and Native Corporate Development," in Native Americans and Public Policy, ed. Fremont J. Lyden and Lyman H. Legters (Pittsburgh, 1992), 85–98; David Rich Lewis, "Native Americans and the Environment: A Survey of Twentieth-Century Issues," American Indian Quarterly 19 (1995): 423–51.

36 John Merritt, Terry Fenge, Randy Amers, and Peter Jull, Nunavut: Political Choices and Manifest Destiny (Ottawa, 1989), 35. Recent Canadian cases include the 1975 James Bay and Northern Quebec Agreement, the Inuvialuit Final Agreement (1984), the Gwich'in Comprehensive Land Claims Agreement (1992), the Sahtu Dene and Metis Comprehensive Land Claims Agreement (1993), the Yukon Final Agreement (1993), and the Nunavut Claims Agreement (1993). Completed concurrently with the Yukon Final Agreement were Aishihik First Nation, Nacho Nyak Dun First Nation, and Teslin Tlingit First Nation agreements.

37 The original case was Passamaquoddy v. Morton. The U.S. Department of Justice reduced the claim to five to eight million acres and, of course, excluded the heavily populated coastal areas.

38 Maine Settlement Treaty of 1980; U.S. Commission on Civil Rights, Indian Tribes: A Continuing Quest for Survival (Washington, D.C., 1981), 130.

39 They are also used as bargaining chips in internal political disputes. Thus federal support for the James Bay Cree provided a powerful counter to the independent-minded Quebecois intent on building a hydroelectric dam in the early 1970s. Public support for the James Bay Cree continues among those opposed to Quebec separatism for the same reason.

40 "Five years after the signing in 1981, it was clear that the federal government had neither budgeted any special funds to meet its new obligations under the agreement, nor had established any agency with responsibility for overseeing its role in the implementation processes. . . . In 1984, after three additional years of negotiation, the Cree-Naskapi Act was signed and passed into law, establishing local self-government for Cree (and adjacent Naskapi) communities, thereby fulfilling one of the obligations from the 1975 agreement." Harvey A. Feit, "Hunting and the Quest for Power: The James Bay Cree and Whitemen in the 20th Century," in Native Peoples: The Canadian Experience, 2d ed., ed. R. Bruce Morrison and C. Roderick Wilson (Toronto, 1995).

41 The economist is the former treasury secretary and noted MIT economist Richard Rubin. The case (Corbett v. Babbit) has yet to be resolved. The Indian Minerals

Development Act of 1982—passed without significant controversy—gives tribes a larger role in managing petroleum rights. The legal presupposition is that, unless otherwise specified, subsoil rights belong to indigenous communities, but the federal government, which often fails to observe basic rules of competitive bidding, manages the income. Felix S. Cohen, *Handbook of Federal Indian Law* (Washington, D.C., 1942), 312–13. In fact, even within petroleum-bearing reservations there is a mix of "headright," allottee, and tribal ownership. See Robert Anderson, ed., *The Oil and Gas Opportunity on Indian Lands: Exploration, Policies and Procedures* (Bureau of Indian Affairs, Division of Energy and Mineral Resources, General Publication G-95-3) (Washington, D.C., 1995). See also the internal document by Pete C. Aguilar, "Oil and Gas Leases on Indian Lands," on-line at http://snake1.cr.usgs.gov/demr/imda/imda%20aguilar.htm. Indians own approximately 3 to 4 percent of oil and gas reserves, 10 percent of the coal, 5 percent of the phosphate, and all of the uranium. See Monroe Edwin Price and Robert N. Clinton, eds. *Law and the American Indian: Readings, Notes, and Cases*, 2d ed. (Charlottesville, Va., 1983), 755–56. On the lawsuit to force the U.S. government to hand over revenue owed Native Americans, see Timothy Egan, "Poor Indians Who Own Rich Lands Try to Break Out of Vast Federal Maze," *New York Times*, March 9, 1999.

42 O sistema jurídico norte-americano exige ser proprietário *antes* de poder vender-o.

43 On Jefferson, see Anthony F. C. Wallace, *Jefferson and the Indians: The Tragic Fate of the First Americans* (Cambridge, Mass., 1999). On Carter, see U.S. Commission on Civil Rights, *Indian Tribes*, 133.

44 Since 1972, the Western Shoshone have spurned efforts by the U.S. government to force them to surrender lands in exchange for payment. When presented with $26 million, which the Indian Claims Commission had determined was the value of the terrain, the Shoshone refused to accept any funds. The federal government then placed the money into a U.S. Treasury account and declared that the government owned the land. The Shoshone argued that placing funds into a U.S. Treasury account failed to constitute "payment" under section 22(a) of the Indian Claims Commission Act, but the courts disagreed. *United States v. Dann*, 470 U.S. 39 (1985); *United States v. Dann*, 873 F.2d 1189 (9th Cir. 1989), cert. den., 493 U.S. 890 (1980). Recently, the Ninth U.S. Circuit Court categorically refused to allow the Shoshone to offer an opinion regarding their rights to the land in *United States v. Nye County*, 178 F.3d 1080 (9th Cir. 1999). The court summarily dismissed Shoshone efforts to offer an opinion as irrelevant. Up-to-date news on this case is available at the following Web site, which is dedicated to litigation concerning Western Shoshone territorial integrity: http://www.nativeweb.org/pages/legal/shoshone/index.html.

45 Even in New Zealand, Maoris largely hold two categories of nonarable terrain: land with moderate limitations and hazards when under a perennial vegetation cover (34 percent) and land that supports only extensive grazing or erosion-control forestry (32 percent). Ministry of Maori Affairs, "Maori Land Use Capability—New Zealand— 1996." Available on-line at http://www.maoriland.govt.nz/stats/landuse.htm.

46 "The 'full exclusive and undisturbed' possession of properties connotes all rights of authority, management, and control." Waitangi Tribunal, *Whanganui River Report* (June 28, 1999), chap. 11. Note that this does not include a possibility of alienation or sale, which would mean ownership.

47 Subcomandante Marcos Selva Lacandona, declaration of war, 1993. See also the subcomandante's *Viento primero* (rendered in English as *Chiapas: The Southeast in Two Winds*) (August 1992).

48 Quoted in U.S. Commission on Civil Rights, *Indian Tribes*, 107.

49 Argentina gave 250 million hectares (617,750 acres) to Mapuche communities, and Chile gave 75,000 hectares. On Argentina, see "Menem devolvió tierras a los mapuches," *La Nacion On Line*, October 26, 1996, at http://www.lanacion.com.ar/96/10/26/p02.htm; on Chile, see "Diario de Sesiones del Senado, Legislatura 339ª, Extraordinaria Sesión 22ª, en martes 9 de marzo de 1999," on-line at http://www.congreso.cl/senado/diarios_sesiones/leg339/sesion22.htm.

50 Alice Littlefield and Martha C. Knack, "Native American Labor: Retrieving History, Rethinking Theory," in *Native Americans and Wage Labor: Ethnohistorical Perspectives*, ed. Alice Littlefield and Martha C. Knack (Norman, Okla., 1996), 3.

Index

120; Protestants, 118; rituals of, 120. *See also* Catholicism; Christians; "Christians, the"; evangelizing

Christianizing. *See* evangelizing

Christians, 60, 61, 62, 63, 73, 75, 76, 77, 79, 84, 85, 87, 88, 92, 93, 101, 103, 104, 105, 107, 114, 115, 116, 125, 126, 133, 177–78; Iberian, 74, 94, 124, 140

"Christians, the," 116, 117, 118, 121, 126, 136, 139

civil rights: of market access, 170; of property ownership, 170; of pursuit of profit, 170, 178; of "recreation," 170

class. *See* middle class

Clenardo, 27

climate, 131

Clinton, George, 25

clothing, 74, 89

coal. *See* natural resources, coal

Coke, Edward, 32, 48

Colbert, Jean-Baptiste, 50

"cold war," 92, 103

Colombia, 179, 180

Colonialism, nineteenth- and twentieth-century European, 7, 168

colonists, xi, 152; Dutch, 8, 36, 45, 55, 56, 71, 107, 110; economic objectives of, 5; English, xi, 2, 3, 8–9, 13, 23, 28, 55, 57, 72, 100, 105, 107, 109, 114, 126, 129, 133, 135, 150; French, 3, 8, 36, 45, 55, 56, 107, 114; Portuguese, xi, 3, 45, 55, 56, 57, 60, 99, 100, 103, 105, 135, 136, 139, 147, 150; Spanish, xi, 3, 45, 56, 57, 60, 62, 67, 72, 97, 100, 103, 105, 118, 125, 150

colonization, 2, 5; English, 3, 9, 13, 14, 29, 92, 152; Spanish, 3, 9

Columbus, Christopher, 63, 77, 83, 101

commerce, 123, 135, 137, 148, 165, 172

commercial model: Dutch, 135; French, 135; Portuguese, 135, 136

commodity, 19; Brazil nuts, 140, 141; brazilwood, 137, 139, 141; coral, 137; hides, 145; pepper, 138; porcelain, 137; shellac, 137; silks, 137; spices, 138; vanilla, 140, 141. *See also* crops; money; presents; purchase

common land, shared, 162

communal use rights, 35

community, 64, 65, 76, 78, 80; subjugated, 73, 84, 87

community autonomy: Muslim, 76; Jewish, 76

Connecticut, 178

conquest: of nature, 160; of people by Spanish, 2, 3; of property by English, 2

conquests: Arabic, 4; Berber, 4; German, 4; Islamic, 75; Scandinavian, 4. *See also* Norman Conquest

conservation, 161

contracts, 23, 75

Cook, James, 110

Copeland, Patrick, 35

Cordoba, 92

Cortés, Hernán, x, 44, 67, 77, 84, 96, 100, 104, 105, 108, 147

cotton. *See* crops, cotton

Cotton, John, 20, 38, 52, 53

courts: Spanish, 84, 87. *See also* legal and economic systems, Spanish

Crashaw, Richard, 101

credit, 21. *See also* money

Croke, George, 14

Cronon, William, 39

crops: coffee, 127; cotton, 127, 169; indigo, 127; sugar, 127, 139, 143, 144, 145; tobacco, 39, 127, 139, 143

Cuba, 67, 173, 179

Cummins, John, 50

Cushman, Robert, 38, 128

customhouses, Brazilian, 138; for South Asian goods, 137, 139; for West African goods, 137, 139

Dakota (badlands), 187

Dakotas (people), 176, 178

Dann, Carrie and Mary, 161, 187

Dawes, Henry, 158

decolonization, 163, 190

de Vries, David, 17

dhimma, 75, 84. *See also* community

Dias, Carlos Malhiero. *See* Malhiero Dias, Carlos

Díaz del Castillo, Bernal, 95 100, 108

PATRICIA SEED is professor of history at Rice University. She is the author of *To Love, Honor, and Obey in Colonial Mexico: Conflicts over Marriage Choice, 1574–1821* and *Ceremonies of Possession in Europe's Conquest of the New World, 1492–1640*.

IMPORTANCE OF TERMS
  AND THEIR CHANGE OF MEANING OVER TIME
   "TREATY", "WASTE LAND"
  ↳ A DIFFERENT LANGUAGE!
    — IMPORTANT TO CONTEXTUALIZE
  ★ BUT WERE THE SETTLERS REALLY WORRIED W/ WORDS?
OR ARE THEY LACANIANLY USED TO LAY BARE
    THEIR UNCONSCIOUS?

   IMPERIAL EYES ALWAYS SEE THROUGH
     SPECIFIC CULTURAL LENSES
     THAT RECONSTRUCT (RE-PRESENT) WHAT
     THEY SEE IN PARTICULAR (CONVINIENT)
     WAYS   APPROPRIATE

SPAIN: GOLD ⇄ RELIGION (p61)

DIFFERENT TRADITIONS — DIFFERENT LAWS
        INDIVIDUAL VS. COMMUNAL
    TOPSOIL/SUBSOIL VS. TOPSOIL ≠ SUBSUELO
        LAND   VS   LABOR
JUXTAPOSITIONS: GOOD WAY OF KEEPING TRACK
        OF THE BIG PICTURE

SPANISH: RELIGION & WAR TIGHTLY LINKED
        SPIRIT OF THE CRUSADE
        + PROFIT (GANADO)
      CONQUISTADORES ⇄ CID
      RELIGION & STATE ENTERPRISE (p117)

DOES NOT REALLY EXPLAIN
WHY TIES WERE NOT CUT B/ ENGLISH
COLONIES & ENGLISH METROPOLE
(AND SKIPS A WHOLE CENTURY!) (p 152)

PERHAPS AN EXCESSIVE GENERALIZATION
OF SPANISH AMERICA? (p 173)

GOOD TO CALL ATTENTION TO
THE IMPACT OF COLONIALISM
ON PRESENT DAY AMERICA

GOOD TO CONSIDER IT IN THE
CONTEXT OF INTERNATIONALIZATION
(NATIVE COMMUNITIES MUST APPEAL
TO INTERNATIONAL ORGS. BECAUSE
NATIONAL LAWS DO NOT PROVIDE
FOR THEM — YET WHO'S INTRESTS DO
THESE PURSUE? AND THE PROBLEM
OF SOLUTIONS FOR EVERYONE
MIGHT NOT ALLOW FOR CULTURAL
SPECIFICITIES...)

IN THE CASE OF SPANISH AMERICA
NEO IMPERIALISM SHOULD ALSO
BE CONSIDERED — EXAMPLE THE
CASE OF VENEZUELA (O IRAK) (p 183)